PERCEIVED IMAGES

Daniel Frei

PERCEIVED IMAGES

U.S. and Soviet Assumptions and Perceptions in Disarmament

Rowman & Allanheld
Publishers

ROWMAN & ALLANHELD

Published in the United States of America in 1986
by Rowman & Allanheld, Publishers
(A Division of Littlefield, Adams & Company)
81 Adams Drive, Totowa, New Jersey 07512

Library of Congress Cataloging in Publication Data

Frei, Daniel.
  Perceived images.

  "Published in cooperation with the United Nations
Institute for Disarmament."
  Originally published: Assumptions and perceptions
in disarmament. New York: United Nations, 1984.
  Bibliography: p. 289.
  1. Disarmament. 2. Arms race. 3. United States—
Foreign relations—Soviet Union. 4. Soviet Union—
Foreign relations—United States. I. United Nations
Institute for Disarmament Research. II. Title.
JX1974.F74 1986   327.1'74   85-14207
ISBN 0-8476-7443-6

88 87 86
10 9 8 7 6 5 4 3 2 1
Printed in the United States of America

CONTENTS

CHAPTER IV

THE AMERICAN VIEW: A SURVEY OF THE ACADEMIC
LITERATURE

CHAPTER V

CONFLICTIVE COGNITION: THE VIEW OF THE ADVERSARY
AND ITS CONSEQUENCES FOR DISARMAMENT

FOREWORD

The international community today finds itself at a crossroads. Two major challenges face it - on the one hand, an unchecked arms race which threatens to destroy human civilization and, on the other hand, the problems of underdevelopment in the countries of Africa, Asia, and Latin America, which threaten the quality of human civilization. In both these cases, the search for solutions appears to have reached a dead end, while the magnitude of the problems increase steadily.

In such a situation, no avenue which offers even the slightest chance of success in tackling these issues should remain unexplored. UNIDIR's mandate is to focus on one of these problems - the arms race, disarmament and related issues. It is in the spirit of the search for solutions to this problem and in an attempt to cast some light on the current deadlock that this study has been prepared.

Most thinking on arms control and disarmament has been dominated by the analysis of what might be called "objective" factors present in the situation - the number of weapons, their characteristics, technological developments, nuclear weapons employment policies and other similar factors. This work is an indispensable part of the international community's effort to understand and eventually control the arms race. But it needs to be supplemented. The "objective" factors in disarmament and arms control are only one part of the complex relationship between security doctrines, technological developments, the growth of armaments and the failure of arms control efforts. "Subjective" factors - such as assumptions and perceptions of threat which compel leaders to seek security in ever growing numbers of more and more sophisticated weapons at an even increasing cost - need to be examined as do the various interests propelling the armament race.

It is an evident fact that nations pile up arms because they feel threatened and feel they need arms for security. But how much of this threat is actual, and how much results from misperceptions, or perceptions which attribute far more hostility to the other side than is actually the case? It would appear that this is a vital question which needs to be answered in the interests of checking the arms race and the tremendous expenditures this race implies.

Other than as part of an explanation for the arms race, a study of perceptions will be invaluable to answer a question which is being increasingly asked by those concerned by the path the arms race is taking - why have arms control and disarmament negotiations had so little success so far? It would appear that success in arms control, or any other form of negotiations for that matter, would depend on an accurate picture of what the other side's intentions, concepts, fears and interests are. Distorted, or incomplete, visions of the other side's goals and ideas can only breed mistrust, hostility and eventual failure.

Understanding assumptions and perceptions is crucially important for understanding the disarmament policies of the powers, especially the two major powers. By providing the overall conceptual framework within which the governments act, the analysis of perceptions helps to come to grips with the often confusing course of the current negotiations.

It would seem that an understanding of assumptions and perceptions and an attempt to relate them to actual situations is an urgent task. This is not to imply that all threats, and all perceptions of threats and hostility, are imaginary and unrelated to facts. On the contrary, nations do undoubtedly face threats to their security, and in the absence of a reliable system of international security they do still require a minimum level of armaments to ensure their independence, sovereignty and territorial integrity. It is essential however to distinguish between actual threats and those which relate mostly to assumptions and perceptions. This is what UNIDIR, through this study, has attempted to do.

A profound understanding of the various factors and processes which fuel the armaments race and impede progress towards disarmament is essential if political action is to change the present threatening trends. The arms race is becoming more complex and more firmly entrenched, more dangerous and uncontrollable. Since the forces that propel it act most frequently together and reinforce each other, it is not sufficient to deal and remove one or some of them only in order to start the long due process of disarmament, but this action should be part of a global disarmament strategy in which partial measures would find their place and supplement each other.

The universality of the goal postulates the universality of participation in efforts aimed at its fulfilment. That is why the United Nations which has a central role and primary responsibility for disarmament should be utilized to the full in this endeavour.

The author, Daniel Frei, Professor of Political Science at the University of Zürich, is an internationally recognized authority in the study of international relations and this is the second study carried out by him within the research programme of UNIDIR. The earlier one is "The Risks of Unintentional Nuclear War", published in 1982. I avail myself of this opportuny to express to him UNIDIR's gratitude for the serious and dedicated work which is embodied in this book.

Besides the extensive survey of literature on the subject, the author conducted interviews with officials and scholars in Washington and Moscow and we are grateful to them for their generous assistance and co-operation.

The particular contribution of this study is a sincere, careful, document-based description of Soviet and U.S. images and conceptions, with special emphasis on how the major powers perceive each other and the kind of assumptions regarding their potential adversary they start from.

The results of this study may seem quite sobering, demonstrating confrontation of irreconcilable views. It certainly is not appropriate to belittle the conceptual gap existing between the two governments. Yet, this does not mean that the road towards further progress in disarmament is blocked. Quite the opposite is true: only by clearly taking these differences into account can meaningful negotiations be conducted. The room available for pragmatic and constructive action thus becomes visible.

In this sense, the present study represents a substantial contribution to ongoing and future negotiations. It helps to identify the common ground. In addition, it promotes mutual understanding by providing an exact description of the complex sets of expectations and assessments held by the two governments.

This study forms part of the research programme approved by the Board of Trustees of UNIDIR. Its content is the responsibility of the authors and not of UNIDIR. Although UNIDIR takes no position on the views and conclusions expressed by the authors of its studies, it does assume responsibility for determining whether a study merits publication.

UNIDIR commends this study to the attention of all those who have responsibilities in the disarmament field or are interested in it - government officials, academics, journalists, members of non-governmental organizations and students. By publishing it, UNIDIR hopes that the study would contribute to promoting the cause of disarmament.

Liviu Bota
Director, UNIDIR

AUTHOR'S PREFACE

Any decision by a Government tends to a considerable extent, to be determined by the way this Government views the intentions, capabilities and expected behaviour of other Governments, in other words by assumptions regarding partners or adversaries. The aim of this study is to identify views and expectations held by the Soviet and the United States Governments about each other, with special reference to assumptions regarding the sensitive field of security, i.e. a field comprising both the strategic rivalry and attempts to tame it by disarmament and arms control negotiations. The rationale for this study is that meaningful disarmament negotiations cannot be properly understood without prior clarification of their premises in terms of perceptions and conceptions that serve as the ultimate basis and starting-point for any proposals regarding steps in disarmament or response to such proposals. This task will be done here by a comprehensive study of the Soviet and American world views as general frameworks for political orientation, the images held about the other side and the expectations expressed with regard to the opponent's disarmament policies and their underlying motives.

Focusing on the views held by the Soviet Union and the United States of America as the subject of the present study does not of course mean that the respective findings apply equally to other countries in East and West as well. It is clear that the allies of the two major Powers may have views that in some respects differ from those presented here. Still, the crucial importance of the policies of armament and disarmament adopted by the two major Powers justifies an examination of their views without looking, for the time being, into the variations existing in and outside the respective alliance systems.

As far as the presentation of this study is concerned, it should be noted that the different chapters serve different purposes; therefore different approaches have been chosen. Chapter I presents a general introduction to the problem to be studied. Chapter II and III offer summaries of the Soviet and the American views of the respective "other side". These two chapters are based, to the largest extent possible, on published and openly accessible source material; this material is also amply quoted and allowed to speak for itself. In view of certain aspects not covered by official source material, the author interviewed Government officials in both Moscow and Washington. The results of these interviews and discussions are also included in chapters II and III; however, no attributions to specific individuals are made. The names of the persons who kindly gave oral information are listed in the acknowledgements (see page xi). As far as the American view of the Soviet Union is concerned, it was felt indispensable to include also the views reflected in the vast academic literature, as the academic experts' opinions very often have an impact on official thinking. This task is performed in chapter IV.

The three chapters II to IV do not lay claim to any originality; on the contrary, the author tried to offer a sincere descriptive account of Soviet and American sources, deliberately withholding his own judgements and comments and proceeding more as a rapporteur than as an author. That is why these three chapters may to some extent appear to be an eclectic gathering of quotations; it is hoped, however, that the selection of these quotations is justified by their being both representative and authoritative and thus reflecting the views of the two Governments as truly and precisely as possible. It is only in Chapter V that the author makes an attempt to draw some conclusions from the material assembled in the preceding chapters.

In considering the methodological approach to be applied in this study, the author gave ample thought to possible alternatives. Being a social scientist with an empirical-quantitative bent, he would very much have preferred to employ one of the more rigorous research techniques available in the field of content analysis. However, none of the techniques concerned was satisfactory because none seemed to be practicable and useful in this case. As the purpose of this study is neither to identify changes and trends in perceptions over time nor to compare perceptions held by different groups within the Soviet Union and the United States, any method based on a frequency count would not yield results commensurate to the effort involved. Rather, the central aim of this study is to discuss the structure and contents of the views held by the two major Powers.

Evaluating the various available methods in this perspective, the author reached the conclusion that the most appropriate method may be a semi-structured content analysis combining a systematic approach with verbal interpretative procedures. The systematic element of this method can be seen in the attempt to structure the contents of each view according to a hierarchical set of issues to be taken into consideration. This set of issues reflects a system of dimensions evolved by theoretical reasoning and based on a broad body of existing theories of perception and cognition. It is represented in a "checklist" (cf. chapter I) which in turn served as a heuristic tool, i.e. as a kind of questionnaire for analysing the texts. Hence the florilegium-like appearance of chapter II, III and IV would be misleading if the reader were to conclude that the result of this analysis merely constitutes a compilation of quotations devoid of any theoretical structure. There is definitely a structure in this analysis - however, within the framework of this structure the author felt free to quote and analyse the source material which, in his opinion, best illustrates and corroborates the specific features of the view to be dealt with in the respective sector of the overall structure.

The selection of the source material was not done with the intention of collecting a sample representative in terms of statistical probability. Rather, the author preferred to work on the basis of the universe of relevant texts by looking at those documents which, due to the specific decision-making processes prevailing in the two countries, reflect the views of the supreme leadership. The specific classes of documents used and the rationale for making this selection are described at the beginning of chapters II and III, respectively. In order to avoid blurring the picture by including aspects belonging to a different historical context, the temporal range of the documents chosen for analysis was, in principle, restricted to the past five years.

For this reason, this study does not examine the evolution of perceptions in the course of history. Of course, perceptions do change. In the period of the cold war, the competitive elements were more manifest and the co-operative elements played a subordinate role. In the early 1970s, perceptions tended to concentrate more on co-operative perspectives, while the present analysis yields a picture where competitive elements seem to have again become more important.

It should also be borne in mind that the documents selected reflect official views only; it is not the purpose of the present study to inquire into the nature of public opinion or specific groups inside the two countries. This also implies that the findings refer to declaratory policy rather than to the actual behaviour of the two Governments concerned. In the field of practical politics there is much more room for pragmatic action and constructive co-operation than one might conclude from the statements analysed in this study. Still, there is no doubt that these statements condition and limit the actual potential for co-operation and agreement in the field of disarmament.

ACKNOWLEDGEMENTS

First and foremost, the author wishes to thank Dr. Liviu Bota (Director, United Nations Institute for Disarmament Research) for all his friendly encouragement and expert suggestions. As head of the institution under whose auspices the author had the privilege to work, Dr. Bota's help has been crucial not only in shaping the approach underlying this study but also in initiating the contacts with Government officials in both East and West necessary for gathering the required information.

This book has been written with the most valuable assistance of five persons to whom the author would like to pay tribute: Dr. Dieter Ruloff (lecturer at the University of Zurich), who shared the author's burden in reviewing the plethora of publications serving as a basis for chapter IV and who wrote several useful extracts which were incorporated in the text of that chapter; Mr. Ednan Agaev, an official of the United Nations at Geneva, who assisted the author in his search for Soviet source material for use in chapter II, kindly translated several passages of texts available only in Russian, and co-organized the author's appointments with officials in Moscow; Mrs. Aurelia Boermans, secretary at the University of Zurich, who patiently and intelligently prepared the various versions of the manuscript; Mr. Christian Catrina, who compiled the bibliography, and Mr. Stephan Kux who took care of the proofreading. I also wish to thank Mr. Gerald Williams of the United States Office at Geneva who co-ordinated publication arrangements.

I also owe a special debt of gratitude to the many Government officials and researchers in both the United Nations and the Soviet Union with whom I had useful and instructive discussions.

In Washington D.C., I had the privilege of consulting with Brigadier-General John W. Nicholson (Joint Chiefs of Staff Representative for SCC), Brigadier-General Donald O. Aldrige (Joint Chiefs of Staff Representative for START), Colonel Richard G. Toye (Chief, Nuclear Negotiations Division, Joint Chiefs of Staff), Major-General (Ret.) Edward B. Giller (Joint Chiefs of Staff Representative for the Comprehensive Test Ban Negotiations), The Hon. Ambassador Jack F. Matlock (Special Assistant to the President for European Affairs, The White House), Dr. John Lenczowski and Mr. Sven Kraemer (both staff members of the National Security Council), Mr. John Hawes (Director, Office for European Security and Bilateral Affairs, Department of State), Mr. Pete Martinez (Strategic Planning, Office of Politico-Military Affairs, Department of State), Mr. Robert Baraz (Director, Office for the Analysis of the Soviet Union and Eastern Europe, Bureau of Intelligence and Research, Department of State), and Dr. Byron F. Doenges, Mr. Al Lieberman, Mr. Donald Silkwood and Mr. Stanley Riveles (Arms Control and Disarmament Agency).

These appointments were kindly arranged by Ambassador Louis G.Fields and Colonel Charles Pearcy (United States delegation to the United Nations Conference on Disarmament), the Hon. Mrs. Faith Ryan Whittlesey (Special Assistant to the President for Public Liaison, The White House), Colonel Roger Scott (Joint Chiefs of Staff), Mr. David Swartz and Mr. David Johnson (both at the Department of State).

In Moscow, I was kindly granted appointments with Mr. Vadim V. Zagladin (International Department, Secretariat of the Central Committee of the CPSU), Lieutenant-General Dimitry A. Volkogonov (Main Political Directorate of the Soviet Army and Navy), Major-General Konstantin Mikhaylov (General Staff of the Soviet Armed Forces), Eugene Silin, E. Juriev and German Ossipovski (Soviet Committee for European Security and Co-operation), Professor Georgii Shakhnazarov (Institute of Law and State, USSR Academy of Sciences, and Secretariat of the Central Committee of the CPSU), Dr. Fyodor M. Burlatsky (Literaturnaya Gazeta), Mr. V.F. Petrovsky (Department for International Organizations, Foreign Ministry of the USSR), Professor Radomir Bogdanov (Institute for the Study of the USA and Canada, USSR Academy of Sciences), Professors Alexander Yakovlev, G.D. Tomashevsky, Vladimir I. Gantman, Nikolai Kishilov, Daniil Proyektor, V. Razmerov, Lev S. Voronkov (Institute for World Economy and International Relations, USSR Academy of Sciences), Professor Yvan G. Tyulin (Moscow State Institute for International Relations), Professor Gennadi Vorontsov (Diplomatic Academy of the USSR), and M. F. Priakhin of the Soviet delegation to the UN Conference on Disarmament, Geneva.

All paragraphs not explicitly based on specific sources identified in the text have been drafted by closely following statements made by United States and Soviet officials; however, it will be understood that no attributions have been made.

In addition, I was offered an opportunity to talk to some key officials concerned with problems of nuclear strategy and nuclear disarmament in Her Britannic Majesty's Government, in particular Mr. John Weston (Head of Defence) and the Hon. Michael Pakenham (Head of the Arms Control and Disarmament Department), both at the Foreign and Commonwealth Office, Mr. J.N.H. Blelloch (Deputy Under-Secretary of State), Mr. D.J. Fewtrell (Head of Defence Secretariate), Mr. Patrick Faults, Mr. Tony Ryan and Mr. Peter Bailey (Defence Intelligence Study Group), all at the Ministry of Defence, Whitehall, London. Mr. Neil Smith (H.M. Consul General, Zurich) kindly arranged these appointments.

Apart from these very thorough and informative discussions I had the pleasure of talking about the subject of this study with many distinguished colleagues, from both East and West, whom I happened to meet in the course of my extensive travels and at conferences and congresses, in particular the Pugwash Conferences and meetings of the Executive Committee of the International Political Science Association. Among the many to whom I owe interesting comments and suggestions I may mention just a few (in alphabetical order):

Academician V. Emelianov (USSR Academy of Sciences, Moscow), Dr. Ellis Morris (Queens University, Canada), Dr. Robert O'Neill (Director, International Institute of Strategic Studies, London), Professor Karl-Heinz Roeder (Institute for State and Law, Academy of Sciences of the German Democratic Republic, Berlin), Dr. J. Simpson (University of Southampton), Academician Yevgeny Velikhov (Vice-President, USSR Academy of Sciences, Moscow), and Dr. David Watt (Director, Royal Institute of International Affairs, London).

I am very grateful to all these persons who offered aid and advice. The published result is, of course, my responsibility.

D.F.

CHAPTER I

INTRODUCTION

THE RATIONALE OF THIS STUDY

It is a truism to say that disarmament presupposes trust. Yet this truism in fact points to the very heart of the matter: any decision to agree on measures of disarmament and arms control relies on specific assumptions regarding the future behaviour of the partners - and so does reluctance or refusal to engage in any such progress. All policies in this delicate field ultimately rest on what one believes about the potential adversary's aims and motives, his capabilities and intentions, his strategic options, his way of waging war should it break out. Everything a Government does depends on how this Government perceives the situation. In other words, behaviour is largely determined by cognition. In the case of the Soviet Union and the United States the processes of cognition are taking place in an environment characterized by an adverse relationship. Therefore, the resulting peculiar type of cognition may be called "conflictive cognition".

Conflictive cognition produces views of the world, 'of oneself, and especially of the adversary that, by their very nature, have a speculative character. At worst, they may represent nothing more than a hazy or imperfectly realized belief or an uncritical acceptance of some hypothesis; at best they refer to something that is taken for granted because some information and clues available at least indicate that some premise regarding the other side may be true. Complete certainty, however, can rarely be established.

The fuzzy nature of such assumptions also makes them susceptible to misunderstanding and - sometimes - misrepresentation. Misperception becomes the more likely the more conflictive the political relationship and the more therefore patterns of conflictive cognition intrude into the views Governments take for granted. Unfortunately there are reasons to suspect that many a deadlock and failure in arms control negotiations has been caused, among other things, by preciseely such processes. They constitute a risk inherent in the very same adverse relationship that makes disarmament so desirable. Hence it is imperative to study the views and assumptions underlying the disarmament and arms control policies of Governments, and especially the Governments of the two major Powers.

Such views and assumptions play a crucial role in all fields related to security, not only in the field of disarmament. There is widespread awareness of their importance for the analysis of capabilities and the shaping of strategic doctrine. Doctrines are generally known to depend on "'scenarios' (hypothetical political-military situations) based on assumptions, some of which are explicit, others implicit and not always recognized" (Garthoff 1983:3). Conflictive cognition as a set of patterns of perception originating in and

3

responding to a situation characterized by an adverse relationship is rooted in a strategic culture which in turn results from socialization processes transmitting "a set of general beliefs, attitudes and behavioral patterns". Conflictive cognition inhibits objective assessment of new problems but lets them be "seen through the perceptual lens provided by the strategic culture" (Snyder, quoted in Gray 1981:21f.). Conflictive cognition as part of the strategic culture and the extent to which it affects disarmament and arms control - that is, in very general terms, the subject of this study.

Such an endeavour may justly claim considerable practical relevance. Of course in most respects "no formula will ... reveal what image is correct" (Jervis 1976:409; Buzan 1983:231). Hence any hope of finding out which views and assumptions correctly reflect the "real reality" would be futile (Boulding 1956:164-175). But one can hope that presenting an analysis of these views will help responsible statesmen and negotiators to reach a better understanding of others' way of seeing the world and the way in which it differs from their own views. They would thereby be practising what is called empathy, i.e. "the self-conscious effort to share and accurately comprehend the presumed consciousness of another person, including his thoughts, feelings and perceptions ... as well as their causes" (Booth 1979:103). Therefore the ultimate rationale of this study is to contribute to the promotion of empathy on the part of all sides concerned. While empathy alone will certainly not solve any of the problems on the agenda of the current arms control negotiations, it will at least be conducive to facilitating the negotiating process.

In addition, some aspects of the views and assumptions underlying policy and negotiation behaviour in the field of disarmament and arms control may be amenable to a critical examination of their accuracy. This can be done by matching corresponding elements of the mutual images held by the two major Powers, for example by comparing the self-image of one side with the image of this side held by the other side, and also the perception of one's opponent's view of oneself with one's self-image.

Furthermore, a sober and sincere analysis of mutually held assumptions regarding the adversary may help to identify areas of potential common understanding and thus contribute towards practical steps aimed at achieving the progress in disarmament which is so desperately needed by mankind.

Related approaches have been and are being widely used in the study of "perception", "misperception", "images", "national prejudice" and the like; they have produced hundreds of books and articles. Most of them refer to the strategy of deterrence, starting from the general hypothesis that "unless statesmen understand the ways in which their opposite numbers see the world, their deterrence policies are likely to misfire" (Jervis 1982:1). The crucial motive underlying these studies, in most cases, refers to the relationship between perception and the causes of war (Levy 1983). However, so far with a few exceptions (Schwartz 1978, Lenczowski 1982, Lockwood 1983) no systematic effort has been made to employ this theoretical perspective and its corresponding analytical tools in the field of disarmament and arms control. This state of affairs is quite astonishing - even more so because the political relevance of assumptions underlying disarmament and arms control negotiations is generally acknowledged. A Soviet publication, for instance, refers to the need "to have correct knowledge of each other":

"... Now, as at all critical junctures of history, it is highly important for Governments and nations to have correct knowledge of each other. Especially when it concerns war and peace." (The Threat to Europe 1981:7)

Similarly, official American sources regularly emphasize the importance of "perceptions" as the very basis for dealing with the potential adversary; as, for instance, Senator John Spakman put it:

"The lesson to be learned here should be self-evident. It is the need for a measure of empathy in our relationship - a willingness to put ourselves in the other man's shoes ... First and foremost, it is a matter of perceptions." (Senator John Sparkman in: Perceptions 1979:vi)

American sources also give ample proof of intensive consideration of the perceptions generated on the "other side" in the field of arms control policy and negotiations; the Arms Control Impact Statements, as a rule, inquire into the impact which specific American defense programs may be expected to have on Soviet perceptions (cf. e.g. FY 1984 Arms Control Impact Statements: XVII).

For many decades, the importance of this approach has also been pointed out in more general terms. The Charter of the United Nations Educational, Scientific and Cultural Organization (UNESCO) aptly observes in its introduction: "War begins in the minds of men" - and not only war, but disarmament as well, one is tempted to add. Many efforts have also been made to promote what is called "moral disarmament", aimed at influencing and changing that very key to a peaceful and disarmed international order: the mind. In this sense, as early as 1936 Governments signed a "Convention in the Cause of Peace" adopted by the League of Nations and aimed at preventing the dissemination of war propaganda. Today, precisely the same rationale underlies the "World Disarmament Campaign" (A/S - 12/27) launched by the Second Special Session of the United Nations General Assembly devoted to disarmament, as well as the Disarmament Week which has as its aim to "mobilize public opinion, and create an atmosphere conducive to progress in disarmament negotiations".

One may justly argue that the study of conflictive cognition underlying disarmament and arms control policies focuses on an essential, and perhaps the most important, link between the somewhat munificent design of creating "an atmosphere conducive to disarmament negotiations" on the one hand, and the harsh reality of the arms control negotiation chamber, on the other hand. As a matter of fact, views and assumptions regarding the adversary, to a considerable extent, reflect moods deeply embedded in national traditions and public opinion. They therefore deserve to be analysed with great care and by rigorous research.

FOCUSING ON CONFLICTIVE COGNITION: SOME CONCEPTS AND DEFINITIONS

Reality and the image of reality

When examining views and assumptions as elements of conflictive cognition it would be wrong, however, to treat them as if they were mere chimeras lacking any substantive relation to reality, let alone to objective evidence. In most cases, fortunately quite the opposite is true: everywhere Governments are making every effort to find evidence about their adversaries' capabilities and intentions. All Governments therefore command a considerable range of evidence. Hence, to a large extent, disarmament policies and strategic doctrines are built on fairly firm ground. Yet there are still some elements that inevitably cannot be grasped easily - and it is here that more or less subjective assumptions and guesses can play a crucial role, and it is here also that all kinds of biases and preconceptions may intrude. These are the elements on which this study is focused.

The problem addressed in this study ultimately has its roots in one of the basic characteristics of the "conditio humana" and man's existence in a societal context: whatever a person does refers to an environment as he or she sees it. For any person, "reality" exists only as reflected in the image he has of this reality. In other words: in order to understand a person's action, one has to know something about how he defines his situation, that is how he perceives himself and others and the relationship between those others and himself. This is virtually a truism, yet an important one which deserves to be recalled again and again. The cognitive process referred to by this insight is probably much more complex and subtle than it might appear at first glance. In particular, reflections on the other's assumptions have to be taken into account, as well as the reflections on reflections. According to a definition of "strategic interaction" offered by Goffman (1970:101), "courses of action or moves will then be made in the light of one's thoughts about the other's thoughts about oneself", and so on - in other words: decisions are based on an "infinite series of probabilities" (Schelling 1963:208). Views tend to influence each other.

The reflexivity of views is of particular importance in the context of all policies related to national security issues, both in the field of disarmament or arms control policies and strategic doctrine: trust and mistrust being the central motives in any strategic relationship are, by definition, expectations that can be

6

believed or contested but which to some extent remain outside the reach of full evidence. They refer to images one has about the other(s). The same must be said about strategies which represent plans contingent upon specific possible moves by the other(s) (Gäfgen 1980:261); by definition, possible future moves do not yet exist objectively but only as images of eventualities. There may be some indications about the relative probability of one or the other eventuality; however, as a rule, the information available is usually short of full evidence.

Hence those responsible for making decisions feel the need to bridge the information gap by a process of inference (Steinbruner 1974:91-109; Watzlawick 1976:142f.), ascribing some wider meaning and significance to the fragments of evidence that can be grasped. It is clear that this process of inference is largely governed by expectations, i.e. by preconceptions. Depending on these preconceptions, the image produced by an inference process will be true or not true. Common ground can hardly be established easily. As Buzan (1983:230) points out, the inevitably different interpretation of reality enhances misunderstandings. Therefore, "international relations cannot be compared to a chess game, in which a struggle for power and position proceeds according to agreed rules which establish a common perception of the significance of events. Instead, security relations are more like a chess game in which the players follow somewhat different rules. Each player believes his own rules to be universally valid, and assumes the other player to know this" (Buzan 1983:230). That is why, in any debate on disarmament and strategy, there are competing policies based on competing views and definitions of the situation. It may therefore be of little use to simply juxtapose the different policies; priority must be given to an adequate clarification of assumptions underlying these policies.

Concepts and definitions

This approach has been widely used in various fields of the social sciences, and academic literature offers an abundance of concepts, terms and definitions relevant in this context. Summing up the work done so far and selecting those concepts that will be used in the present analysis, the following concepts seem to be of central importance; they reflect the current discussion of the problem in the social sciences in East and West:

| Cognition: | Transformation of neural signals into recognized codes that then become the basis for various symbolic operations (Bennett 1981:83); discerning of factual reality (Gibert 1977:3); any knowledge, opinion, or belief about the environment, about oneself, or about one's behaviour (Festinger, quoted in Hveem 1972:13) |

Cognitive process:	Various activities associated with problem-solving, including perception, appraisal, interpretation, search, information processing, strategies for coping with uncertainty, decision rules, verification, etc. (Holsti 1976:20; Holsti 1977:12); Perception and representation, with subsequent or preceding inferences, attributions and concept formation (Kaufmann 1981:134)
Cognitive style:	The way in which the individual modifies external stimuli through the selection, connection, and interpretation of information (Bennett 1981:145f.); A consistent pattern of organizing and processing information (Bennett 1981:145f.)
Perception:	Selection and reception of sensory inputs and the transmission of these inputs to various centers in the brain (Bennett 1981:83)
Perceptual process:	Acquiring, classifying, evaluating and integrating or rejecting information (Gibert 1977:2)
Code:	A means for reducing the complexity of information at hand or to be sought (Heintz 1982:12)
Belief:	The subjective probability of a relation between the object of the belief and some other object, value, concept, or attribute (Fishbein/Ajzen 1975:131); Conviction that a particular description of reality is true, proved and (usually) obvious (Gibert 1977:4)
Belief system:	All the beliefs, sets, explanations, or hypotheses, conscious or unconscious, that a person at a time accepts as true of the world he lives in (Rokeach, quoted in McGinnis 1978:3)
Image:	The total cognitive, affective and evaluative structure of the behaviour unit, or its internal view of itself or the universe (Boulding 1969:423); Something material that has been transformed and reprocessed in the brain of the individual (Fundamentals of Marxist-Leninist Philosophy 1982:83)

8

Definition of the international situation:	A set of images possessed by an individual, representing his view of what other nations are like, what relevance they have to the goals of his own nation, and what behaviour would be appropriate for his own nation (Pruitt 1965)
World outlook:	A set of views on the world, nature and society (Political Terms 1982:90)
World view:	That construction of reality within which an individual perceives and chooses among policy alternatives (Cottam 1977:10)
Prevailing world view:	That construction of reality which is most congruent with the choice among policy alternatives that a decisional group makes (Cottam 1977:10)

Related to the above are a number of other terms such as "operational code", "perspective", "filter", "screen", "orientation", "preconception" "premise", "bias", (Frei 1977:11f.) "tacit knowledge" (Polanyi, quoted in Wolf 1983:148), "convictions" (Goldhamer 1978:3f) and "schema" (Thorndyke/Hayes-Roth 1979). It should be noted that these concepts partly overlap, and some of them are often used synonymously. Yet they obviously share a common denominator inasmuch as they all refer to what a particular observer selects, perceives and interprets. They must be distinguished from approaches or techniques for presenting them, such as "maps", "scripts", "plans", "schemas", "frames" (Seiler 1973:10; Sieber 1978; Bennett 1981:169).

Corresponding concepts in Marxist philosophy

In connection with the nature and dynamics of cognition, it is interesting to note that the perspective underlying this approach is to some extent shared by all leading schools of thought in both East and West. Marxist philosophy also generally distinguishes between the "objective world" and the "subjective image of the objective world"; the two concepts are linked by "consciousness":

"Consciousness is the subjective image of the objective world. When we speak of the subjectivity of an image, we have in mind the fact that it is not a distorted reflection of reality, but something ideal, that is, as Karl Marx noted, something material that has been transformed and reprocessed in the brain of the individual. A thing in a person's consciousness is an image, and the real thing is its prototype." (Fundamentals of Marxist-Leninist Philosophy 1982:83)

Marxist philosophy also emphasizes the importance of selectivity inherent in any process of cognition:

> "Consciousness is characterized by an active creative attitude to the external world, to oneself, to human activity. The activeness of consciousness can be seen in the fact that a person reflects the external world purposefully, selectively. He reproduces in his head objects and phenomena through the prism of the knowledge he has already acquired - his representation and concepts. Reality is recreated in human consciousness not in the dead form of a mirror-like reflection, but in a creatively transformed state." (Fundamentals of Marxist-Leninist Philosophy 1982:87)

So far, the Marxist approach generally concurs with the approaches developed by Western social sciences. Both stress the crucial role of selection in inference in the process of acquiring consciousness. However, while Western approaches are generally characterized by what might be called an attitude of "relative objectivity", the Marxist view is more radical in this respect and assumes an "objective relativity" of any cognition. In other words: while Western approaches assume the possibility of perceiving at least some aspects of objective reality and offer a variety of (more or less tentative) explanations of how and why this process occurs, the Marxist approach tends to assume that it is "determined by the historically conditioned structure of man's cognitive abilities, the level of development of cognition, which in turn is determined by the existing social conditions" (Fundamentals of Marxist-Leninist Philosophy 1982:152). It also suggests criteria by which one can separate true knowledge from the untrue and the false : coherence (ibid.: 165f.), verification (ibid.: 166) and, foremost, "the activity which is the basis of knowledge, that is,... social historical practice" (ibid.: 166f.). This points to the high degree of practical relevance of the problem of cognition; far from constituting merely a subject of purely academic interest, cognition and cognitive processes constitute key elements of any practical policy. Again, this conclusion, although resting on a basis different from Western assumptions, can be said to coincide with corresponding conclusions reached by Western social scientists. It may therefore provide common ground for further research in the field of cognition.

Another interesting insight important in this context is offered by Marxist philosophy with regard to the "objective" and "subjective factors" dichotomy. Politics and social life, according to the Marxist view, are shaped by two types of factors:

> "Objective factors are the conditions which are independent from the individuals and which determine the direction and the scope of human actions. Such are for example the natural conditions, the stage of economic development, the needs of material, political development. The subjective factors are the actions of the popular masses, of classes, of parties, of States, the individuals, the conscience and the ability to act. Objective factors are always

the determining factors, but their influence is applied through the subjective factors. The subjective factors may play a determining role only when there are necessary objective conditions for this action." (Filosofsky Slovar 1980:25 9)

In Marxist terms, therefore, this study refers to the "subjective factors" shaping policies in the various fields related to security. More precisely, its purpose is to identify the "world outlook" of which military strategy and disarmament policies are constituent parts.

Theoretical assumptions

The purpose of this study is to find out to what extent and how the world outlooks or world views determine and affect the way in which policies related to security are formulated. This has an exclusively descriptive orientation. The aim is to analyse and offer a sincere account of the contents of the Soviet and American views. In other words, the study will avoid assessing or judging whether the views held by the two major Powers are "true" or not. However, the study will show where they and their underlying cognitive processes coincide and where they tend to reflect conflicting positions. The emphasis, of course, is on finding areas of actual or potential common understanding.

The utilization of terms mentioned in the preceding sections is usually associated with more or less specific theoretical arguments about the nature, the causes, the consequences and the interrelations of cognition and action, of understanding and misunderstanding. Some of these theoretical arguments will be taken up at various stages of the following analysis and in particular in the concluding chapter when it comes to interpreting the findings. At this point, it may be sufficient to draw attention to the following three main lines of theoretical argument:

(a)   "The greater the ambiguity, the greater the impact of preconceptions." (Betts 1978:69ff.). Ambiguity, in turn, in most instances is generated by either lack of information or excess of information accompanied by deception and "noise" (Betts 1978:69ff.; Knorr 1979:74ff.; Heuer 1982). Tension too leads to ambiguity and hence misperception (Mandel 1979, ch.II). That is why conflict situations are situations where peculiar patterns of cognition play an important role.

(b)   The cognitive process comprises various patterns some of which must be said to be downright inappropriate and thus leading to misperception, in particular (Holsti 1967; Steinbruner 1974:109-122; Axelrod 1976c:57; Jervis 1976:319-408; Hart 1978; Heradstveit 1980:273-292; Clarkson 1981:32f.; Vertzberger 1982): reinforcement of beliefs, overcoming inconsistency by arguments from analogy, wishful thinking, "worst-case" thinking, stop thinking, discreditation of discrepant information, reinterpretation of information, susceptibility to deception and other processes. Such adaptation processes have repeatedly been studied in connection with the thinking of defence planners who for instance, starting from a prudent and conservative attitude, characteristically deal with "worst-case" situations and underestimate their own capabilities (Garthoff 1983:3).

(c) Definitions of situations lead to actions that may precipitate the perceived condition (Keys 1981:18); this is the well-known logic of the self-fulfilling prophecy (Boulding 1956:112f.; Goffman 1970:101; Heradstveit 1980:273-292). Assumptions and discussions about these assumptions induce specific actions that in turn may have an effect on the potential adversary (Wells 1981:69) and thus ironically precipitate a situation which would not otherwise have arisen. Insights into a society's self-image and view of the world may therefore be helpful for a better understanding of this society's behaviour (von Beyme 1983:7f.).

Most of these and other theoretical propositions refer to the inherent logic of cognition, i.e. they ascribe the outcome and consequences of cognition to the very nature of cognition itself. It goes without saying that the validity of this position may be rather limited and that additional explanations must be included. Among them, the nature of the political and social system plays an important role in determining the specific patterns of cognition. Furthermore, cultural factors are to be taken into consideration whenever we are trying to offer insights into the causes of a particular kind of cognition, because "men tend to create the social universe in their own images" (Booth 1979:13). The most crucial determinant, however, is the state of political tension or detente existing between the adversaries.

As the main thrust of the present study is to identify and describe the contents and structure of the Soviet and the American views and their underlying cognitive patterns, no systematic effort will be made to explain why the Governments concerned perceive the strategic situation in their particular way. Yet some interpretative steps towards explanation will be offered, most of them based on the academic literature available on the subject.

DIMENSIONS OF CONFLICTIVE COGNITION: EVOLVING A CHECKLIST FOR ANALYSING SOURCE MATERIAL

The foregoing discussion of definitions of the various concepts and terms used for grasping conflictive cognition has clearly demonstrated that both the cognitive process and its outcomes, the views or images always represent highly complex phenomena. Complexity implies multi-dimensionality. Hence, in order to describe and to analyse conflictive cognition, the various dimensions involved must first be identified. Just as one requires three dimensions for describing the size of the room in which one is sitting (length, height and width), so one also needs a number of dimensions for

12

exploring the "space" of the intellectual construct called "conflictive cognition".

Based on the results of two decades of cognitive analysis (cf. Holsti 1962; Pruitt 1965; Finlay 1967:2; Holsti 1967:50; White 1968; Goffman 1970:101; Stoessinger 1974; Kirkpatrick 1975:56f.; Axelrod 1976c; Hart 1976:17-20; Snyder/Diesing 1977:308; Sienkiewicz 1978; Hart 1978; Reychler 1979:64-111 and 273; Gäfgen 1980:261; Hopple/Rossa 1981:74; Clarkson 1981:10; Lukov/Sergeyev 1982; Jervis 1982/83) and summarizing these results in a comprehensive and coherent way, it makes sense to subdivide the whole complex of views produced by conflictive cognition into three major subsets of images, each of them combining a number of dimensions or themes. These three subsets are :

(1) The view held about the international system in general;

(2) The view held about the adversary (including also, as a sub-subset, the so-called "meta-perspective", i.e. what one thinks the adversary thinks about oneself);

(3) The view of one's own role and choices with regard to the adversary.

Mapping the view and its subsets in graphical form, they may be represented as follows :

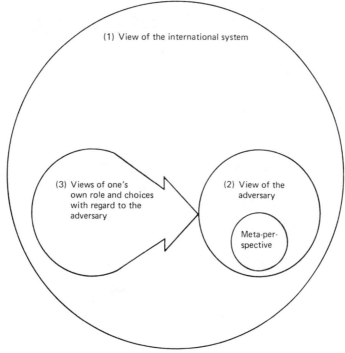

13

The three subsets of conflictive cognition are much broader in scope than assumptions regarding disarmament and arms control in the more restricted sense only. The reason for preferring such a comprehensive approach is that the views held with regard to disarmament and arms control cannot be properly analysed and understood independently of other elements of an overall view. The latter to a great extent determine the more specific views underlying policies and negotiations in the field of disarmament and arms control.

Within each of the three subsets, a number of specific dimensions or themes can be discerned. They are identified in the following checklist. This checklist, in turn, serves as a heuristic tool for analysing official texts, i.e. each text will be carefully read with regard to its potential contribution to answering the questions raised by the checklist. This analytic approach not only helps to extract important elements from sometimes rather bulky texts; more importantly, it also makes different texts comparable to each other and offers a basis for further conclusions, based on a semi-structured content analysis. It has been drafted with a view to serving the purpose of description without necessarily making a commitment to one of the specific epistemological or philosophical theories and concepts mentioned above.

Dimensions of conflictive cognition : a checklist

Dimensions (themes)	Key questions and possible categories (examples)
Views of the national system	
(1.1) Basic pattern of aggregation of the international system	How is the world organized? What are the basic units of the world system? Types of "actors" ? Dual structure/ plural structure What are the subunits of the basic units?
(1.2) Nature of relations among basic units	How do the basic units interact? (basically competitive, conflictive, tense or basically harmonic, relaxed)

14

(1.3)
Nature of the system,
trends and tendencies

How can the overall nature of the system be described? (dynamic, constant change/ static).

(1.4)
Evaluation of system
structure

In what direction does the world political system evolve? How is the present state of the system evaluated? (just, basically acceptable, good/ unjust, reactionary, undesirable, to be overcome, evil)

2) Views of the adversary

(2.1)
Aims

What are the adversary's indispensable key values? What are the adversary's aims or interests on the international level? What are the adversary's aims or interests with regard to specific fields of action (military-strategic position, both nuclear and non-nuclear, economic position, political position, etc.) and specific geographic regions?

(2.2)
Motives underlying aims

Are there contradictions between his aims? How does he rank-order these aims (priorities)? Why does the adversary have these aims? How does he justify them? Are the adversary's aims rooted in general dispositions or in the situation?

(2.3)
Structure of adversary

Is the adversary a unitary actor pursuing an integrated overall strategy, or are there internal cleavages?

(2.4)
Predictability and
trustworthiness

To what extent is the adversary's behaviour predictable (or incalculable)? To what extent can the adversary be trusted to respect agreements?

(2.5)
Capabilities

What are the basic capabilities the adversary relies on? On what basis rests his strength? What are his weaknesses? What is the priority rank-order of the adversary's capabilities for pursuing specific aims or interests? What are his specific strengths and weaknesses with regard to specific fields or levels of action and specific geographic regions?

(2.6)
Choice of strategies

What strategies has the adversary at his disposal (rank-order hierarchy)? What strategies promote best which of his specific goals with regard to specific fields or levels of action and specific geographic regions?
To what extent are there alternatives at his disposal? To what extent is the choice of his strategies determined by the nature of the challenge? Has the adversary certain general principles for selecting strategies? How does the adversary qualify and justify the pertinence of his decisions (experience? lessons of history? pragmatism? general rules?).

(2.7)
Disarmament and arms control policies

What are the adversary's primary objectives in the field of disarmament and arms control? What are the basic features to be observed in his conduct of negotiations? How does he approach the problem of verification? Why did he sign arms control agreements? Can the adversary and his attitude to arms control agreements be trusted?

(2.8)
Meta-perspective

How does the adversary see us (dimensions regarding aims/intentions, capabilities, strategies/ strategy choice as in groups)? Are the views held, by the adversary, about us appropriate or inappropriate (misrepresented, distorted, selective)?

What are the specific deficiences of his views about us? What information sources does the adversary rely upon, and how are these to be qualified? To what extent is our information available about the adversary sufficient or insufficient?

If the adversary misrepresents our intentions, might this be due to certain types of our behaviour which are in fact prone to misperception and misunderstanding?

(2.9)
Assessment of information about the adversary

How do we reach these assumptions and conclusions (historical experience, causal inference, etc)?

What proofs are quoted? To what extent can the adversary's declaratory strategy be trusted as reflecting his genuine views? To what extent is it appropriate to distinguish between declaratory strategy and real intentions? How can real intentions be inferred if they are not publicly expressed? Are there any uncertainty gaps regarding the information about the adversary? What aspects do they concern?

3) Views of one's own role and choices with regard to the adversary

(3.1)
Aims

What are the absolutely indispensable goals cherished by us? What are our aims or interests on the international level, especially with regard to the adversary? What are our aims or interests with regard to specific fields of action (military-strategic position, both nuclear and non-nuclear, economic position, political position, etc.) and specific geographic regions? Are there contradictions between aims? How do we rank-order these aims (priorities)?

17

(3.2)	
Motives underlying aims	Why are our aims or interests justified and necessary? Are our aims rooted in our genuine disposition or in the situation?
(3.3)	
The nature of one's own system	Are there internal cleavages relevant for relations with the adversary? To what extent is our behaviour predictable?
(3.4)	
Capabilities	To what extent, if at all, can the behaviour of the adversary be influenced by us? What are the basic capabilities we rely on? On what basis rests our strength? What are our weaknesses? What is the priority rank-order of our capabilities for pursuing specific aims or interests? What are our specific strengths and weaknesses with regard to specific fields or levels of action and specific geographic regions?
(3.5)	
Principal political strategies for shaping relations with the adversary	What strategies are at our disposal (rank-order hierarchy)? What strategies promote best which specific goal with regard to specific fields or levels of action and specific geographic regions? Can the adversary be influence better by negative sanctions (punishment) or positive sanctions (rewards)? To what extent can alternative strategies be freely chosen? To what extent is the choice of strategies determined by the nature of the challenge? Are there certain general principles for selecting strategies? How should the strategies be applied? How is the pertinence of decisions qualified and justified (experience, lessons of history, pragmatism, general rules)?

(3.6)	
The role of force and principles of military strategy	What is the role of the military factor in contemporary relations with the adversary? What military actions should we choose in different hypothetical situations? What will be our reponses to specific challenges emanating from the adversary? If information about what the adversary intends is inadequate, what ought to be done on our part? What is the role of disarmament as a strategy?
(3.7)	
Disarmament and arms control policies	What are our objectives in disarmament and arms control negotiations? What are the appropriate means to achieve these objectives in negotiations with the adversary? What is the proper approach to verification?

THE SOURCE PROBLEM: DOCUMENTS AND THEIR VALIDITY

Thoughts and words

As a matter of principle and throughout this study, the contents of views will be identified on the basis of official statements made by authorized spokesmen of the Governments concerned or the heads of Governments themselves. However, at this point an important question must be raised: can such material really be used for evidence? Or, to put the question more bluntly: do Governments really tell the truth when talking and writing about their views and assumptions? How reliable are official statements and can they be trusted in all circumstances? Can thoughts be inferred from words? This question is far too general to be answered by a wholesale argument for or against the doubts and criticisms it obviously implies.

The fundamental issue of the validity of texts can be clarified by first considering the worst case - outright deception. Public statements may be aimed at leading an addressee astray by hiding one's true intent and by reinforcing the target's erroneous beliefs (Heuer 1982; Whaley 1982). In the context of global strategic competition this possibility must not prematurely be ruled out; its occurrence cannot be said to be absolutely remote. "Disinformation" in this context is too familiar to be ignored.

Even if there are no reasons to suspect arrant deception or disinformation, one may still wish to make a reservation when reading and interpreting a document on disarmament policy or strategic doctrine, as there exists the possibility of the respective document merely serving a propaganda purpose. It is clear that any author of such a document writes with his audience in mind. It may be intended "to persuade, justify, threaten, cajole, manipulate, evoke sympathy and support, or otherwise influence the intended audience" (Holsti 1977:45). Truth may then become quite relative in this case, as has been pointed out by a Marxist-Leninist philosopher:

> "Truth is the prerequisite and basis of our agitation. The latter's quality, however, cannot be assessed only in terms of its truth but also in terms of its ability to make truth operational in thought and action of men. The point is to bring about change in the consciousness of men, i.e. to generate positive appraisors and prescriptors and, with their help, to achieve a modification in the behaviour of the addressee according to the aims of the agitation." (Klaus 1971:200)

Documents written with a specific agitation purpose in mind can hardly claim to have a high degree of validity. Yet the problem is how to distinguish documents comprising an element of propaganda from documents truly and sincerely conveying objective information. There are no convenient criteria to be found.

A third cause for reservation stems from the fact that Governments generally try to avoid committing themselves verbally when not forced to do so. Therefore, statements on policy and strategy may be so diffuse and ambiguous that they are virtually useless for any further conclusions (Bryder 1981:76).

This line of sceptical reasoning about the validity of written documents can be said to constitute a common practice in all fields of scientific inquiry where documents serve as the main source of information, such as history and many branches of the social sciences. It would be hard to disprove and unwise to discard these caveats in principle.

Words and deeds

However, some additional aspects should be taken into consideration that lead to more refined conclusions (cf. Mouritzen 1981; Bonham and Shapiro 1977; Trout 1975) : First of all, Governments have a strong interest in continuity and consistency in making foreign policy statements because any statement deviating from previous ones generates the need for additional justification, and, in the absence of such efforts, may be followed by negative sanctions from the domestic and foreign receiver groups. No Government can afford to merely "play around" with disarmament policy and strategic doctrine without losing its internal and external credibility as a responsible actor. After all, "Governments are nevertheless at great pains to communicate a desired image of their intentions by means of 'doctrinal' statements" (Hart 1979:75f.) Outright lying, on the other hand, implies costs, of which a Government is usually well aware (Neubauer 1977).

Furthermore, it cannot be denied that Governments in fact tend to limit their freedom of choice and action in the future. In other words, official doctrines can be expected to induce, to some extent, self-fulfilling prophecies. With considerable probability, words are followed by deeds. Hence words, whatever their original purpose, are not simply irrelevant for future behaviour; they tend to create a reality of their own. In more general terms, one can argue that attitudes to some extent determine behaviour namely, to the extent that the behaviour is embedded in a social context (cf. Meinefeld 1977:177f.) This is definitely the case in the context of international relations.

This does not, of course, imply that assumptions and their verbal expression have a direct and immediate impact on foreign policy actions and actual strategic behaviour. The role which beliefs may play in policy-making is much subtler and less direct (Holsti 1977:31). Rather than directly guiding action, they serve as "a lens or prism through which information is processed and given meaning; as a diagnostic scheme; as one means of coping with the cognitive constraints on rationality; as a source of guidelines that may guide or bound - but not necessarily determine - policy prescriptions and choices" (ibid.:31). Still, in this relative role, they are clearly vitally important, and even more so in a field characterized by such a high degree of uncertainty as that of security.

When discussing the relevance of published official statements we do not inevitably have to rely on mere speculation only. Especially in the study of Soviet foreign policy, the link between words and deeds has become a central theme. In an empirical study by Zimmerman (1983) the relation between changes in Soviet press reports and changes in actual Soviet defence spending was examined, analysing in particular the changing characterization of the United States and "imperialism" as well as the presentation of Soviet military intentions. Statistical correlations calculated by relating these changes in content to changes in the Soviet defence budget explained more than four fifths of the variance in the change of Soviet ruble expenditure for defence. That means that Soviet statements provide quite ample information about subsequent behaviour in the field of armaments.

Such close links between words and deeds are even more obvious in the case of the United States. Words ought to be taken seriously. It therefore seems that, despite the various reservations with regard to the suspected deception and/or propaganda purpose of official texts, it is nevertheless meaningful to base a study of conflictive

21

cognition on official statements, keeping in mind, however, the caveats which follow from these reservations.

In all probability, the delicate nature of strategic communication expresses itself less in outright deception, lying and propagandistic abuse than in ambiguity. As a matter of fact, as will be shown repeatedly in the following chapters, the information content of official statements is very often quite poor or very general, and the information provided therein sometimes diffuse and ambiguous. This fact poses a serious obstacle to any attempt at a comprehensive description of the nature and dynamics of conflictive cognition. But it certainly does not mean that a description based on such texts is doomed to be beside the point. It may also be meaningful and revealing to pay attention to those elements of conflictive cognition which deliberately or unintentionally remain fuzzy.

CHAPTER II

THE SOVIET VIEW

REMARKS ON THE SOURCES AND CHARACTERISTICS OF THE SOVIET VIEW

Types of documents used

The Soviet view as presented in this chapter can reliably be grasped in a considerable number of official documents reflecting the conceptions held by the supreme leadership of the country. The documents on which the following analysis will be based and which will also be amply quoted in this chapter comprise reports by the General Secretary to the Congresses of the Communist Party of the Soviet Union (CPSU), public statements made by the General Secretary, the Minister of Defence and leading CPSU, Government and Army officials on various occasions. Use will also be made of official communiqués and articles containing declarations of principles published in leading Soviet daily newspapers and political journals, as well as handbooks, dictionaries and textbooks and materials published by the staff of the leading academic institutions active in the field of international politics (Institute of World Economy and International Relations, Institute for the Study of the USA and Canada, Moscow State Institute of International Relations, etc.). These texts offer a comprehensive insight into the contents, structure and nature of the official Soviet view of the international situation.

They can be said to be fully representative of Soviet views. These views are evolved in a complex and constant process of discussions held on various levels of the ministerial and Party organizations and academic institutions. They are then synchronized, adjusted and go through a process of authentication by the Party leadership. Once a decision has been taken, the ensuing directives constitute binding guidance or "general line" for all the following statements on the subject.

Therefore, in the Soviet Union, all published statements on problems of national security reflect a unity of views and ultimately rest on key concepts adopted by the highest authorities. By their very nature they directly or indirectly refer to these officially sanctioned concepts to which they have a deductive relationship and which they often quote at length. Hence they can all be said to reflect the authoritative standpoint truly and sincerely.

Depending on their direct or indirect relationship to the ultimate key concepts adopted by the supreme leadership, three types of texts may be distinguished: the most immediate reflection of these views can be found in Party documents and speeches made on important occasions; these texts provide the constants or the "general line", i.e. the fundamental principles of the Soviet view which are characterized by a high degree of stability over time. Secondly, there are speeches and articles by the Head of State, the Ministers of Defence, Foreign Affairs and other branches of government, as well as the high commanders of the Soviet Armed Forces; such texts analyse specific contemporary problems in the light of the "general line". The third category comprises scientific source material; it also deals with more or less specific questions, again interpreting them within the framework of the "general line", and looks at them in a prospective or retrospective manner.

Characteristics of Soviet statements

The documents convey a picture of the Soviet perception which is striking by both its coherent and systematic character. Coherence is provided by the absence of contradictory or dissenting views, i.e. the statements available are characterized by a high degree of harmony and mutual compatibility. The systematic nature of the views conveyed by the documents stems from a rigorous effort to utilize a generally binding terminology and even more so by the systematic reference to the basic propositions of Marxist-Leninist philosophy and its current interpretation by the CPSU leadership.

The specific origin of all officially published material in the Soviet Union also suggests that looking for discrepancies reflecting latent tensions between different "wings" may probably be nothing but a futile task. Western observers sometimes try to identify different and conflicting perspectives, using the labels "hawks" vs. "doves" or "traditionalists" vs. "realists" or "the military" vs. "the Foreign Ministry apparatus" and the like. However, there are compelling reasons to assume that interpretations of this kind are ultimately based on wishful thinking and may be simple projections of the pluralistic Western approach on to Soviet reality, which works in a completely different way, at least as far as the elaboration and publication of political and military statements are concerned.

It must also be noted that Soviet statements exhibit an impressive degree of continuity. This feature, too, reflects the nature of the Soviet political system: as any abrupt change or reversal of the "general line" would indicate that the previous "general line" was to some extent incorrect or at least has to be seen in a relative way, this would implicitly question the authority and leading role of the Communist Party. Thus the CPSU's claim to exclusive and scientifically based leadership necessarily leads to a strong emphasis on continuity.

In the West, many commentators sometimes feel inclined to ask whether Soviet leaders really act in accordance with what they say. More often than not this question is motivated by the implicit assumption that Soviet policy statements merely serve purposes of external propaganda and internal legitimation, thus constituting something not to be taken seriously. However, as has already been pointed out in the preceding chapter, it is hard to believe that the constant reference to a specific pattern of perception and evaluation of the international situation and the policy of disarmament and arms control has simply no impact whatsoever on the real perception and evaluation.

In addition, another important feature of Soviet statements must be borne in mind when reading Soviet source material: when talking about "assumptions" underlying policies in the field of national security, and when implying that the value judgements inherent in such assumptions may be rather relative, one has to be aware that Soviet spokesmen tend to think of themselves and of their foreign and military policies in terms of objective, scientifically based knowledge rather than of hypothetical assumptions regarding a context dominated by uncertainty. They emphasize their claim to correct understanding, also with regard to foreign policy and military strategy:

> "Lenin attached special importance to the need for a strictly scientific approach to the phenomena of international life and foreign policy, an approach which is incompatible with voluntaristic attitudes, opportunistic considerations, superficial improvisation, and scholastic speculation... In their entire activities on the world scene the CPSU and the Soviet State are invariably loyal to Lenin's behest: to correctly determine the leading trend in social development by giving a scientifically sound definition of the character of the modern epoch." (Gromyko 1984:64)

> "Soviet military science and doctrine can successfully resolve their task because they rely on a correct understanding of the essence of wars, their sources, the laws governing their emergence, the political motives and 'mechanisms' of their unleashing. ...This doctrine is a scientifically based and harmonious system of ideas and principles defining the basic tasks of strengthening the country's defensive capacity and military development." (Marxism-Leninism on War and Army 1972 :301 and 303)

In a more generalized form, the claim to present a "scientifically based" doctrine reflecting "correct understanding" of all its aspects originates in the philosophical positions of Marxism-Leninism, as pointed out for instance by Ponomarev:

> "Marxism-Leninism derives its vitality and force primarily from the essence of its scientific method of knowing and transforming the world.... The Marxist-Leninist method of analysing the life of society is tied up with the theory of Marxism-Leninism, with its postulates, which show the common historical regularities in the development of society. How these regularities operate in concrete historical and national conditions is determined by creative scientific analysis. This is why the Marxist-Leninist method is a creative method requiring tireless search for answers to new questions arising in the surrounding world. Yet it is also a strictly scientific method, based on integral and consummate theory - dialectical and historical materialism, political economy, and scientific communism." (Ponomarev 1979:147 and 149)

Another Soviet author, comparing various epistemological approaches, claims that "only one scientific theory, Marxist-Leninist theory, has succeeded in learning this character <of modern society>, all its complexity and diversity." (Shakhnazarov 1979:23). Still, according to Marxist-Leninist epistemology, the assumption of an objective and scientifically corroborated law of historical evolution does not exclude the fact that there are also subjective and accidental factors at work shaping the course of events. As this second category of factors determining the course of events cannot be grasped as easily as the "historical regularities", Soviet thinking and writing on these matters tend to concentrate on the "regularities" or "general law", and it does not always commit itself to precise conclusions regarding "subjective factors". Therefore, the task of analysing Soviet statements is not as easy as it might seem at first glance.

Finally, it should also be noted that Soviet strategic thinking, although characterized by an impressive degree of systematic coherence and a deductive structure, is far from being rigid and inflexible. Soviet authors constantly draw attention to the innovative, dynamic and mobile nature of the political situation in general:

> "The fact is that military doctrine is not static. Its content changes with the change in the political situation and alteration of economic and military-technical factors." (Zavizion/Kirshin 1972:80)

Therefore, when defining concepts, Soviet sources always point to the temporal limits of the validity of such definitions. This can be seen, for instance, in the definitions offered by the Soviet Military Encyclopaedia (1977) and the Great Soviet Encyclopaedia (1976):

> "... a system of views adopted by a State in a certain period <emphasis ours>, concerning the aims and character of a possible war, the preparation of the country and its army for war, and the methods of waging it." (quoted in Siegmund/Kleine 1982, English translation by Lider 1983:338)

> "... the system of official views and propositions that determines the direction of military development, the preparation of the country and its armed forces for war, and for the method or forms of conducting the war. The military doctrine is developed and defined by the political leadership of the State. The principal propositions of a military doctrine are formed and changed in accordance with politics and the social structure, the level of development of the productive forces, new scientific achievements and the nature of the anticipated war." (Great Soviet Encyclopaedia, Vol. 5:258)

Given the dynamic evolution of Soviet strategy, the selection of documents used for the analysis of the Soviet view will therefore basically concentrate on the past five years in order to avoid misrepresentation of contemporary Soviet doctrine by confusing statements valid today with statements made some time ago in a rather different historical context. When faced with the ample quotations from Soviet sources presented on the following pages, the reader may find the author's inclination to use cited material somewhat excessive. However, when analysing texts it is clear that the nature of the material must be taken into account. Based on the preceding reflections on the characteristics of Soviet texts, and after thorough examination of all alternative methods available for analysing the content of such texts, the author concluded that frequently quoting representative extracts from authentic texts constitutes the method which can be said to be most appropriate to the specific structure and nature of the material to be analysed.

THE SOVIET VIEW OF THE INTERNATIONAL SYSTEM

Assumptions regarding the basic patterns of global politics: a dichotomy

In order to acquire a proper understanding of how the Party, State and military leadership of the Soviet Union perceives the adversary and its own choices and options, the Soviet view of the international system as a whole must first of all be ascertained, for this general view represents a framework within which all other views are placed. Fundamental elements of such a world view are the views of how the world is organized, of how the political "world map" looks, of what basic units the global system is composed, and of the type of actors which determine the world scene. In the standard presentations of Soviet political and strategic thinking one clear-cut and constant image of the world can be seen to dominate: a world characterized by the "main contradiction" between two oppposing classes - "the working class, which along with other classes and groups of society holds power in socialist countries", on the one hand, and the "monopolistic bourgeoisie, ruling in imperialist States" (Nauchnye Osnovy 1982:47) on the other hand. In other words, the world is seen as a dichotomous structure which has existed ever since the first socialist State was established:

"The battle between the two lines in world politics - our policy of peace, on the one hand, and the aggressive, hegemonistic imperialist policy, on the other - is not something that began today or even yesterday. It began in October 1917 with the birth of the world's first socialist State ..." (Gromyko 1980:449; 1983b:4f.)

This fundamental split rooted in the "main contradiction of international relations" (Arbatov 1973:33f.) is held to be more significant than any other type of cleavage which might be envisaged, in particular national differences existing between sovereign countries:

"Consequently the axis of antagonism in the world arena has

29

gradually shifted from the national into the class sphere."
(Shakhnazarov 1983:279)

As national differences have no pre-eminence, "a new type of socialist international relations" has developed between the socialist
countries; it is based on their political and ideological unity
(Kulish 1982:84) and "the vital class interests of these countries'
peoples" (Novopashin 1982:63). That is the meaning of the term
"internationalist" frequently associated with the notion of the
"international class conflict":

> "The Marxist-Leninist method is essentially an internationalist
> method. It proceeds from the objective fact that there is an
> international working class and that there are united imperialist
> forces, and maintains therefore that the interests of the working
> class and all other anti-imperialist forces are international, and
> that these forces must act in common within the frame of the
> single, objectively conditioned world revolutionary process."
> (Ponomarev 1979:149)

The "world map" as perceived through the prism of Soviet political
thought therefore remains basically dichotomous although there may be
some secondary cleavages, especially inside the "non-imperialist"
part of the world, i.e the part dominated by "revolutionary forces".
The latter is said to be composed of "the world of socialism" (comprising the countries belonging to the Warsaw Treaty Organization
plus Afghanistan, Laos, Kampuchea, Cuba, the Democratic People's Republic of Korea, Yugoslavia, Mongolia and, with some reservations,
the People's Republic of China plus the "republics on the way to
construct the elements of socialist society" (such as Angola and
Mozambique). In addition, the "working-class movement" in capitalist
countries is as a rule also included in the camp of "revolutionary
forces" (Ponomarev 1979:19-33; Brezhnev in: Documents and Resolutions
1981:15-21). Similarly, the "anti-war movement" operating in the West
is seen as an integral part of the forces in favour of peace and
social progress; any attempt to distinguish between Western and
Eastern peace movements is criticized as a plot against the unity of
the anti-war movement, an attempt to split it and to advocate
division in this movement (Lokshin/Oryol 1984:21). Still, despite the
"basic contradiction" dividing the world Soviet leaders concede that
some problems are common to all mankind, irrespective of the social
and political system to which peoples belong. With particular reference to the environmental challenge of our time, General Secretary
Brezhnev said:

> "We are not alone on the planet, and the conservation of nature
> calls for the efforts of all peoples inhabiting the earth. A wound
> inflicted on nature on one continent would inevitably spread its
> infection to another." (Brezhnev 1978:49)

It is, however, very important to note that in the Soviet view the
awareness of global interdependence, as expressed in this and other
representative statements, does not necessarily imply a shift from
the dual image of a world dominated by the "main contradiction of
international relations" to the vision of "one world" or "spaceship

Earth", as many in the West would like to see it. In this respect, Soviet sources draw a clear and distinct line. They reject any idea of perceiving the contemporary and future world in terms of the technocratic logic of modern civilization and global interdependence. "Bourgeois" theorists are sharply criticized for their ideas:

"Limited by their class interests and lacking a scientific method of cognition... bourgeois sociologists seek to prove that the nature of the modern epoch is determined by technical discoveries, chiefly by the discovery of atomic power. No more and no less than the atomic bomb is regarded as being at the hub of the modern epoch, which these sociologists call the 'technical age', the 'nuclear age', the age of the 'atomic bomb'. Yet the development of society cannot be reduced to technology, to technical discoveries, despite the fact that in the conditions of the present scientific and technological revolution they play an immense role in social development. But technology influences the historical process not by itself but through the relations of production, that are predominant in society. These relations and the class forces behind them must be primarily taken into consideration when we analyse the modern epoch." (Afanasyev 1981:40)

Soviet spokesmen hold that the conception of the "nuclear age" is a mere fabrication of bourgeois propaganda aimed at diverting attention from the real issue of world politics - the "main contradiction" of the "international class struggle". Likewise, they refute the conception of a world divided into a "poor South" and a "rich North". In his report to the 26th CPSU Congress in 1981, General Secretary Brezhnev made this quite clear:

"And certainly, the issue must not be reduced, as this is sometimes done, simply to distinctions between 'rich North' and 'poor South'." (Brezhnev 1981:21)

It is even bluntly said that:

"The concept of war between 'the South and the North', preached by the revisionists, plays into the hands of the bourgeoisie and exploiters both in capitalist and in developing countries. This theory meets with the interests of the imperialists, who dream of disuniting the proponents of peace, social and national progress and socialism." (Belov/Karenin/Petrov 1979:182)

According to other authors (e.g. Schachnasarow 1982:328), any attempt to put the socialist countries into the same category as the imperialist countries, by referring to their developed economy, merely presents a futile trick of bourgeois propaganda. From a Marxist-Leninist point of view, it is completely wrong to structure the world according to the criterion of per capita income. Rather, the decisive question is who owns the means of production, and hence the nature of the ruling class. Distinguishing between "rich" countries and "poor" countries, according to Soviet spokesmen, only serves to split socialism from the national liberation movements (Iwanow 1983:778-786).

Therefore, neither the term "third world" nor the term "developing country" involve concepts acceptable to the Soviet view (Shakhnazarov 1979:298f.)

In sum, in analysing world society, there is one cleavage definitively seen to prevail. In Marxist-Leninist theory, the class cleavage is, under all circumstances and at all times, assumed to be the predominant factor shaping the world: there are socialist countries and capitalist countries - and perhaps "mixed" or "transitional" countries in between (Shakhnazarov 1979:300). It is very important to keep in mind this basic assumption because it implies a number of highly relevant conclusions, chief among them the idea that neither the "nuclear age" nor the "North-South conflict" has any logic of its own. According to this view, the nature of the world political system as determined by the existence of the international class conflict cannot be altered by the consequences of the nuclear era or disparities of economic development.

The fundamental class cleavage characterizing the nature of the world political system, in the Soviet view, may be conditioned, however, by the "common interests in the progressive development of human civilization". In practical terms, common interests may be served by the principle of "peaceful coexistence" (Fedoseyev 1983:44f.). The Soviet conception of "peaceful coexistence" will be dealt with below. It basically means that the confrontation between the two opposed social systems will go on but must not escalate into a war, i.e. the international class struggle must be fought by peaceful competition.

When further analysing the global political system and its underlying "main contradiction", Soviet sources point to the special role of the two major Powers. Their relationship is held to have a decisive impact on the state and evolution of international relations in general as they are "the most powerful States" (Alexandrov V. 1982:248).

"US-Soviet relations are of great importance for vital problems of the modern world- the problem of war and peace, the international atmosphere in general, functioning and development of the system of international relations. The character of US-Soviet relations, the tendencies of their evolution largely influences the evolution of international relations and the perspectives of détente." (Razriyadka mezhdunarodnoy napriyazhennosty i ideologicheskaya borba, 1981:193)

Yet this does not mean that the Soviet view of the world assigns any particular importance to the two major nuclear Powers. On the contrary, Soviet authors vigorously disclaim: "We are against the 'superpower' concept." (Sivachev/Yakovlev 1979:269) All they concede in this respect is the fact that the confrontation of two very powerful States "complicates the situation"; for this reason the two great nations share a special responsibility in international relations for preserving world peace (ibid.) and for promoting disarmament

(Abarenko/Semeyko/Timerbayev 1983:85).

But this is not to say that the two major Powers share equal
responsibility with regard to the increasingly dangerous military
situation and the arms race. Representatives of Western peace movements appealing on the very same terms to both the United States and
USSR leaderships are criticized for not paying due attention to the
fact that one side is heating up the arms race while the other is
basically peace-loving and reluctantly being forced to react. As a
group of Soviet scholars puts it :

"All the blame for the current speed-up in the arms race and
rising world tensions rests with the militarist circles of those
States <meaning the United States and its allies>". (Kalyadin/
Bogdanov/Vorontzov 1983:2)

Assumptions regarding global political relations: basic antagonism

From the foregoing assumptions it logically follows that the
"international class struggle" will inevitably continue - between the
two forces true and definitive "peace" is held to be neither feasible
nor thinkable. According to the fundamental concept reflected in
official Soviet statements, the relationship between the two forces
representing the "basic contradiction" is dominated by an inherent
and incessant antagonism. Of course, the actual manifestation of this
antagonism is said to differ according to historical conditions; as
will be shown below, the particular type of manifestation of this
antagonism genuine to our time can be described in terms of the
concept of "peaceful coexistence". This principle is said to be valid
at least for the time being and until the end of the process of
transition to socialism. It means "rivalry - yes, military hostility
- no" (Burlatsky 1983b). While continuing rivalry results from "the
objective sources of contradictions between the two powers", Soviet
sources indicate a vast field of proximity of interests where the
rivals could act as partners: prevention of a nuclear war, economic
co-operation, co-operation in the sphere of science, culture and the
arts, and ecological problems (ibid.). In brief, as Burlatsky points
out, "the existence of social contradictions in the world arena does
not rule out political accord and compromise" (Burlatsky 1982).

Yet Soviet sources never fail to emphasize clearly and distinctly
that the paramount nature of the "basic contradiction" must never be
mitigated by any adaptation to this period of transition. In particular, they warn that "peaceful coexistence" and "détente" should not
be taken to mean the abrogation of the "international class struggle":

"The relationship between détente and the class struggle was
clearly defined at the 25th Congress of the CPSU. It was stressed

that détente did not and could under no circumstances annul or modify the laws of the class struggle." (Ponomarev 1979:62)

The basic nature of the antagonism is also held to be the ultimate and fundamental cause of all wars. A war is simply an acute, "extreme intensification of the antagonistic contradiction between classes and States" (Sowjetische Militärenzyklopädie 1980, Vol. 26:69). More specifically, under present historic conditions, the outbreak of war, according to the Soviet view, can result from three types of contradictions: between imperialism and socialism, between new nations or colonial or dependent countries and imperialist States, and between the ruling class and the revolutionary masses (ibid.:71).

More particularly, the concept of the "international class struggle" also means that the Soviet leadership wishes the "struggle of the peoples for national liberation" to go on unaffected by any restrictive considerations associated with détente. As was mentioned in an important statement of the Soviet Government:

"Détente does not and cannot mean the freezing of objective processes of historical development. It is not a safeguard for decayed regimes. Nor does it grant an indulgence for the right to suppress the just struggle of the peoples for national liberation." (Pravda, 22 May 1976, quoted in: Luzin 1981:144)

As far as the relations between the Soviet Union and developing countries are concerned, the Soviet view can be stated as follows:

"The political relationship between the USSR and recently declared independent countries is primarily concerned with providing comprehensive, disinterested assistance to the process of decolonization and independent development, consolidating a new type of equal and mutually beneficial relationship based on the principles of non-interference." (Anatoly Gromyko 1982:118)

In Soviet writings, the relations among socialist countries and the alliance of world socialism with national liberation forces as well as the unity of the world communist movement are generally summed up under the heading "proletarian internationalism":

"Loyalty to it <i.e. proletarian internationalism> is the main condition for ensuring the interaction of the three main revolutionary streams of our time - world socialism, the international working class and the national liberation struggle." (Ponomarev, quoted in: Proletarian Internationalism 1980:129)

In other words, the Soviet Union assumes the existence of a high degree of unity and cohesion among all "revolutionary forces" opposed to "imperialism" as its main adversary. This assumption also implies an elaborate theory about the types of relations prevailing and desirable between the three "revolutionary forces"; the essence of their interrelations is unity and solidarity in the fierce antagonism generated by the world's "main contradiction".

As was mentioned before, the world seen through Soviet eyes is fundamentally dichotomous and conflictive. The dividing line between the two opposing forces, however, has to be identified in a rather refined and precise way, because it does not simply coincide with any national border. It sometimes also separates people within capitalist countries. That is why, with regard to the long period of peace achieved in Europe, General Secretary Andropov said that this has been made possible

"... by the consistent peace-loving policy of the countries of the socialist community, the efforts of the continent's peace-loving forces and also the realistic position adopted by sober-minded politicians in the West." (Andropov 1983d:5)

The assumption is that there are "peace-loving forces" and "sober-minded" elements in the West thinking and acting in accordance with the aims of the "progressive world" and its leading country, the USSR. This assumption has some practical implications with regard to the approach chosen by Soviet foreign policy to deal with the West. In particular, it implies a special approach to addressing and encouraging these "sober-minded" groups in the West.

Assumptions regarding global trends and tendencies: irreversible change of the correlation of forces and ultimate triumph of socialism

Soviet sources maintain that the world as seen in the Soviet perspective can, as a matter of principle, never be stabilized as long as the "main contradiction" continues to exist. Yet this does not mean that the future simply depends on the more or less capricious outcome of what happens here and there. Soviet statements point in quite an opposite direction by proposing that the past, present and future course of events is largely determined by the "laws of social progress":

"Scientifically analysing the historical process and social phenomena of the capitalist society of their time, Marx and Engels revealed the general tendency of the development of the productive forces which sooner or later unavoidably abolish capitalist relations of production. In turn this means that communism is a historical inevitability." (Kortunov 1979:323)

This is how Foreign Minister Gromyko describes the phenomenon:

"Socialism is gaining and will continue to gain strength. The world is developing according to the objective laws discovered by Marxism-Leninism." (Gromyko 1983b:22)

According to a general tenet central to Marxist-Leninist philosophy and especially historical materialism (cf. Fundamentals of

Marxist-Leninist Philosophy 1982:195-431), the present epoch which began in 1917 is ingressing the gradual "transition from capitalism to socialism on a world scale". More precisely, and quoting the words of Ponomarev, it is the epoch

"... of victorious socialist revolutions in many countries, of the establishment and powerful growth of the world socialist system, of the building of socialism and communism. It is the epoch of the steady crumbling and decline of capitalism..., of the aggravation of that system's general crisis... Lastly, it is the epoch of radical change in the alignment of forces in the world, of the mounting influence of existing socialism on the course of social development..." (Ponomarev 1979:7f.)

This assumption is absolutely crucial for a proper understanding of the Soviet world view and Soviet political concepts based there upon. Soviet spokesmen are convinced that "the transition to socialism and communism is the road of development of all mankind" (Afanasyev 1977:49). From their observation of world history since 1917 they infer that the "correlation of forces" has steadily been shifting in favour of socialism; in their eyes this process constitutes nothing less than an objective necessity :

"The change in the correlation of forces in favour of socialism is an objective and natural law of world development." (Lebedev 1982:141)

The concept of "correlation of forces" ("sootnosheniye sil") in Marxist-Leninist thought serves as the yardstick for observing and measuring the state and evolution of world social development; its precise meaning will be dealt with below.

In the context of understanding the more general aspects of the Soviet world view, it is indispensable to realize that the concept of correlation of forces has an inherently dynamic nature: as it refers to the relationship between socialism and capitalism in the historic struggle for the triumph of the former, any attempt to deny or halt this process is simply called an "absurdity" - it would be as foolish as denying the law of gravity. This also means that the "law of world development" is working irrespective of whether or not the Soviet Union and its allies make efforts to promote it. Soviet spokesmen emphasize that they do not want to "export revolution"; for instance, any changes in the correlation of forces such as the revolutionary change in Central America are surmised to result from an autonomous process of objective necessity. Capitalism is assumed to be losing ground not only because of the growing strength of the socialist community, but also because of the internal contradictions of capitalism, ensuing crises, and the accelerating pace of social revolutions taking place in Africa, Asia and Latin America.

For a proper understanding of the Soviet view it is indispensable not to confuse the Soviet term "correlation of forces" (in Russian:

"sootnosheniye sil") with the Western term "balance of power" (in Russian "ravnovesiye sil" or "balans sil"). While the first connotes an inherently dynamic conception, the second, in its Western usage, implies that the preservation and stabilization of the "balance of power" is something desirable. As will be demonstrated further below (p. 43ff.) this second meaning is forthrightly and unanimously repudiated by Soviet spokesmen. From the Soviet point of view, the concept of "correlation of forces" also conveys a clear and distinct design for political action.

The process of the change of the correlation of forces is furthermore held to be irreversible:

"Marked by competition between the two social systems, it is developing under the banner of the epoch's main law - the steadfast and ever more decisive and irreversible change in the correlation of forces on a world-wide scale in favour of peace, democracy and socialism." (Gromyko 1980:415)

More importantly, the resulting shift in the correlation of forces in favour of socialism is believed to import even greater momentum to this process; "counter-revolution" will lose its chance. These considerations are aptly expressed by Shaknnazarov:

"If we project the clear tendency of the faster development of the socialist countries in comparison with the capitalist countries, the conclusion suggests itself that some time in the foreseeable perspective the correlation of world forces on the whole and in each non-socialist country will make impossible any counter-revolutionary actions such as occurred e.g. in Chile."
(Schachnasarow 1982:344)

Zagladin considers that, by recognizing the principle of "peaceful coexistence of the two systems", the world has also recognized "the irreversibility of the conquests made by socialism" (Zagladin 1981:167). The very same process of an ongoing change of the "correlation of forces" is usually also projected into the future.

Yet Soviet spokesmen do not wish to foretell precisely when and how this change will occur because it may be a long and difficult process. This has been expressed by General Secretary Chernenko:

"We do not doubt in the least that socialism will eventually win that competition. At the same time, while emphasizing that modern capitalism is historically foredoomed, we must take into account the fact that, in the context of its general crisis, it still has substantial and by no means depleted reserves for development." (Chernenko 1984b:6)

In a more detailed view, the following observations are adduced as proof of the evolution of the "correlation of forces" in the direction of the "ultimate triumph of socialism":

"The modern era is characterized by the following principal features:

- transition from capitalism to socialism on a world scale, victorious revolutions in a number of States, formation and evolution of world systems of socialism, and construction of socialism and communism;

- decline of a social system of exploitation - capitalism -, aggravation of its general crisis, successful struggle of the working class and its allies against monopolies for democracy and social progress, peace and socialism;

- collapse of a colonial system of imperialism, powerful advance of the national liberation movements, access of the peoples of Asia, Africa, and Latin America to independent social, economic, and political development;

- radical change in the alignment of forces in the world, and the growing influence of real socialism on world development with its struggle for the elimination of war from the life of humanity." (Nauchnye Osnovy Sovetskoy Vneshney Politiki 1982:20)

The "general crisis of capitalism" constitutes the subject of many elaborate studies (e.g. Schachnasarow 1982:190-261). They conclude that, although the system of contemporary capitalism may still have some strength, the tendencies leading to its decay clearly prevail (ibid.: 259): the decay of capitalism, on the one hand, signifies the growing predominance of the forces of socialism, on the other hand (ibid.: 344). While Soviet sources always stress the validity of this general trend, they are still very careful not to oversimplify its significance. Referring to Lenin's dictum that "history does not evolve like Nevsky Prospekt" (i.e. not in a strictly linear fashion), they draw attention to setbacks, phases of showdown, ups and downs. They suggest that global developments rather have the shape of a spiral.

Finally, it should be noted that theoretical assumptions similar to the one underlying the idea of the changing correlation of forces also apply to war itself should it occur. In the article devoted to the "laws of war" of the Soviet Military Encyclopaedia, the most important law is said to be one "according to which, historically, the side wins which represents a new and more progressive social and economic system and effectively utilizes the means at its disposal" (translated from the German edition: Sowjetische Militärenzyklopädie 1980, Vol. 10:9f.).

Evaluation of the international systems structure: distinguishing between good and evil

The foregoing analysis has already made it amply clear that the Soviet image of the international system does not merely serve as a framework for understanding the world. Its task clearly transcends simple perceptive, cognitive and interpretative functions. It also offers criteria for evaluation and judgement. This approach to evaluating what one perceives in world politics is strongly reflected in the type of terminology used: world politics are not just described in neutral terms - the words employed to describe the two systems usually signal positive or negative feelings, thus suggesting a clear distinction between what is to be considered as good or as evil.

The basis for such implicit and explicit qualifications is also reflected in what is called the "moral code of the builders of communism" which includes aspects absolutely essential to the evaluation of politics in general and particularly world politics:

"Morality ... has a class character, and so different classes have different views of what is moral and immoral, what is good and evil... The moral code of the builders of communism calls for devotion to the communist cause, friendship and fraternity of all the peoples of the USSR, irreconcilability towards national and racial enmity and towards the enemies of peace and the freedom of the peoples, and fraternal solidarity with working people of all countries." (Political Terms 1982:47f.)

This also implies that any other evaluative perspectives, in particular the one adopted by "bourgeois" society, are rejected outright. Soviet political thinking explicitly dismisses the relevance of the Western approach to and Western interpretation of "freedom" and "human rights":

"Bourgeois ideology, which proceeds from rather vague and amorphous premises to proclaim the ideals of equality and humanism as it talks about 'pure' freedom and 'pure' democracy, 'universal' human rights and so forth. To such abstract notions of good and evil and the innumerable delusions stemming from them, the communist ideology counterposes the objective laws of the historical process... If this reference point is missing, then freedom, democracy, equality, human rights and so forth are empty words devoid of meaning." (Kortunov 1979:18)

The general tendency, inherent in the Soviet view, to evaluate many aspects in positive or negative terms also leads to an incisive definition of differences between just and unjust wars. This constitutes a logical consequence of the whole approach prevailing in Soviet political and strategic thinking. As a rule, Soviet spokesmen start from the assumption that:

"... any war that is waged by a people for the sake of freedom and social progress, for liberation from exploitation and national oppression or in defence of its State sovereignty, against an aggressive attack, is a just war." (Marxism-Leninism on War and Army 1972:63)

Applying this general rule, any war can then be classified by "taking into account the main contradiction" and also "the social forces clashing in the armed struggle", i.e. by distinguishing between "progressive" and "reactionary forces" (ibid.:69; cf. also Afanasyev 1981:100f). Soviet sources thus offer elaborate typologies and classifications of wars: just and unjust wars, progressive and reactionary wars (Sowjetische Militärenzyklopädie 1980, Vol. 5:36f.). Just wars are:

"(1) The wars defending the socialist fatherland, the countries of the socialist community; (2) the revolutionary wars of the working class and of the entire working people against the exploiter classes; (3) the wars of national liberation; (4) the wars in the defence of national sovereignty of a capitalist State against an imperialist aggression. Accordingly, the unjust wars are the following: (1) the wars of imperialist States against the socialist countries; (2) the wars of the exploiter classes against the working class, the entire working people in the antagonist States; (3) the colonialist and neocolonialist wars; (4) the aggressive imperialist wars within the capitalist system". (Marksistsko-Leninyskoye ucheniye o voyne i army 1984:49)

It should be borne in mind that the classification of wars according to their just or unjust character is a reflection of a universal tendency in evaluating what is perceived. Seen in the Soviet perspective, almost every phenomenon in world politics somehow carries the mark of acceptability or unacceptability in terms of socialist objectives. The affirmation of this quality is particularly salient and explicit in the case of Soviet theories of just war, but it can regularly, albeit less explicitly, and in most cases only implicitly, be found in practically all statements explaining the Soviet view of the international system.

This perception of the world political system also has far-reaching consequences for the understanding of policies of armament and disarmament. In particular it leads to a repudiation of suggestions regarding equal responsibility for the arms race. Any such suggestion is dismissed as a devious manoeuvre for diverting attention from the real cause of the arms race and putting the Soviet Union and the United States on an equal footing as far as their contribution to the arms race is concerned:

"Of special importance in the ideological struggle on the problems of war and peace is the denunciation of the false thesis concocted by imperialist propaganda about the 'equal responsibility' of the Soviet Union and the USA for the arms race and heightening international tensions... The political and ideological purpose of the 'equal responsibility' thesis is to shift the blame from imperial-ism, the true source of wars, and the danger of war, to socialism as the 'focus of evil', to quote the American President, and the cause of all conflicts in the world." (Kapchenko 1983:1/ 1)

Likewise, pacifism and the radical anti-war movement are criti-cized for not being able "to perceive the true causes and the class-political nature of wars" (Sowjetische Militärenzyklopädie 1980, Vol. 19:53). It is therefore held to be "unscientific". Soviet theoretical writings accept it only to the extent that it contributes to the "anti-imperialist struggle", its relative utility being determined by "its objective role in the struggle between progressive and reac-tionary forces" (ibid.:54).

On the other hand, Soviet sources often refer to the desirability of heroism - provided that "heroism" is defined properly, i.e. as proposed by the Soviet Military Encyclopaedia, as an "outstanding action in the interest of the popular masses and the progressive classes..., founded on firm communist convictions, fidelity and love for the Communist Party and the socialist homeland, on political consciousness and proletarian internationalism" (Sowjetische Mili-tärenzyklopädie 1980, Vol. 4:102-105; and a similar article on "anti-militarism", ibid.: Vol. 2:36-40).

In sum, in the Soviet view, any issue related to international politics and problems of war and peace can be evaluated properly and conclusively by applying certain key criteria such as the basic distinction between "progressive" and "reactionary" classes.

The notion of the "social character" of any phenomenon always serves as the evaluative yardstick, i.e. Soviet sources examine and qualify everything according to "whether or not the main political objectives (as well as the realisation of those objectives) ... correspond to social progress" (Marksistsko-Leninskoye ucheniye o voyne i army 1984:46).

THE SOVIET VIEW OF THE ADVERSARY

Assumptions regarding American aims: aggressive anti-communism and superiority

The basic assumption regarding American aims and intentions, as expressed and reconfirmed repeatedly by Soviet sources, is that any "imperialist society", and foremost the United States as the leader of "imperialism", by its very nature and ideological orientation, is inevitably committed to the spirit of aggression. Aggressiveness is said to be rooted in the fundamental nature of "imperialism": "As long as imperialism exists, there also remains the danger of war and military conflict" (Sowjetische Militärenzyklopädie 1980, Vol. 12:113).

More precisely, aggressiveness is aimed at communism as its principal or exclusive enemy. Soviet sources constantly assert that American foreign and military policy is driven by incessant "agressive anti-communism":

"What all bourgeois theories of war have in common is their class essence - all are permeated with anti-communism, all serve as a basis for the aggressive policies and aims of the imperialist States." (Marxism-Leninism on War and Army 1972:47)

In the Soviet view, American aggressiveness cannot be ascribed to momentary circumstances - it constitutes a constant element inherent in American policy irrespective of the personality and personal ideology of the President in office. As striking proof, Soviet sources recall that immediately after 1917, when the Soviet State was born, it promptly became a victim of American and Allied intervention and armed aggression. In Soviet eyes, the ultimate and most recent proof of American anti-communism is the statements made, by President Reagan, on the Soviet Union as the "focus of evil" and the present Administration's denial of the right of existence of socialist society. Soviet spokesmen express the conviction that today the United States is really committed to putting socialism on the "ash heap of history" and liquidating socialism in the Soviet Union and elsewhere, and perceives the emergence and success of socialism as a "historical anomaly". All this, they conclude, gives the Soviet Union plenty of reasons for now being on high alert. In other words, they think that traditional American anti-communism has been reinvigorated by the spirit of crusade.

General Volkogonov distinguishes between "theoretical anti-communism" and "empirical anti-communism". The first is said to "parasitize mainly in the sphere of political consciousness, philosophy, sociology, history and law" by attempts to "disprove" Marxism-Leninism (Volkogonov 1983:86). Recent theories such as the theory of "convergence", "de-ideologization" and "industrial society" are objects of particular condemnation as they are charged with "reflecting the long-term aims of imperialism which seeks to damage real socialism in every possible way" (ibid.). On the other hand, "empirical vulgar anti-communism" is defined as an imperialist instrument serving the psychological struggle by peddling various myths about Soviet realities and reviving national prejudices (ibid.:87).

In sum, Marxist-Leninist theory asserts that "imperialism" cannot and will never give up its aggressive anti-communism. It believes that the rest of the world has to reckon with this fact for an indefinite future, i.e. as long as "imperialist society" continues to exist. Semyonov expresses this assumption in the following laconic formula:

"Imperialism cannot change - its antipopular nature and aggressive propensities are too deeply engrained." (Semyonov 1979:262)

In other words : aggressive anti-communism is assumed to represent a general disposition of "imperialist society". From this general disposition, in turn, a number of additional and more specific aims are said to depend; they follow logically and deductively from the general aim of anti-communism.

In the Soviet view, the first specific aim underlying American political and military strategy is "resistance to progress" (Chernenko 1984a:15) and to "the historically inevitable progress of mankind towards socialism" (article on "Military doctrine" in the German edition of the Soviet Military Encyclopaedia: Sowjetische Militärenzyklopädie 1980, Vol. 12:8). More specifically, this implies resistance to and possibly attempts to reverse the change of the "correlation of forces" in favour of socialism. Soviet sources and other statements available in official publications from socialist countries repudiate the notion of "balance of power" as used in American political terminology. In an analysis published in the German Democratic Republic, "balance of power" is dismissed as being

"...a construct serving the purpose of concealing the intent to secure and, if possible, promote the imperialist sphere of power and influence. It serves the purpose of declaring unchangeable the social status quo in that part of the world directly or indirectly dominated by imperialism and making this unchangeability the terms of business of détente." (Schwarz et al. 1981:47)

The rejection of the American understanding of the "balance of power", and in particular the refusal to accept the balance as something to be stabilized, has to be seen in the context of the dynamic interpretation of the Soviet concept of the "correlation of forces" mentioned above: by assuming that the future evolution of world politics must and will further advance the shift of the correlation of forces in favour of socialism as the "objective and natural law of world development", Marxist-Leninist theory rejects the Western meaning of the concept of "balance of power" as something static and therefore neither understandable nor acceptable:

"The 'balance of power' doctrine is ultimately to prevent any strengthening of socialism's position, hold up the growth of the revolutionary anti-imperialist and national liberation movements and thereby block any further change of the alignment of strength in favour of peace, democracy and progress. This, properly speaking, comprises the doctrine's class essence." (Belov/Karenin/Petrov 1979:281)

The dynamic interpretation of the "correlation of forces" and the rejection of anything remotely suggesting a stabilization of the present power relationship has of course immediate practical consequences for the political and military strategies envisaged by the Soviet authorities with regard to the adversary (cf. below pp. 87ff.)

It also has considerable relevance with respect to the scope of détente. As "peaceful coexistence" under all circumstances, and necessarily so, is "not simply co-operation, but a close interlacing of co-operation and political and ideological struggle between capitalism and socialism in the international arena" (Obchennovost i problemy voiny i mira 1978:46), any idea of interpreting it as a reason to refrain from competition in the "third world" is vigorously rejected. The Soviet view does not regard peaceful coexistence as a policy of stabilization in general. For this reason, Western suggestions for agreement on a kind of "code of conduct" are strongly condemned as being an unabashed "imperialist" plot to halt progress in the shifting of the correlation of forces in favour of socialism and to preclude Soviet assistance to peoples struggling for "just liberation":

"One has to overcome the intense opposition of those influential circles in the bourgeois States which, while admitting that détente has no reasonable alternative, often try to impose their own egoistical "rule of conduct" profiting from the slackening of international tension. For example, under the defence of détente they ... are worried about human rights or propose that socialist countries not unite themselves with the just liberation struggle of the peoples of Africa, the Middle East and other regions of the world." (Obchestvennost i problemy voiny i mira 1978:46)

The specific interpretation of détente as ascribed to the United States view also helps to explain why, in the Soviet perspective, the policy of détente failed: namely, because it was sabotaged by the West. The West and particularly the United States are assumed to have accepted détente only in order to obstruct "the onward march of history". They are held to have abandoned détente when this aim proved to be unattainable - an attitude clearly unacceptable to the Soviet Union:

"The main reason underlying the reconsideration of the attitude with respect to détente of those who define the internal and foreign policy of the United States has been and still is their unwillingness to accept the onward march of history. Some of them regarded détente from the very outset as only a forced measure and a conjunctural phenomenon. Détente has been considered as an opportunity 'to sit out' to go through the consequences of Viet Nam and Watergate, hampering the military and political adventures of American imperialism, and to accumulate force. The others have accepted détente since, as they have projected, détente could be used for breaking the process of national liberation and of social renovation of the world. When these hopes appeared to be groundless, their enthusiasm towards détente changed into irritation." (Ovinnikov 1981:76)

For the same reason, in a Soviet perspective, the American formula of "peace built on strength" means nothing else than "a modern version of Pax Americana" designed to justify aggressive expansion, impose one's will on all countries and pin down the revolutionary and national liberation forces (Sovetov 1984). The Soviet view derides the American pledges to the maintenance and defense of the status quo as nothing but a cover for a highly "pragmatic" approach to international politics: the American intervention in Grenada is quoted as a particularly vivid example of how United States policy is eager to torpedo the status quo whenever this seems convenient. In other words, it is assumed that the United States is not even really interested in the status quo which it proclaims by proposing to maintain a "balance of power". In the standard presentation of the Soviet view, the ultimate aim underlying American policy is said to be superiority, not equality:

"Superiority has always been and still remains a symbol of aggressive aspirations." (Ogarkov 1982:20)

"The present Administration has proclaimed the achieving of US military superiority over the Soviet Union as the primary goal in the next few years." (Ustinov 1981:10)

"What is now being done by Washington has one principal aim: to achieve military superiority over the Soviet Union, to deal with the socialist countries from a position of strength and, generally, to try to impose American will on the rest of the world." (The Race Against Reason 1983:3)

The accusation that the United States is striving for superiority can be found in various Soviet comments and interpretations of American behaviour. Having been accustomed to be superior, one Soviet argument runs, the Americans are now neither able nor willing to accept that this is no longer so - they are in effect suffering from a "superiority complex" and continue to dream about superiority although the realities have changed. Therefore, frustration generates anger and aggression. The American leadership, for the first time for 150 years, meets opposition to their policy of "liberating people", and they feel that they have lost their power - which in turn leads them to cling even more desperately to their vision of superiority. For the same reason, United States policy is also believed to incessantly deny the Soviet Union the acquisition of those arms which the USSR feels are necessary for its defence.

Any assertions made by United States authorities about not being interested in strategic superiority are rejected as mere fabrications designed to conceal their true intentions. That is why Soviet spokesmen refuse to take at face value concepts such as "strategic sufficiency":

"Hence, the concept of 'strategic sufficiency' is by no means as harmless as its name might imply... Yet the unpopularity of the US aggressive course, the mounting desire for a peaceful solution of controversial issues fostered by the peaceful policy of the USSR and other socialist countries compelled the Pentagon to conceal the true substance of its schemes from the American people." (Luzin 1981:102)

45

The Soviet view therefore starts from the assumption that whenever American foreign policy has an opportunity to do so, it tries to take the offensive in order to roll back the might of the socialist countries on a global scale (Schwarz et al. 1981:8), and to "liquidate or weaken the socialist system, suppress the national liberation movement of the peoples" (Sowjetische Militärenzyklopädie 1980, Vol. 12:8). According to Soviet spokesmen, the United States follows the Clausewitzian principle of "war as a continuation of policy by other means". In the Soviet perspective, the United States' entire strategic planning is geared to the offensive, to preparing and unleashing an attack for restoring superiority. As will be shown below (p. 66ff.), American behaviour in the field of disarmament and arms control negotiations can, from a Soviet point of view, only indicate the very same desire for maintaining or regaining superiority.

Additional aims underlying American policy and strategy are also held to be rooted in the specific nature of capitalism - namely "plundering nations" (Gorshkov 1979:3). Admiral Gorshkov accuses the United States of being driven by the will to exploit other countries:

"Here the navy is given the role of a guarantor of the economic expansion of the American monopolies, the role of an accomplice in robbing the peoples of many countries dependent on the USA in economic, political and military fields." (Gorshkov 1979:4)

The aims of American military policy are thus seen to be identical with or subject to the interests of American business.

Assumptions regarding American motives: external and internal crisis of capitalism

Soviet assumptions regarding American aims rest on assumptions regarding the motives underlying these aims. As a matter of fact, Soviet spokesmen devote considerable attention to analysing the reasons why American foreign policy strives to achieve these aims as they are perceived. The results of the respective analytical efforts are very subtle and complex: they refer to a variety of aspects and one would hardly do justice to them by trying to sum them up in a single overall formula. Nevertheless, they all share one important element which may be said to constitute a kind of common denominator for all Soviet statements regarding American motives.

This common denominator is the axiomatic assumption that it is the nature of capitalism which ultimately determines the motives. Hence these motives are seen as being unavoidable, as are the ensuing aims and strategies chosen in American foreign policy. In other words, the central motive behind American foreign policy and strategy is believed to be rooted in the ideological predisposition of the capitalist system:

46

"There is no doubt that the foreign policy of any State is to some extent based on ideological considerations, related to the class character of the State. But in US foreign policy, the ideological factor has always been hypertrophied due to the fact that the US has always been sure of its messianic role and has considered it necessary, if not obligatory, for all countries to follow the US' way of thinking." (Razriyadka mezhdunarodnoi napriyazhennosti i ideologicheskaya borba 1981:143)

When elaborating this basic assumption further, Soviet spokesmen usually point out that the nature of capitalism necessarily generates aggressive motives via two mechanisms (cf. Schwarz 1981:11). The first is held to be the decline, on a world-wide scale, of the position of "imperialism". The second is said to originate in the "internal contradictions" and crises from which capitalism increasingly suffers:

"Imperialism is progressively losing ground on the world scene, the sphere of its domination is contracting, and capitalist society is deep in crisis. All this prompts the militarist and reactionary quarters in the West to step up the arms race and to try to secure military superiority. This reflects the frantic desire to stop or, better still, turn back the clock of history... In other words, a truly global attempt is now under way to change the course of history, extend the life span of capitalism and destroy socialism. Naturally, this attempt is doomed to failure." (Zagladin 1982:43f.)

This first main motive is declared to be intrinsically interconnected with the second, the "crisis of capitalism"; the two are said to constitute "a knot hard to undo" (Burlatsky 1983:326). As far as the first motive is concerned, Soviet authors think that the United States, and imperialism altogether, increasingly find themselves on the losing side owing to a considerable weakening of their position and many politico-strategic losses in all parts of the world, in particular in Viet Nam, Kampuchea, Iran, Afghanistan, Angola, Mozambique, Ethiopia, Zimbabwe and Nicaragua. They are convinced that the revolutionary process is also putting imperialism on to the defensive (Schwarz et al. 1981:11; Tolkunov 1984:64). The most important factor, however, is said to be the change in the correlation of forces in favour of socialism and the continuing loss of United States military superiority. This evolution is considered to be hard to accept for the American leadership - hence its enraged aggressive reactions:

"The military strategic equality which has arisen between our countries does not suit the belligerent leaders of the present Administration, because it hinders the United States' aggressive intention in the world arena, and limits its expansionist actions." (Ustinov 1981:11)

Therefore, when referring to the "American psychology", Soviet spokesmen have in mind a general political disposition towards aggressiveness, generated and mediated by the specific nature of the capitalist social and economic system.

Based on the premise that capitalism is doomed to decline and extinction and that the "triumph of socialism" is inevitable, American resistance to this irreversible trend is described as being very desperate. This is also believed to have implications for the conduct of American diplomacy, which has the task of "fighting doggedly against the fate of history". It goes without saying that this premise has far-reaching practical consequences for the actual conduct of diplomatic negotiations by Soviet diplomacy.

The aggravation of the general crisis of capitalism is assumed to be the second driving force behind the aggressive thrust character-istic of American foreign policy: analysing it systematically, the Soviet Military Encyclopaedia presents four groups of causal factors: "political (aggravation of the aggressiveness of imperialism), socio-economic (tendency by the bourgeoisie to solve internal contradic-tions and difficulties by the arms race), military-technological (ab-breviation of the innovation cycle of military technology), and ideological (the culmination of the class struggle on the level of ideology)." (translated from the German edition: Sowjetische Mili-tärenzyklopädie 1980, Vol. 7:128).

According to Marxist-Leninist theory, the system of capitalism is simply no longer capable of coping with the requirements of the modern age, thus producing a deterioration of productivity, growth and welfare:

"There is a growing conflict between, on the one hand, an objec-tive need for systematic development, which is essential given the present level of productive forces, and the commercial anarchy characteristic of capitalism, on the other hand.

The scientific and technological revolution aggravates the funda-mental contradictions of the capitalist system, since it calls for ever greater integration of production, long-term forecasting and planning, and improved management." (Semyonov 1979:245)

In particular, Soviet authors tend to surmise that the intrinsic deficiencies of capitalism will inevitably aggravate the law of unequal development prevailing in the capitalist system. Furthermore, this evolution is said to lead to economic and political liability which, in turn, fosters unemployment and inflation, the growth of déclassé elements, deterioration of housing, healthcare and education, and moral degradation (Diligensky/Yaropolov 1982:131f.; Schwarz et al. 1981:11; Burlatsky 1983a:326; Tolkunov 1984:64). Typical indications of the latter are seen in what Foreign Minister Gromyko calls "ideological emptiness, cultural decay and the mental maiming of youth" (Gromyko 1984:81).

A further explanation in this context concerns the undermining of the "myths describing the United States and Western Europe as the technotrone and post-industrial society and the 'society of prosperity' which have been for many years successfully propagated among the population." (Lukov 1979:42)

Finally, the Soviet view likes to assume that the inner crisis of the West has also affected the cohesion of the Western alliance, thus giving the American "ruling circles" additional incentives to adopt or reinforce warmongering policies:

"The aspirations of Washington to minimize the centrifugal tendencies in NATO, maintaining the US domination of the Atlantic alliance (in the first instance by means of an artificial rise of military factors within the system of the Atlantic relationship, by the removal of the balance of military forces in Europe towards the direction preferable to the West, by forcing new, large military programs of NATO, by advancing the decision of NATO concerning the deployment of new US intermediate-range nuclear missiles in Western Europe) has in large part contributed to the negative position taken by the US vis-à-vis the policy of military détente in Europe and all the political activities in the field of disarmament." (Razryadka mezhdunarodnoy napryazhennosty i ideologicheskaya borba 1981:128f.)

Soviet scholars analyse the crisis of the Western alliance in terms of what they call the "increasing inter-imperialist rivalry" which in turn is said to reflect the "uneven development of capitalism" making rivalry virtually inevitable (Bunkina 1979:17f.). The "separation or disunification of imperialist forces" is assumed to be countered by the arms manufacturing business circles which allegedly try to "instigate a further and even more dangerous arms race and the production of new types of weapons" (ibid.:24).

Similarly, a vicious circle is seen to operate inside the United States, as "the aggravation of social calamities is used to justify militarism, while the latter diverts resources, funds and public attention from the burning social and political questions and deepens the crisis of society" (Fedoseyev 1983:45f.). At the same time, this situation is seen as promoting a growing influence of the "socio-political forces" which have an interest in rising tension and aggressiveness (Zagladin 1981:135) in order to profit from the boom in the armaments industry.

"The confrontation with the socialist world is becoming a source of high profits for a handful of tycoons of the cosmopolitan arms industry. Behind the highly dangerous course followed by the leaders of the US Administration, therefore, stand the material, super-enrichment interests of the more aggressive groups of monopoly capital which seek to impose their will on all countries and continents." (Ponomarev 1983:3)

In the Soviet view, the "military-industrial complex" constitutes something like the "missing link" connecting the general nature of the capitalist system with its aggressive anti-communism. This insight has the function of a basic axiom underlying all Soviet assumptions regarding American motives. It is considered universally valid as long as capitalism exists:

"The following idea of Lenin sounds as topical as ever today: 'Interlinked on a worldwide scale, capital is thriving on armaments and wars' (Vol.21, p.227)." (Ponomarev 1983:3)

The "military-industrial complex" is defined as the "union of the major monopolies of the war industry with militaristic circles in the State apparatus of imperialist powers" (Petit Dictionnaire Politique 1982:83f.). It is held to reinforce the domination by the "monopoly-bourgeois class" by pressing for a continuing increase of military might:

"Like a carnivore smelling blood the capitalist pounces on the chance to increase his profits, and enters into a vicious competitive struggle for war orders." (Kortunov 1979:271)

On the basis of this assumption, another Soviet author draws the conclusion that "war is a function of Big Business" (Pumpyansky 1983:45). Soviet analysts see this general assumption corroborated today by close links existing between President Reagan and the "financial and military-industrial circles of the 'California group'" backing Reagan right from the start of his political career (Henri 1983:8f.). In their view the "California group", by pushing Reagan into the presidency, won access to the Pentagon "as a kind of Ali Baba's cave" (ibid.:36).

In sum, analysing the motives underlying American aims, Soviet political thinking proposes that the continuing, and perhaps intensified pursuit of those aggressive aims cannot be expected to slacken let alone to cease unless capitalism is liquidated. Aggressiveness, in this view, is believed to be deeply embedded in the objective nature of the "capitalist class society"; "imperialism" by definition is assumed to have a "rapacious nature" (Ogarkov 1982:17).

Soviet leaders and Soviet specialists commenting on the United States think that their analysis of motives goes much deeper than any Westerner might attempt. This claim is supported by the conviction of having the proper instrument for analysis available - Marxism-Leninism. Therefore, in the Soviet view, Western thought and action regarding any aspect of foreign policy and strategy will necessarily be wrong unless the West accepts the basic truths discovered and taught by Marxism-Leninism.

Assumptions regarding the American internal structure: rivalry between reactionaries and realists

The Soviet diagnosis of the essence of capitalist society as presented in the preceding section does not, however, lead its authors to wholesale generalizations about the structure of that society. On the contrary, they pay much attention to discerning differing and even contradictory "factions" in "bourgeois society" cherishing differing values and aims with regard to foreign policy and strategy. They perceive a fundamental contradiction between the "extremist and adventurist 'war party'" (Ponomarev 1983:10), on the one hand, and the "large groups of the population in favour of détente" (Schwartz et al. 1981:44, cf. also Luzin 1981:187). The intensity of the contradiction between the two forces is viewed as a function of East-West détente as opposed to cold war policies:

> "The cold war gave capitalism broad opportunities to hold back the aggravation of social conflicts by distracting the working people from their economic and social problems. Détente tended to deprive capitalism of this opportunity... In recent years, there has been a growing tendency to dampen the mass social protest by undermining détente and whipping up anti-Sovietism." (Diligensky/Yaropolov 1982:131f.)

Therefore, as the peace-loving mass social protest is assumed to pose a threat to the privileged position of the military-industrialist complex, the latter is believed to be reviving the spirit of the cold war and aggressive anti-communism in order to discipline those who dare cast doubts on the ever-growing arms race (Matveyev 1984:75). From this perspective, Soviet criticism is also directed against the alleged "Soviet threat". In their view, this "threat" constitutes nothing more than a fabrication which is instrumental in misleading the protesting working class in capitalist countries :

> "The reactionary ideologists and policy-makers of the capitalist countries try to drown the discontent of the working masses due to the deterioration of the ecological situation, the lowering of the level of living, resulting in particular from the energy crisis and the aggravation of all other global problems of modern times, by initiating all kinds of anti-Soviet campaigns and by intimidating the population by the mythical so-called 'Soviet threat'. The result of such a propagandistic campaign is the acceleration of the arms race." (Razryadka mezhdunarodnoy napryazhennosty i ideologicheskaya borba 1981:19)

The Soviet view also makes a distinction between two different tendencies to be identified within "the ruling circles" of the United States - "realists" and "reactionaries":

> "There have always been at least two tendencies within the ruling circles of the US which, while aiming at the same imperialistic objectives, advocate different ways and methods of realizing such

51

policy objectives. On the one hand, we see the realistic policy-makers who take into consideration the real alignment of forces in the world and recognize the need for the peaceful coexistence of States. But on the other hand, there is another point of view, reflecting the aspirations of the most reactionary and militaristic circles which refuse to face reality and still hope to restore, even if it requires resorting to military force, the imperialistic order of the past when the imperialist Powers were the incontestable rulers of the world." (Alexandrov V. 1982:254)

The influence exerted by "realists" is deemed slight for at least two reasons. Firstly, their relative importance is seen to be lagging behind the power of the "aggressive imperialistic circles":

"The process of realizing détente is complicated by the fact that it is subject to attack by the most aggressive imperialistic circles which, although they do not hold the absolute majority, have a position strong enough to directly influence the official policy of the main capitalist Powers. Nor can we ignore the fact that realistic Western policy-makers are often subject to growing pressures by aggressive circles and military-industrial concerns." (Razryadka protiv antirazryadki 1982:144)

The last remark concerning "military-industrial concerns" is central to the Soviet line of argument. According to the Marxist-Leninist view, in a capitalist society there are always some "who benefit from anti-détente, i.e. from the arms race and the aggravation of tensions among States". (Luzin 1981:187). That is why the monopolies of the military-industrial complex are assumed to be interested in a booming arms race, and they constantly produce what in Soviet terminology is called the "myth of the Soviet threat".

Secondly, within the "ruling circles" Soviet analysts also discern those who, although initially inclined to adopt a liberal attitude by the logic of the situation, face nothing but disincentives and are constantly discouraged from speaking out about their realist way of seeing things. They are afraid of being accused of being too soft on communism and therefore finish up thinking and behaving like the hardliners. This interpretation is offered by Academician Arbatov who quotes the American economist Galbraith:

"It is significant to recall an observation by Professor J.K. Galbraith that the arms race in the USA is stimulated by the economic interests of influential groups and the economic interests of these groups are, in turn, maintained by two great fears underlying American political life. The first is the fear of communism typical of conservatives. The second is the fear of being considered too soft on communism, the typical situation for liberals, and this situation is even more dangerous according to Galbraith, since it is hard to find anyone as irrational as a liberal trying to show that he is as much a hardliner towards reds as anyone else." (Arbatov 1980:70)

Ultimately the official Soviet view tends to surmise the existence of two principal groups:

"The line between common sense and folly in the industrialized capitalist countries lies between the bulk of the population and the military-industrial complex." (Luzin 1981:191)

The tendency towards internal dissension originating in the social contradictions of capitalism is declared to be also responsible for the instability observed in American foreign policy:

"Therefore, it is quite natural that the positions of realists are not stable, are subject to fluctuations, are fraught with risks of conjunctural alternations and are as heavily dependent upon the prevailing tendencies in the internal political arenas as they are in the international scene." (Razryadka protiv antirazryadki 1982:144)

As will be demonstrated in the following section, this diagnosis of instability has further implications once it becomes generalized.

Soviet observers are by no means confused by the pluralism prominent in Western thought and especially in the American political and strategic debate. As one high-ranking military spokesman remarked, dissension and the existence of opinions opposed to the Administration's views clearly prove that the Administration is wrong. The same holds true, according to a Soviet spokesman, for the fact that every newly elected United States President denigrates the policies conducted by his predecessor as totally inadequate: this is said to prove that these policies never reflect the true interests of the American people. In the same sense, according to a high-ranking Soviet official, the fall of President Nixon in the aftermath of the "Watergate" scandal was engineered by conservative circles unhappy about Nixon's policy of détente, which would have curbed the arms race.

A similar approach is used for analysing the problem of coherence and dissension within the West more generally. The United States is said to exert "pressure on its allies to draw them into the aggressive policy of direct confrontation with the socialist countries" (Matveyev 1984:77). With great satisfaction, Soviet observers note a steady growth of "inter-imperialist contradictions" tearing apart the capitalist world. They are aware, however, that this very tendency is giving rise to "attempts to counter the centrifugal trends in the capitalist camp and to mobilize all the forces against the USSR" by launching an unprecedented campaign against a "Soviet military threat" (ibid.).

Assumptions regarding American trustworthiness: predictable unreliability

The foregoing analysis leads to the question of how the Soviet

leadership evaluates American trustworthiness. Soviet sources generally complain about "US instability, unceremoniousness vis-à-vis its
partners, lack of reserve, willingness to neglect important foreign
policy questions in favour of short-lived considerations, related to
internal political struggle and rivalry" (Arbatov 1980:76; cf. also
Schwartz et al.1981:33f.). They also accuse United States foreign
policy of being "subject to opportunist zigzags" (Kortunov 1979:244).
According to the Soviet view, this tendency is reinforced by the
nervousness of periods of presidential elections, which are "bad
periods for good policy and good periods for bad policy" (Arbatov
1980:72). Similarly, the simultaneous availability of official and
non-official sources of American doctrine is regretted, particularly
because, depending on the weight the unofficial sources have, they
may influence the official standpoint to a greater or lesser extent
(Siegmund/Kleine 1982:73).

In sum, as a consequence of its crisis-ridden domestic structure,
plagued by the fundamental internal contradictions of capitalist
society, the United States is perceived to be "unreliable as a partner" (Arbatov 1980:76). It goes without saying that this conclusion
has grave consequences if taken as an assumption underlying any
further assessment of the adversary and his policies. The assumption
that the United States is an unreliable partner must necessarily
affect the way one prefers to deal with such a partner. The image of
the partner of course also has an impact on the approach chosen to it
in both the fields of military strategy and disarmament.

The question whether or not the adversary can be trusted is
closely related to the problem of predictability, as trust, by definition, means nothing else than reliance on expectable behaviour. In
this respect, however, the conclusions to be drawn from Soviet source
material are somewhat ambiguous: on the one hand, Marxist-Leninist
theory makes for full and correct understanding of the structure and
processes of capitalist societies - and Marxist-Leninist authors are
convinced that they even have a better understanding than "bourgeois"
social scientists themselves. The propositions expressed about the
future of capitalism and in particular the future evolution of the
United States are therefore commonly put forward in a firm and
assertive way, as they ultimately rest on what these authors consider
to be certain knowledge of objective factors. As far as United States
strategic doctrine is concerned, Soviet sources seem to assume a
definite continuity and hence predictability in as much as the key
elements of United States nuclear strategy are held to be basically
stable and not affected by changes of Administrations. According to
Academician Arbatov:

"Thus those conceptions are neither the strategic views of one
particular individual nor of an Administration or political party.
As a matter of fact this is a net tendency in strategic thinking,
which has been in some way or another approved by the three or
even four Administrations - the Republicans as well as the Demo-
crats - and which is already deeply rooted in US political life

and is not greatly influenced by the presidential elections."
(Arbatov 1981c:103)

On the other hand, however, there are bitter complaints about the inherent instability of politics in the United States and doubts about its unreliable nature. This instability is said to have various causes. First of all, Soviet observers note with dissatisfaction that in the United States the presidential holders of the executive power change at regular intervals, hence confronting the Soviet Union with new negotiating positions and new personnel every few years. Therefore the Americans are said to be incapable of conducting any continuous long-term policy. More particularly, it is complained that, for instance, the SALT II negotiations were conducted by no less than three American Presidents.

Secondly, the Soviet leadership seems to have increasing doubts about the reliability of its American partners. Attention is drawn to the cancellation of the MFN agreement due to congressional intervention led by Senator Jackson, and the non-ratification of the SALT II treaty. While originally assuming a kind of American "mirror image" of their own stable society, Soviet experts are now becoming more and more aware that the American system is completely different.

Yet Soviet spokesmen understand the instability of United States foreign policy not primarily as a function of regular changes of power holders. In their view, the instability vis-à-vis the USSR stems from the uncertainty of United States imperialism about how to deal with the Soviet State - either by a policy of strength or by trying to undermine it by "peaceful means". In sum, while on the one hand the Soviet Union has deep-rooted doubts about United States reliability, on the other hand Marxist-Leninist theory presumes to be capable of perfectly understanding the complexities of capitalist society and policies. How is this ambiguity to be resolved ? The answer probably is that Soviet leaders assess the Americans as being predictably unreliable.

Assumptions regarding American capabilities: weapons for world supremacy and resistance to progress

In the Soviet view, the present military situation existing between East and West is characterized by "rough parity on all counts". In this perspective, therefore, American capabilities are assessed as being equal to Soviet capabilities. There are, however, two important qualifications to this analysis to be found in Soviet sources. The first refers to the current trend which Soviet observers discern in the evolution of American capabilities, while the second points to some special features of these capabilities which are accused of serving an offensive purpose.

As far as the current trend in United States armaments policy is concerned, Soviet observers believe that enormous efforts are being made to challenge the existing parity:

"Peace 'from a position of strength' is what the men in Washington would like to have. These days they are not concerned about the equality and equal security of the sides, and are ben on developing new, increasingly destructived weapons of mass annihilation, on securing military superiority over the Soviet Union, and on establishing hegemony and direct domination over other countries." (Whence the Threat to Peace 1982:94)

The article on "military doctrine" in the Soviet Military Encyclopaedia laconically sums up this hypothesis by stating that "the military doctrine of the USA is subordinate to the idea of world hegemony" (Sowjetische Militärenzyklopädie, Vol. 12:8). This aspect of perceived American capabilities has already been dealt with above in connection with Soviet assumptions regarding American intentions (pp. 41ff.). At this point it is sufficient to state that in the Soviet perspective such an attempt is bound to be futile because the Soviet Union counts on having both the firm intention and the capabilities to thwart this attack on equality.

American military capabilities are assessed by being interpreted in the context of the Western concept of escalation. To Soviet observers, acquiring capabilities suitable for a strategy of escalation clearly proves the willingness to obtain the freedom to act from a position of strength in the pre-war period (cf. article on "escalation" in: Sowjetische Militärenzyklopädie 1980, Vol. 23:9). In the same way, the capabilities acquired in the context of the strategy of "flexible response" are perceived as serving the "American drive for world domination" (ibid.: Vol. 7:32).

More important are the Soviet allegations about the specific nature of United States capabilities. The "US war machine", in the Soviet view, is geared to implementing a "global aggressive design", especially in overseas territories (Whence the Threat to Peace 1982:17); it aims "to secure 'world leadership'" and to deploy forces "to any region of the globe that it may declare a sphere of its 'vital interests'" (ibid.: 28). According to General Secretary Andropov:

"Military bases are set up for the purpose of direct armed interference in the affairs of other states, and for the use of US weapons against any country which rejects Washington's diktat. The result of this is that tension has grown throughout the world - in Europe, Asia, Africa, the Middle East and Central America." (Andropov 1983c:11)

The "far-flung network of military bases and installations" is also held to be used by the United States:

"...to further its expansionist global policy... to exert direct pressure on the Governments of these States, keeping them within the mainstream of US policy, to threaten progressive and assist reactionary regimes in the region concerned, and to oppress national liberation movements by armed force." (Whence the Threat to Peace 1982:29)

Consequently, American seapower is scorned as "an instrument of the policy of aggression and for exploiting and subjugating liberated and developing countries, for supporting reactionary regimes and for the struggle against national liberation movements" - ultimately "for providing the US monopolies with a dominant position and influence" (Sowjetische Militärenzyklopädie 1980, Vol. 20:41f.). At any rate, the evolution of the United States Navy, seen through Soviet eyes, cannot but indicate offensive intentions, and this is particularly true of the deployment of aircraft carriers to the Mediterranean and the Pacific from where bombers with nuclear capability can directly threaten Soviet territory. To Admiral Amelko, Deputy Chief of Staff of the Armed Forces of the USSR, the present American naval capability clearly shows that the United States "from Mahan to Weinberger" has steadily clung to the same conception - commanding the sea and thus commanding the world (Amelko 1984). Similarly, the development of the United States' General Purpose Forces is said to serve to "back up its position-of-strength policy" (Whence the Threat to Peace 1982:41). Moreover, Japanese-American defence efforts are seen as being intended "to revive Japanese militarism and link it up to the bloc's military-political machine" (Andropov 1983c:12).

The Soviet assessment of American nuclear capabilities is not less critical: American plans to upgrade the strategic missile capability are allegedly intended for a "disarming strike" (Whence the Threat to Peace 1982:37). Soviet military writings constantly express concern about the true nature of United States strategic capabilities, which are interpreted as instruments suitable for launching a "first strike" or "preventive war". According to the Soviet Military Encyclopaedia, the American concept of "realistic deterrence" is aimed at acquiring capabilities "having sufficient efficiency not only to launch a first, i.e. preventive strike with nuclear weapons but also to make a second, i.e. retaliatory strike impossible and thereby guarantee the annihilation of the opponent" (Sowjetische Militärenzyklopädie 1980, Vol. 24:98). Even the American preference for sea-based strategic weapons is interpreted in this perspective: by decentralizing a large number of missile systems in the ocean, United States strategists are believed to acquire the capability to attack the opponent by nuclear strikes from various sides; "at the same time the vulnerability of strategic offensive forces is thus diminished and the probability of a hostile nuclear strike against one's own territory is reduced" (ibid.:Vol. 19:19f.).

In sum, the Soviet view is that American capabilities, especially in the field of nuclear weapons, clearly exceed the requirements of deterrence. They are said to indicate a strange definition of equality as "equality plus one" and hence obviously serve for more than mere deterrence. According to the Soviet interpretation, the United States have given up the concept of "mutual assured destruction" in favour of a capability going far beyond defensive insurance against an attack, i.e. a capability that can be used politically for exerting pressure on the Soviet Union, blackmailing it and ultimately launching a surprise attack against the homeland of socialism. As seen from Moscow, American nuclear capabilities clearly do not serve for "sderzhivaniye" ("keeping out") but for "ustrasheniye" ("intimidating").

At is hardly surprising that in the Soviet view American anxieties about existing or potential "windows of vulnerability" are dismissed outright as mere fabrications and, worse, as direct falsifications based on misinformation with the purpose "of justifying the continued arms race, deceiving the peoples, including its own, and achieving a steep increase in military spending." (Whence the Threat to Peace 1982:69). Again, the American reference to "windows of vulnerability" is identified as having the same ulterior motive as the United States efforts increase its capabilities, namely to secure military superiority and thereby restore "US world leadership" (ibid.:71).

Assumptions regarding American strategies: from ideological provocation to surprise attack

The question of how the United States tries to realize its aims is amply dealt with in official Soviet statements and in Soviet academic literature. In general, four types of political strategies are said to be utilized by the United States: ideological provocation, sowing disunity among and destabilizing the socialist countries, acquiring a position of strength by a massive military build-up, the threat to use force and ultimately unleash a war by a surprise attack. The following paragraphs describe these Soviet beliefs.

The first political strategy which the West purposedly uses is ideological provocation aimed at eroding or destroying socialist society. In the Soviet view, the "ideological battle" is now acquiring an unprecedented scope because the imperialists are becoming nervous about the successes of the USSR and the crisis of the capitalist system (Tolkunov 1984:64). Therefore they base foreign policy "on countering at all costs the revolutionary process" (Vidyasova 1984:71). Consequently, the United States is believed to have "announced a 'crusade' against socialism as a social system" (Andropov 1983c:6). This policy allegedly dominates all aspects of United States foreign policy:

"In ideological terms, it is clearly manifest in the incessant propaganda of anti-communism and anti-Sovietism, though its concrete forms and methods at different times change within fairly broad limits, from comparatively moderate and more or less camouflaged concepts to openly aggressive and provocative ones." (Kortunov 1982:85)

Among the "more or less camouflaged concepts" serving anti-commu-

nist propaganda and "psychological warfare" (Rashlev 1984:95) attention is focused mainly on the idea of the "convergence of the two
systems" and the idea of a "multipolar structure" (Kortunov 1982:85);
both ideas are held to be particularly insidious inasmuch as they are
designed to confuse and seduce the citizens of socialist countries.

According to Soviet sources, the policy of détente requires that
the United States should completely refrain from organizing "subver-
sive propagandistic campaigns" (Razryadka mezhdunarodnoy napryazhennosty i ideologicheskaya borba 1981:169). In this connection the
"pretext of 'defending human rights'" is said to be a mere instrument
serving "to legalize interference in the affairs of socialist countries" (Luzin 1981:279).

According to Soviet sources, the same plot against socialism is
also at the heart of another political strategy: the policy of interference in the domestic affairs of sovereign States by "the reactionary attempt to deepen the difficulties and contradictions in the
socialist world" (Burlatsky 1983a:325). The main instruments used in
this context are the arms race, economic pressure and political
blackmail - all designed to impede the development of the socialist
world (ibid.:325). American initiatives in the arms race are viewed
as a peculiarly dangerous instrument in the service of this strategy
because their aim is:

"... to disrupt the Soviet economy by extending the scale and
accelerating the rate of the arms race, to impair Soviet social
programmes, and to complicate economic ties within the socialist
community." (Bykov 1982:84)

Soviet spokesmen also express abhorrence of the linkage method by
which American diplomacy tries to tie economic exchanges to political
concessions. This is "as a rule, accompanied by blatant interference
in the internal affairs of other parties to the negotiations"
(Petrovsky 1982a:18). It must therefore be rejected. Soviet observers
attach great significance to the general disposition of the United
States to perceive itself as a "world leader" and the American
inclination towards hegemonic great power policy (Trofimenko 1982).
In practice this is said to mean an "increasing military build-up"
and efforts by the United States to "improve the flexibility and
effectiveness of its military force as well as enlarging the scope of
that force in US global strategy" (Problemy voyennoy razriadky
1981:77). These efforts are explained as serving the aim of attaining
superiority. The rationale of this strategy is described as follows:

"The truth is that the aggressive quarters of US imperialism and
NATO are counting on the force of arms in their bid to halt social
progress, and are hoping to acquire predominant influence on world
development, to suppress the movement for social and national
liberation, and even to manage to eliminate the socialist system,
to send world socialism to the 'junk yard' of history." (Ponomarev
1983:9)

"Imperialism" is said to have always resorted to war in order to achieve its sinister goals:

"In its struggle for a redivision of the world for the purpose of achieving world supremacy and its attempt to settle the contradiction inherent in its system by means of armed violence, imperialism resorts to war. Wars have become its constant and invariable feature." (Ogarkov 1982:6)

In the Soviet view of the adversary, the aggressive thrust inherent in United States strategy can be discerned in the global dimension of American military activities. This aspect of United States strategy is held to be aimed at encircling the Soviet Union. According to Foreign Minister Gromyko,

"... it is common knowledge that a circle of American military bases surrounds the Soviet Union." (Gromyko 1983a:15f.)

The vision of encirclement also includes the aspect of the nuclear threat. In fact, Soviet spokesmen perceive the policy of nuclear blackmail and nuclear aggression to be the prime rationale for the chain of military bases surrounding Soviet territory:

"Our country is encircled by American military bases. More than 12,000 warheads of different nuclear strategic missiles are spearheaded against our territory. Since the day the US acquired nuclear arms they have always declared their readiness to use them first. The stake on the first nuclear strike has transcended all the American doctrines of the period after the Second World War: 'doctrine of massive retaliation', 'doctrine of flexible response', 'realistic deterrence'. And during the 1940s, 1950s and 1960s, the US has many times been on the verge of practical use of nuclear arms against the USSR." (Akhromeyev 1983)

Apart from bases, the "camp of imperialism" is said to employ oceanic strategy for intimidating the Soviet Union and other socialist countries; Admiral Gorshkov states:

"This strategy starts from the premise that practically all land objectives are within the reach of attack from the ocean... Therefore, even now, extensive areas of the world ocean have already been turned by the imperialists into launching points for highly mobile, covertly acting carriers of long-range strategic missiles launched from under water and always ready for combat." (Gorshkov 1979:X)

The most dangerous instrument in the hands of American leaders is held to be the use of force. Statements by socialist authors tend to assume that "monopoly capital, by relying on military power, hopes to have a variety of options at its disposal" (Schwarz et al. 1981:72-75). This general tendency is said to apply under all United States Administrations, but it is alleged to have become particularly grave in the case of the Reagan Administration:

> "The Reagan Administration has not only inherited the aggressive directions of the Carter Administration, but has made them more dangerous. The apparent tendencies of the Administration's approach to crisis situations and its apparent preference for the policy of military force is, given the actual international conditions, one of the most dangerous sources of military conflicts and a threat to peace. The Administration's position complicates the adoption of effective mesures in the field of military détente and disarmament." (Problemy voyennoy razryadki 1981:79)

Soviet spokesmen also accuse the West of using its naval capacities for projecting power in different parts of the world (Gorshkov 1979:2). More specifically, Admiral Gorshkov views the function of Western navies as "showing force" and "intimidation", thus "achieving political ends without resorting to armed struggle":

> "In conditions of opposition to socialism, the ruling circles of the countries of capitalism are resorting to ever more ingenious ways of showing force and using intimidation, going as far as nuclear blackmail in an attempt to preserve or restore their dominance over the peoples of former colonies or other countries tearing themselves from the clutches of capitalist exploitation." (Gorshkov 1979:251)

Admiral Gorshkov affirms that American bases abroad serve to "guarantee the permanent presence of US Navy" and thus represent "an important component of US foreign policy of expansionism, aimed at achievement of world domination" (Gorshkov 1983). Worse, according to many representative Soviet sources, the very climax of all strategies planned by the United States leadership is to unleash a war:

> "The US Administration and the Pentagon have elaborated plans which envisage the unleashing of a war aimed at the defeat of the Soviet Union and the liquidation of socialism as a social system." (Akhromeyev 1983)

More particularly, the United States is accused of planning and preparing for a preventive nuclear war against the Soviet Union and other socialist countries - and is said to have done so ever since the United States Government succeeded in constructing nuclear weapons. Of course, one might ask why it did not make such a strike while enjoying a nuclear monopoly, i.e. during the time between Hiroshima and the manufacture of nuclear weapons by the Soviet Union in 1949. Soviet sources claim that, in the 1950s, the United States did contemplate "in all earnest" a preventive war (Luzin 1981:29), yet felt restrained by the fact that the American nuclear forces of that period had only a limited range and therefore could not hit Soviet territory from air bases on United States soil without stop-overs or refuelling in flight (ibid.:30). After the Soviet Union had become a nuclear Power, American "illusions of world domination suffered a crushing blow. The policy of attempted nuclear diktat and blackmail failed." (ibid.:31) In this way, Soviet sources refute the argument that the United States gave proof of its peaceful intentions by not attacking the Soviet Union when it still had the capability to do so with impunity. Furthermore, they criticize the West for hypocritically using this argument in order to mislead today's public opinion. In the view of a high-ranking Soviet military officer, quite a different conclusion must be drawn from the fact that the United States has so far not attacked the Soviet Union - this fact only proves that the United States has not felt capable of daring to launch an attack, but it does not prove that it did not have such an intention. With this kind of argument, the Soviet interpretation of American intentions does not give the Americans any chance of presenting evidence of peaceful intentions - simply because Soviet leaders are convinced that the United States cannot be peaceful. If it nevertheless happens to behave in a peaceful way, this can only be explained by American inability and/or Soviet resistance.

America is also said to have continued to try to find ways and means "of averting a Soviet nuclear retaliation strike" by its strategy of "realistic deterrence" and "counter-force doctrine" (Sowjetische Militärenzyklopädie 1980,Vol.12:9). Moreover, Soviet sources clearly express the assumption that the United States is firmly engaged in preparing a surprise attack, i.e. preparing to launch a pre-emptive nuclear first strike:

"Soviet military doctrine proceeds from the assumption that the imperialists are preparing a surprise nuclear attack against the USSR and other socialist countries. At the same time they consider the possibility of waging military operations with conventional weapons and the possibility of these operations escalating into military actions involving the use of nuclear missile weapons." (Marxism-Leninism on War and Army 1972:304)

Again and again, Soviet military publications stress the importance allegedly given by "bourgeois" theorists to the "surprise start of military actions and preventive war by massive use of the most modern means of annihilation" (Sowjetische Militärenzyklopädie 1980, Vol. 24:30). The assumption that the United States is planning a surprise attack on the Soviet Union is also supported by ideological arguments referring to the law of history: as capitalism is approaching its historical end, its policies reflect despair and folly - hence the danger of the United States launching a preventive attack has to be taken seriously (Henri 1983:93-99).

This assumptionis further substantiated by reference to two specific aspects of American nuclear force policy on both the Eurostrategic and central balance level. As far as the Eurostrategic context is concerned, the deployment of Pershing-2A missiles and cruise missiles is interpreted as a clear indication of such a first-strike strategy, as either missile is considered to be a first strike weapon:

"Pershing-2A missiles:...The capability to enfeeble the Soviet strategic forces in a matter of minutes makes a pre-emptive strike considerably more 'tempting'.

...A cruise missile is unspottable until it reaches the immediate proximity of the target. Consequently it is also a first-strike weapon like Pershing-2." (The Threat to Europe 1981:24)
"The Pentagon considers the installation of the new long-range theatre nuclear forces in Europe as one of the channels leading to the creation of the potential for the first nuclear strike against the USSR, claiming that if nuclear war begins, it would be limited to Europe." (Pravda, 10 February 1982)

The Soviet view emphasizes the willingness of the United States to acquire these nuclear warfighting capabilities that would help keep the United States homeland outside a potential "local" nuclear war:

"Preparing for nuclear war, the US Administration and the US Army staff attach great importance to the survivability of the US in such a war. Therefore, they are elaborating the theory and practice of the conduct of a limited nuclear war in Europe. They are finishing the process of preparing for the installation of many hundreds of long-range nuclear missiles in Europe which will, according to the US administration, allow them to achieve a limited nuclear war in Europe, the political objective of the US without the escalation of this into a world war and thus without the risk of nuclear retaliation against the US' own territory; the Pershings and cruise missiles are a real technical base for limited nuclear war." (Akhromeyev 1983)

The Soviet view establishes a close association between the concept of "local" or "limited" nuclear war and the concept of a pre-emptive nuclear strike. According to the Soviet interpretation of the American Presidential Directive 59 (PD-59) of August 1980, the "pre-emptive strike concept holds top priority", and "a surprise attack to destroy almost all Soviet nuclear devices is expected to prevent a return strike against cities in the United States with America retaining the capability of hitting vital enemy centres" (Luzin 1981:213).

This interpretation of NATO's nuclear policy is strikingly different from NATO's own ideas regarding this subject, which are basically oriented towards preventing any war and securing a "linkage" or "coupling" mechanism between the United States nuclear deterrent providing a nuclear guarantee and the European territory to be protected by this kind of guarantee. Soviet leaders explicitly accuse the United States of abusing its European allies and not refraining from even risking their existence in order "to unleash nuclear war" against the Soviet Union. As General Secretary Andropov put it:

"In the two World Wars the flames of destruction had spared the territory of the United States of America. And today Washington would like to think that by deploying its medium-range missiles in

63

Europe and thus creating an additional nuclear threat to the socialist countries it could divert the retaliatory strike from its own territory. As to the security of the West European allies of the United States, it seems that this interests the American leaders only to the extent to which the West Europeans will be able with their lives and their cities to lessen the retribution for the United States, should Washington yield to the temptation to unleash nuclear war in the illusory hope of winning it." (Andropov 1983c:6)

In sum, Andropov accuses the United States of regarding "the European allies as hostages" (Andropov 1983c:16). While NATO's concept of "flexible response" provides for nuclear guarantees by the United States for the benefit of its European allies, the Soviet perspective sees the United States-European linkage quite differently: in the Soviet view, the stationing of American nuclear weapons on the soil of Western European members of NATO has the function of a "magnet", i.e. it would immediately provoke Soviet retaliation. The entire premise of NATO's doctrine of "flexible response" which involves preparing for a nuclear response in case of a Soviet conventional or nuclear attack against Western Europe, is alleged to be built on completely false grounds - for the simple reason that there will never be a Soviet attack. Hence the only mission which NATO's intermediate-range nuclear force can conceivably have is, according to Soviet spokesmen, its utilization for a surprise attack, i.e. a first strike. Such a contingency is also regarded as conceivable in connection with an armed confrontation between the two major Powers outside Europe, e.g. in connection with a severe crisis in Latin America or Africa. Taking up a term familiar to Western strategic terminology, Soviet experts call the stationing of nuclear-capable systems close to the Soviet homeland inherently "destabilizing".

Not only do these systems pose a deadly threat to some of the Soviet strategic weapon bases, but Soviet analysts also surmise sinister American plans for a "decapitation" strike:

"...the stationing of qualitatively new missiles in Western Europe is conceived as a means of strengthening the US potential for what may be called a 'decapitation' strike, that is, a nuclear strike that is meant to instantly destroy the centers of political and military leadership, and command and communication centers." (How to Avert the Threat to Europe 1983:34)

More specifically, Soviet sources expect the thrust of an enemy nuclear attack will be designed to:

"...disrupt the political leadership of the country, undermine its military-economic potential, deter employment of the armed forces, and seize the strategic initiative in the war." (Yegorov/ Shlyakhov/Alabin 1970:1)

It is interesting to note, in this context, that Soviet sources use the two terms "first use of nuclear weapons" and "nuclear first strike" in a rather indiscriminate way. Sometimes these terms seem to be employed as if they were synonyms, especially when talking about the first-use concept as adopted by NATO as one of the key elements of the Western "strategy of flexible response". A Soviet study calls NATO's policy of not refraining from the use of nuclear weapons in case of an armed attack against a NATO member simply "the first strike capability concept" (How to Avert the Threat to Europe 1983:15). This peculiar usage of strategic terminology may also reflect the deep concern felt by the Soviet leadership about the possibility of a surprise attack.

Corresponding indications are surmised on the central balance level, where the new American emphasis on ballistic missile defence (BMD) technology is considered to constitute striking proof of the intention of "securing first strike impunity" (Ponomarev 1983:8). This assumption has been voiced at the highest political level by General Secretary Andropov:

"In fact the strategic offensive forces of the United States will continue to be developed and upgraded at full tilt and in quite a definitive direction, namely that of acquiring a first nuclear strike potential. Under these conditions the intention to secure for itself the possibility of destroying with the help of the ABM defence the corresponding strategic system of the other side, that is of rendering it incapable of dealing a retaliatory strike, is a bid to disarm the Soviet Union in the face of the US nuclear threat." (Andropov 1983a:33)

Whatever type of nuclear war the United States may be envisaging, Soviet analysts at any rate believe that American and NATO strategic doctrine definitively wishes to:

"...make nuclear war, and first use of nuclear weapons, thinkable and ...postulate the drive to gain an edge in the quantity and quality of nuclear weapons in the belief that a nuclear war is winnable." (How to Avert the Threat to Europe 1983:13)

When making this analysis, however, Soviet sources never fail to stress that "as the strategic conceptions of Washington become more sophisticated and complicated they become more unrealistic" (Arbatov 1981c:105). This lack of realism is held to be the consequence of Western underestimation of the Soviet Union's intention to "counter-balance" any new weapon introduced on the other side by corresponding systems on its own side. Soviet spokesmen, as a consequence, expect a sobering-up process to start in the United States - owing to the insight that the Soviet Union is strong enough to counter any American aggression. This change of American psychology in a more and more realistic direction is also expected to have a mitigating impact on the United States Administration's behaviour.

Assumptions regarding American disarmament and arms control policies: achieving military superiority

Viewed in the perspective outlined in the preceding sections, Soviet spokesmen conclude that the American drive for a military build-up also sheds serious doubts on the American willingness and seriousness to engage in constructive arms control negotiations. The basic assumption to start from, according to a distinguished Soviet chief negotiator, must be as follows:

> "They <US arms limitation proposals> must be compatible with US military aims, and ensure Western military superiority over their rivals, that is, the countries of the socialist community." (Issraelyan 1982:118)

Therefore the Soviet Union is afraid that the United States is in effect "not interested in agreements limiting strategic arms" (Ustinov 1981:12), and, worse, as expressed by General Secretary Andropov:

> "The purpose of the United States at the Geneva talks, as it has transpired, is at all costs to add new powerful armaments to the vast nuclear arsenal of NATO that already exists, and it is only Soviet missiles that it wants to reduce." (Andropov 1983a:67)

> "While calling for 'radical reductions' in word, what it really has in mind is essentially a reduction of the Soviet strategic potential." (ibid.:14)

> "In brief, we are being invited to talk about how to help the NATO bloc upset to its advantage the balance of medium-range nuclear weapons in Europe." (Andropov 1983b:12)

In the Soviet view, it is an "undeniable truth" that United States resistance to signing treaties such as SALT II is ultimately rooted in the United States refusal to accept "equality in strategic weapons possessed by the two countries and equal security for both the USA and the USSR." (Trofimenko 1983:23). This assumption again comes down to the general premise that the United States is aiming at military superiority:

> "Yet it turns out that the beneficial and progressive effect of that principle was recognized by American political leaders only as long as the principle remained but a figure of speech, a semantic ruse designed to comfort or console the other party, while at heart the American leaders actually assumed that the USA far surpassed the USSR in terms of potential ability to get off cheap in case of their nuclear attack against the USSR. They believed that they could disarm the Soviet Union to such an extent that the Soviet return strike against the USA would be 'acceptable', whatever this word means. In those days the American leaders loved to talk of the mutual assured destruction principle and its merits. But as soon as MAD became a reality for both parties ...

those in the USA who still think in 'imperial' categories and cannot reconcile themselves to the erosion of American strategic superiority made up their mind to ruin SALT II in the futile hope that a new spurt in the strategic arms build-up would enable the USA to regain a position of unilateral deterrence." (Trofimenko 1983:23f.)

Therefore American arms control policies are alleged to serve only to achieve and secure military superiority. Soviet commentators regularly tend to interpret particular features of the current arms control negotiations in terms of this assumption. Deadlock in the negotiations are ascribed to machinations "towards curtailing and blocking negotiations, pursued by NATO", which reflect "the desire of that military bloc's leaders to upset the existing military balance in their own favour" (Petrovsky 1982a:11). Most Soviet comments on the current arms limitations and disarmament negotiations fit into this pattern. Thus they demonstrate the importance of basic assumptions underlying and policies adopted with regard to the adversary.

The basic Soviet assumption is summed up by Foreign Minister Gromyko's statement that the United States Administration, in its arms control policies, is proposing nothing less than "the Soviet Union's unilateral disarmament" (Gromyko 1983b:17), or, as another Soviet observer puts it, that United States policy is "geared entirely not to an honest agreement but to gaining one-sided advantage" (Petrovsky 1984a:83). As one significant indication corroborating this hypothesis, Soviet sources point to the alleged plan of American officials to maintain "a margin of superiority".

For these reasons, Soviet sources, as a rule, blame the American side for the absence of progress in the field of disarmament and arms control. They accuse the Western partners to arms control negotiations of having failed, in most cases, to reciprocate Soviet good-will gestures and of discontinuing important negotiations (Trofimenko 1983:20f.). In general, the American leadership is denounced as only "paying lip service to strategic arms reduction" while in fact aiming at a higher level of nuclear confrontation (Disarmament: Who's Against? 1983:22). The Geneva talks and the accompanying propaganda are said to "serve as a smokescreen to disguise these true intentions of the United States" (ibid.:23). As General Secretary Chernenko puts it, the participation of the United States in talks on this subject has been turned "into a propaganda tool and cold war policy" (Chernenko 1984a:17). Soviet experts generally reproach the United States with negotiating only for the sake of negotiating, in order to calm the yearning of the American people for disarmament and peace.

Western politicians are accused of "using major international talks... for internal political purposes so as to save their damaged reputation" (Petrovsky 1982b:293). This and other domestic determinants of American policy in the field of disarmament and arms limitations appear particularly irritating from a Soviet viewpoint. The domestically motivated non-ratification of treaties signed with the

Soviet Union, and more generally, counterproductive tendencies originating in the American political system, are regarded as a second
major characteristic of United States policy. As a distinguished
Soviet commentator puts it, the United States behaviour in this
respect is hard to understand from a Soviet point of view:

"What sort of country is it where the president signs something,
and then they say that the president was a fool and signed something he did not know about? ... I do not understand it." (Zhukov
1984)

Soviet spokesmen generally criticize the United States leadership
for "scrapping the treaties previously concluded with the Soviet
Union" and "breaking off the talks on the limitation and reduction of
armaments" (Ogarkov 1982:18). When the United States is rebuked for
not having ratified some treaties signed, such as SALT II, and
refusing to sign treaties which have nearly been agreed upon in
principle, such as the comprehensive test-ban, from a Soviet point of
view it is quite clear why the American authorities suddenly became
reluctant to proceed: obviously their constructive efforts must have
been blocked by interventions by the military-industrial complex.

Thirdly, Soviet observers are very upset by what they consider a
sabotaging of any progress in disarmament by using all kinds of
strange pretexts. To them, the refusal to ratify signed treaties
based on reference to the situation in Afghanistan "can hardly have
anything to do with the subject matter of the treaty itself"
(Disarmament: Who's Against? 1983:22). In Soviet eyes, this
constitutes a typical feature of the Western approach to negotiations
which, referring to the United Nations Committee on Disarmament, the
Soviet representative describes in the following terms:

"The USA and certain of its NATO allies impose discussions of
matters that have no bearing at all on the functions of the
Committee, fruitless procedural debates and the like. The foes of
military détente have mounted a head-on attack on the very possibility of business like dialogue concerning topical problems of
disarmament." (Issraelyan 1982:116)

"The US and some of its military and political allies are attempting to replace businesslike discussion by debates on secondary,
minor problems often of a procedural nature, which introduce
red-tape into discussions on critical issues." (Petrovsky
1982b:293)

These and other claims and tactics are said to be "pure
demagoguery" (Disarmament: Who's Against? 1983:23).

A fourth unfair trick of which Soviet spokesmen accuse the United
States arms control negotiators is their intention:

"...to subject to limitations only specific components of strategic forces suiting the American side, while leaving other compo-

nents outside the framework of agreement, simply turning a blind eye to them. In effect, the United States would like to destroy the existing structure of the Soviet strategic potential, while retaining a free hand to build up its own corresponding armaments" (Gromyko 1983b:17f.)

A fifth trick that Soviet experts identify is the American nego-tiators' practice of withdrawing previous proposals once they have been accepted by the Soviet Union. In particular, in the context of the Vienna talks on mutual force reductions, Soviet observers think that the Soviet Union has made proposals which are very similar to previous United States proposals - and which were then promptly rejected by the American delegation. Viewed in the Soviet perspec-tive, all these tricks clearly demonstrate that the United States is not interested in genuine disarmament negotiations, let alone in concrete results. Worse, they also prove that the original American proposals right from the beginning were not meant seriously but were put forward only to create difficulties for the Soviet Union.

Given the basic assumption regarding American disarmament policy - according to which the United States aims at achieving "unilateral superiority" - it is hardly surprising that Soviet statements also dismiss the idea of "deep cuts" in strategic arsenals put forward by the United States Government. In the Soviet view, this proposal merely serves the purpose of:

"...exploiting differences in the geopolitical positions of the two powers and the composition of the respective strategic 'triads' to the maximum unilateral advantage of the USA." (Trofimenko 1983:24)

The same perspective is also relevant when Soviet spokesmen interpret more specific aspects of the American conduct of disarmament negotiations. They suspect American behaviour in this field to be not only dishonest but also constantly inspired by an attempt at "securing one-sided advantages at the expense of other countries" (Petrovsky 1982a:16, Petrovsky 1984a:81) and, worse, blackmailing the USSR. Foreign Minister Gromyko expressed the feeling that the adversary thinks that:

"... the thing to do is to pressure the Soviet Union and to strike a tougher posture, and then everything will be all right. They even claim: 'The more pressure we put on the Soviet Union, the better the chances of agreement'." (Gromyko 1983a:11)

General Secretary Andropov explicitly rebutted the American approach which, as he sees it, is characterized by the principle of "strength and dialogue go hand in hand":

"The American leadership, as all signs indicate, has not given up its intention to conduct talks with us from positions of strength, from positions of threat and pressure. We resolutely reject such an approach. And, in general, attempts to conduct 'power diplomacy' in respect of us are a hopeless thing." (Andropov 1984:135)

In general, the American "style" in arms control negotiations is thus alleged to be dominated by "a predilection for looking at the tactical side of things, which means that those who express themselves in that way give little thought to the substance of the matter at hand" (Gromyko 1983a:22).

Another feature of the American "style" which annoys Soviet experts is what they call the "poker approach" to negotiations, where everything is conceptualized as though there were no alternatives to winning at the other side's expense or losing - instead of aiming at a compromise on the basis of equal security and legality.

As far as the specific aspect of verification or, in Soviet terminology, "control of disarmament", is concerned, United States insistence on strict verification procedures is derided as either "the Philistine side of arms control" (Arbatov 1981a:140) and "unrealistic" or as merely representing a "tactic of obfuscating the substance of negotiations and torpedoing talks by exaggerated demands concerning control" (Issraelyan 1982:118). In other words, it is held to be an artificial pretext fabricated in order "to disrupt the solution of questions of arms limitation" (Batsanov 1982:28) and to "wreck the talks" (Arms Control-Disarmament 1983:7). Any American reference to the inadequacy of verification procedures is therefore criticized as "false and hypocritical" (Disarmament: Who's Against? 1983:42), an "imaginary problem" only (Petrovsky 1984a:82). In addition, Soviet spokesmen are afraid that the reason why the United States is putting so much emphasis on verification is that it erroneously believes this to be the Soviet Union's "weak point" or, worse, it merely provides an opportunity for spying on the Soviet Union:

"Control becomes legalized espionage the moment its scope, the competence of controlling bodies, the methods of inspection and so on go beyond what is actually necessary to verify agreed disarmament measures." (Arms Control-Disarmament 1983:5)

Soviet sources also point to the charges put forward by the United States concerning alleged Soviet violations of existing treaties; these charges are vigorously rejected as being nothing but an attempt:

"to shift the blame from the guilty to the innocent" in order "to camouflage their policy aimed at undermining the agreements already signed on limiting the arms drive, and at the same time to conceal their own sins in defaulting on their legal and political commitments in this field". (Kortunov/Sokov 1984:9)

Seen from the Soviet point of view, therefore, the conclusion cannot be avoided that the United States and especially its arms control diplomacy do not deserve to be trusted. According to the USSR Minister of Defence this conclusion is supported by a "conspicuous trend" in United States foreign policy: the "gradual undermining of many treaties and agreements" (Ustinov 1981:13). Hence the Soviet Union believes it to be all the more important to rely on the change of the "correlation of forces" rather than giving unlimited credit to verbal promises offered by the "imperialists".

Considering all these difficulties, obstructions and acts of trickery and sabotage deeply embedded in the "imperialist" nature of the West, one might ask why, in the Soviet view, it nevertheless makes sense to negotiate with the United States and its allies. How does the Soviet Union explain the rationale and significance of the agreements signed so far? This question may seem even more pertinent in the light of the severe criticism expressed by Soviet sources that:

"The frivolous approach of the United States to the 1974 and 1976 treaties, which it had previously signed, is giving it the reputation of an unreliable negotiating partner." (Disarmament:- Who's Against? 1983:42).

The Soviet attitude in this respect has to be seen in the context of the overall concept of the "correlation of forces"and the dynamic nature of this concept. Seen in this context it is clear that according to the Soviet view the piecemeal progress achieved so far must not be ascribed to a change of mind on the part of the "imperialists". Quite the opposite holds true: according to the Soviet interpretation, the West was compelled to sign these agreements by the growing might of the socialist camp. A Soviet author expresses the relationship between the change in the "correlation of forces" and disarmament in the following unambiguous terms:

"Government leaders in the West were compelled to acknowledge the West's losses of its military advantage and admit an objective necessity for peaceful coexistence with the Soviet Union and other socialist countries... This realisation has had matching political consequences as it prompted Western politicians to look for ways of strengthening national security not by whipping up the arms race but through reaching agreement with the other side, at least on the limitation of armaments." (Mamontov 1979:131)

In sum, although the Soviet leadership feels extremely sceptical about American reliability and American willingness to engage in arms limitation and disarmament measures, they think that these negotiations should nevertheless continue because the United States Administration is increasingly realizing the constraints of the situation. Soviet spokesmen are rather confident in this respect: not only does the general evolution of the "objective forces", i.e. the correlation of forces, lead the American Administration to some sober insights, but they feel that the United States President is also becoming increasingly sensitive to the declining popularity of his stubborn approach in the field of disarmament. So they trust that sooner or later the American Administration will again accomodate itself to the realities of life.

71

The meta-image - assumptions regarding the American view of the
Soviet Union: misrepresentations, distortions, lies

When offering their reflections on the adversary, Soviet spokesmen
never fail to point to the crucial role played by American assumptions about the Soviet Union and Soviet intentions - assumptions
which, not surprisingly, are harshly criticized for being wrong,
distorted and even deliberately mendacious.

The cardinal aspect usually taken up in the context of such statements about what might be called the Soviet "meta-image" refers to
the alleged aggressiveness of the Soviet Union and the nature of the
Soviet threat. More often than not allegations of this kind are
simply rejected as representing nothing but "lies", or more specifically "imperialist lies" (Mamontov 1979:89f; Zukunft 1982) or "myths"
or "false allegations" or "fabrications" (e.g. Yefremov 1979:251ff.).
Some statements very explicitly discuss the main features of these
"lies":

> "The main emphasis is laid not on analysis of the material and
> factual side of the matter, that is, on the actual possibility of
> any one-sided military build-up, but on speculation about 'inten-
> tions' slanderously ascribed to the Soviet Union. In other words,
> the main thrust of the arguments in favour of escalating the mili-
> tarist preparations of the USA and NATO is lodged in the gratui-
> tous assumption of a Soviet military threat". (Bykov 1982:81)

According to General Volkogonov, all the talk about the "Soviet
threat" can only be explained in the context of United States
psychological warfare against the Soviet Union :

> "Having developed psychological warfare into State policy and
> trying to make it even tougher, Washington's leaders are directing
> the efforts of USIA, CIA and other propaganda and intelligence
> establishments in the first place to sell myths about the Soviet
> threat. In fact, one of the major tasks of psychological warfare
> in the opinion of its creators or inspirers is to create in the
> world an atmosphere of war hysteria, uncertainty and fear."
> (Volkogonov 1983:196)

Soviet authors seem particularly enraged by the West's presuppo-
sition of Soviet "aggressiveness" to the extent that it serves as
the rationale for the Western concept of "deterrence". They claim
that there is absolutely no reasonable justification for such a
strategy of deterrence; the situation is held to be as simple as
this:

> "But 'deterring' the USSR from 'aggression' is a trumped up, need-
> less undertaking. This should be clear to any unprejudiced student
> of the Soviet policy of peace... This judgement is based on the
> absurd idea that the Soviet Union has aggressive intentions in
> Europe or elsewhere. It has no such intentions, because they are
> contrary to the very principles of the Soviet policy of peace."
> (How to Avert the Threat to Europe 1983:13f.)

Similarly, Soviet spokesmen criticize the West's distorted view of the meaning of the concept of "world revolution". They assert that the Soviet Union has never nor will it ever strive for expansion by exporting revolution. They refer to the "Peace Programme" and the concept of "peaceful coexistence" which, they complain, are not taken seriously by Western politicians. Another indication of the non-expansionist attitude of the USSR, as suggested by a Soviet spokes-man, is the failure of Trotsky to launch a programme of exporting revolution.

Apart from this general denial of aggressive intentions, Soviet spokesmen also often object to the American view of specific Soviet policies, such as the one adopted vis-à-vis the Middle East. Here, too, they repudiate the constant American obsession with alleged Soviet aggressive intentions:

"Washington is spreading the story of a 'Soviet threat' to the oil wealth of the Middle East or the oil supply lines. That is delibe-rate falsehood, because its authors know perfectly well that the Soviet Union has no intention of impinging on the one or the other." (Brezhnev 1981:28f.)

Furthermore, Soviet statements put particular emphasis on the American perception of Soviet military doctrine. They express regret at what they call misrepresentations and distortions of Soviet doctrine, as this "is the artificial prime cause of many of the fears cultivated in the West" (The Threat to Europe 1981:6) to "create a perverse image of the Soviet Union as a 'militaristic power' guided by a 'doctrine of conquest'." (How to Avert the Threat to Europe 1983:15) Two blunders are held responsible for the West's distorted view of the allegedly aggressive nature of the Soviet doctrine: the first is the - unintentional or deliberate - confusion of strategic doctrine with works devoted to battlefield tactics. According to Soviet spokesmen, such works do stress the importance of surprise, offensive actions and camouflage, but they have nothing to do with doctrine. Therefore, it is:

"... a simple ruse to adduce that Soviet doctrine is aggressively offensive. They do so by quoting from works of Soviet military theorists devoted not to doctrine or military policy but to parti-cular aspects of combat, such as tactics in the battlefield. These quotes are passed off as Soviet doctrine, though that is a deli-berately incorrect and specious approach." (The Threat to Europe 1981:10)

The second blunder of which Soviet statements accuse the West is reference to outdated Soviet publications:

"Passages out of the works of Soviet military experts, even such as were published in the 1960s, are being dished up as representing Soviet military doctrine." (How to Avert the Threat to Europe 1983:16)

The third feature of the Western image of the Soviet Union, according to Soviet statements, is the "screaming about the alleged military superiority of the 'Soviet bloc in Europe'". Soviet sources hold that "facts prove that the claim of an 'imbalance' in favour of the Warsaw Treaty is nothing but a lie" (Luzin 1981:312). In Soviet eyes this aspect of the Western image seems to constitute the main trick used by Western propaganda. Therefore great efforts are made to disprove the West's claim that the Soviet Union is superior in military forces. Again and again Soviet sources contend:

"The Soviet Union - as this has been repeatedly declared at the highest levels- has never sought, and does not now seek, military superiority, but neither will it allow anyone to win such superiority over itself." (Whence the Threat to Peace 1982:5)

Western assessments of the military balance are held to "deliberately exaggerate the armaments of the Warsaw Treaty, while downgrading the corresponding NATO figures" (ibid.:80). By contrast to the American picture of the situation, Soviet sources conclude:

"Thus, irrespective of whether we compare strategic nuclear weapons or medium-range nuclear weapons in Europe or conventional forces of NATO and Warsaw Treaty countries, there is evidence of rough parity on all counts. The USA and NATO are not lagging behind." (ibid.:81)

When commenting on the Western view of the military balance, Soviet sources also like to refer to a feature of strategic discussions in the West: they amply quote dissenting opinions expressed by distinguished Western personalities such as Helmut Schmidt, Robert McNamara, McGeorge Bundy, George F.Kennan and Gerard Smith (ibid.:82) who have questioned the existence of Soviet superiority and are now quoted as witnesses for the Soviet view (e.g. How to Avert the Threat to Europe 1983:23f. quoting also Jimmy Carter, Harold Brown, Alexander Haig and even Caspar Weinberger).

Another subject of complaints by Soviet authors is the way in which the United States depicts Soviet policies in the field of disarmament and arms limitation:

"In the Western literature ... the position of the USSR on disarmament is often wrongly portrayed as inflexible and intransigent. Therefore, even the informed reader is liable to form a false impression about the Soviet position, although the Soviet Union and her allies actually approach such issues in a thoroughly constructive way." (Trofimenko 1983:19; cf. also Gromyko 1983a:16f.)

74

In connection with the thoroughly negative assessment of the United States view of the Soviet Union and Soviet policies, the question arises of how Soviet spokesmen explain the constantly "wrong" and "slanderous" character of the American view. They perceive the main reason to lie in the American unwillingness to give an objective description of Soviet policies. In addition, Soviet authors concede that the information about the Soviet Union available in the West may sometimes not be as comprehensive and exhaustive as one might wish, because secrecy is given much importance in the Soviet Union. Yet they argue that there are good reasons for this attitude: given the many occasions when the country has been the victim of foreign invaders, and the fact that it lived for a long time in a virtual state of siege, it is deemed to be quite natural that the Soviet authorities should be very cautious in deciding what can be disclosed and what ought to be kept secret. (Arbatov 1981c:191)

It is characteristic of the systematic nature of Soviet political thinking that consistent efforts are made to interpret the meta-image within the broader framework of Marxist-Leninist thought. In practice this means that the perceived American tendency to misrepresent and distort Soviet political and military strategy is assumed to serve a specific purpose. According to the Soviet Military Encyclopaedia it is aimed at undermining the moral strength of the peoples and armies of the socialist States by distorting Marxist-Leninist theory, slandering the socialist social system and falsifying the policy and aims of communism (Sowjetische Militärenzyklopädie 1980, Vol.10:44). The "Soviet military threat lie" is alleged to "nourrish militarism, the policy of military blocs and preparations for a new 'crusade' against socialism" (Kortunov 1982:87) and to have been fabricated in order to outmanoeuvre the Western peace movement and enhance "imperialist defense motivation" (Zukunft 1982). Its main function, however, is to serve as "a screen for the revival of the imperialist 'position of strength' policy" (Bykov 1982:79) and a "camouflage" by "trying to put the blame at the wrong door and to 'prove' that the Soviet Union is behind the aggravation of international tensions" (Tolkunov 1984:64). In sum, the Soviet evaluation of the American image of the Soviet Union assumes the "imperialists" to be attempting to justify and legitimize American aggressiveness. Accordingly, American leaders are charged with "smearing the Soviet people" in order to divert attention from their own provocative and dangerous course:

"In attempting to justify in some way their dangerous, inhuman policies, the same people pile slander upon the Soviet Union, upon socialism as a social system... One must say bluntly that it is an unattractive sight when, intent upon smearing the Soviet people, the leaders of such a country as the United States resort to what amounts almost to obscenities alternating with hypocritical preaching about morality and humaneness." (Andropov 1983b:6)

In the last resort, the American image of the USSR is believed to represent a typical consequence of capitalist contradictions:

"Intimidation by a Soviet 'threat' in the struggle against socialism is a 'universal method' of imperialist reaction. It is used
most vigorously when contradictions in the capitalist world are
aggravated and the ruling circles of imperialist States cannot
cope with the difficulties inherent in the capitalist system."
(Nalin 1982:73)

Another variant of this general tendency is said to reside in
certain alliance problems: as Europe has been living in peace for 40
years, NATO is assumed to suffer from a lack of cohesion - hence the
American wish to fix in the minds of the Europeans the idea of a
Soviet menace.

As these and other Soviet statements suggest, American perceptions are usually ascribed to deliberate machinations designed to
achieve the aggressive aims of "imperialism". As such, they are seen
to vary according to the foreign policy adopted by the American
Administration: while in the period of détente, due to the increase
in contacts, there were "signs of a change for the better" in the
field of perceptions, the attempts being made by the Reagan
Administration to "reverse this process" are said to have again
produced more one-sided and distorted perceptions (Arbatov, in:
Perceptions 1979:297). Soviet experts therefore discern a cyclical
process, whereby the alleged "Soviet threat" is brought up again
every 10 to 15 years.

Furthermore, in a Marxist-Leninist perspective, the Western image
of the Soviet Union is also interpreted by looking at economic determinants shaping this image. As Academician Arbatov points out, the
information delivered to the American public is strongly influenced
by "direct or indirect pressure of the forces that have a vested
interest in creating a distorted picture of the Soviet Union". He has
in mind first and foremost economic forces. As "the biggest business
in the USA is military business", it is clear to him why there are so
many "distorted ideas about the Soviet Union, artificially bloated
fears of the 'Soviet military threat' and continuously fanned
animosity and distrust toward the USSR" (ibid.). Other American
pressure groups responsible for the "blatant disinformation" about
the Soviet Union are, according to Arbatov, all "groups benefiting
from the cold war", in particular ultra-conservative elements, organizations representing anti-communist emigration from Eastern Europe
and the Israeli lobby (ibid.:298).

The interests of the military-industrial complex are thus held to
be the prime impetus behind the tendency to create a myth about the
"Soviet threat". The whole mythology serves to justify the
ever-rising defence expenditure. The press and the media are then in
turn bribed and manipulate public opinion. Disinformation is said to
be facilitated by the need of many people to think in terms of simple
images. The United States Administration is believed to exploit this
disposition by projecting the simplistic image of a Soviet State that
is the ultimate cause of all evils. In sum:

"The anti-Soviet myth as a specific means of policy and ideological and psychological manipulation of social consciousness performs a rather definite concrete function in a bourgeois society. This function is used to fulfil the myth's social role. It represents a strategic lever by means of which monopolies influence the internal and external policies of an imperialist State." (Volkogonov 1983a:204)

Soviet authors tend to suppose that ultimately Western observers are in fact simply unable to grasp the essence of Soviet policy. "Bourgeois" theory in general is said to be based on false premises and wrong assumptions (Marxism-Leninism on War and Army 1982:301). Worse, "bourgeois theorists" approach the problem "from a metaphysical viewpoint" (Zagladin 1982:39) quite distinct from the much superior epistemology offered by materialist dialectics (cf. Fundamentals of Marxist-Leninist Philosophy 1982: ch. VII). Inevitably and as a matter of principle, bourgeois approaches "are superficial, lacking any power of penetration into the essence of things" (ibid.:476). This is believed to be the reason why the American view of Soviet policy is bound to be fundamentally erroneous although it is sometimes conceded that the American people, by contrast to American leaders, have a clearer picture of the peaceful intentions of the Soviet Union. In addition, Soviet authorities also tend to assume that the American leadership suffers from "a lack of knowledge about the Soviet Union, a lack of knowledge, if you wish, about our character" (Gromyko 1983a:17). In other words, the Americans are suspected not to be in a position, for reasons of cultural difference, to understand their Soviet partners. This theory is further elaborated by Academician Arbatov, who points to certain "peculiarities of their <the Americans'> history and traditions", especially the United States remoteness, almost complete self-sufficiency and isolation that for a long time did not encourage much interest in the outside world but resulted instead in a particular concentration on domestic affairs. In addition, Arbatov condemns traditional American "messianism together with the faith in America's 'manifest destiny'" (Arbatov, in: Perceptions 1979:299).

Nevertheless, Soviet spokesmen concede that the American perception of the USSR, although basically incorrect and inaccurate, does offer a certain variety of outlooks. Praise is expressed for those Americans who "voice sound, realistic judgements" (ibid.:300). They are sharply contrasted to American Sovietologists who, in Soviet eyes, are virtually "anti-Sovietologists" - most of them émigrés from socialist countries who have lost contact with their mother countries and, driven by hate and resentment, provide a completely distorted picture of life in the Soviet Union and other socialist countries. These elements are severely criticized for having no interest in discerning reality and for being, at least in part, guilty of the slanderous image held of the Soviet Union.

Although, on the whole, Soviet spokesmen completely repudiate the American image of their own country, they do concede some understanding for at least part of Western fears. But it is not the armed might of the socialist countries of which the West is afraid, they say. Rather, the Western obsession with the "Soviet threat" simply reflects the fears of a system in hopeless and irreversible decline. In the same way as the English aristocracy felt frightened by the French Revolution, the leaders of capitalist society rightly have a "logical fear". This explanation of Western images again refers to the fundamental assumption underlying the entire structure of Marxist-Leninist thought about world politics: the law of history. Seen in this framework by Soviet observers, the American image - as distorted and slanderous as it may be - once more confirms the basic truths of world development.

Assessment of information about the adversary: a clear grasp of a confusing partner

From the foregoing it follows that the Soviet leadership and Soviet authors of academic studies assume that they have a propor understanding and correct view of the American adversary. Given the enormous amount of information available about the United States, they also feel perfectly able to expose stratagems, to penetrate the "bourgeois smoke-screen", to rip off "the mask of peaceableness" (Ponomarev 1983:16) and to see into the heart of American society, politics and strategy. In general, the Soviet view of the potential adversary is based on the premise that everything one perceives is true and sound in practice and theory, because before an eye armed with the conceptual instruments of Marxism-Leninism, it is impossible for capitalism to hide its true intentions. In this connection it should also be borne in mind that Soviet leaders, claiming a scientific approach, are not accustomed to acknowledge potential information gaps or to complain about poor intelligence. This generally confident attitude has some implications for the way in which sources of information about the potential adversary are selected and evaluated.

According to a Soviet expert, the best sources for identifying American intentions and capabilities are concrete facts such as the number of newly deployed missiles, and declarations of intent such as can be found in presidential statements, the Military Posture Statements, the Annual Report of the Secretary of Defense, the Military Budget and the related Congressional Hearings. As operational policy and declaratory policy are held to rarely match, Soviet experts argue that information about the two policies must always be "correlated". On the whole they prefer to judge "the ruling circles in Washington... by their deeds (rather than statements)" (Whence the Threat to Peace 1982:94) because they claim to discern "a gap between the policy statements and actual military policies of the NATO countries" (How to Avert the Threat to Europe 1983:13). It is hardly surprising that Soviet observers exhibit an attitude of profound mistrust towards verbal statements made by Western spokesmen. This attitude necessarily follows from their assumption that Western sources are seeking to conceal the truth, deceive their own peoples as well as the outside world, and generally hide their true intentions.

Soviet observers are also convinced, on the basis of their scientific Marxist-Leninist analysis of Western societies, that they are
well equipped to infer the ultimate aims and motives of Western
Governments. These assumptions in fact offer the very basis for their
analyses. Hence, for theoretical and conceptual reasons of a very
fundamental nature they feel no urgent necessity to learn more about
the adversary's intentions, which they assume they know much better
than the adversary himself.

THE SOVIET UNION'S VIEW OF ITS OWN ROLE AND CHOICES

The principal aim: promoting the victory of communism

In its officially published statements, the Soviet Union projects
an image of itself that is strikingly elaborate and systematic. It is
intimately connected with Soviet assumptions regarding the adversary
and with the Soviet view of the international system, providing a
basis for both areas of the Soviet world outlook. The Soviet
self-image also offers insights into how the Soviet leaders wish to
react to the nature of the world scene and the adversary as they
perceive it. The ultimate basis of the Soviets' view of their own
role and choices can be found in the Soviet conceptions of the
principal aims to be pursued.

There is one single paramount aim, according to the Soviet view,
which dominates everything else: to struggle for "the complete disappearance of the capitalist system and the victory of communism"
(Fundamentals of Marxist-Leninist Philosophy 1982:425). This implies
that the Soviet Union, jointly with the other socialist countries,
and with the international proletariat, declares itself called upon
to fight in the "international class struggle". It goes without
saying that the Soviet Union, being the most important socialist
country, feels it plays a leading role in this struggle. By adopting
this central objective, the Soviet Union draws operational
conclusions from what is believed to be the objective necessity of
the "law of historical progress" which, in Marxist-Leninist
philosophy, is assumed to make capitalism "a historically doomed
system" (ibid.:430; Zagladin 1981:14). Hence the predominant aim
underlying Soviet foreign policy and military strategy is seen to be
rooted in the very nature of history in general.

Yet Soviet sources again and again point to a second aim dear to
the Soviet leadership: the promotion of peace, claiming also nothing
less than a leading role for the Soviet Union in the "struggle for
peace" (Problemy voyennoy razryadki 1981:14). For an innocent observer, the two basic aims - the victory of communism in the international class struggle and the promotion of peace - may seem contra-

dictory, but in the Soviet view they are not. Soviet political thinking has evolved a sophisticated and complex conception of establishing a "dialectical" relationship between the two aims resulting in a coherent policy programme; this programme is called the "Leninist principle of peaceful coexistence" and will be presented below (pp. 89 ff.). At this point it may suffice to confirm that the Soviet view does not assume any contradiction between the two aims and tends to rank-order them in a clear hierarchy:

"General peace, yes - but no conciliation. General peace which excludes war among States as a means for achieving the goal of social transformation, but still leaves scope for action for the class struggle within the antagonist society, for social revolutions and national liberation movements." (Burlatsky 1983a:328)

The pursuit of the victory of communism not only does not conflict with the pursuit of peace - in the Soviet view quite the reverse holds true. The policy of peaceful coexistence is hold to be clearly conducive to the promotion of the transition from capitalism to socialism:

"Peaceful coexistence facilitates the struggle and victory of the international working class, all the working people, over the bourgeoisie, furthers the world socialist revolution and helps mankind to accomplish the transition from capitalism to socialism." (Afanasyev 1981:104)

When Soviet source material is scrutinized hardly any reference to "national interests" or related aims can be identified. If Soviet statements refer to lessons to be drawn from national experience and to patriotism and national interest; they constantly do so by explicitly linking the national perspective with those universal aims and the frame of reference of the "law of history". This can be seen, for instance, in the following paragraph extracted from a statement made by Soviet Minister of Defense Ustinov:

"What lessons can one learn from the experience of the Great Patriotic War, from the war itself? The victory gained by the Soviet people and their Armed Forces in the Great Patriotic War graphically showed the indestructibility of socialism, the great force of communist ideas, the invincibility of the Soviet Armed Forces. German fascism, having encroached upon the progressive social system, doomed itself to an inevitable defeat, because the emergence and development of socialism that has come to replaced the old capitalist society which outlived itself is an irrepressible, law-governed process. It is impossible to arrest this process. Such is the law of history which manifests itself with ever greater force in our time, in conditions where the community of socialist nations, the mighty revolutionary, national liberation and anti-war movements, and the progressives forces of all the world oppose world reaction. The outcome of the last war is a stern warning to imperialism's aggressive forces." (Ustinov 1983a:4)

Putting this relationship into a more generalized wording, Marxist-Leninist philosophy asserts that "internationalism and patriotism are inseparable" and proclaims "a correct and fully consistent solution" of this problem by "its <i.e. the nationality's> subordination to the task of the struggle and the interests of the working class" (Fundamentals of Marxist-Leninist Philosophy 1982:290f.). In more operational terms, the principal aims underlying Soviet foreign policy and strategy can be described by the wording of the relevant passage of the Soviet Constitution. This is how Foreign Minister Gromyko prefers to define these aims:

"The most important directions of Soviet foreign policy are inscribed in truly golden letters in the Constitution of the USSR. They are:

Safeguarding the State interests of the Soviet Union and consolidating the position of world socialism;

Supporting the struggle of peoples for national liberation and social progress; and

Preventing wars of aggression, achieving universal and complete disarmament and consistently implementing the principle of the peaceful coexistence of States with different social systems." (Gromyko 1983b:4)

The ultimate justification of Soviet aims: the scientific base of an objective principle

The foregoing analysis has made it amply clear that the principal aim of Soviet foreign policy, in the view of the authors of the respective statements, is supported by very strong motives requiring no additional justification. It finds itself deeply embedded in the assumed necessity of the "law of history". In this capacity it cannot be subject to discussion - it is an absolute, objective principle, not a relative one. More precisely:

"Socialist foreign policy is intrinsically scientific, in other words it is founded on a knowledge of the objective laws governing the development of society and international relations ... This knowledge of the laws of social development allows Soviet foreign policy to look confidently to the future and gives it the strength of scientific prevision." (A Study of Soviet Foreign Policy 1975:12)

This also means that Soviet foreign policy is perceived and evaluated in strictly moral terms - it is positive and good, while everything impeding it must be condemned as being evil in terms of socialist morality.

These features ascribed to the principal aims of Soviet foreign policy have further implications with regard to the Soviet assessment of international politics. It has already been mentioned that the world of sovereign nations is not merely seen as a system of units placed side by side and existing with the same right. Such an attitude has already been denounced by Lenin as "agnosticism", qualified as "thoroughly reactionary" (Fundamentals of Marxist-Leninist Philosophy 1982:438). With regard to the evaluation of contemporary international relations, there is a definite rejection of perceiving the two major Powers to be on an equal moral footing. Even if they seem to be adópting the same policies - for instance, acquiring new nuclear arms - the significance of this policy is believed to vary according to the "class character" of the State concerned; one side is right and the other wrong:

"It is most important ... to combat efforts ... to impose upon it <the public> false political doctrines such as the ideas of 'equidistance' from the USSR and the USA, and the 'equal responsibility' of NATO and the Warsaw Treaty Organization for the worsening of the international situation, and so on." (Ponomarev 1983:17)

Another consequence of this approach to justifying the principal aim of Soviet foreign policy has to do with the premise of the scientific basis it is supposed to have. Someone has to decide about the proper use of the scientific method. Its application and interpretation require a competent authority in charge of finding out the ultimate, authentic truth. For the Soviet leadership it is obvious and beyond any doubt that this authority is represented by the Communist Party of the Soviet Union:

"The Communist Party is armed with the knowledge of the Marxist-Leninist theory, knows the laws of social development and war, of military science." (Marxism-Leninism on War and Army 1972:131)

"The foreign policy of the CPSU and the Soviet Government has a solid scientific base. Analysing the world development process and determining foreign policy strategies and tactics, the CPSU and the Soviet Government base their actions on the Leninist conception of international relations in the transitional period from capitalism to socialism and communism. The scientific methodology, approved by the experience of CPSU activities, is of great importance for analysing the complicated phenomenon of international life, the modern world revolutionary process and its motive forces, the general crisis of capitalism and the different level and nature of capitalist development within capitalist countries." Narochnitsky 1982:7)

The reasoning reflected in these texts also explains the unitary structure of Soviet political thinking and argumentation, as mentioned in the introductory remarks in this chapter (cf. above pp. 26ff.). The key elements of all conceptions have gone through a process of authentification involving also the highest Party organs and then serve as yardsticks and points of reference for any further statement made by other spokesmen of the Party, Government, Army and the academic institutions. At any rate they never convey simply the private opinion held by the author:

> "Soviet foreign policy is charted collectively by the Party, which generalizes the experience of the Soviet Union and of the entire world communist and working-class movement. In foreign policy the CPSU Central Committee and the Soviet Government are steadfastly guided by the theoretical propositions and basic principles worked out by Lenin, creatively enlarging upon and applying them in the new conditions." (A Study of Soviet Foreign Policy 1975:16)

The CPSU is therefore called the "leading and guiding force of Soviet foreign policy" (ibid.:16) applying a "profoundly scientific approach to questions of Soviet foreign policy on the most complex issues" (ibid.:85). As

> "the communists... rely on a science-based method of cognition, on their revolutionary theory and on the more than 60 years' experience of building a new world, they are fully entitled to say that they know where and how to lead mankind." (Kortunov 1979:344)

In the same way, the CPSU claims an indisputable leadership in the evolution of military science and military policy, as "the military policy of the CPSU is profoundly scientific, taking into full consideration the effects of the objective laws of the military structure, the specific historical situation as well as the requirements of the liberation struggle of the working people" (translated from the German edition of the Soviet Military Encyclopaedia 1980, Vol. 6:59; cf. also Ogarkov 1982:55f.).

The Soviet Union's view of its own system: unanimity of leadership and peace-loving masses - firm predictability

The insistence on the absolute superiority and moral exclusiveness of the principal Soviet aims in world politics not only implies the assumption of infallible leadership by the CPSU; it also means that - by contrast to assumptions regarding Western society - Soviet statements clearly deny the existence of any contradiction between leadership and the "masses" as far as the foreign policy objectives of socialist States are concerned. Again, any imputation of symmetry between East and West is forthrightly rejected.

A vivid illustration of this attitude is how Soviet statements qualify the peace movement. They warmly welcome the activity of the peace movement in the West as unmasking the evil militarist policy pursued by the "ruling circles" in the capitalist system. However, they do not believe that similar or parallel peace movements are necessary and justified in socialist countries as well, for here the conditions are held to be quite different:

> "The peace movements in various countries are taking place in different, sometimes greatly different, conditions. ... The over-whelming majority of Soviet people cannot agree with the idea that the battle for peace would always and everywhere have an anti-governmental thrust..." (How to Avert the Threat to Europe 1983:89)

In other words, the Soviet Union's view of its own structure starts from the premise of full unity between the Soviet leadership and the Soviet masses, which share a common consciousness of the true way to promote the cause of the supreme aim, the world-wide victory of communism. The reason justifying this premise, in the Soviet view, is patently obvious. As

> "in a socialist society ... the State Power is in the hands of the working class and all the other working people allied with it..., one of the cardinal features of that policy is that it is profoundly and genuinely democratic and serves the working people." (A Study of Soviet Foreign Policy 1975:11f.)

In other words, as in the Soviet Union, since 1917, all class differences have been abolished, there is no longer any reason for having different opinions regarding political aims and methods. On the other hand, in this perspective the pluralism of political opin-ion prevailing in the West signifies nothing else than an expression of diverse class interests. Hence pluralism is by no means a virtue. On the contrary: a really classless society is held to be a basically unanimous society. That again implies that the Soviet leadership most truly interprets and represents the interests of the Soviet people.

Another area where Soviet spokesmen wish to dismiss any insinu-ation of symmetry between East and West has to do with the conti-nuity, calculability and reliability of foreign policy. As has already been noted above (pp. 53ff.), Soviet assumptions regarding the West's nature reflect strong criticisms of Western instability and unreliability. By contrast, Soviet spokesmen think of their own conduct of foreign policy as being utterly steady because it origi-nates in the eternal "law of history". According to the Soviet view, Soviet policy has been made amply explicit and offers no scope for surprise:

> "Our ideology is a reflection of what is objectively taking place in human society. Our policy is an open book and everyone can read it." (Gromyko 1983a:27)

Soviet authors also claim that the Soviet State always "proclaims its foreign policy objectives" and has "nothing to hide from its people", providing the world with the maximum information about these objectives. (Kortunov 1979:244) The assertion of Soviet foreign policy being "an open book" somehow seems to contrast with the fact that the Soviet Union, for historically understandable reasons, appreciates secrecy. However, the "open book" aspect refers primarily to the principal foreign policy objectives, while of course foreign policy methods are not disclosed so easily.

The Soviet Union's assumptions regarding its own capabilities: sufficient strength for all contingencies

As far as the Soviet Union's capabilities are concerned, all available Soviet statements confidently suppose it to be adequately prepared for all contingencies. It is not customary in the Soviet Union to complain publicly about "gaps" of all kinds and to lament one's "vulnerability". Again, this attitude must be seen against the philosophical background of Marxism-Leninism. As it is assumed that no one can "turn back the course of historical development", and as the change in the "correlation of forces" is thus held to be irreversible, it is virtually unthinkable that socialism can be defeated - hence socialism is supposed, by necessity, to have sufficient strength. This view has been expressed by General Secretary Andropov, quoted by Defense Minister Ustinov:

"And all this is being done ⟨by the West⟩ for the purpose of establishing world supremacy, of raising a barrier in the way of progressive changes in the world. 'Of course, these plans are sure to fail,' Comrade Y.V.Andropov emphasized. 'It is not given to anyone to turn back the course of historical development. Attempts to 'strangle' socialism failed even when the Soviet State was still getting on its feet and was the only socialist country in the world. So, surely, nothing will come of it now.'" (Ustinov 1983:5)

The feeling of being sufficiently armed for meeting any contingency of a war unleashed by the "imperialists" has a corollary with regard to the arms race: here, too, Soviet sources emphasize that any theory of dealing with the Soviet Union from a position of strength or, worse, the intention "to drive the 'Russian bear' into the corner" is based on an absolutely false foundation (Burlatsky 1983b). As a Soviet spokesman very clearly points out, "in the same way as it is impossible to win a nuclear war, it is impossible to win the nuclear arms race" (Zagladin 1983:28). When assessing the Soviet Union's capabilities, Soviet statements proudly profess that due to its ideological superiority the Soviet Union enjoys a considerable advantage, first of all by fighting for a just cause, and secondly also by guaranteeing full unity of and support by the Soviet people:

"It is the defence capacity and economic strength of the Soviet Union, together with the ideological and political unity of the Soviet people, which guarantee that the influence of the USSR in world politics steadily grows... They force the ruling circles of capitalist States, in all circumstances... to reckon with the USSR." (Lebedev 1982:15)

As far as the military capabilities of the Soviet Union are concerned, the Minister of Defense confirms:

"Our allegiance to the cause of peace is consistent and unshakable. But it also presupposes constant concern for ensuring the country's security. V.I. Lenin taught us: 'Prepare seriously, vigorously and unwaveringly to defend the fatherland, to defend the Soviet Socialist Republic!' (V.I. Lenin, Collected Works, Vol.27, p.66). This behest of Lenin and the lessons of the Great Patriotic War demand that we constantly preserve high vigilance and keep a watchful eye on the intrigues of the enemies of socialism so that no aggressor could catch us unaware.

The Soviet people have come to know the adventurism of the imperialist policy from their own experience. They are well aware that strength, and no small strength, is needed to safeguard peace, to defend the socialist gains, and to bridle the imperialist aggressors. Such strength is constituted by the Soviet Army and Navy which vigilantly keep combat watch shoulder to shoulder with the armies of the fraternal States - members of the Warsaw Treaty Organization. The amassed historical experience, the complicated international situation and the growing military threat on the part of the USA and NATO oblige our Armed Forces to be on the alert, to keep the powder dry.

It is beyond doubt that any attempt to take aggressive action against our country will encounter a most resolute rebuff of the Armed Forces of the USSR and of all the Soviet people, and will prove to be fatal for its initiators. Retribution will hit the aggressor inevitably and without delay.

The Soviet Union has never rattled the sabre and does not intend to do so. Sabre-rattling would conflict with our principles. We have to speak about our readiness for defence and about the combat might of the Soviet Armed Forces for cooling some hotheads overseas and in Europe, who have imagined themselves to be the rulers of mankind's destinies and who place the world on the brink of a universal nuclear catastrophe by their reckless actions." (Ustinov 1983:7f.)

Does the Soviet Union have any reservations with regard to its own strength and capabilities? As has already been mentioned, official Soviet sources practically never complain publicly about weaknesses and uncertain elements in the range of Soviet capabilities. The only reservations that can be found are expressed with regard to the geographic situation, which is held to be rather unfavourable. The USSR, the argument runs, is surrounded by unfriendly States to both East and West. This disadvantage is felt to be particularly grave if viewed in a comparative perspective because the United States is seen to be in a much happier geographic position - an insular position with thousands of kilometres of ocean keeping any opponents at safe distance.

However, apart from this reservation assertions of strength and capabilities clearly predominate. Confidence is expressed not only with regard to the Soviet capability to thwart any provocation by "a most resolute rebuff" but also with regard to the capacity of the Soviet arms industry:

"It is more than obvious that in the present conditions no one will succeed in upsetting the existing military-strategic equilibrium and winning superiority. And those who nurse any such plan are clearly exaggerating their own capacity and overlooking the capacity of the other side, which will not remain passive in face of war preparations aimed against it." (Whence the Threat to Peace 1982:94)

Pointing at its economic and technological potential the Soviet Union has repeatedly announced the inevitability of "appropriate steps" in the event of new Western moves in the field of strategic arms deployment, thus indicating that American intentions are doomed to fail. More generally, Soviet sources describe any acquisition of a new capability on the part of the USSR as being purely reactive and defensive, i.e. responding to corresponding prior American steps and never initiating any new round of the arms race:

"Throughout the postwar years the Soviet Union has never initiated the development of new types of weapons. In structuring its armed forces it was forced merely to respond to the threats created by the United States and take steps to ensure Soviet security." (Disarmament: Who's Against? 1983:14)

This theme is very often elaborated in Soviet publications and statements by recalling the beginning of the nuclear age, when the United States was first to develop a nuclear bomb. It is also remembered that, whenever the United States developed and deployed a new weapon system, the USSR first tried to cope with it by suggesting a mutual renunciation by an arms limitation agreement; yet, as the West constantly rejected any such proposals, the Soviet Union each time was left no other choice than, albeit unwillingly and reluctantly, to respond with appropriate counter-measures to the new round in the arms race. So the Soviet Union perceives itself to have been obliged to counter-balance each new weapon system introduced by the West with a similar system of its own.

Purely defensive intentions are also declared to underlie the build-up of the Soviet Navy, despite its global deployment. The missions of Soviet naval capabilities, according to Admiral Amelko, are (1) to counter the threat emanating from strategic nuclear-capable aviation aboard American aircraft carriers, (2) to interdict transatlantic communications which do "not serve for the transportation of tourists" but for the transfer of combat material for military operations against the USSR and other socialist countries (Amelko 1984). Soviet amphibious landing capabilities are affirmed to have a restricted operating capacity as they can assume missions on a limited tactical scale only (ibid.).

When talking about Soviet military capabilities, Soviet sources also never fail to emphasize that they do not consider armed force as the best means of achieving Soviet aims but that they would prefer disarmament because they have much more urgent tasks to accomplish at home. However, in their view, this desire is unfortunately foiled by the incessant drive of the West in heating up the arms race.

The principal political strategies for shaping relations with the adversary: peaceful coexistence, strengthening might and shifting the correlation of forces

The term "strategy", in Soviet usage, has to be understood in a very broad sense encompassing nothing less than "the general and basic task (Lenin) of the working class". The transition between "strategy" and "tactics" may be fluent:

"To define strategy means to define the principal goal of the movement, to distinguish the main class enemy against whom revolutionary efforts must be directed and to determine allies in the struggle against this enemy...

tactics: ... they are the totality of forms, methods, and means of attaining the main goal in concrete circumstances." (Afanasyev 1981:73)

The priority of political objectives is always stressed in Soviet writings on war and peace. This also applies to military doctrine:

"The determining factor in the formulation of military doctrine is State policy. The State's military doctrine is the reflection of its social nature, social system and policy, as well as its dominant ideology." (Akhromeyev 1983)

The main political strategy officially adopted by the Soviet Union is the principle of "peaceful coexistence". Soviet authors emphasize that it goes back to V.I. Lenin, who said that "the desire of the Soviet Republic is to live in peace with all nations and to direct all its energy to the construction of socialism in the country" (Lenin, Vol. 39:413; cf. also Belov/Karenin/Petrov 1979:29-34; Afanasyev 1977:119-127). The principle of peaceful coexistence is defined as follows:

"Peaceful coexistence of States with different social systems: the fundamental foreign-policy principle of the socialist countries in the period of transition from capitalism to socialism on a world scale; the peaceful form of the struggle between the opposing social systems (socialist and capitalist) in the political, economic and ideological spheres. The principle was formulated by Lenin.

The main task of P.C. is to avoid armed conflict in settling disputes between States... The strengthening of the positions of socialism in the world arena creates favourable conditions for gradually eliminating the use of force in international relations and for putting an end to all armed conflicts between countries." (Political Terms 1982:60)

It is important to note that "the strengthening of the position of socialism" is held to be a crucial cause of the process that led to détente. The assumption regarding the relationship between the change of the "correlation of forces" in favour of socialism and the growing relaxation of tension constitutes a topical element in Soviet writings about international politics, as will be shown below.

As, according to the Soviet view, the main problem is to cope with imperialist aggression, the USSR, in co-operation with the other socialist States and "all progressive and peace-loving forces" of the world, seeks to "force imperialism to renounce its aggressive plans and compel it to painstakingly respect the agreements signed by States, belonging to different social systems as well as to implement a realistic limitation of the arms race." Ultimately, however, "when socialism will have reached its victory on a global scale, all sources of war will be removed" (translated from the German edition of the Soviet Military Encyclopaedia: Sowjetische Militärenzyklopädie 1980, Vol. 12:114).

The principle of peaceful coexistence was explicitly made part of Soviet policy in the "Peace Programme" put forward by the 24th CPSU Congress in 1971, in the "Programme of Further Struggle for Peace and International Co-operation and for the Freedom and Independence of Peoples" adopted by the 25th CPSU Congress in 1976, and in the "Peace Programme for the 1980s" put forward by the 26th CPSU Congress in 1981 (Lebedev 1982:154f.; Political Terms 1982:60-62). Peaceful coexistence, as amply expounded by Soviet sources, first of all signifies a continuation of the "international class struggle" by ways and means suitable to the nuclear age:

"Peaceful coexistence as a specific form of class struggle is very synthetic and many-sided. It includes elements of political, theoretical and diplomatic struggle and of peaceful economic competition of the two systems, as well as many other elements, but not armed violence. In this sense peaceful coexistence as a competition of the two systems assumes the characteristics of a specific form of class struggle. At the same time it makes it possible to a certain extent to work for restricting and blocking the manifestations of the major reason for wars in modern times, which is rooted in the system of exploitation." (Volkogonov 1982:12)

As has already been noted above (pp. 33ff.), although sometimes employed synonymously with "détente", "peaceful coexistence", by contrast to Western conceptions of "détente", has nothing to do with preserving or stabilizing the international situation. It does not envisage recognition of freezing of the status quo, nor does it guarantee the present distribution of "spheres of influence". As General Secretary Brezhnev very clearly pointed out:

"Détente does not in any way abolish nor can it abolish or change the laws óf class struggle." (Brezhnev, Leninskim kursom Vol. 5:485)

This is further substantiated by General Volkogonov in his article on "peaceful coexistence" in the Soviet Military Encyclopaedia:

"Peaceful coexistence does not mean a 'ban' on revolutionary civil wars of the working masses for their social liberation nor wars of national liberation against imperialist domination. The struggle for peaceful coexistence in international relations creates favourable international conditions for the evolution of the revolutionary and the national liberation movement." (translated from the German edition: Sowjetische Militärenzyklopädie 1980, Vol. 15:73)

In order to make the dynamic nature of "peaceful coexistence" perfectly clear and highlighting the unacceptability of the status quo orientation of Western concepts of détente, Soviet spokesmen also explicitly criticize the "imperialist" policies of détente:

"They hoped to compel the Soviet Union and the other socialist countries to renounce their class goals, proletarian internationalism, backing of the national liberation movements, to make the socialist community 'deideologize' its internal and external policies in return for Western 'concessions' to détente." (Tolkunov 1984:69)

Ultimately, this theory is rooted in the firm belief that in social relations everything is in flux according to the law of history. Any attempt to stabilize the social status quo nationally or internationally would therefore be futile and doomed to fail. An armistice in the international class conflict, let alone its cessation, is held to be objectively and inevitably impossible as long as the "period of transition to socialism" prevails, i.e. as long as capitalism is not yet extinguished (cf. Golubnichy 1978:59).

Peaceful coexistence, in other words, is assumed to be fully compatible with and also conducive to the world revolutionary transformation; the choice of this strategy necessarily results from present historical conditions:

"The disintegration of the capitalist system and the formation of a world socialist system is a gradual process. It is, therefore, inevitable that countries with different social systems must coexist for a period of history. Of course, this does not mean that in the period of peaceful coexistence the process of revolutionary transformation stops." (Lebedev 1982:11)

In more precise terms, the process of transformation in the framework of peaceful coexistence, to Soviet authors, seems to be a continuing shifting of the "correlation of forces" ("sootnosheniye sil") in favour of socialism by all means short of war. The existence and direction of this movement results from the basic premises of the Marxist-Leninist theory of history: according to this view, since the laws of history prescribe a constant shift of the correlation of forces in favour of the socialist system, only such a development of the correlation of forces is legitimate. To attempt a social and political change in the opposite direction or even to preserve the existing status quo in the correlation of forces amounts to nothing else than "a modern version of the imperialist policy of exporting counter-revolution" (Shakhnazarov, quoted in Lider 1981, pp. 232f.). The concept of the correlation of forces must therefore be seen as an inherently dynamic one. This also applies to the reverse of the concept, i.e. the preservation of the balance of power which Soviet authors blame for being, from this point of view, "precisely the same as the previous 'liberation' and 'roll-back' doctrines". (ibid.:233)

Marxist-Leninist theory is so convinced about the idea of inevitable progress in the change of the correlation of forces that it also concludes "that the relation of world forces will soon make counter-revolutionary interventions such as in Chile wholly impossible". (Shaknazarov 1979:326)

In the Soviet perspective, the relationship between peaceful coexistence and the change in the correlation of forces is even closer. While, on the one hand, the policy of peaceful coexistence is believed to facilitate the further shift of the correlation of forces in favour of socialism, precisely this process of shifting the correlation is held to contribute to further consolidation of peaceful coexistence, on the other hand. In fact, the shift in the correlation of forces now taking place is assumed to constitute a prerequisite for the adoption of the policy of peaceful coexistence by the West.

According to many representative Soviet statements, it is precisely the growing strength of the socialist world that has forced the West to accept peaceful coexistence:

"Only upon losing their military superiority did the ruling circles of the capitalist countries come to realize the inevitability of peaceful coexistence." (Shakhnazarov 1983:280)

"The peaceful coexistence of States with different social systems is closely linked with the alignment of the class forces in the world. Peace is more consolidated when this alignment of forces changes in favour of socialism. Peaceful coexistence results not from spontaneous development but from the stubborn struggle of the socialist countries, which forces the capitalist countries to accept a policy of peaceful coexistence." (Agayan 1982:40)

In other words, the cold war, according to the Soviet view, was overcome and followed by a period of détente because of the change of the correlation of forces in favour of socialism (Sowjetische Militärenzyklopädie 1980, Vol. 24:70). This has been officially stated in the report of the Central Committee of the CPSU to one of the Party congresses:

"The transition from the cold war, from the explosive confrontation of two worlds, to relaxation of tension most importantly depended on the change of the correlation of world forces" (Brezhnev, quoted in: Sowjetische Militärenzyklopädie 1980, Vol. 17:111)

These and other authoritative statements (cf. Hoffmann 1974:546, 492) indicate that the utilization of power is not excluded from the strategies envisaged for achieving the ultimate goal of the victory of communism. However, this does not mean the same as the "use of force" in terms of actual military operations or violent "export of socialist revolution". Rather, the significance of the notions of "power", "strength" or "force(s)" in this context is related to the notion of the "correlation of forces" mentioned above (cf. p. 90). The "correlation of forces" concept is a broad concept comprising economic, political and psychological factors, such as expansion and consolidation and unity of the socialist community, the decline of the West due to the crisis of capitalism and many other factors (Afanasyev 1981:103; Schmidt 1982; Schwarz et al. 1981:20-24).

"The correlation of forces in the world can no longer be assessed only in terms of military power. The importance of political, economic and ideological factors has grown sharply and continues to grow." (Shakhnazarov 1983:280)

The progress achieved in the initiation and implementation of the policy of peaceful coexistence in the early 1970s is ascribed to a shift in the correlation of forces due mainly to the defeat of the United States in Viet Nam. The "military factor", and especially the loss of strategic superiority by the West, is perceived as one among other factors contributing to "force" in general, although it is widely assumed to represent the "decisive" factor (Schwarz et al. 1981:75). Although all Soviet sources clearly disagree that the correlation of forces should be considered to be identical with the military balance, they assign a relatively crucial importance to the military factor. That is why Soviet authors so often refer to the "defence might" of their country :

"The defence might of the Soviet Union and the whole socialist community and inevitable retaliation in the event of aggression against them are a new and weighty factor in the system of international relations today which sober-minded Western political leaders cannot ignore." (Kortunov 1983:9)

In this relative sense only, military power, military preparedness and armaments are said to be an important instrument for shaping the political relationship between the Soviet Union and the other socialist countries on the one hand, and the adversary, the United States and its allies, on the other hand.

The Soviet leadership assumes a political utility of military power short of war. This insight is based on historical experience:

"The growing power of the Soviet State enabled the victory of socialism in Eastern Europe and in a number of countries in Asia and then in Latin America." (Lebedev 1982:13)

In a more general perspective, Soviet theorists start from the premise that:

"if the forces of the working people predominate overwhelmingly over the forces of the bourgeoisie, and the latter, realizing that resistance is useless, prefer to concede power to the working class, a peaceful transition to socialism is possible... The new balance of forces between capitalism and socialism that took shape in the world after the Second World War has appreciably advanced the possibilities for a peaceful transition to socialism." (Afanasyev 1981:70)

The direct link existing between military power and the change in the correlation of forces is also confirmed by Admiral Gorshkov:

"The invincible military power of the Soviet Union forms an integral part of the military potential of the whole socialist community, it ensures the safety of fraternal countries and radically alters the balance of forces in the world arena in favour of a peaceful revolutionary process and world peace." (Gorshkov 1979:246)

Strengthening the might of socialism, i.e. both the economic and defence forces, and thus shifting the correlation of forces in the contemporary period is therefore presumed to be in the interest of the world-wide transition to socialism and the ultimate victory of communism. Assumptions regarding the law of history are closely intertwined with conclusions as to what ought to be done - prediction presupposes prescription, and vice versa.

According to the Soviet view, therefore, the growing strength of the Soviet Union and the socialist States ultimately constitutes a direct and substantive contribution to preserving world peace: as imperialism is the cause of any risk of war, peace is in jeopardy as long as imperialism exists. This inevitably leads to the conclusion expressed by the authors of the Soviet Military Encyclopaedia:

"The most important guarantee for peace is the ongoing strengthening of the defensive power of the States of the socialist community, the consolidation of the armed alliance of the member States of the Warsaw Treaty Organization and the general promotion of the state of battle-readiness of the Soviet armed forces." (translated from the German edition: Sowjetische Militärenzyklopädie 1980, Vol. 15:70)

Yet, when explaining the role of the military factor in shifting the correlation of forces, Soviet spokesmen invariably make two important reservations: the first is that, although the overall correlation of forces must and will be constantly changed in favour of socialism up to its ultimate triumph and the world-wide disappearance of capitalism as a social system, this does not imply that the Soviet Union intends to strive for military superiority. According to the Soviet view, the USSR has been catching up from a position of military inferiority and has now reached parity with the United States; it wants to maintain this state of parity and equal security, putting the emphasis of the continuing international class struggle on non-military factors of the correlation of forces and pursuing the competition by peaceful means. It is also hoped that the confrontation of arms can be thereby be stabilized at a lower level by arms limitation agreements. Ultimately, Soviet policy wishes to exclude the military factor altogether from the competition between the two systems. However, for the time being the military factor is said still to constitute the basis of the correlation of forces.

The extended role of conventional military power: supporting the struggle for national liberation in distant regions

As far as the more extended political significance of conventional military power is concerned, Soviet sources usually refer to the commitment felt, according to the fundamental Marxist-Leninist orientation, to assist people fighting for "national liberation" and against "counter-revolution". In theoretical terms, Soviet sources refer to what they call "internationalist duty" which, among other things, obliges the States of the socialist community "to strengthen the anti-imperialist national liberation movement by all means in order to promote the world revolutionary process" (translated from the German edition of the Soviet Military Encyclopaedia: Sowjetische Militärenzyklopädie 1980, Vol. 10:71). This theory had practical implications in the economic, political and military assistance given to North Korea, Viet Nam, Cuba and also to Afghanistan, where the objective of fighting against counter-revolution was declared to be one of the two motives for rendering military aid. In his report to the 26th Party Congress, General Secretary Brezhnev summarized the two motives in the following terms:

"Imperialism launched a real undeclared war against the Afghan revolution. This also created a direct threat to the security of our southern frontier. In the circumstances, we were compelled to render the military aid asked for by the friendly country." (Documents and Resolutions 1981:18)

In addition, the dispatch of military advisers and, in particular, the shipping of arms to various places in Africa and Latin America are viewed in the same perspective of what in Soviet terminology is called the "fulfilment of an internationalist duty". It derives from the principle of "proletarian internationalism" as the cornerstone of Soviet foreign policy which calls for "consistent support for the revolutionary and liberation movement of the working masses and oppressed peoples." (Gromyko 1984:67)

The general principle of "proletarian internationalism" has been reconfirmed by General Secretary Chernenko:

"One of the fundamentals of the foreign policy of our party and the Soviet State has been and will remain solidarity with the peoples who have shattered the fetters of colonial dependence and embarked on the path of independent development. Especially, of course, with the peoples who have to repel the attacks of the aggressive forces of imperialism which is creating very dangerous seats of bloody violence and war conflagration in one part of the world after another." (Chernenko 1984:28)

What is the exact function of the Soviet armed forces in this context? There were some very explicit answers to this question in the first half of the 1970s; for instance, Marshal Grechko pointed out:

"At the present stage the historical function of the Soviet Armed Forces is not restricted to their function in defending our motherland and other socialist countries. In its foreign policy activity the Soviet State purposefully opposes the export of coun-ter-revolution and the policy of oppression, supports the struggle for national liberation, and resolutely resists imperialist aggression in whatever distant region of our planet it may appear." (Grechko in: Voprosy istoryi KPSS, May 1974, quoted in Holloway 1982:48)

Similarly, the "Officers Handbook" (1971:7) stipulates that the principle of internationalism "provides for assistance to young national States in ensuring their security against the intrigues of the colonial Power, and military development aid". The objective of preventing and opposing "the aggressive aspirations of imperialism" continues to constitute one of the primary functions of the Soviet military forces and especially the Soviet Navy.

"The Soviet military forces and the Soviet Navy - as one of their components - serve a cause of peaceful policy and policy of friendship among peoples, a policy of prevention of aggressive aspirations of imperialism and of deterring its military adven-tures and of decisive counteraction to any threats to the security of peoples." (Gorshkov 1983)

The main instrument serving this policy is the Soviet Navy. The Soviet Military Encyclopaedia defines "sea-power" as serving the "safeguarding of the interest of the States of the socialist community as well as the establishment of favourable conditions for the building of socialism and communism in peace" (translated from the German edition: Sowjetische Militärenzyklopädie 1980, Vol. 20:42). Admiral Gorshkov, in his book on The Sea Power of the State devotes much attention to the role of the fleet in peacetime, which he describes in the following general terms:

"Ships appearing directly offshore represent a real threat of action... And if such a threat was quite great in the past, it has now considerably grown... Demonstrative actions by the fleet in many cases have made it possible to achieve political ends without resorting to armed struggle, merely by putting on pressure with one's own potential might and threatening to start military operations. Thus the fleet has always been an instrument of the policy of States, an important aid to diplomacy in peacetime." (Gorshkov 1979:247f.)

In the case of the Soviet Navy, this key role is affirmed as serving the aims of socialist foreign policy:

"The Soviet Navy is also used in foreign policy measures by our State. But the aims of this use radically differ from those of the imperialist Powers. The Soviet Navy is an instrument for a peace-loving policy and friendship of peoples, for a policy of cutting short the aggressive endeavours of imperialism, restraining military adventurism and decisively countering threats to the safety of peoples from the imperialist Powers." (Gorshkov 1979:251)

What Gorshkov terms "cutting short the aggressive endeavours of imperialism" and "restraining military adventurism" has to be seen in the context of the Soviet policy of "proletarian internationalism". This principle calls for assistance to "progressive forces" all over the world, whenever these forces are perceived to be jeopardized or attacked by the "imperialists". In particular, Gorshkov emphasizes the will to "resolutely protect socialist gains" (ibid.:278) and "exert a sobering influence" on "expansionist ambitions of imperialists on the oceans" (ibid.:281).

The most explicit expression of this political intent so far made can be found in General Secretary Brezhnev's report to the 25th Party Congress of 1976. After mentioning that "Angola's struggle for independence was supported by the world's progressive forces", he made the following statement:

"In the developing countries, as everywhere else, we are on the side of the forces of progress, democracy and national independence, and regard them as friends and comrades in struggle. Our Party supports and will continue to support peoples fighting for their freedom." (Brezhnev 1976:16)

The same line of argument is employed again in General Secretary Brezhnev's report to the 26th Party Congress of 1981, where he made special reference to military aid:

"Together with the other socialist countries, we are also helping to strengthen the defence capabilities of newly independent States if they request such aid... We are against the export of revolution, and we cannot agree to any export of counter-revolution either." (Documents and Resolutions 1981:17f.)

While this statement refers only to military assistance and does not indicate a direct commitment to send Soviet troops, the same document contains another less ambiguous reference to the necessity to intervene "when victims of aggression have to be helped" - an obligation felt by the Soviet soldier in his role as an "internationalist":

"Whenever the interests of the nation's security and the defence of peace require it, and when victims of aggressions have to be helped, the Soviet soldier appears before the world as a disinterested and courageous patriot and an internationalist prepared to face any hardship." (ibid. :85; cf. also other statements by Brezhnev, quoted in Luzin 1981:202)

Again this right and obligation to assist others by military means has to be seen in the context of the Marxist-Leninist theory of just wars. Viewed in this perspective it is not primarily a Government's formal request for outside armed assistance which justifies such actions but mainly the "class nature" of the Government and hence the "class nature" of the conflict. Therefore the Soviet view strongly emphasizes the difference between Soviet armed assistance and Western armed assistance:

"There is a striking difference between the assistance which is rendered by the socialist States to the peoples of Africa, and the West's self-seeking armed interference in Africa's internal affairs. The assistance of the socialist countries promotes the just cause of liberating the peoples from racist and colonialist slavery and protecting the sovereignty and territorial integrity of States from external encroachments." (Luzin 1981:203)

Seen in this perspective, Soviet military assistance represents an act of "internationalism" required as an "internationalist duty" (see article on "military assistance" in the Soviet Military Encyclopaedia; Sowjetische Militärenzyklopädie 1980, Vol. 17:90f.).

Here the question arises to what extent this principle must be conditioned by the historical situation. In more practical terms, what is meant by "doing one's internationalist duty" without "exporting revolution" ? The rule, as defined by Soviet spokesmen is that the Soviet Union will offer military assistance if the revolutionary achievements in a country are jeopardized by counter-revolution or external aggression and if the revolutionary Government explicitly asks for help. Such was the case in Afghanistan, where the

Soviet Army felt obliged to intervene. Similar situations occurred in Angola and Mozambique; as Soviet spokesmen point out, here Soviet and allied military assistance was in full accordance with United Nations resolutions on decolonization. Soviet spokesmen also emphasize that the Soviet approach is pragmatic, especially with a view to the "close linkage with the general system of international relations" which may easily lead to a "globalization of conflicts" (Problemy voyennoy razryadki 1981:54), i.e. the risk of escalation of local conflicts into a general nuclear war, a risk to be avoided.

Elements of military policy and strategy on the nuclear level: preparing for the worst, but preserving parity

In order to obtain a clear picture of the Soviet view it is indispensable also to devote some attention to certain basic conceptions underlying Soviet military policy and strategy to the extent that they represent assumptions constitutive of Soviet behaviour vis-à-vis the potential adversary. As in the case of the choice of political strategies, the most fundamental premise adopted by Marxist-Leninist theory is that everything must be seen as conditioned by the historical situation and its ongoing change:

> "Security as a policy is not static but is, rather, dynamic. There is no security guaranteed indefinitely. Its realization requires a political will and constant political efforts. Different periods and different circumstances create different ways of realizing and guaranteeing security. They are subject both to the class structure of a society, to dominant economic and social relations. History has known many ways and methods of realizing security which have always changed their forms and character when their historical environment has necessitated it." (Problemy voyennoy razryadki 1981:41)

The principles of military policy and strategy are thus held to be basically relative, or they have to be modified according to changing historical conditions. Such is the case, first of all with the very concept of war itself. The traditional Marxist-Leninist assumption regarding the relationship of war and politics used to refer to Clausewitz:

> "'With reference to wars', Lenin wrote, 'the main thesis of dialectics... is that 'war is simply a continuation of policy by other (i.e. violent) means'. Such is the formula of Clausewitz ... and it was always the standpoint of Marx and Engels ..." (Marxism-Leninism on War and Army 1972:7)

Contemporary Soviet authors maintain that this Clausewitzian hypothesis is no longer valid without restrictions today, considering the existence of nuclear weapons:

> "According to von Clausewitz war is the continuation of policy by

other means... These ideas have once appeared to be as irrevocable as war itself. Only when war, in its nuclear variety, began to seem unthinkable, did the postulates of Clausewitz first show a chink... Here, Clausewitz is out of date. It is impossible to find arguments, to single out a goal that would justify nuclear war and yet remain within the bounds of reason... In sum, nuclear parity has enabled the world to 'overcome' Clausewitz." (Bovin 1982:97f.)

Other authors go even further by stating that:

"... the harsh reality of today is that, in contrast to the past, the correlation of the extremely important concepts of 'war' and 'politics' has changed completely in international relations. The revolution that has been going on for several decades in the means of warfare, the vast accumulation of nuclear missiles makes it suicidal to rely on armed force and hope it would bring victory." (Inozemtsev 1982:32)

In the Soviet view, however, this insight does not completely in-validate Clausewitz's maxim. For, after all, the Marxist-Leninist standpoint always starts from the assumption that "the central ques-tion in any analysis and evaluation of war is that of its socio-political nature" (Marxism-Leninism on War and Army 1972:8) - a cri-terion far more relevant than the military nature of war. That is the meaning of the following statement by a leading Soviet philosopher:

"The fact that, because of the existence of massive means of destruction, war as a means of policy carries a threat to human civilization does not mean at all that, from the standpoint of its class content, war has ceased to be a continuation of a definitive policy by other, non-peaceful means." (Fedoseyev 1981:20)

Similarly, the Soviet Military Encyclopaedia says that "armed force serves political and class aims, it is a continuation of poli-cy" (translated from the German edition: Sowjetische Militärenzyk-lopädie 1980, Vol. 14:82). "War" is simply defined as a "socio-political phenomenon, continuation of policy with the means of force" (ibid. Vol. 5:33). There appears to be a contradiction between these statements and the statements quoted previously. Yet this is only seemingly so, for in the Soviet concept, should a war nevertheless be forced upon the Soviet Union, it will be a just war serving the supreme cause.

In view of the general approach deemed to be proper and adequate by Soviet leaders when thinking about nuclear war, the present situ-ation calls for a comprehensive view of security. According to Gener-al Secretary Andropov, security in the nuclear age can no longer mean national security only:

"The well-being of our people, the security of the Soviet State we do not separate from, nor, the more so, do we set them against, the well-being and security of other peoples, of other countries.

One should not in the nuclear age look at the world through the narrow crack of one's selfish, egoistic interests. Responsible statesmen have only one choice, that of doing everything possible to prevent a nuclear catastrophe. Any other position is short-sighted - more, it is suicidal." (Andropov 1983b:9f.)

It goes without saying that Soviet military strategy is perceived as purely defensive in nature:

"The Soviet military doctrine is an exact antipode of the US military doctrine. The political content of the Soviet military doctrine is defined by the socialist system, the policy of the Soviet State and the CPSU, and the vital interests of the Soviet Union which are: to live and work for the welfare of the Soviet country and for humanity in conditions of stable peace.

The political content defines, in the final analysis, the defensive character of all the military theory and practical activities of our State. Aggressive wars, hatred, nationalistic prejudices, a sense of superiority are alien to the Soviet Union. We have no plans to attack any States, including the United States. The attempts to attribute to our military doctrine any insidious projects of preparation of the first strike against the US are nothing but lies, intended for deceiving world public opinion.

The main task of Soviet military doctrine is to avoid the first strike as well as the second and, in fact, nuclear war in general. Our approach to these problems has been formulated by the Soviet Government in the following terms: the defense potential of the Soviet Union must be sufficient to prevent anyone with such an intention from disturbing our peace. The very sense of our doctrine and of our policy is not a course towards military superiority, but a policy towards arms control, disarmament, and a slackening of military confrontation." (Akhromeyev 1983)

The Soviet Union's pledge, in 1982, never to be the first to use nuclear weapons is held to represent striking proof of the purely defensive motives underlying Soviet nuclear armaments. Soviet efforts to prepare for military defence are affirmed to be necessary because of the Soviet Union's strategic situation, which is characterized by a deadly threat by the West and by the West's plot for the military encirclement of the territory of the socialist States:

"The Soviet Union's strategic situation compels it, for purposes of defence, to ensure not only a general equilibrium of strength between it and the USA... but also a regional equilibrium in separate theatres... The armies of the Warsaw Treaty countries have a territory of 23,500,000 sq km to defend... This is more than the area of the United States, Europe, and China combined... ... the Soviet Union is simultaneously exposed to danger in the East from the American Pacific nuclear fleets and from China with its growing nuclear potential and the world's most numerous army..." (The Threat to Europe 1981:12; How to Avert the Threat to Europe 1983:19f.)

This implies that any steps undertaken by the Soviet Union in the armaments field constitute only a response to Western challenges. As a rule "socialism was forced to take up the manufacture of these weapons because they had appeared in the West" (Zagladin 1983:36; Diatchenko 1978:52).

What, then, is the function of nuclear weapons? According to Soviet sources, they clearly and exclusively serve a defensive purpose, i.e. their task is deterrence, although Soviet sources do not explicitly refer to the notion of "deterrence" (there are two distinct terms in Russian "sderzhivaniye" meaning "restraining, keeping out, holding back, dissuasion" and "ustrasheniye" meaning "intimidation"; cf. Holloway 1983:33).

However, the way in which the function of nuclear weapons is described obviously rests on assumptions reflecting the concept of deterrence or "war prevention".

High-ranking Soviet military officers in fact confirm that the term "sderzhivaniye" comes quite close to the Soviet conception of preparing for nuclear war, while at the same time the Americans are accused of preparing for a nuclear strategy in the sense of "ustrasheniye". In more general terms the Soviet concept means "constant readiness to give a determined rebuff to any aggressor" (Ogarkov 1982:58).

A similar conclusion is drawn by Arbatov, based on an examination of various official statements on Soviet military doctrine:

"The essence of those statements is that we see the mission of our strategic forces as deterring war. The Soviet Union considers it senseless to strive for military superiority. 'Its very notion', as President Brezhnev emphasized, 'loses any meaning in a situation where tremendous arsenals of nuclear weapons and their means of delivery have already been stockpiled'." (Arbatov 1981c:94)

This basic orientation of Soviet military strategy also implies that the Soviet Union declares itself not interested in achieving military superiority:

"The military and strategic equilibrium prevailing between the USSR and the USA, between the Warsaw Treaty and NATO, objectively serves to safeguard world peace. We have not sought, and do not seek, military superiority over the other side." (Brezhnev 1981:30)

The emphasis on the renunciation of the attempt to achieve superiority in Soviet theory is relatively new. It should be noted that some years ago representative and authoritative authors from socialist countries reached a conclusion quite different from this one, yet nevertheless compatible with the overall framework of the theory of "correlation of forces". For instance, in 1974, the Minister of Defense of the German Democratic Republic, General Heinz Hoffmann, referring to authoritative Soviet statements, wrote that:

"... On balance there is no military equilibrium between the camps of imperialism and socialism... On balance there is military superiority of the socialist community of States... There is no 'equilibrium of forces', and it is quite good that this is so - good for socialism, good for peace and good for the peoples of Europe." (Hoffmann 1974:459 and 463)

On the basis of this assumption, General Hoffmann concluded that "superior socialist military strength will also be necessary in future for preserving peace among peoples and for promoting the requirements suitable for the evolution of socialism" (ibid.:594f.).

In contemporary Soviet military theory, the nature of the "military and strategic equilibrium" is further interpreted in terms of the "capability to destroy each side", mutual "vulnerability" or "unavoidable retaliation" or "roughly equal risks". These terms very much resemble the American concept of "mutual assured destruction" and the insistence prevailing in American strategic doctrine on preserving a sufficient "second strike capability". This is also expressed by the following two quotations from the writings of an academic expert :

"The parity of military forces existing in the main areas of military opposition is guaranteed by the availability of mutually counterbalancing material means of war, primarily nuclear forces. The objective conditionality of parity consists of the fact that the tremendous power of modern arms of mass destruction is accompanied by the lack of any effective defense against it. In any case, if war is unleashed, the aggressor using such an arm has no chance of avoiding retaliation. Even in the worst cases, the opposing side is capable of using the surviving nuclear arms for retaliatory purposes. This means that the first pre-emptive strike cannot go unpunished." (Bykov 1980:135)

"There is no chance of exploiting the vulnerability of the other side before one eliminates one's own vulnerability, and that will not be feasible in the foreseeable future." (Bykov 1982:83)

This also means that in Soviet strategic doctrine the alleged United States intention of launching a pre-emptive nuclear strike against the Soviet Union is held to be completely worthless, first because "the hope of destroying all or almost all enemy military targets in a first nuclear strike is not sound", and secondly because "there is absolutely no reason to believe that the enemy, aware of your plans for a pre-emptive strike against its nuclear arsenal, will do nothing to ensure the capability of delivering a return strike" (Luzin 1981:213). These views were also confirmed by the Declaration of the Warsaw Treaty Countries of 5 January 1983, which laconically said that:

"All expectations, on starting a nuclear war, to score a victory in it, are foolhardy. There can be no winners in a nuclear war should it ever break out."

In more technical terms, Soviet leadership wishes to give priority to landbased nuclear weapons:

"The United States ... believed that its nuclear weapons should be more invulnerable if it installed them on submarines. And they did this. This is understandable because the United States is a sea power. We are a continental power and most of our nuclear weapons were deployed on land." (Andropov 1983a:80)

In the standard presentation of modern nuclear strategy this situation is said to be new, replacing the former situation of American superiority. The evolution of the "fundamentally new strategic equilibrium" is again ascribed to the "change in the balance of military strength, compounded with the steady invigoration of socialism's position and with other progressive changes in the modern world" (Bykov 1982:77f; cf. also Alexandrov 1982). In other words, the central concept of the "change of the correlation of forces" serves once more as the interpretative framework for explaining the nature of the present strategic relationship.

At this point one might ask whether there is not a contradiction between the assertion that the USSR is not interested in military superiority, on the one hand, and the declared intent of further changing the correlation of forces in favour of socialism, on the other hand. As has been pointed out in the preceding section, in this connection Soviet spokesmen point to the fact that the correlation of forces is a broad concept, encompassing a variety of military, economic, political, and psychological factors; the military factor, however, is said to be made relative and to be stabilized by achieving and maintaining rough military parity and refraining from striving for military superiority. It must also be recalled that (as pointed out above pp. 89f.), Soviet spokesmen harshly criticize the Western concept of "balance of power", with its implied meaning of maintaining the status quo. They utterly reject the use of this term whenever it seems to be synonymous with the attempt by the "imperialists" to halt the steady progress of socialism. In the Soviet view, the desirability of the "equilibrium" is thus seen to be quite relative: the preservation of the military balance in the narrow sense may seem desirable, at least for the time being. Furthermore, acceptance of the existence of this equilibrium by no means entails acceptance of the stabilization of an overall "balance of power" or "correlation of forces".

Another aspect of the Soviet use of the concept of "military balance" lies in the fact that, in the Soviet view, the preference for parity and the commitment to refrain from aspiring to superiority is not tantamount to agreeing that such a military balance constitutes something desirable. As will be shown below, Soviet political and military thinking dismisses the idea of the "balance of terror" being a good and durable method of preserving peace.

An important element in Soviet strategic doctrine relates to the hypothetical situation in which, despite all precautions, a nuclear war breaks out. Should Soviet nuclear forces, in view of this eventuality, also be prepared to fight a nuclear war beyond the capacity to merely deter an attack? Although some Soviet sources clearly state that "there can be no winners" in a nuclear war, other representative statements indicate that, in the event of nuclear war being unleashed, the Soviet Union wants to achieve victory; this is emphasized by Marshal Ogarkov in an article published in the 1979 edition of the Soviet Military Encyclopaedia:

> "Soviet military strategy proceeds from the fact that if nuclear war is forced on the Soviet Union, then the Soviet people and its Armed Forces need to be ready for the most severe and prolonged trial. The Soviet Union and the fraternal socialist States in that case will, by comparison with the imperialist States, possess definitive advantages, conditioned by the just goals of the war, and the progressive character of their social and State order. This creates for them objective possibilities for attaining victory. However, for the realization of these possibilities timely and all-round preparations of the country and the Armed Forces are necessary." (Ogarkov in: SVE Vol. 7, Moscow: Voyenizdat, 1979, p. 564; translated by Holloway 1983:54)

In this connection, one might ask how this attitude to nuclear war relates to the assertion that, should a nuclear war break out, there will be no victory. Does it not mean that the Soviet Union is never-theless preparing to fight a nuclear war and "ride out" a nuclear attack with the firm determination of emerging from the ordeal as the ultimate winner? A high-ranking Soviet military officer qualifies this conclusion by two arguments: firstly, he says, the essential message conveyed by those statements is that the Soviet Union is willing and is preparing herself to annihilate the enemy should he dare to attack the territory of the USSR. This does not necessarily mean "victory", but it does mean readiness to inflict unacceptable losses upon the enemy - and thus keeping his aggression away. This is said to be even more indispensable today in view of the shrinking early-warning time available to the Soviet Union in the event of an attack. Secondly, those statements are to be seen in a specific context and as addressing specific audiences. "One does not train soldiers for their defeat." Hence, some of them merely serve the purpose of military education with a view to strengthening morale and giving the individual soldier the feeling of having a chance of survival.

In more specific strategic terms, Soviet military authors tend to think along the lines of classical concepts such as superiority and surprise. In the article on "superiority over the opponent" ("prevoskhodstvo nad protivnikom") in the Soviet Military Encyclopaedia, the following paragraph can be found:

"In nuclear war, superiority over the opponent can be achieved in selected directions mainly by employing nuclear weapons. The following elements are of great significance for establishing and maintaining superiority: effective struggle against the opposing means of mass destruction, measures for averting a mass breakdown of troops and military technology on one's own side, and re-establishing the fighting strength of those troops subject to hostile nuclear strikes. The high degree of troop mobility and the long range of the means of destruction (rockets, planes) allow for achieving a superiority in the desired direction without prior concentration of large masses of troops in a limited space of the sites used for the initiation of operations." (translated from the German edition: Sowjetische Militärenzyklopädie 1980, Vol. 20:127)

Similarly, the general importance of surprise is emphasized, and even more so with reference to nuclear weapons:

"In the course of the development of the means of armed struggle the significance of surprise has steadily grown. Especially after the introduction of nuclear rocket weapons and other powerful means of annihilation its role has increased. Nuclear rocket forces and aviation, in conjunction with high mobility and manoeuvring capability of the troops, allow the application of a variety of methods of surprise actions." (translated from the German edition: Sowjetische Militärenzyklopädie 1980, Vol. 7:84)

As far as the criterion of stability is concerned, it has already been pointed out that the Western concept of "stability" as used in United States strategic doctrine is not fully compatible with the Soviet notion "stabilnost" (Frei/Catrina 1982:74). "Stability" in the Western sense refers to the absence of any incentive to strike first in order to prevent a disarming first strike by the other side. Yet it should not be overlooked that Soviet sources in fact reflect full awareness of this problem. This can be inferred from the frequent reference made to the nightmare of surprise attack. In his book on the lessons to be drawn from the Great Patriotic War, Marshal Grechko devoted a special chapter to this issue (Grechko 1977:95-100) and concluded that "now high combat readiness has an even greater significance". Soviet spokesmen are also aware of the necessity of minimizing the vulnerability of strategic nuclear weapons. They point to the fact that land-based missiles are not necessarily always fixed-site missiles.

As far as the Soviet Union's attitude towards surprise attack or first strike strategies is concerned, Soviet statements firmly deny any intention of this kind (cf. Problemy voyennoy razryadki 1981:148). This coincides with the declaratory defensive orientation of Soviet military policy as mentioned previously:

"Our strategic doctrine, as Leonid Brezhnev has said, has a thoroughly defensive orientation. This is reflected in the Constitution of the USSR. The essence of Soviet military doctrine is that, guided by the principle of the Leninist foreign policy of peace and international security, it aims at defending the Soviet Union and other socialist States and at preventing imperialist aggression. Preventive expansionist wars of any type and any scale and the concepts of pre-emptive nuclear strikes are alien to Soviet military doctrine." (Ustinov 1981:27)

A practical application of this principle has been the Soviet pledge, made in 1982 "not to be first to use nuclear weapons".

Another feature of Soviet doctrine related to nuclear war is the rejection of the idea of limited nuclear war. As has been conveyed by a large number of official statements, Soviet leadership assumes that once a nuclear war breaks out it cannot be kept limited; there is a high degree of continuity in this assumption, as expressed in the following statements made by General Secretaries Brezhnev and Andropov:

"They ⟨the Americans⟩ want people to believe that nuclear war can be limited, they want to reconcile them with the idea that such a war is permissible. But that is sheer deception of the people! A 'limited' nuclear war as conceived by the Americans in, say, Europe would from the outset mean the certain destruction of European civilization. And of course the United States, too, would not be able to escape the flames of war." (Brezhnev 1981:28)

"Official spokesmen in Washington are heard to discourse on the possibility of 'limited', 'sustained', and other varieties of nuclear war... Veritably, one has to be blind to the realities of our time not to see that wherever and however a nuclear whirlwind arises, it will inevitably go out of control and cause a world-wide catastrophe." (Andropov 1982:22)

This view is reconfirmed by Marshals Ogarkov and Akhromeyev, who state:

"A new world war, if the aggressive forces of imperialism nevertheless succeed in unleashing it, would be a decisive conflict of the two opposite social systems. It would envelop all the continents and would be conducted by the coalition of the armed forces with the most decisive objectives and with the use of all means of armed struggle. It would maelstrom many hundreds of millions of people. Its bitterness and scope could not be compared with any war of the past. The very character of modern arms means that if they are used, it will be very dangerous for the future of humanity." (Ogarkov 1981:85)

"...as a military man, I can declare that a limited nuclear war is impossible. What is the sense of the notion of limited war in the actual conditions, when there are enormous quantities - many thousands - of nuclear ammunitions? If war is declared, it will certainly be a general war with all the consequences." (Akhromeyev 1983)

Western references to the possibility of "limited" or "controlled" or "local" nuclear war are discarded as deceptive and serving only the purpose of causing the masses of the people to acquiesce (Sowjetische Militärenzyklopädie 1980, Vol. 11:49; Vol. 14:66-68). This view also implies the rejection of any idea regarding the "rules of the game" in the event of an armed conflict (Sivachev/Yakovlev 1979:249f.). "War is war", as a distinguished Soviet expert puts it. Other Soviet spokesmen refer to the fact that, today, there is "no more time for aristocratic duels".

In this context, too, it might be helpful to discern how the Soviet leadership sees the congruity or incongruity existing between its declaratory policy and actual force deployment. The Soviet forces are known to be equipped with a variety of tactical nuclear arms, ranging from nuclear artillery shells and torpedoes armed with a nuclear warhead to short- and medium-range nuclear missiles. If there was only one type of Soviet response to a nuclear attack of any kind - namely a "devastating retaliatory attack" (Ustinov 1981:7) - it would be hard to envisage the mission of these "small" nuclear weapons, and emphasis would be laid exclusively on the means for delivering a massive, devastating retaliatory attack. The published materials about Soviet military doctrine, however, do not offer detailed information about the specific missions ascribed to the various types of weapons available in the Soviet nuclear arsenal.

According to a high-ranking Soviet military officer, however, the tactical and intermediate-range nuclear weapons deployed in the territory of some Warsaw Pact member countries have a mission to be assessed primarily in a political context, i.e. they serve to "counter-balance analogous weapon systems deployed in Western Europe". From a purely military point of view this seems to have only slight significance, as the Soviet Union has pledged never to be the first to use nuclear weapons and hence in theory excludes the possibility of attacking NATO's nuclear arsenal in Western Europe by a preventive strike. In a very general way, Soviet spokesmen explain this situation by the intention to have all means at its disposal for retaliation in case the "imperialists" unleash a war. Renouncing this means is considered to amount to "a luxury which the Soviet Union cannot afford".

From deterrence to disarmament

As a matter of principle, the Soviet concept of "rough military equilibrium" must not be confused with the Western concept of "strategic stability" or, in its vulgar form, the "balance of terror". According to the Soviet approach to military strategy, the present approximate parity achieved on the nuclear level represents nothing to be welcomed let alone to be preserved. Soviet sources clearly indicate that the present strategic system must be overcome, and they forthrightly contest Western assumptions as originally expressed by Churchill in his famous statement about the "balance of terror":

"The core of détente is not to be found in maintaining this equilibrium, but in the complete elimination of the military factor from the practice of international intercourse... In adopting the 'equilibrium of fear' thesis as axiomatic, bourgeois ideologists arrived at the conclusion that they needed not only to perpetuate the 'balance of terror'... but also constantly to build up military power." (Lebedev 1982:255)

"The feverish military build-up has historically been neither a guarantee of stable peace nor a path to peace. It has always reflected not a concern for peace, as some Western policy-makers have claimed, but rather a material preparation for war." (Razryadka protiv antirazryadki 1982:141)

In particular, Soviet sources criticize the Western concept of "mutual assured destruction" which, in their view, is completely unacceptable:

"'guaranteed mutual annihilation capability': essentially this theory is a version of the balance-of-terror doctrine widely publicized in the West today. But fear can never be a guarantee of a durable peace... On the contrary, fear will make the opposing sides build up and improve both nuclear and conventional weapons..." (Mamontov 1979:87)

Any system based on deterrence or "balance of terror" is said to be "a fragile, unsafe construction, no more than a surrogate of true peace" (How to Avert the Threat to Europe 1983:11; cf. Burlatsky 1983a:329; Petrovsky 1980). Soviet authors reason that the nuclear balance of power is insufficient because, in addition, the further stockpiling of nuclear weapons intensifies the risk of an outbreak of an unintentional nuclear war - hence the "doomsday machine" is thoroughly unsatisfactory (Burlatsky 1982). Likewise, the American approach to arms control by promoting "stability" is charged with being unsatisfactory because it merely serves the needs of United States geopolitical and technological assets:

"From the first glance it is clear that the American concept of strategic stability and arms control basically is not the product of abstract logical reasoning, as its authors try to prove. This concept is closely connected with the particular characteristics of US military policy which in turn is conditioned by the specifics of its geographical position, technical development, etc." (Arbatov, quoted in Kober 1984:158)

What then, do Soviet authorities recommend as an alternative? The answer is clear: one has to strive to achieve disarmament or, more precisely, Soviet sources suggest: "moving toward a proportional lowering of defence levels and elaborating an agreement concerning the preservation of this parity" (Problemy voyennoy razryadki 1981:47). This has been pointed out, on the occasion of the sixtieth anniversary of the Bolshevik Revolution, by General Secretary Brezhnev in the following representative terms:

> "Needless to say, maintaining the existing balance is not an end in itself. We are in favour of starting a downward turn in the curve of the arms race and of gradually reducing the level of military confrontation." (Brezhnev 1977, quoted in Garthoff 1981b:109)

His successor, General Secretary Andropov, outlined this vision by proposing, as the ultimate goal, "the attainment of accords on a radical reduction of nuclear and other arms" (Andropov 1983d:11). By adopting such a policy, Soviet leaders claim "to be thinking not only of the security of the USSR and the States of the socialist community, but also of the security of all other countries", as General Secretary Andropov (ibid.) put it.

It is in this context that the USSR Supreme Soviet, in December 1983, solemnly declared that "the Soviet Union is not encroaching on the security of any country" (Andropov 1983d:29). The general formula for any progress in the field of disarmament and arms limitation is therefore "the principle of equality and equal security and seeking, on this basis, mutually acceptable accords" (cf. e.g. Andropov 1983d:28). In other words: the ultimate achievement of military policy and strategy is to guarantee parity at a lower level. This of course excludes any unilateral steps, as pointed out by General Secretary Andropov:

> "But let no one expect unilateral disarmament from us. We are not naive. We do not demand unilateral disarmament from the West. We are for equality, for taking account of the interests of both sides, for honest agreements. We are ready for this." (Andropov 1983a:8)

Lowering the defence level on a mutual basis by simultaneously preserving parity is thus proposed as the main principle of Soviet policy in this field. Here the question arises whether the Soviet leadership, apart from these very general assumptions, applies additional and more operative criteria in this context.

According to the Soviet conception of disarmament one has to take into account the actual feasibility of the moves it demands. That means that "general and complete disarmament cannot be brought about by a single effort but can be attained through a long stage-by-stage process" (Disarmament: Who's Against? 1983:7f). Therefore, partial measures are recommended "as steps ultimately leading to general and complete disarmament" (ibid.:8).

As already mentioned, the key notions from which Soviet thinking about disarmament starts are the principles of "equality and equal security" (cf. Gromyko 1983b:17). The principle of equality, according to the Soviet view, has been formally recognized in the 1972 "Basic Principles" agreement signed by the United States and the USSR (Mamontov 1979:111). A Soviet author describes the place of these principles in disarmament negotiations in the following terms:

> "Progress in limiting the arms race and then in disarmament requires that the existing correlation of forces should be taken into account, that the level of the military confrontation should be reduced on the principles of equality and equal security, and that no side should seek military superiority, so that the adopted measures would result in more reliable security both of the signatory States and the international community as a whole; the principle of not impairing the security of any of the parties must be observed at every stage of the negotiations." (Petrovsky 1980:150)

In more practical terms, this implies the rejection of any proposals insisting on "asymmetrical force reduction" (Mamontov 1979:113). Practical definitions of "equality and equal security" are difficult to find. One Soviet source offers the following definition, using identical words for the term to be explained as well as for the term explaining it:

> "To the Soviet Union, equality in international affairs is precisely equality, parity in the alignment of forces is precisely parity, equal security is precisely equal security." (Disarmament: Who's Against? 1983:8)

So far, the most precise interpretation of this concept has been suggested by Zagladin who defines it in terms of the impossibility of obtaining "the security of one country by creating a threat against the other countries". He points out that any attempt to achieve this end by accumulating new types of weapons would be promptly offset by corresponding developments and deployments on the other side, due to the "scientific-technological revolution". (Zagladin 1983:28)

As to the primary practical implication of the principle of equality, Soviet negotiators ask for a true, frank dialogue between equal partners, i.e. an approach to negotiations aimed at finding a compromise and strict observance of the legal commitments made. Another necessary principle derived from the concept of equality is reciprocity, as Soviet spokesmen frequently underline. Only if the will to respect these principles is assured can progress in the field of disarmament be expected - otherwise the Soviet Union would not agree. In particular, Soviet spokesmen reject any idea of being treated, by their American counterparts, from a "position of strength", which they consider to be a completely futile approach.

As far as the question of verification is concerned, spokesmen of the Soviet Union strongly repudiate the Western allegation that it is not interested in "control" :

"It is alleged that the USSR is against control. Meanwile the Soviet Union, too, wishes to be sure that others are fulfilling their obligations. It is therefore no less, and maybe more interested in control than is, say, the United States." (Batsanov 1982:28)

It must be noted that Soviet terminology does not usually employ the term "verification" and prefers the term "control over dis-armament". The Soviet usage of the term "arms control" is therefore distinct from its American, and generally, Western usage. The equivalent of the Western term "arms control" in Soviet terminology, is "arms limitation" which, however, seems to represent a slightly narrower concept than "arms control" in the Western sense. Similarly, Soviet sources refer to the notion of "arms reduction".

The Soviet position with regard to "control" or "disarmament control" (or "verification" in Western usage) is conditioned by two important considerations. First of all:

"... the control problem can be solved only when specific disarmament commitments of the contracting parties have been defined, as only then does it become clear what form control over the fulfilment of these commitments should take." (Mamontov 1979:115)

In other words, the Soviet Union wishes to give priority to the concrete steps to be agreed upon, while "control" is considered to have a "subsidiary role". A Soviet author goes on to add the follow-ing explanation:

"Control per se is not an independent factor separated from prac-tical measures envisaged in a particular agreement." (ibid.:115)

Or, as General Secretary Andropov put it:

"We approach questions of control concretely and not on the plane of general declamations." (quoted in: Disarmament: Who's Against? 1983:8)

The suggestion that disarmament and verification should be treated as an integral whole seems to be quite close to the American position, which also seeks a consolidation of disarmament and verifi-cation arrangements.

Nevertheless, the apparent similarity is confined to a superficial level only. As a matter of fact the priorities are altogether differ-ent, as pointed out in an official Soviet information brochure on problems of disarmament:

"Different views on the relations between arms control and disarmament are a stumbling block: the United States and its NATO allies put CONTROL first; the Soviet Union and its Warsaw treaty allies put DISARMAMENT first." (Arms Control-Disarmament 1983:3)

Disarmament, in turn, is perceived to be dependent on more general principles of mutual trust and relaxation of tension. That is why Soviet officials again and again emphasize the necessity of first improving the international climate. In order to achieve this goal, they propose measures such as the signing of a treaty of non-aggression between the two military alliances, the unilateral pledge of never being the first to use nuclear weapons, and related proposals aimed at laying a basis for further negotiations. When asked about the value of a pledge without a corresponding and verifiable removal of capabilities, Soviet officials agree that such pledges ought to be followed by additional measures concerning capabilities, but at the same time point to the intrinsic value of pledges in improving the climate and building confidence.

The second feature of the Soviet position with regard to verification or "control of disarmament" reflects a considerable sensitivity to what, in the Soviet view, constitutes "interference in the internal affairs of sovereign States". According to a Soviet author, a "definitive line of distinction" must be drawn between "control" and "interference" (Mamontov 1979:115). Soviet statements stress the necessity of basing verification or "disarmament control" on principles of international law such as sovereign equality and non-interference in internal affairs (Arms Control - Disarmament 1983:5).

In more practical terms, this fundamental consideration leads to the following position:

"It follows then that an international control agency cannot usurp the functions of a supranational body and cannot impose its will on sovereign States. Therefore, it is important to define clearly the terms of reference and rights of a disarmament control body which should be based on respect for sovereignty and equality of both sides in exercising control in such a way that neither enjoys unwarranted privilege. In other words, control should be mutual and based on voluntary agreement." (Mamontov 1979:116)

These principles lead to a clearly defined order of priority regarding the various approaches to verification: (1) national technical means of control, (2) exchange of information, (3) bilateral or multilateral consultations, (4) on-site inspection, (5) special control bodies or international organizations (such as the IAEA), (6) regular conferences. As far as on-site inspection is concerned, the Soviet position is clear:

"For several reasons this method is advisable only in exceptional cases when all other methods fail to establish confidence that commitments are being fulfilled." (Arms Control-Disarmament 1983:15)

112

In early 1984, the Soviet Union expressed readiness to agree to on-site verification of the destruction of chemical weapons, as part of an agreement prohibiting the production and deployment of such weapons to be negotiated by the United Nations Conference on Disarmament. The main reason for this step, according to Soviet officials, is the fact that chemical weapons can only be verified on site. Yet they indicate that a transfer of this particular on-site procedure to other issues of disarmament and arms limitation is not necessarily excluded.

When interpreting Soviet texts on disarmament and arms limitations, the specific Soviet definitions of "peaceful coexistence" and "shift in the correlation of forces" (to which they always refer) should be kept in mind. It is very important to note that the shift of the correlation of forces in favour of the socialist countries is assumed to be a crucial factor conducive to the progress of disarmament (Mamontov 1979:128). Soviet authors believe that the change in the correlation of forces compelled the "imperialists" not only to accept the policy of peaceful coexistence but also to reach agreement on arms limitation. This has been stated by the highest Soviet political authorities such as General Secretary Brezhnev:

"The forces of socialism and peace exercise such powerful influence that the progress towards this cardinal goal <disarmament> for all mankind is shifting to the realm of the possible, even though progress is slow and is in evidence in some areas only. The ruling circles of the capitalist countries are increasingly coming to realize that in this nuclear age to stake on unleashing a new world conflagration is as hopeless as it is perilous and criminal." (Brezhnev, quoted in Mamontov 1979:132)

Hence the conclusion is self-evident and imperative that, from the Soviet point of view, the best and most efficient method of promoting the cause of disarmament is to continue shifting the correlation of forces in favour of the socialist countries. Progress in the field of disarmament is held to be a direct function of the changing correlation of forces. Apart from strengthening the might of the socialist countries, the growing influence of the peace movements and other domestic factors in the West are also considered to be conducive to the progress of disarmament. Soviet spokesmen note with satisfaction that the United States Administration has been forced to change at least its tone vis-à-vis the Soviet Union, owing to the healthy influence of the mass protest. For the same reason, the Soviet Union decided to continue to negotiate in the multilateral contexts of the United Nations Conference on Disarmament and the Vienna talks on mutual force reductions although it had decided to stall all negotiations owing to the deployment of Pershing-2 missiles and cruise missiles in Europe, since late 1983. The rationale given for continuing Soviet participation in these talks refers to the potential healthy influence of third States on the United States delegations which, in a multilateral context, would be expected not to remain indifferent to being isolated in their inflexibility. The Soviet

Union firmly counts on the United States Administration sooner or later being forced to recognize reality - that is the essence of the motive justifying ongoing Soviet co-operation in the various negotiating forums focusing on disarmament. Thereby, the Soviet Union, as Foreign Minister Gromyko proudly asserts, "firmly retains the initiative in questions of disarmament" (Gromyko 1984:78).

CHAPTER III

THE AMERICAN VIEW
AN ANALYSIS OF OFFICIAL SOURCE MATERIAL

REMARKS ON THE SOURCES AND CHARACTERISTICS
OF THE AMERICAN VIEW

The "flea market" of the strategic debate in the United States: implications of pluralism

When analysing source material and literature covering the American view of the strategic situation and the potential adversary, it would be futile and erroneous to begin by looking for the American view. No such thing exists. While the Soviet views are expressed in a coherent body of carefully drafted, highly co-ordinated statements evolving within a more or less centrally controlled framework and in accordance with binding guidelines, the American views and their verbal reflections constitute an inherent part of a rather broad public debate often lacking consensus. While Soviet sources are sometimes said to be regrettably secretive or ambiguously brief, one cannot help observing that the overall picture available from the American debate may be said to be confusing, at least to a certain extent.

The pluralistic nature of the American view(s) originates in the fact that both strategic and arms control policies are the object of intensive and sometimes heated domestic competition and bargaining. The outcome of this process can usually neither be predicted nor said to be overwhelmingly consistent over time. It simply mirrors the pluralistic structure of democratic discussion peculiar to a pluralistic society.

In addition, views also vary within the bureaucracy. This is of particular importance in the context of the assessment of Soviet intentions and capabilities; it seems that, for instance, Department of State officials often think the Soviet Union to be behaving in terms of a great Power, while in other branches of the administration the assessment is done in more ideological terms. In the context of this study this fact has two important implications.

First and foremost, one has to keep in mind the multitude of functions which any American statement may have. While Soviet statements of any kind can be expected to have been drafted with a view to - or at least by duly taking into consideration - their impact on perceptions by the outside world and in particular the potential adversary, statements made in the United States may be aimed at a particular audience and may serve primarily domestic purposes at a particular time. Their style and content then may be primarily determined by the intent "to persuade, justify, threaten, cajole, manipulate or otherwise influence the intended audience" (Holsti 1976:43-46; 1977:44ff.). The main difficulty, when trying to interpret such texts, stems from the fact that one never knows for sure to what extent and how domestic considerations did in fact shape the respective text. This reservation must be kept in mind also with regard to official documents. As a distinguished American specialist argues, "it is clearly insufficient to rely on offical statements or documents at any level of classification or authority" (Ermarth 1981:54). This precludes an analytical approach identical to the one employed in chapter II with regard to the Soviet view.

Secondly, one must never forget that, outside the realm of official authorities, there are private élites and counter-élites that may have a considerable and sometimes decisive influence on the process of doctrine-making. Some individuals working within the framework of specialized research and academic institutions and thus outside and sometimes in opposition to official governmental views may suddenly become crucially influential once a new Administration appoints them to important government positions. For this reason, the American view (or views) will be analysed twice: first (in the present chapter) on the basis of official source material including non-official statements published by Government agencies, and secondly (in chapter IV) by studying a number of books and articles published by the various academic institutions concerned with the analysis of Soviet policy and strategy.

Furthermore, it must be borne in mind that even without changes in the Administration, the mechanics of Congressional decision-making give diverging views a certain impact, depending on the configuration of alignments; they are therefore hard to predict. In sum, one feels tempted to agree with the sarcastic conclusion reached by an American expert complaining about "this virtual flea market of conflicting influences and processes that affect American defence decision-making ... where it frequently seems that everybody is a strategic expert after a fashion". (Lambeth 1980:31)

The question, however, is how to discern the key elements in American strategic and arms control doctrine and its underlying assumptions despite all the diversity.

Therefore the present chapter will not focus on the diversity of views, and it does not aim at identifying the various positions expressed in the broad debate about United States security and the problems arising from the perceived Soviet threat. Rather, it sets out to identify the common denominator shared by the various tendencies manifest in the debate.

Classes of documents and literature used

There are various approaches to overcoming the problems generated by the plurality of American views in the field of strategy and arms control. A first and obvious solution is to compare statements across audiences (Holsti 1977:44f), thereby trying to identify what might be called the "common denominator" underlying the debate. Related to this is, secondly, the task of generalizing a body of policy concepts and values that govern United States strategic behaviour, in other words to identify those strong tendencies and central concerns that dominate United States strategic behaviour in the areas of declaratory policy, force acquisition and arms control policy (Ermarth 1981:55). Thirdly, one may focus on those official statements that announce reassessments of general guidelines for military policy and, in particular, the missions of armed forces (Lider 1983:310). There are regular occasions when Administrations feel obliged to present these guidelines, such as the yearly preparation of military budget and other statements made on an annual basis (ibid.:311).

As has already been pointed out, in this study an attempt is being made to combine the advantages of all these approaches by analysing the American view(s) twice: first on the basis of highly representative official source material (chapter III), secondly by presenting the array of views to be discerned in the public discussion or, more precisely, in the academic literature produced by the various élites competing for attention in the American debate about security policy (chapter IV). While the second analysis will be based on an extensive bibliography, the first is elaborated by extensively quoting official source material, in particular the following annually published documents: US Military Posture Statement, Department of Defense - Annual Report to the Congress, Arms Control Impact Statements and the verbatim records of the congressional hearings on these documents (especially testimony by Government officials). Also included are official materials released by the Bureau of Public Affairs of the Department of State and other governmental institutions, and finally publications issued by the National Defense University and written by Government officials (although there is usually a disclaimer regarding the responsibility of Government agencies). This selection of sources reflects the insight that the military and the presidency constitute the key actors. Among them, the Secretary of Defense is of particular importance because he has much the same inside information as the military, he is powerful in espousing strategic theories, and he plays a dominant role in the public debate (Carter 1978:21f). The President is of course the decisive actor, but only when he wants to be, and similarly, other actors in the executive branch, e.g. the Secretary of State, play roles from issue to issue (ibid.: 22).

When quoting crucial extracts from these documents, however, the style of the following presentation should not be confused with the scholastic approach it apparently exhibits. It must always be kept in mind that the American documents do not have the same significance as corresponding Soviet texts. It would be quite misleading to consider these statements as parts of a flawless doctrinal whole - which would definitely not correspond to the American style of political and strategic thinking.

More importantly, a mental reservation also seems appropriate with regard to the relative place such statements have in the process of decision-making: rather than being solely the representative out-come and ultimate product of a complex bargaining process among interests and pressures of various kinds, they always are, to some extent, also an input into this process. In this capacity they risk being modified in many respects in the course of the decision-making process before a final decision emerges.

THE AMERICAN VIEW OF THE INTERNATIONAL SYSTEM

Assumptions regarding the basic pattern of global politics: a world of free nations

An inquiry into American views of the international system depends very much on the framework within which such views are being evolved. When official American spokesmen have their potential adversary and American-Soviet relationships in mind, they often tend to think in terms of a dichotomy: on this side there is the "free world" or the "cause of freedom", on the other side is Soviet power, "slavery" and "oppression". The dichotomy is seen as a fundamental contradiction of ideas, an inextricable difference of "views of the rights of men and nations", leading to a "protracted conflict" between the United States and the Soviet Union (General Lewis Allen, Chief of Staff of the Air Force, in: Hearing, HASC 1983, part 1:850):

"It is a classic confrontation between radically different sys-tems: individual liberty contrasted to repression; free enterprise versus a command economy; national self-determination opposed to Russian imperial hegemony. It is a contest which we cannot wish away." (Verne Orr, Secretary of the Air Force, in: Hearings HASC 1982, part 1:854)

When talking about the "freedom" vs. "repression" dichotomy, what American spokesman envisage is primarily the existence of two funda-mentally different and irreconcilable principles for justifying power, i.e. a diffeence in legitimacy. Sometimes this dichotomous view leads to a straightforward "zero-sum" image of international relations. This was pointed out by Secretary of Defense Weinberger in his 1982 Department of Defense report:

"I must also remind you that whatever strengthens the Soviet Union now, weakens the cause of freedom in the world." (Weinberger 1982: I-23)

Still, the dichotomous structure prevailing in the American view of the world is quite explicitly conditioned by a clear refusal to see "two empires" or even to treat them as though there were symmetry between them. In his address to the United Nations General Assembly in 1983, President Reagan said:

"The United States rejects as false and misleading the view of the world as divided between the empires of the East and West. We reject it on factual grounds. The United States does not head any bloc of subservient nations, nor do we desire to. What is called the West is a free alliance of Governments, most of whom are democratic and all of whom greatly value their independence. What is called the East is an empire directed from the center, which is Moscow." (Reagan 1983a:8)

The ideal world therefore, in the American perspective, is not a dichotomous world, but a world of free, sovereign and equal nations:

"The United States today, as in the past, is a champion of freedom and self-determination for all people. We welcome diversity; we support the right of all nations to define and pursue their national goals. We respect their decisions and their sovereignty, asking only that they respect the decisions and sovereignty of others". (ibid: 8)

Furthermore this dichotomous view of the world is also considerably conditioned by taking into account the fundamental trend towards "multipolarity". American observers note a growing diffusion of power among many unstable and sometimes antagonistic States. The two trends are seen to be closely intertwined because the Soviet Union is accused of benefitting from the opportunities that these instabilities offer (ibid.: II-3; US Military Posture for FY 1982: 12).

In addition, the American "map" of the world seems to be largely determined by perceptions of regional cleavages. Much emphasis is given to United States interests in the American hemisphere. The Administration has the explicit intention of "viewing Latin America not as a third world area... but as a contiguous region whose future bears directly on the security of the hemisphere as a whole" (ibid.: 11).

Canada, Mexico, Central America and the Caribbean Islands are perceived as the "American heartland, the Monroe Doctrine defense zone", and any direct military threat to countries in this area would be viewed as a vital United States defence interest (Nuechterlein 1983: 42). The significance of this area is sometimes compared with what Eastern Europe is to the Soviet Union: "a vital defense zone which it <the US> will not permit to be turned into a military base of operations by a hostile power" (ibid.)

Another area seen to be of vital interest to the United States is Western Europe. East Asia and the Pacific basin are also considered to be of vital or major interest. In particular, China is regarded as an important nation indirectly contributing to global and regional security objectives (US Military Posture for FY 1983: 10). Finally, in the American political map of the world, South America, the Middle East and Southern Africa are given special emphasis as major interest regions (Nuechterlein 1983: 61).

Assumptions regarding global trends and tendencies: interdependence and decline of United States military strength

Official American sources usually discern two main trends characteristic of the contemporary international system. A first global trend is the growing global interdependence making the world more fragile. This also implies a serious vulnerability, mainly in the field of access to energy and mineral resources.

The second trend as diagnosed in the American perspective looks like the precise equivalent of the Soviet hypothesis of the shifting "correlation of forces". Again and again, American spokesmen assert that the overall military balance did in fact shift in favour of the Soviet Union as a result of both "the greatest build-up of military power seen in modern times", on the part of the Soviet Union, and the continuing decline of American investment in forces and weapons (Weinberger 1982: 1-4; US Military Posture for FY 1983: 15). This trend resulted in the "loss of US strategic superiority" (US Military Posture for FY 1982: i). The United States is no longer "the preeminent military power in the world", and "had the overall trends in the military balance been permitted to continue, the ability of the United States and its allies to maintain a credible deterrent posture... would have been questionable" (Weinberger 1984: 21).

American observers expect this trend nevertheless to continue at least until later in the decade. This continuing trend is perceived to have profound effects on the political and military competition characterizing the global scene in the 1980s. One of the key paragraphs in the 1982 Military Posture Statement outlines the following assumption:

"Adverse trends in the military balance and emerging incentives for Soviet aggression and intimidation suggest that the 1980s will be a period of greatly increased risk. The United States and its allies are taking important steps to reverse the trends, but significant aspects of the military imbalance will not and cannot be overcome until later in the decade. Thus the Soviet Union may see the early and middle 1980s as a period of transitory but useful military advantage. During the period, there will be no shortage of opportunities for potential exploitation by the Soviet Union and its allies and clients. The underdeveloped world is rife with political, economic, and social instabilities; and the developed and underdeveloped nations alike are dependent on oil from the Persian Gulf. It would be optimistic to assume that a militarily superior Soviet Union will be willing to forgo all such opportunities to diminish the global presence of the United States and to extend its own influence over additional peoples and resources". (US Military Posture for FY 1982: 53f.)

A further implication of the continuing shift of the balance of power between the United States and the Soviet Union towards the latter is suggested with respect to the perception of their relative military capabilities by other States. It is argued that the evidence of these developments will bear heavily on their attitude and behaviour, and the respective effect is surmised to be profound and dangerous (ibid.: 23).

As far as the Soviet Union as the ultimate cause of this trend is concerned, American officials are convinced that future trends in Soviet military expenditures are unlikely to deviate substantially from past trends in spite of economic difficulties (US Military Posture for FY 1983: 19). In summary, the combined results of these two main trends in world politics offer a rather gloomy picture:

"The interaction of the threats to peace and stability posed by the realities of Soviet military power and intransigent third world problems makes the 1980s a potentially explosive decade. Because the factors that give rise to threats to free world security are not transitory phenomena, the US and its allies clearly face a protacted period of challenge. Neither the Soviet Union nor its surrogates can be expected to abandon their efforts to exploit the vulnerabilities of the third world or to extend their influence in areas vital to free world security."
(ibid.: 3)

Apart from these two trends the American view also signals awareness of considerable uncertainties, especially with regard to strategic systems. According to the Secretary of Defense, "the full sweep of technological change... cannot be predicted", and this may in turn bring major geopolitical change (Weinberger 1982: I-19).

On the other hand, the American Administration affirms that for the long term the prospects are bright. The "great assets of the Free World - the resilience of democratic nations, the productivity and innovativeness of capitalism, the vigor of free society" give reasons for quite an optimistic picture. As President Reagan said:

"The West won't contain Communism, it will transcend Communism."
(quoted by Weinberger 1982: I-22)

Similarly, a message of hope is expressed with regard to the future of communist dictatorships which are seen to completely contradict human nature which wants freedom. It is assumed that in the long run the Soviet empire cannot maintain its iron grip over dozens of oppressed nations.

Evaluation of the international systems structure: against value indifference

It has always been a striking feature of American political culture that it is highly value-oriented. This of course has paramount implications for the way in which the global scene is interpreted and evaluated. The most explicit evaluation of the international system's structure has been offered by President Ronald Reagan in his famous allusion to communism as the "focus of evil", rejecting altogether the adversary's moral base and the principles of political legitimacy (Reagan 1983b). To a greater or lesser extent, this evaluative approach has always characterized the American view. It has been rooted in the history of the American nation ever since the Bill of Rights and the Declaration of Independence and it constitutes an intrinsic element of American identity.

It is hardly surprising that this clear commitment underlying American foreign policy and strategy also leads to some misgivings with regard to those who seem to remain indifferent. American spokesmen do not like other Governments to put the United States on the same footing as the USSR. Former Secretary of Defense Brown criticizes:

> "... nations who are still unsure of any distinction between the motives of the US and the USSR. In my travels through the Middle East, in particular, I have seen evidence of the 'plague on both your houses' attitude... We must broaden our efforts to identify and nurture the community of political, economic, and security interests with these and other nations of the world." (US Military Posture for 1982: iii)

The issue of value indifference and double standards is also increasingly becoming a source of bewilderment, frustration and anger for American observers, especially with regard to Europe. As a Congressman asked himself at a hearing:

> "... rocks were thrown at our Embassy about El Salvador... Why don't they chunk rocks at the Russian Embassy or the Cuban Embassy or other embassies? Are they just down on us more than anybody else in the world? Aren't they supposed to be our allies? (Congressman Spence in: Hearings HASC 1982, part 1: 950)

Yet this does not mean that the United States expects a general and full-fledged adherence to its goals and policies on the part of all allies and friends and third parties. Rather, the American approach towards attitudinal positions taken by others is determined by a large sense of tolerance and a commitment to the necessity of a free debate among free nations - in the same way as freedom of thought and speech are cherished as the most fundamental and absolutely irrevocable principles of the American political system.

Nor does the American evaluation of the present world situation signify a belief that this situation is unalterable. The negative assessment of the Soviet cause on the contrary implies a strong commitment to change the situation for the better: as the Soviet Union has placed itself virtually outside the world community, as a kind of "outlaw" or "empire of evil", it has to be brought back to more moderate and civilized behaviour. In the words of President Reagan:

"Until they are willing to join the rest of the world community, we must maintain the strength to deter their aggression.
But while we do so, we must not give up our effort to bring them into the world community of nations. Peace through strength, as long as necessary but never giving up our effort to bring peace closer through mutual, verifiable reduction in the weapons of war." (Reagan 1983a)

In this statement it is interesting to note how closely assessment and policy implications relate to each other. Because the Soviet Union is assumed not to conform with universal norms, there is only one policy to be considered appropriate - maintaining strength to deter aggression, and ultimately inducing the adversary to comply with the universal norms as one sees them.

THE AMERICAN VIEW OF THE ADVERSARY

Assumptions regarding Soviet aims: long-term goals incompatible with American goals

Official American sources reflect considerable awareness of Soviet aims, even quoting specific Soviet terms such as "correlation of forces" (US Military Posture for FY 1983: 2) and "world revolutionary process" (ibid. 1982: 111). There is also evidence of an awareness, by persons responsible for the American government of "a clear recognition that we face adversaries with serious long-term goals incompatible with our own" (Weinberger 1982: I-10). Summing up the divergencies existing on the level of fumdamental political objectives, the following observation may be significant from this point of view:

"When we sit down to negotiate with the Soviets we negotiate for peace, they negotiate for victory". (Hearings on Military Posture 1981, Part 4: 216)

United States sources do not usually spend much time analysing and assessing the essence of Soviet goals. They also rarely pay attention to the philosophical claims underlying Soviet objectives. On the other hand they strongly emphasize the instrumental consequences of Soviet goals in terms of power politics. The essential nature of Soviet global aims is thus described by referring to Soviet ambitions to become the dominant Power in the world:

"While a set-piece mentality should not be attributed to Soviet leaders, it seems evident that over the long term the Soviets intend to become the dominant power in the world. In furtherance of this general objective, Soviet leadership seeks continued enhancement of its power and prestige, probing at weakness, pausing before strength, but relentlessly pursuing its goals". (US Military Posture for FY 1982: 7)

125

This assumption has also been expressed in most concise terms by Secretary of Defense Weinberger who, when asked the reason behind the Soviet military build-up, said: "World domination, it's just that simple." (quoted in the New York Times, 11 April 1984: A1) The Soviet claim not to be interested in superiority is rejected outright as a lie, a typical propaganda ploy aimed at deceiving the West (Sorrels 1983: 10). American spokesmen perceive strong indications that the Soviet Union does not accept equality, pointing to Soviet complaints about shrinking early-warning time due to the stationing of Pershing-2 and cruise missiles in Western Europe; in this view, such complaints reveal the implicit Soviet assertion that their security needs are greater than those of the West, where Bonn or Brussels or Rotterdam are certainly not accorded more warning time from a potential Soviet attack by SS-20 missiles (ibid.: 14).

The American assessment of what the Soviet drive to expand military strength ultimately means is somewhat ambiguous. While some sources (such as the ones just quoted) start from the premise that the USSR aspires to military superiority, others prefer the less clear notion of the Soviet Union having "a determined commitment to achieve a military posture second to none" (Gen. Kelly H. Burke, Deputy Chief of Staff, US Air Force, in: Hearings HASC 1981, part 4: 372).

At any rate, the feeling prevails that:

"The Soviets have not accumulated this awesome military arsenal solely for defense of the Fatherland or even their swollen empire. Their military forces far exceed those required for defensive purposes. Instead, these growing forces are designed to support the Kremlin's unmasked aspirations for imperial expansion." (General Lewis Allen, Chief of Staff of the Air Force, in: Hearings HACS 1982, part 1: 850)

Whatever interpretation is preferred for understanding Soviet behaviour in international politics, it generally leads to the conclusion that the Soviet Union is primarily and uniquely committed to pushing forward in terms of power and influence, provided it does not meet resistance. It is this assumption which has an immediate bearing on practical policy conclusions, as expressed by former President Gerald R. Ford:

"The Soviet Union pushes as far as it can. As long as you react with weakness, they'll push further. On the other hand, if you react with a display of strength, at least they begin to have reservations." (Ford 1983)

The Soviet expansionist course of action is interpreted as being deeply rooted in classical historical patterns with antecedents as old as the Russian State itself. A US National Defense University publication recalls that as early as in 1552, only five years after he had claimed the title of Tsar, Ivan the Terrible captured and annexed the Mongol Khanate of Kazan, beginning an expansion which is still continuing (Grayson 1982: 5).

When assessing the global challenge arising from Soviet goals, American sources clearly indicate that this challenge is not perceived in military terms only but "as a more comprehensive struggle involving political, economic, social, and ideological factors", including also activities in the third world, exploitation of political developments in the West and influencing world public opinion (Soviet Military Power 1984: 113). The Soviet notion of the "correlation of forces" is thus interpreted properly according to its Marxist-Leninist meaning (ibid.). US Government spokesmen increasingly point to the non-military aspects of the Soviet drive for political power and do not hesitate to criticize previous American perspectives focusing exclusively on the Soviet military threat and failing to understand the political meaning of this threat.

American observers note with satisfaction that, despite the basically aggressive aims of the Soviet Union, the main adversary has made little progress in recent years. Yet this state of affairs is deemed to be a problem because it might lead to the conclusion that in fact the Soviet Union is not as aggressive as it was believed to be:

"Indeed, it is a paradox of deterrence that the longer it succeeds, the less necessary it appears. As time passes, the maintenance of peace is attributed not to a strong defense, but to a host of more facile assumptions: some imagined new-found 'peaceful intent' of the opponent, or the spirit of détente, or growing economic interdependency." (Weinberger 1984: 8)

Hence the implication is that basically and beyond any doubt the Soviet Union is expansionist. To the extent that it does not behave in an altogether expansionist way, restraint is attributed to American resistance only and certainly not to the absence of expansionist goals.

Assumptions regarding Soviet motives: the self-perpetuating quest for power

The analytical reflections offered by official American statements on Soviet motives concentrate heavily on what might be called the "logic of power". There are various approaches to support this view. The most simple and obvious one assumes that:

"Increased Soviet prestige and freedom of action have probably confirmed their belief in the tenets of their strategic approach and reinforced their justification of the sacrifices required to implement that approach." (US Military Posture for FY 1983: 2)

In other words, the positive experience made with developing and utilizing military might is held to foster the belief that this rep-

127

resents in fact the key to further success. According to this view, therefore, the Soviet "style" in using force for political ends is presumed to become self-perpetuating and self-reinforcing.

Additional and more specific incentives conducive to a power-oriented approach to international politics are assumed to originate in specific characteristics of the Soviet political system, such as succession problems in the aging Soviet top leadership. It is suspected that contenders for top positions in the Soviet leadership will be "tempted to bolster their international position through international adventurism". (Verne Orr, Secretary of the Air Force, in: Hearings HASC 1981, part 1: 1355). Thus the conjecture is that each time a Soviet leader passes from the scene, external instability and possibly adventurism will be the consequence.

Another motive suggested for such behaviour is "the limited appeal of ideology, political structure, and economic system" which is said to lead the Soviet Union to resort to its very trump, the threat or actual use of force, in order to assert its influence (ibid.: 1354). American observers think that the Soviet leadership cooly calculates the costs and gains of armed adventure (Brown 1982: 19) and never hesitates to employ military strength as an essential instrument for the attainment of political objectives (US Military Posture for FY 1983: 2).

Sometimes American spokesmen concede that the USSR might have a different outlook on military force due to its difficult geographic position and a host of historical adversaries. In this connection, attention has been drawn to the Russians' "almost paranoid desire to protect their nation from the devastation that would follow another conflict fought on Russian soil" (Grayson 1982: 6) which may explain their extreme concern about any power potential situated nearby but beyond the reach of Soviet control. The US Military Posture Statement for FY 1982 (p.ii) says that this accounts in part for the significant force deployments along the lengthy Sino-Soviet border and for "the 'buffer' role imposed by force on the 'captive nations' in Eastern Europe". But the same source very much questions the validity of this argument as a necessary and sufficient motive. Even if the intent of "defensive entrenchment" is fully taken into consideration, it is held that one has to look for additional factors to explain the sustained build-up of Soviet offensive capability (ibid. : ii; Gen. Donald R. Keith, Deputy Chief of Staff, Department of the Army, in: Hearings HASC 1981, part 4: 581).

Thinking about motives behind Soviet behaviour very often leads also to more specific propositions related to particular regions. For obvious reasons, in recent years, much attention has been focused on Soviet motives with regard to the Arabian Gulf. The explanations offered by American sources range from the alleged Soviet desire to ameliorate possible long-term Soviet bloc energy deficiencies to the need to contain the forces of Islamic resurgence and ethnic self-determination that threaten to spill over into the USSR (US Military Posture for FY 1983: 7).

When attempting to dwell more thoroughly on the principal motive forces behind Soviet foreign policy and strategy, however, American sources address the fundamental question whether the Soviet Union is ultimately driven by the sense of mission genuine to any ideological creed or by her status and self-awareness as a great Power guided by national interest and pragmatism. American Government officials specializing in Soviet affairs agree that it may be wrong to put this question in such an exclusive manner. Rather, they argue that both ideological motives and considerations of power politics determine Soviet decisions in the field related to security. One has to assume that many Soviet leaders, as "true believers", in fact regard for instance "fomenting of national liberation struggles in the Third World and subverting democracies in the West" as "altruistic undertakings, just as imposing restraints upon cannibals and eliminating the slave trade appeared to our ancestors" (Grayson 1982: 6). Of course, to other Soviet leaders and officials this justification may be nothing but cynical propaganda for actions they know to be motivated by other interests. Yet American sources caution against underestimating the "deep sense of mission" in Soviet policies imparting consistency of action over a long time (Soviet Military Power 1984: 116).

On the other hand, American officials, especially among those directly involved in arms control negotiations, are struck by their Soviet counterparts' strong need for superpower status; they report that any hesitation or refusal to treat the Soviet Union as an equal leads Soviet negotiators to repel vigorously what in their eyes represents a kind of condescension. Hence either motive has to be taken into account.

The two motives may be interlinked to a much greater extent than one might assume at first glance. As a leading US Government expert argues, ideology represents an important determinant of Soviet policy not because the Soviet leaders necessarily believe in the theories of dialectical materialism but because it provides a set of world views which they cannot give up for psychological, motivational and legitimatory reasons and which inevitably affects perceptions. Ideology does not offer a guideline which is implemented stringently and on a step-by-step basis through practical actions. Hence ideology hardly serves to predict future Soviet decisions. However, it does lead Soviet decision-makers to view the world in terms of the "correlation of forces" - and they will make advances and retreats according to their perception of this correlation. Ideology also affects the Soviet leaders' interpretation of the world situation in the context of a protracted systemic struggle. Within this context and based on their assessment of the "correlation of forces" both globally and regionally they act pragmatically and even cynically, accepting temporary retreats when necessary, but swiftly pushing forward when an opportunity arises and are often incredulous and contemptuous about their Western foes who seem to be unable to exploit their own opportunities.

Some aspects of this general Soviet disposition towards expansionism, as seen by US Government officials, may be traced back to traditional Russian attitudes of orthodoxy and an exaggerated sense of security. They are simply reinforced by Marxist-Leninist ideology and now constitute elements of a complex amalgam of motives. A powerful reinforcing mechanism originates in the problems of internal security which, according to American experts, constitutes the number one threat to the CPSU which rules on a shaky legitimatory basis: as Soviet communist leaders are afraid of their own people, they are even more inclined to feel distrust of anything they do not control.

This attitude, coupled with situations where they enjoy a superiority of forces which is not counterbalanced, makes them feel irresistibly tempted to advance. That is how American officials explain the motives that led the Soviet Union to launch an enormous arms build-up program after 1974, i.e. at the same time that the West engaged in a policy of détente and the United States, after its withdrawal from Vietnam, made considerable arms cut-backs. In more general terms, the Soviet threat, as viewed by American experts involved in shaping United States policy vis-à-vis the Soviet Union, result from a combination of two motives: an inherent drive to push forward, fuelled by an amalgam of ideology, a traditional Russian sense of mission and feelings of insecurity, on the one hand, and cynical assessment and exploitation of opportunities, on the other hand.

Again, this set of assumptions regarding Soviet motives has direct implications for the conduct of United States policy with respect to its adversary, as is the case with regard to assumptions on Soviet long-term goals. From this analysis American officials draw the practical conclusion that United States policy must be aimed at inducing and maintaining an environment within which the Soviet expansionist drive is contained.

Assumptions regarding the Soviet internal structure: dismal implication of authoritarian centralism

American official statements on the Soviet Union very often draw attention to the type and implications of a system of government described, in Soviet terminology, as "democratic centralism", i.e. the existence of a central, authoritative control by a leadership determining decisions about the allocation of society's resources devoted to defence (Brown 1981: 18). It is striking that perceptions of the Soviet domestic power structure are almost always made in a comparative perspective. Comparing it with American decision-making structures, the latter are believed to have considerable disadvantages with respect to the ability to cope with the harsh reality of the international rivalry for the acquisition and projection of military power. As John F. Lehman, Secretary of the Navy, very pointedly put it: "We debate, they build". (Hearings HASC 1981: part 1)

Although, in a comparative perspective, the role of American citizenry is of course highly appreciated, American observers tend to think that "the Soviets have a highly centralized and authoritative apparatus to coordinate the applications of their activities, directed to basic goals" (Weinberger 1982: II-16). This fact is held to have most dismal implications harmful to the West, especially with regard to the Soviet ability to focus all energies on the goal of increasing its military capability (Soviet Military Power 1984: 3). American sources frequently remind their audience that the Soviet decision-making process must not be confused with the American way of life in the field of politics. In particular, they surmise that within the Soviet "party-military amalgam" it is hard to imagine any independent military voice given the tight party control and the communality of interests (Dziak 1981b).

The main asset of the Soviet internal structure, they maintain, is not a hypothetical strong influence of a "military-industrial complex", but the high degree of "national mobilization that penetrates every sector of Soviet life" (Soviet Military Power 1984: 3). The constant reminders of the Great Patriotic War and the glorification of the Soviet Army serve the purpose of reminding Soviet citizens of the necessity of making sacrifices and always being prepared for war (ibid.: 17). As a result of this structure, "Soviet leaders today perpetuate a powerful and rigidly centralized State that strives to control every national resource, under the guise of ensuring national survival in a hostile environment." (ibid.: 11)

Still, some additional aspects are suggested which somehow modify this picture. It is argued that the unitary leadership, notwithstanding its enormous potential for a coherent, goal-oriented co-ordination of national resources, may have difficulties in overcoming problems of inflexibility (US Military Posture for FY 1982: 9) and flaws of the central planning system (Weinberger 1982: I-23). As American officials realize that the Soviet Union cannot reform its system without liberalizing its society as a whole, it is very much regretted that, "by allowing access to a wide range of advanced technologies, we enable the Soviet leadership to evade the dilemma... of being forced to choose between its military-industrial priorities and the preservation of a tightly-controlled political system" (Weinberger 1982: I-23). In that sense, the West is assumed to be at least responsible for the continuing centralized structure of Soviet Government and the ensuing global political drive; this has been clearly expressed by Secretary of Defense Weinberger in his first statement on US Military Posture:

"Thus, the infusion of new technology from the West helps preserve the Soviet Union as a totalitarian dictatorship. And, of course, if the Soviet Union were less totalitarian, it would also be less of a military threat, since a less controlled and more liberalized regime could not possibly allocate so much of the nation's resources to military expenditures." (Weinberger 1982: I-23).

Roughly the same analysis as in the case of the Soviet domestic structure is made with regard to the structure of the Soviet sphere of influence. Yet here the conclusions drawn are even more ambiguous: on the one hand, American sources express respect for the high degree of Soviet military standardization which makes military programmes more additive in the Warsaw Pact since "the Soviet Union can impose standardization" on her allies (Weinberger 1982: II-7). As a consequence this implies a more efficient and effective use of resources, less duplication and less redundancy in force and military capabilities (Alton G. Keel, Assistant Secretary for Research and Development, US Air Force, in: Hearings HASC 1982, part 5: 471f.). On the other hand, the fact that "the Soviet empire, unlike the alliance, is not a voluntary association of democratic nations" (Weinberger 1982: I-16) is considered to lead to a fundamental weakness and important Soviet vulnerabilities (cf. Verne Orr, Secretary of the Air Force, in: Hearings HASC 1981, part 1: 1355), and the Soviet Union is assumed to be obliged to question the reliability of some of its allies (US Military Posture for FY 1983: 5).

While most American officials tend to see the Soviet internal structures as having dismal consequences, there are others who think that the domestic dilemmas faced by the Soviet leadership may mitigate the Soviet drive for external power. Former Secretary of Defense Harold Brown argues that, even though Soviet leaders consider it their duty to work towards world revolution and the triumph of Marxism-Leninism:

"There have always been limits to their dedication. Preserving their power in the USSR is more important to the Soviet leaders than increasing it elsewhere." (Brown 1983: 12).

This aspect is in fact emphasized by many United States Government officials in charge of assessing the Soviet Union and its political system. They point to the internal threat the Soviet population constantly poses to the ruling party. This fact is said to compel the Soviet leadership to spend an enormous amount of attention and resources on maintaining internal security by imposing conformity and watching that every member of society strictly respects this conformity. Nevertheless, American experts do not see any reasonable prospects of changing the fundamental "engine of Soviet politics", although they expect that the spirit of freedom innate in human nature will in the long run overcome this system.

However, as long as the Soviet system in its present form prevails, it is held to have grave consequences for the external behaviour of the Soviet Union. This is how President Reagan links Soviet domestic rule to further Soviet aggressiveness, thus aptly summing up the essence of the American view of the Soviet internal structure:

"We know it will be hard to make a nation that rules its own people through force to cease using force against the rest of the world." (Reagan 1983a)

Assumptions regarding Soviet trustworthiness: nothing particularly surprising

Not suprisingly, American assumptions regarding Soviet trustworthiness are again centred around the issue of Soviet military power and its political utilization. In the general mood expressed in American official statements, disappointment prevails. According to Secretary of Defense Weinberger, the Americans expected too much from the arms control agreements and other understandings with the Soviet Union. While the West gradually reduced the proportion of national income devoted to defence, "the Soviet continued to amass force without slackening; and they have already exploited their power in several areas of the world" (Weinberger 1982: I-9f.). Hence, the Soviet emphasis on power is held to be so predominant that anything else becomes relative - and so do any Soviet promises and agreements.

Frequently, American sources also refer to another element of Soviet theory and practice relevant in this context: the emphasis put, in Soviet military doctrine, on deception and surprise. In view of this salient feature of Soviet military thinking it is argued that the United States should soberly expect "a massive and skillful effort at deception" (Weinberger 1982: I-12).

As far as the risk of surprise is concerned, American experts start from the premise that "the first strategic principle for the Soviet Union is that now the main law of war is to attack first with a surprise and devastating blow." (Bathurst 1979: IX)

American observers feel that the Soviet predilection for surprise tactics and the use of "tricks" is not just a superficial phenomenon but is ultimately rooted in the fundamentals of Marxism-Leninism and its peculiar definition of morality and truth. They point to what Kolakowski called the "lie syndrome" in Soviet society: as the touchstone of truth is what the party says is true, the individual citizen comes to believe psychologically that this is in fact the truth. Once a decision has been taken about a particular version of reality, Soviet spokesmen go on propagating this version although it might represent nothing but a big lie. In this respect, United States officials consider the Soviet reaction after the shooting down of a Korean airliner in September 1983 as very indicative: once the Soviet leadership decided to "explain" that incident by accusing the United States of using the plane for a spying mission (rather than preferring another lie such as knowing nothing about and having nothing to do with the "accident"), they continued to lie to the outside world and to their own people although the United States Government has clear indications that the Soviet leaders knew very well that the aircraft was not on a spying mission. Some United

States officials tend to assume that, in this respect too, Russian traditions much older than Marxism-Leninism may still influence Soviet behaviour; they refer, for instance to the Potemkin tradition and to certain characters known for their lying such as in Gogol's "Inspector". Whatever the cultural and ideological background of this attitude, to Americans the conclusion seems to be clear: the Soviet leaders cannot be trusted.

On the whole there is a tendency, on the part of American officials, not only to deny Soviet trustworthiness but also, to dismiss altogether the idea of showing trust when dealing with the Soviet leaders. As Secretary of Defense Weinberger put it:

> "The critically important and really new factor is that we now recognize that we need not trust the Soviet leaders' peaceful intentions to believe that they will not seek a conflict they cannot win." (Weinberger 1983a: 3)

Many American political leaders and Government officials seem to be so sure of meeting this attitude when dealing with Soviet leaders that they ultimately reach the conclusion that "nothing about the Soviet approach is particularly surprising" (Nitze 1980: 83) - every step undertaken by the Soviet leadership follows from the sheer logic of basic Soviet guidelines.

In this respect at least, the Soviet modus operandi seems predictable - a conclusion that is also shared by American officials with long experience in negotiating with Soviet delegations on issues of disarmament and arms control.

Assumptions regarding Soviet capabilities: inexorable military build-up for the sake of imperialist reach

Statements reflecting the official views of the American Government clearly and unanimously stress the massive Soviet build-up of military capabilities. In doing so, they usually speak in terms of financial investments, which are estimated to be about 50 per cent higher than corresponding United States investments (Brown 1982: 15). More recent estimates even point to an "overspending" by 80 per cent or 90 per cent (Weinberger 1982: II-5).

This overspending continues despite the economic hardships imposed on the people of the USSR. American observers perceive what they call "the Kremlin's single-minded devotion to the accumulation of military power" (General Lewis Allen, Chief of Staff of the Air Force, in: Hearings HASC 1982, part 1: 850). As a result of these efforts, the Soviet Union is said to have achieved a completely new order of capability:

> "To date, this massive effort has brought the Soviets from inferiority to essential equivalence in strategic nuclear forces,

has strengthened in a major way the theater nuclear and conventional capabilities of the Warsaw Pact both quantitatively and qualitatively, and has given new power and reach to their naval and other force projection capabilities. "(Brown, 1981: 4; cf. eq also US Military Posture for FY 1983:1)

Sometimes it is even argued that the Soviet Union has moved from a position of relative inferiority in the strategic nuclear field to "a position of equivalence, or superiority" (US Military Posture for FY 1983: 106). More precisely, it is felt that "the Soviets have now developed strategic offensive and defensive capabilities that erode the credibility of the US deterrent and increase the risk that Soviet leaders would consider launching a nuclear attack" (US Military Posture for FY 1985: 1). The most decisive impact, however, which the growing Soviet power is assumed to have lies in the political significance of military power: "At the very least, Soviet advantages increase their coercive power, while decreasing the options available to US and allied leaders during confrontations with Soviet power". (ibid.). Worse, it is assumed to reflect "a clear and determined attempt to blunt the effects of a possible US retaliation" (Weinberger 1984: 55). Unless this trend is matched by corresponding Western efforts, the United States Administration is afraid that "we would face the very real danger that the Soviet leadership could at some point come to believe that it could blackmail us by threatening to use nuclear forces to gain its military or political ends" (ibid: 56). Soviet theories about the "shift of the correlation of forces" seem to attract considerable attention from American observers. At least they express an awareness of the Soviet use of the concept (cf. for instance Alton G. Keel, Assistant Secretary for Research and Development, US Air Force, in: Hearings HASC 1982, part 6: p. 474; Nitze 1980: 83), although tending to understand it primarily in military terms rather than in the broad meaning given to it in Soviet thinking. In the American view, the growth of Soviet military capability has a decisive impact on the balance of forces in Europe where NATO used to compensate the Soviet advantage in conventional arms by nuclear arms. According to Secretary of Defense Weinberger, the West has now lost this compensating advantage (Weinberger 1982: II-17) or its ability to maintain a credible deterrent is at least dramatically declining due to the growth of Soviet capabilities (US Military Posture for FY 1983: 39). All this is seen to amount to one large single thrust underlying the Soviet global design - "military imperialism" through the use of military strength:

"The only domain in which Soviet communism has not proved to be a failure is the practice of military imperialism. In this domain, the Soviet Union has steadily moved ahead. It has conducted, and is still conducting, the biggest military buid-up of modern times. It has expanded, and is still expanding, its imperial reach by establishing or consolidating military outposts throughout the world - in the Middle East, Africa, Indochina, and elsewhere. If the Soviet military buildup continues unabated, if Soviet imperialism expansion is not reversed, if the Soviets see

135

themselves steadily and easily gaining in military strength, our ability to deter aggression will be inexorably weakened. Moreover, the Soviet incentive for arms control would vanish." (Weinberger 1982: I-22)

When evaluating the size and significance of Soviet capabilities, American commentators also take great pains to take the qualitative side of Soviet armaments into consideration. They implicitly or explicitly refer to the belief, widely held in the West, that the Soviet build-up of armed might represents a primarily quantitative phenomenon which the West can still easily match by its qualitative technological superiority. However, in the 1981 Hearings on the Military Posture, one of the United States' leading scientists, Professor Eduard Teller, questioned this view as being basically misleading, and perhaps even amounting to a kind of self-delusion:

"Many people have consoled themselves with the statement that while the Soviets are ahead quantitatively, we are ahead in a qualitative manner. Indeed, the quality of their technology as it appears in their civilian activities would make such a statement plausible. Unfortunately, the statement will not hold up... I know that there is a great deal of evidence for Soviet qualitative excellence in the military field. Unfortunately, we are keeping the Soviet secrets more vigorously than we are keeping our own, and the general public is not aware - and many policymakers even are not aware - of the increasing danger that both quantity and quality favor the Soviet Union. For quantity, it's an established fact. For quality, it is an ongoing and most dangerous development." (Hearings HASC 1981, part 4: 1031)

In this context, attention is also being drawn to the large proportion of its defence effort which the Soviet Union is devoting to investment in research, development, testing and evaluation, all of which contribute to increased future military capabilities (US Military Posture for FY 1982: 8).

The relative success of this effort by the Soviet Union is supposed to have been "made possible by a national policy that has consistently made military material production its highest economic priority" and placed "the highest priority on the utilization of science and technology for military purposes" (Weinberger in: Soviet Military Power, 1984: 3). Ultimately, the main advantage of the Soviet system must be seen in the fact that "the Soviet Union has in place a national mobilization system that penetrates every sector of Soviet life" (ibid.). That is why, "even with a smaller economic base than the United States, the USSR can direct more peacetime resources to military requirements" (US Military Posture for FY 1985: 11).

Here, too, complaints are expressed about Western credits propping up the Soviet Union's economy, thus enabling it to divert more of its resources to its military build-up. Worse, the Soviet Union is said to obtain advanced technology from the West and thus can threaten it with advanced weaponry (Weinberger 1982: I-22f.).

In this connection, American sources point to the "elaborate network for the collection of foreign scientific and technological information", with KGB and GRU agents targeted against Western sources for critical technologies (Soviet Military Power 1984: 108). To United States observers, it is of particular concern that "the Soviet military posture has become increasingly offensive in orientation" (Weinberger 1984: 21).

Still, American spokesmen are not insensitive to the factors in the Soviet system impeding a continued and fast military build-up. The Secretaries of Defense, when assessing the Soviet Union's capabilities, have repeatedly drawn attention to inherent weaknesses and liabilities, foremost among which are demographic trends, problems within its own alliances, economic difficulties, mainly in the field of agricultural production, dissidence among intellectual and ethnic groups and other domestic problems (Brown 1981: 19f.; US Military Posture for FY 1982: 8 and FY 1983: 2). Yet American sources warn against overestimating this type of problems, noting that "reports of industrial malaise and disruptions have primarily concerned the civilian sectors" which have always been given a much lower priority in research, development and investment (Soviet Military Power 1984: 101). The decision-making process in the Soviet forces is seen as constituting another liability: political orthodoxy is said to have a negative effect on the ability of officers to make quick, independent decisions. Furthermore, for the same reason, logistics are called "the Achilles heel of Soviet ground forces" (Understanding Soviet Military Developments 1977: 53f.).

In specific strategic terms, the American assessment of Soviet capabilities tends to attach great importance to geographic and geo-strategic considerations. By contrast to the Soviet view which, in this respect, is dominated by the vision of encirclement and threat, the American interpretation of the very same geo-strategic situation perceives disadvantages for the West exclusively which are summed up in the key notion "geographical asymmetry". Such a geographical asymmetry is believed to exist because the United States has vital interests far from American shores and close to the Soviet Union, "most pronounced in Southwest Asia where it is only a few hundred miles from their border into the Gulf and many thousand miles from us" (Gen. David C. Jones, Chairman, Joint Chiefs of Staffs, in: Hearings HASC 1981, part 1: 74f.). Generally, the relative proximity of the USSR to the United States and allied interests is held to introduce a serious asymmetry between the Soviet potential for aggression and United States capacity to help to resist external interference (US Military Posture for FY 1982: ii). American officials therefore assume that the Soviet Union in fact has the capability to "militarily interfere with our access to vital requirements simultaneously" (John F. Lehman, Secretary of the Navy, in: Hearings HASC 1981, part 3:574).

Also, specific Soviet weapon capabilities are constantly monitored and evaluated. For instance, American sources repeatedly
express concern about the provision made, in Soviet military doctrine, for the use of chemical weapons (CW). Soviet forces are
alleged to be the best prepared and equipped in the world to operate
in a CW environment. Hence American policy-makers see the necessity
to deter the use of CW in any conflict by adequate preparation for CW
retaliation (FY 1984 Arms Control Impact Statements: XXII).

Assumptions regarding Soviet strategies: the political and actual utilization of military power

One of the striking features of the American view of Soviet military strategy is the prominence of assumptions regarding the
"non-violent" utilization of military power as a political instrument
in the overall conception of Soviet foreign policy. This premise may
be said to constitute virtually a standard theme in American thinking
about the potential adversary. It is constantly pronounced,
irrespective of the political orientation of the American
Administration in office. Secretaries of Defense Brown and Weinberger
have in fact put it in almost identical words:

> "This robust growth in military power yields potential benefits
> for the Soviets in at least two ways: in any number of scenarios,
> it could alter the outcome of a war, and as important, although
> more difficult to ascertain (by us, by the Soviets, or by
> others), this augmented military power, if not offset by our
> collective efforts, could translate into enhanced political power
> for the Soviets in situations short of war." (Brown 1982: 19)

> "I think it is neither reasonable nor prudent to view that
> build-up as defensive in nature. I think it would be extremely
> naive, dangerously naive, if we expected the Soviet Union, once
> it achieves clear military superiority, not to try to exploit it
> even more fully than they are now doing.
>
> I think we have to assume that there is some rationale behind
> their enormous allocation of resources to the military at the
> expense of their other basic human needs." (Secretary of Defense
> Caspar Weinberger in: Hearings HASC 1981, part 1: 976)

American spokesmen have precise ideas about the basic mechanisms
underlying the Soviet Union's strategy to reap the political benefits
of its growing power, and for transforming military power into the
Soviet Union's most effective instrument for advancing its interests:
it is seen in the deliberate attempt to undermine the resolve of
other nations to resist Soviet pressures, more particularly by
influencing their "perception of Soviet superiority, whether global
or local, nuclear or conventional", thus having far-reaching effects
on the attitude and actions of nations actually or potentially
exposed to the pressure of Soviet power (US Military Posture for FY

1982: 23 and 53). The peacetime political utility of military power for supporting political objectives under conditions short of war is perceived to be increasingly more sophisticated and growing in both efficiency and geographical scope (ibid.: ii and 7). According to American sources, the political thrust of Soviet military strength must be interpreted as a long-term process designed "in a more comprehensive way than commonly understood in the West", promoted, in addition, by persistent diplomatic efforts, covert action, and pervasive programmes of propaganda and disinformation (US Military Posture for FY. 1983: 2 and 105f.). The comprehensive Soviet strategy is also reproached with including more insidious elements, in particular the support of terrorism and revolutionary warfare (ibid.: 116; and FY 1982: 111). For instance, the store of Soviet weapons discovered in Grenada reminds American officials of "the USSR's willingness to extend its military influence" (Weinberger, in: Soviet Military Power 1984: 5). Treaties of friendship and military assistance are said to represent additional instruments of power projection used in this connection (Soviet Military Power 1984: 116-119). American officials also surmise that the shooting down of a Korean civilian airliner may have been at least in part motivated by the Soviet intention to impress third world countries by an act of massive assertion of power, and the fact that the Soviet leadership, immediately and unreservedly embraced that incident as an act of State policy is seen as an indication that they want to exploit terror in all its forms.

The overall results is "greater assertiveness and worldwide adventurism by Soviet leaders" (US Military Posture for FY 1984: 1). In addition, the Soviet military build-up and the utilization of military force for power projection are thought to have a cumulative effect:

> "The gradual shift in the global military balance in favor of the Soviet Union has facilitated, and helped to consolidate, the geographic expansion of Soviet influence and presence in many regions of the world. This expansion of Soviet dominion, in turn, has further strenghtened Soviet military power and influence. Because these two fundamental trends are mutually reinforcing, our response is all the more difficult and more urgent. For example, the Soviets' increased ability to project power at a distance made easier their expansion into Afghanistan, South Yemen, and Ethiopia. This, in turn, has provided them with bases and ports strategically located near the world's major trade routes and mineral and energy resources." (Weinberger 1983: 29)

With regard to the practical effects of Soviet power projection by region, the American view puts particular emphasis on Europe (highlighted by the expansion of Soviet theatre nuclear forces), Asia (highlighted by the Soviet involvement in Afghanistan, increased presence in South Yemen and co-operation with Syria), Africa (rapidly expanding support for Libyan adventurism and sponsorship of Cuban and East European proxies in Ethiopia, Angola, and Mozambique) and, last but not least, the Caribbean Basin (Soviet-Cuban instigation of violence in Central America, particularly Nicaragua). In all these regions, American officials anticipate a critically growing destabilization due to increased assertiveness of Soviet foreign policy buttressed by massive military power (US Military Posture for FY 1982: 1, 1983: 8f. and 12f., 1984: 10). In sum, American officials perceive the USSR "pursuing the development of a global client-state system" (US Military Posture for FY 1984: 5). Concern is also expressed with regard to the newly emerging Soviet Navy which, in American eyes, seems to have been assigned a backbone function in the grand strategy of power projection for the attainment of political objectives short of war. In the Congressional Hearings on the US Military Posture Statement (HASC 1981, part 3: 3f. and 25) Admiral Sumner Shapiro, Director of Naval Intelligence, quotes extensively from the works of Admiral Gorshkov and the Soviet Navy periodical "Morskoy Sbornik", saying that the Navy must be able also to "support State interests at sea in peacetime" and that "sooner or later the United States will have to understand it no longer has the mastery of the seas". Other American officials refer to the favourable terms in which Admiral Gorshkov cites historic examples of "gunboat diplomacy". According to Gorshkov, they say, "countering Western 'aggression' by interposing Soviet naval forces between a threatened client State and Western naval forces is another of his Navy's missions" (Hibbits 1978: 16).

It is interesting to note that American officials study authoritative Soviet source material very carefully; they explicitly argue that by studying such writings of Soviet authors, and by analysing Soviet naval exercises and activity, "a reasonable understanding of their naval missions" can be determined (Understanding Soviet Naval Developments 1981: 7f.). Based on these types of information, they conclude that Soviet naval missions are expanding, especially with respect to strategic offence, maritime security of the Soviet Union, interdiction of sea lines of communications, support of the ground forces and, in situations short of general war, the support of State policy (ibid.: 8-12). They expect the Soviet Navy to seek "to expand their now limited capability to extend conventional power ashore to areas distant from the Soviet Union into a full-fledged seaborne projection capability with its attendant sea control, amphibious assaults and sea-based aviation forces" (ibid.: 13). Thus, American experts feel alarmed at the rapidly growing naval strength deployed by the adversary. In particular, they express concern about the build-up of an offensive capacity exhibited by carrier construction of the Kiev class, a new class of amphibious assault ships, naval aviation capabilities and the world-wide Soviet use of naval bases (Weinberger 1982: II-14; US Military Posture for FY 1983: 10). All these considerations ultimately lead to the question to what extent, if at all, the Soviet Union accepts parity. American observers seem to be confused by what, in their view, represents contradictory evidence regarding the issue of parity or superiority. A former CIA expert for Soviet military and economic affairs holds that:

"Realistic Soviet assessments of the status quo should not be interpreted as Soviet acceptance of the status quo as the permanent strategic relationship between the two superpowers and their allies." (Lee 1981: 78)

Repeated Soviet denials that the Soviet Union is seeking military superiority are dismissed out of hand as "an obvious ploy" for purposes of disinformation and of propaganda (Lee 1981: 78f.). While the "peaceful" use of Soviet military power constitutes one major theme in American preoccupation with the potential adversary's strategies, another one refers to the question to what extent Soviet leadership would be willing to actually use force, in other words Soviet risk-taking behaviour. In this respect, American official sources indicate the assumption that Soviet military doctrine always calls for forces structured to fight and win at any level of conflict. The direct Soviet military intervention in Afghanistan is said to reflect a growing degree of Soviet confidence to operate by the actual use of force, provided that the Soviet Union holds great geostrategic advantage and there would be no direct confrontation with the United States (US Military Posture for FY 1983: 2 and 6; Gen. David C. Jones, Chairman, Joint Chiefs of Staff, in: Hearings HASC 1981, part 1: 75). American spokesmen suspect that "the Soviet leaders know that their increased military power has permitted them to undertake politico-military initiatives that would have been too risky only a decade ago" (US Military Posture for FY 1983: 2).

An ominous sign is also perceived in the fact that "Soviet military mobilization and logistic plans, critical elements in waging war, reflect their concepts for the conduct of theater-strategic offensive operations" (Soviet Military Power 1984: 82). Recently American sources have placed increasing emphasis on what, in their view, clearly constitutes an offensive orientation of Soviet armed forces. Significant indicators corroborating this assumption are seen in the "offensively oriented doctrine emphasizing armoured attacks, manoeuvres, and firepower", improvements in tactical aircraft designed and equipped specially for offensive operations, the deployment of heavy-lift vehicles that can rapidly move tanks and other heavy equipment to the front, the threat posed by offensive chemical and biological weapons, and organizational changes such as the establishment of the Operational Manoeuvre Groups (OMG's) taking advantage of surprise and moving forward rapidly, and the reorganization of Soviet airforces that has produced reserve strategic air armies tailored, as self-contained "strike packages", for long-range attacks. All these preparations are alleged to perfectly support a conventional "blitzkrieg" strategy (Weinberger 1984: 24f.). The United States Administration is somewhat puzzled by this offensive orientation:

"We cannot know for certain why the Soviet Union emphasized offensive planning... The Soviets may not seek war, but their belief that conflict is a continuous possibility leads them to build forces designed to prevail in any war." (Weinberger 1984: 26)

Here again, the American view stresses the political function of Soviet military power:

"Apart from hedging against the possibility of war, they undoubtedly also believe that establishing a position of military dominance will give them the leverage in peacetime that will permit them to achieve their aims without war." (Weinberger 1984: 26)

At any rate, American officials tend to diagnose an adverse trend in the evolution of United States and Soviet capabilities to fight a conventional war. In the American view, this adverse trend impairs the United States and allied ability to maintain a credible deterrent and, consequently, threatens stability world-wide (ibid.: 30). All this can be summed up in what an official United States publication calls "the grand strategy of the USSR":

"The grand strategy of the USSR ... is to attain its objectives, if possible, by means short of war - capitalizing on the coercive leverage inherent to superior forces, particularly nuclear forces, to instill fear, to erode the West's collective security arrangements and to support subversion. Thus, the primary role of Soviet military power is to provide the essential underpinning for the step by step extension of Soviet influence and control." (Soviet Military Power 1984: 10)

This is expected to have grave consequences in the European theatre where NATO's qualitative edge has been diminishing and where the Warsaw Pact is "becoming even better aligned with its military doctrine of defeating NATO quickly and decisively by means of fast-moving 'blitzkrieg-style' offensive operations" (Weinberger 1982: II-18). One scenario suggested by an American official therefore refers to the possibility of an "updated version of the summer of 1914", assuming that, if NATO forces are not strong enough at the conventional level, the Soviets "could miscalculate that they can make limited moves in a crisis and produce faits accomplis" (Abshire 1984). On the other hand, American observers also acknowledge a sense of caution in Soviet political and military leaders, who are not held to be "reckless men" and who, even in military operations, tend to be extremely cautious (Chaney 1983: 32). Still, incidents such as the shooting down of a Korean civilian airliner serve as reminders "of the USSR's willingness to use military force" (Weinberger, in: Soviet Military Power 1984: 5).

The paramount issue, however, crucial to all American concerns about the potential adversary's strategies, is of course the problem of how the Soviet leadership might see the role of nuclear forces. American sources repeatedly note the fact that Soviet doctrinal writings assign little importance to the concept of deterrence and talk instead of "sufficiency to achieve objectives by the possession of credible warfighting capabilities" (US Military Posture for FY 1983: 20). It is also emphasized that Soviet policy develops both offensive and defensive forces, paying increasing attention to civil

142

defence and a wide variety of measures designed to enhance the prospect of survival of key elements of Soviet society after the outbreak of a nuclear war (Weinberger 1982: II-11).

This analysis leads to a general conclusion shared by Secretaries of Defense Brown and Weinberger; they both seem basically inclined to assume a Soviet intention to fight and win a nuclear war:

"Several Soviet perspectives are relevant to the formulation of our deterrent strategy. First, Soviet military doctrine appears to contemplate the possibility of a relatively prolonged nuclear war. Second, there is evidence that they regard military forces as the obvious first targets in a nuclear exchange, not general industrial and economic capacity. Third, the Soviet leadership clearly places a high value on preservation of the regime and on the survival and continued effectiveness of the instruments of state power and control - a value at least as high as that they place on any losses to the general population, short of those involved in a general nuclear war. Fourth, in some contexts, certain elements of Soviet leadership seem to consider Soviet victory in a nuclear war to be at least a theoretical possibility." (Brown 1981: 38)

"There are many reasons to believe that Soviet assessments are likely to be different from those usually made in the United States. United States assessments have focussed on dealing with the 'out-of-the-blue' surprise attack and on the associated problem of ensuring the survival of our long-range nuclear forces. Soviet assessments, by contrast, may focus on outcomes of large-scale, global war in which both conventional and theater nuclear forces are also involved." (Weinberger 1982: II-10)

In a nutshell, the essence of Soviet nuclear strategy as seen from an American perspective can be summed up as follows, quoting from a statement made by Donald H. Latham, Deputy Under-Secretary of Defense for C^3I at the Department of Defense:

"Variant Forms of Soviet Attack Objectives
Objective: Preempt ability to attack USSR.
US targets: Nuclear forces; and C^3I system.
Tactics: Deception; surprise and decapitate C^3I system.
Objective: Reduce damage potential to USSR.
US targets: Nuclear and conventional forces; theater nuclear forces; and C^3I system.
Tactics: Strike first; urban withhold; and limit fallout.
Objective: Degrade/deny protracted option and US recovery.
US targets: All forces and C^3I; and urban and industrial targets.
Tactics: Generate heavy fallout; and barrage ground mobile operating areas." (Hearings HASC 1982, part 5: 1107)

Preventive "destruction or neutralization of as many of the

West's nuclear weapons as possible on the ground or at sea before they could be launched" is assumed to constitute a central element in Soviet strategic doctrine (Soviet Military Power 1984: 19). It is further assumed that the Soviet leaders believe that any conflict between the Soviet Union and the West could easily escalate to the nuclear level. They may then feel tempted to be first in escalating in order to negate the other side's nuclear capability. In addition, as even on a nuclear battlefield final victory could only be won by ground armies reaching and controlling their ultimate objectives, Soviet doctrine is said "to call for continuing conventional arms offensives during and after any nuclear phase of a general war" (Soviet Military Power 1984: 11) - a perfect nuclear war-fighting concept. Still, United States officials generally propose that the Soviet leaders would probably not launch a preventive nuclear attack unless they felt forced to do so - a contingency that, however, might arise in any crisis confrontation where Soviet leaders perceive the Soviet Union to be seriously threatened.

According to Weinberger, one should start from the premise that:

"We are faced with an adversary who does not necessarily share our abhorrence of war, even nuclear war. In fact, there is ample evidence that the Soviets have a very different view, and that they regard nuclear weapons as no different than other weapons. The Soviet leadership, through its actions, force deployments, and writings, has in fact given us the clear perception that it believes a nuclear war may be fought and won under certain circumstances" (Weinberger/Draper 1983, letter of 13 July 1983).

Official analysts start from the assumption that in Soviet perceptions "even nuclear weapons do not negate the Marxist teleology of history, that a war between the two superpowers and their allies will be the final decisive clash between the two antithetical social systems" (Lee 1981: 76). Hence the assertion that Soviet politico-military thinking is characterized by the idea that the objective of nuclear war is "victory":

"To the Soviets, nuclear war is a catastrophe they very much want to avoid, but it is no apocalypse. Like any other war, nuclear war between the two camps would be a continuation of politics by violent means." (Lee 1981: 76f.)

Some United States officials even believe that the "Russians tend to view atomic weapons as another type of firepower" (Sollinger 1983: 7), i.e. simply as a category of weapons new in quantitative but not in qualitative terms. On the basis of this assumption, they conclude that a strategy of surprise attack should not be excluded and "an opening nuclear salvo is at least a possibility" (ibid.: 8). In more operational terms this means that official American strategists are afraid of a Soviet first strike or "bolt from the blue", likely to come after a period of tension or perhaps limited hostilities (Congressional Budget Office 1983: 19f.) even though a "nuclear Pearl

Harbour" is not believed to be the greatest danger (Abshire 1984).

Nevertheless, for American officials, the nightmare of a pre-emptive nuclear strike by the Soviet Union is too serious to be lightly discarded. They affirm that "in the context of a nuclear war, the Soviets believe the most favorable circumstance would be a pre-emptive strike" (Soviet Military Power 1984: 20). They point to the Soviet leadership's routine practising of command and control under various conditions (ibid.), and to extensive Soviet "plans either to preempt a NATO nuclear strike by launching a massive attack, or to launch a massive first strike against prime NATO targets" (ibid.: 50). Soviet strategic defensive programmes to protect the key civilian and military leadership are viewed in the same perspective (US Military Posture for FY 1985: 30). However, what from an American point of view has the most severe consequence is the fact that "the Soviets have rejected mutual vulnerability as a continued basis for the strategic balance" (ibid.).

In addition, Soviet nuclear strategy is perceived as a means to undermine Western deterrence, or, in other words, to "deter deter- rence", especially in the Euro-strategic context. As Secretary of Defense Weinberger puts it, "the Soviet attempt to acquire a monopoly of longer-range intermediate nuclear forces, and especially the enor- mous and rapid build-up of the accurate and mobile and therefore sur- vivable SS-20" threatened to undermine the whole strategy of deter- rence and upset the balance (Weinberger 1983a: 2).

On the level of global strategy, it is assumed that the Soviet Union:

"could now begin to envision a potential nuclear confrontation in which they would threaten to destroy a very large part of our force in a first strike, while retaining overwhelming nuclear force to deter any retaliation we could carry out. This ability to conduct a first strike also threatened to make less credible the deterrent linkage between our strategic nuclear force and our forward-deployed conventional and nuclear forces. In addition, the increasing Soviet emphasis on blunting the effects of US retaliation held open the prospect of undercutting deterrence further, because the Soviet leaders could come to believe that their hardening programs would permit them to emerge from a major conflict with their forces, control, and war supporting capabilities damaged but still functioning." (Weinberger 1984: 554)

When discussing the Soviet inclination to launch a pre-emptive nuclear attack, American officials tend to assign little value to the Soviet Union's pledge never to be the first to use nuclear weapons. They recall a statement made on September 5, 1961, by General Secre- tary Khrushchev, who referred to the "logic of the struggle" which forces the decision-makers to act even if they have not planned to do so: "Even if I make a promise, I may not be able to keep it. The struggle has its own logic." They also caution against forgetting the high degree of flexibility and opportunism in Soviet decision-making (Greyson 1982:7). They argue that the Soviet leadership has always exhibited the ability to shift swiftly to a surprising new strategy whenever this seems necessary. Previous pledges therefore do not count much because Soviet leaders are expected to provide a new ideological justification without any great problems.

In an American perspective, pledges made by the Soviet leaders merely serve propaganda, which is in fact held to be an important ingredient in the overall Soviet strategy. American spokesmen warn against the potentially confusing impact of Soviet propaganda on Western audiences. Propaganda and "active measures" of disinformation, forgery and other operations are declared to be of very great importance to the Soviet Union (Sorrels 1983: A1).

Assumptions regarding Soviet disarmament and arms control policies: compromise and compliance by pressure only

In American eyes, the Soviet record in the field of disarmament and arms control cannot be said to be very positive. Rather, the prevailing attitude seems to be disappointment - up to the point of openly and explicitly admitting this feeling of disappointment, as indicated by Secretary of Defense Weinberger:

"Today, we have come to recognize the full extent of our disappointment. Despite the agreements we negotiated, the Soviet Union steadily increased its investment in nuclear strategic forces even though we reduced ours. Our landbased deterrent forces have become highly vulnerable even though one of our main purposes in SALT was to prevent such vulnerability. And Soviet nuclear offensive capabilities now exceed by far our most pessimistic forecasts of 15 years ago, when we estimated what might happen should our SALT efforts fail - as indeed they have." (Weinberger 1982: I-19).

Generally, responsible American officials believe that the United States might have made a major mistake by relying too much on unilateral self-restraint and hopes for peace and security - which were not honoured by the Soviet Union. It is thought that the Soviet momentum, if unchecked and unmatched, will lead to superiority (Gen. Kelly H. Burke, Deputy Chief of Staff, United States Air Force, in: Hearings HASC, 1981, part 4:431). In summary, the adversary is not deemed to deserve to be trusted as he does not reciprocate unilateral concessions and never voluntarily refrains from pursuing his ultimate objectives at the expense of the United States.

What, then, made the Soviet Union nevertheless agree to the more than one dozen arms control agreements negotiated and signed so far? What are the motives of the Soviet leadership in engaging in further arms control negotiations in various negotiating settings (START, INF, MBFR, CSCE, United Nations, etc.)? American officials, when faced with this question, may differ with regard to their rank-ordering of the motives underlying Soviet arms-control behaviour, but there seems to be a clear convergence of views and assumptions with regard to the nature of those motives. There are five assumptions to be discerned:

The first assumption refers to the political impact which arms-control negotiations tend to have on the Western public. It is said that by conducting arms-control negotiations and concluding agreements, the Soviet Union sucessfully lulled the West into a period of complacency, into a warm sense of security which in turn reduced Western vigilance and the Western commitment to national defence. More generally, it is assumed that the Soviet Union conducts negotiations not with a tangible result in mind but by aiming at a propaganda campaign for the sake of "peace", addressing itself to the Western public, thus scoring political points, especially with the European audience. The Soviet Union is blamed for being primarily interested in utilizing the very fact of the conduct of negotiations, irrespective of the substance of any agreement reached as a result of these negotiations. American observers also acknowledge that the Soviet negotiators, being well acquainted with Western perceptions, are in a position to manipulate them.

One of the most questionable efforts undertaken by Soviet propaganda, in this respect, is said to be the "campaign to persuade public opinion in the West to believe that their own Government's actions responding defensively to Soviet power and conduct are instead provocative of a Soviet response and that the Soviets are the aggrieved party, reluctantly forced to consider or pursue countermeasures" (Sorrels 1983:1). Other typical propaganda themes are: "NATO's deployment of INF missiles will increase the likelihood of conflicts" - thereby stimulating fear of war or increased tension (ibid.:26); "NATO's decision will make impossible or complicate arms control negotiations" (ibid.:32), and others. The most sophisticated element in Soviet propaganda, however, is seen to be the Soviet attempt to define the terms of the international debate, mainly by describing it as an issue of war and peace exclusively, with the implicit understanding that the Soviet government acts on behalf of "peace". In this way, the Soviet Union is seen to distract attention from other, more fundamental issues such as the struggle between freedom and slavery; after all, American spokesmen emphasize, conflict and the arms race originate in the basic contradiction, not in the existence of weapons as such.

Secondly, it is felt that by having such a political impact, the Soviet Union tries to divide the West, in particular to divide the United States from Europe and the nuclear countries from non-nuclear countries. Some officials even suspect that in some cases the Soviet Union may right from the start have approached negotiations without any serious intention of reaching agreement - just to exploit the potential for propaganda. For instance, it is believed that in the negotiations on Intermediate-Range Nuclear Forces in Europe (INF) the

Soviet Union does not really want an agreement, but is interested only in benefiting from the opportunity to polarize Western society, ultimately with the purpose of outwitting the West and inducing it to accept unilateral limitations:

"The Soviet Union seems to approach arms control less as a tool for achieving stability and balance and more as a political instrument to be used to secure advantages whether through actual agreements or through the politics of the negotiating process itself. This has been evident in Soviet conduct on INF: Soviet proposals seem to have been designed not to narrow differences between East and West but to generate tensions among members of NATO, to stimulate public concern, and to achieve a limitation on Western forces without accepting reciprocal limits on Soviet forces." (Security and Arms Control 1983:14)

Thirdly, American officials are convinced that the Soviet desire to obtain recognition and legitimation of its "super Power" status played a decisive role in the USSR becoming involved in arms control negotiations. Being the exclusive interlocutor with the United States meant to the Soviet leadership affirming their status as an equal; it is noted that the Soviet Union increasingly and explicitly puts emphasis on "equality" and "parity".

Fourthly, it is supposed that the Soviet Union, by engaging in negotiations with the West, hopes to achieve outcomes that would be more constraining on the United States than on the Soviet side. In the context of the Strategic Arms Reduction Talks (START) a genuine Soviet interest is held to exist with regard to deflecting what the Soviet leadership may believe to be the beginning of heavy United States investment. However, American observers are convinced that the Soviet Union does not even distinguish between systems that are more destabilizing than others; Soviet START proposals are said to have always been aimed at perpetuating the current Soviet throw-weight advantage (Arms Control 1984:7).

According to American officials, among the Soviet motives for arms control, the fifth motive, i.e. interest in making real "cuts" and finding limiting agreements on substantive fields of arms production, ranks very low. Of course American observers concede that the Soviet Union is inclined to avoid "unnecessary" expenditures in the arms race; yet they warn that the urgency which financial considerations sometimes have in the West should not be confused with the situation in the East, where serious economic problems exist but do not translate as easily into political problems of domestic demands and articulate opposition. If the Soviet leadership is seriously interested in a substantive agreement, the motives may not only be fuelled by economic constraints but also by the desire to avoid another round of the arms race where the Soviet leaders might be afraid of Western technological superiority.

Furthermore, from an American point of view, the Soviet attitude to verification and enforcement of arms control agreements is declared to be particularly inappropriate. It is strongly felt that the Soviet Union very often refuses to accept effective verification procedures (Soviet Military Balance 1984:117). American observers concede that to the Soviet Union the traditional belief in secrecy and the insistence on having everything classified may lead the Soviet negotiators to perceive verification as a very difficult and burdensome task. However, they ask themselves whether the reluctance to accept verification may not mean that there is something to hide. Soviet behaviour in the field of arms control is seen to be characteristically oriented towards being declaratory in nature, focusing on unenforceable promises of good will and pacific intent (Security and Arms Control 1983:14). At this point, however, one may ask why the United States Government nevertheless engages in arms control negotiations with the Soviet Union at all and, more precisely, what are the premises American negotiators act upon in this context. The answer has been clearly given repeatedly, especially with regard to the Strategic Arms Reduction Talks (START) and chemical weapons (CW) negotiations within the framework of the Conference on Disarmament (CD). Summarizing the various statements made in this respect and trying to extract their intrinsic message, one may say that United States arms control policy starts from the following assumption regarding Soviet behaviour in this field: the Soviet Union accepts and keeps agreements on arms control only to the extent it is forced to do so. Or, as Secretary of State Shultz puts it:

> "In arms control, successful negotiation depends on the perception of a military balance. Only if the Soviet leaders see the West as determined to modernize its own forces will they see an incentive to negotiate agreements establishing equal, verifiable and lower levels of armament." (quoted in International Herald Tribune, 5 April 1984)

In more specific terms this assumption has four important policy implications: firstly, for example in negotiations on the limitation of strategic delivery systems, United States policy aims at "creating incentives for the Soviets to enter meaningful negotiations for arms control treaties" by continuing programmes such as the MX missile (FY 1984 Arms Control Impact Statements: XVIII). In the American perspective, the historical record of previous arms control agreements also demonstrates "that the Soviets have agreed to real arms control only when it was clear that the West had the political will to preserve the military balance" (Sorrel 1983:32). In other words, United States arms control policy starts from the premise that one cannot negotiate with the Soviet Union because one trusts Soviet negotiators, but one has to create situations where they find it in their own self-interest to reach agreements, and to comply with them.

(Secondly, this assessment implies that the Soviet Union is held to be basically responsive in the future provided that the United States is willing and able to launch new programmes today in order to have "leverage" tomorrow (ibid. 1982:IX).

149

Thirdly, it means that United States programmes (such as upgrading American CW systems) must be designed to discourage Soviet "breakout" from a concluded treaty (ibid. 1984:XVII) - assuming implicitly that the Soviet Union will break out if it is not properly deterred from doing so.

Fourthly, this also leads to the conclusion that it would be naive to assume that the Soviet Union would not risk violating existing arms control provisions since there would always be some risk of detection and to be caught could have damaging political consequences for it - in particular a vigourous condemnation by world opinion; this "theory" is held invalid (Weinberger 1982:1-21) because the alleged pressure by "world public opinion" is believed not to be strong enough to deter the Soviet Union from cheating. In other words, the American Government thinks that the Soviet Union will conform solely to agreements which are not only comprehensively verifiable but which are, in addition, supplemented with an adequate American retaliatory capacity to be activated in case of a Soviet "breakout". In brief: "The U.S.S.R. will repeatedly test our resolve before responding constructively." (Weinberger, in: Soviet Military Power 1984:5). Nevertheless, American officials view the future arms control with confidence because they think that by now "a realistic appraisal of Soviet negotiating behaviour has improved the prospects for arms reductions" (Weinberger 1984:4). American officials in charge of arms control negotiations complain about the Soviet Union's general attitude with regard to the details of the agreements reached. They doubt whether the Soviet Union, while respecting the letter of the agreement, really does abide by the spirit of the agreement, or rather uses loopholes and surprising interpretations from which it can profit to its own advantage.

Whenever the Soviets negotiate something, they are said to use the agreement right to the limit, "stretching" it as much as feasible and trying to exploit every opportunity to reap one-sided benefits. Worse, the Soviet Union is held to stretch the provisions of arms control agreements even to the brink of violation and beyond. American officials increasingly express concern about what they perceive to be clear violations such as non-compliance with the norms regarding chemical, biological, and toxic weapons, the notification of military exercises, a large new Soviet radar being deployed in the Soviet interior, encryption of data needed to verify arms control provisions, the testing of a second new intercontinental ballistic missile, the deployment status of an existing Soviet ICBM, and the yield of underground tests (Weinberger 1984:33). The conclusions to be drawn from this behaviour seem clear:

"Such violations deprive us of the security benefits of arms control directly because of the military consequences of known violations, and indirectly by inducing suspicion about the existence of undetected violations that might have additional military consequences." (Arms Control 1984:10)

Generally, the American evaluation of Soviet willingness and trustworthiness in the field of disarmament and arms control is thus characterized by deep mistrust. When reflecting on Soviet behaviour in this field, American experts sometimes refer to Admiral S.G. Gorshkov's considerations on the history of naval arms limitations. They stress Gorshkov's emphasis on diplomatic and propagandistic measures which, according to Gorshkov, in the case of Great Britain were successful during the inter-War period (Shulsky 1978:250). They also point to Gorshkov's allusion to arms control negotiations as a means in the "prolonged struggle" to have equality recognized - and, perhaps, even to acquire superiority (ibid.:258). In this connection, an official pamphlet points out that in 1979 the Soviet party leader said that "a balance of forces has taken shape in Europe" and that similar statements about "approximate parity of forces" and the "currently existing equality" were continuously repeated at regular intervals through to 1983, while at the same time the number of nuclear warheads on the Soviet side grew from 800 to 1400 (Arms Control 1984:2). This greatly reinforces the American view that, in Soviet arms control policy, words and deeds are not the same thing.

As far as Soviet arms control negotiations behaviour in a more restricted sense is concerned, it is felt that the Soviet counterparts, instead of adopting a business-like approach to negotiations, prefer to operate by skilfully orchestrating public campaigns and generating fear about the consequences of a failure of the negotiations. The patterns with regard to influencing Western public opinion are:

"- unveiling the details of Soviet positions over an extended period of time to foster the appearance of a dynamic, flexible reaction;
- advancing positions in public before tabling them in Geneva;
- evading clarification of such proposals at the bargaining table unless the United States accepts the Soviet framework for an agreement; and
- refusing to cooperate in resolving 'secondary' issues until the central issues are resolved on their terms." (NATO Special Consultative Group 1983:36f.)

According to leading United States participants in many arms control negotiations, the Soviet approach has the following 10 characteristics:

(1) The Soviet negotiators always seek agreement on broad principles - but resist putting forward details. Ambiguity serves their purpose.

(2) They insist that national means of verification are sufficient, expressing strong dislike of any on-site inspection activity which, when it becomes inevitable, is said to be "completely voluntary".

(3) To Soviet negotiators, negotiations are part of a larger struggle.

(4) They seek simultaneous understanding on all important issues, exerting pressure on the Americans to show their cards, while at the same time making only very small moves which they then present as "major concessions".

(5) They seek United States packages - in order to pick the package apart and select those elements that please them most.

(6) They constantly reinterpret the past, for instance previous United States statements, also trying to quote dissenting opinions from the domestic United States political scene which may support their cause.

(7) They prefer short-term solutions and seem to be basically uncomfortable with solutions covering a longer period because they do not think that they can predict United States technology over an extended period.

(8) They behave in a very inflexible way, while at the same time calling for more flexibility on the part of the United States. One of the reasons for Soviet inflexibility may be the bureaucratic resistance which their apparatus meets when faced with the necessity of changing positions.

(9) They are unwilling to understand the Western position and reject the premise of American terms. It remains open whether this is because of the philosophical content of the United States proposal or due to merely tactical reasons.

(10) They are very sensitive and patriotic about Russia's image, conscious of being treated on a strictly reciprocal basis.

In other words, American officials assume that their Soviet counterparts in arms control negotiations always start from a political position which they want to apply irrespective of the American attempt to use a more business-like approach. Seen in an American perspective, this suggests an attitude of extreme caution and care which seems even more indispensable as the Soviet Union is accused of never having divulged its data voluntarily and therefore always trying to hide certain things.

The specific operational implications that follow from this set of assumptions regarding the adversary's arms control policies and negotiating behaviour will be examined below in connection with the analysis of official American views about the appropriate approach to these negotiations.

The meta-image - assumptions regarding the Soviet view of the United States: beware of underestimation!

American official sources express awareness that the perception of American intentions and capabilities by the Soviet leadership plays a major role in shaping Soviet policy and strategy with regard to the United States. In general, American observers think that the Soviet image of the United States is basically correct, at least as far as Soviet perceptions of United States power are concerned:

"The Soviet Union views the United States as its primary potential enemy and its most formidable obstacle to increasing Soviet global influence." (United States Military Posture for FY 1982:7)

American officials tend to assume that the Soviet perception of United States and NATO military forces and capabilities appears to be "a mixture of sober realism and 'worst case' fantasy" (Lee 1981:70). They suggest that this may be the outcome of a fundamental attitude which is said to be a kind of "love-hate" or "love-fear" relationship. Soviet leaders are believed to envy the United States, perceiving their empire to have an inferior status.

Many American officials assume that those responsible for making decisions on behalf of the Soviet Union do not fully grasp the essence of Western society although some of them quite frequently travel to the West. Yet some suspect that the Soviet view of the United States and the West in general may be too accurate and hence also disclose the basic weaknesses of the West. They think, for instance, that "the Soviets fully comprehend Western dependence on resources from the less developed world" (Lee 1981:8). The adversary is therefore held to be tempted to exploit Western vulnerability, looking carefully for opportunities and skilfully playing on Western weaknesses.

The "meta-image" is deemed to be crucially important with respect to the American strategy of deterrence, for the effectiveness of deterrence essentially depends on the perceptions held by the power to be deterred. The 1984 Department of Defense Annual Report indicates a clear awareness of the crucial role of a proper grasp of the situation by the adversary, quoting from the Scowcroft Commission on Strategic Forces' report:

"Deterrence is not an abstract notion amenable to simple quantification. Still less it is a mirror image of what would deter ourselves. Deterrence is the set of beliefs in the minds of the Soviet leaders, given their own values and attitudes, about our own capabilities and our will. It requires us to determine, as best we can, what would deter them from considering agression, even in a crisis - not to determine what would deter us." (Weinberger 1984:27)

With regard to the practical implications of this principle, American sources do not express an unanimous view. While some spokesmen alarm their audience by pointing to the possibility that the perceived credibility of NATO's deterrent is declining (Gen. Bernard W. Rogers, Commander in Chief, United States, European Command, in: Hearings HASC 1981, part 1:654), others assume that "the Soviets have underestimated our resolve" (Gen. Kelly H. Burke, Deputy Chief of Staff, Air Force, ibid. part 4:431). This debate about Soviet perceptions looks quite confusing - and in fact, personalities such as Secretary of Defense Brown have criticized its detrimental impact on the Soviet leadership and warned of the danger to Western security and Western deterrence of making "inaccurate, disparaging, and mis-leading charges about either our national will or our military cap-abilities." (Brown 1981:29)

It seems that, as far as shaping the Soviet perception of Western power is concerned, responsible American officials are facing a par-ticularly difficult task. On the one hand, they have reasons to alarm their domestic audience by depicting Western power as being in a deplorable state; on the other hand, however, they must take care not to shake Soviet belief in America's determination and resolve to resist Soviet global aspirations. The difficulty of this task is reflected by a subtle and sometimes ambiguous balancing between con-tradictory elements discerned in the Soviet image of the West.

In sum, there seems to be agreement among official American observers that the Soviet Union may be somewhat confused by Western pluralism and "contradictions" which to Soviet eyes are held to be fascinating but hardly understandable. American officials therefore conclude that Soviet leaders may be tempted to simultaneously overes-timate and underestimate the West: They are assumed to overestimate, for instance, the American influence on the allies as well as the scope of action available to the American President, whose entangle-ment in a system of checks and balances they are not likely to understand, based on their own experience with almost unlimited power. On the other hand, American officials are aware that in the Soviet perspective some important features of Western society may well be underestimated. In particular, United States officials sus-pect Soviet leaders of underestimating Western vitality and resi-lience. It is surmised that, if the Soviet élite really believes in what their ideological creed tells them about the "decline" and "de-cay of capitalism" they might feel induced to take actions against the West which they would realize too late to be based on a tragic misunderstanding and underestimation of Western strength and resolve.

Yet the ideological preconceptions discerned in the Soviet image of the West might equally well lead to an opposite conclusion - i.e. the assumption that the "decaying" West is even more dangerous because it is trying desperately to avert its fate. American officials are aware of what this interpretation means in Soviet eyes, and they are also aware of the Soviet fear regarding an American sur-prise attack - and the frightening conclusion the Soviet leadership may draw from this belief. As a former CIA expert for Soviet mili-tary and economic affairs put it, the Soviet Union for this reason feels urged to "be ready either to pre-empt a United States/NATO attack, if adequate warning is available, or to retaliate" (Lee 1981:70). This sequence of considerations and its reflection in the meta-image points to the importance of perceptions.

Some American analysts also draw attention to the fact that what Soviet authors write about the United States may perhaps be an indi-cation of future roles and missions for the Soviet Union's own forces as new weapons systems are deployed (Scott/Scott 1981:109). The argue that at least:

"There is a danger that what is said about United States military intentions is merely a cover to justify, and in a sense conceal, actions that the Kremlin itself may plan against the West. If these written perceptions do represent the true views of the Kremlin leaders, there is an even greater danger they might begin a war, or precipitate a surprise nuclear attack, through miscalculation of the intentions of the United States." (Scott/Scott 1981:110)

In other words, some themes in the Soviet image of the United States are believed to be virtual "projections", i.e. attributions to another of what is actually one's own perspective or inclination or intention. This is held to be particularly relevant with regard to the alleged United States intention to launch a pre-emptive or first strike, a concept that, according to American sources, is precisely consistent with long-standing tenets of Soviet military doctrine (Sorrels 1983:13). Or it may at least constitute an argument which serves to dissimulate and rationalize facts which the Soviet leaders have chosen for different reasons, because for many American experts it is hard to believe that the Soviet Union really assumes an American first strike policy, which is unthinkable given the nature and orientation of the American political system.

When pondering the enigma of the Soviet image of its United States adversary, American experts increasingly think that more specific conclusions are required: those elements of information about the United States which are amenable to numerical indicators - such as the number of missiles - may be perfectly grasped by Soviet analysts who seem to have a thorough knowledge of the United States congressional process. Still, some American officials acquainted with Soviet negotiators have reservations as to the internal distribution of such knowledge within the Soviet bureaucracy; they are inclined to conclude that, based on a rigid application of the principle of the "need to know", only a handful of Soviet personalities really have all the information about the United States which is available.

In terms of the more qualitative aspects of the assessment of United States strength American officials expect the Soviet analysts to use a prudent approach, i.e. certainly no underestimation, yet a tendency to employ a kind of worst-case approach. They will therefore not misunderstand Western complaints about "gaps" and "inferiority".

As far as the political and social assessment of the United States is concerned, American experts doubt whether their Soviet partners really believe what they proclaim about the "decadence of capitalism". It is considered that, while still continuing to talk about this "decline" for propaganda purposes, they are perfectly well aware of the fact that the West is not weakened by social tensions. As many travel frequently to the West, they may be expected not to have a completely unrealistic view of social conditions in the West, although not being really capable of understanding the "fluid" societies of the West. American experts assume that Soviet leaders

155

perceive the West as ideologically weak yet at the same time still capable of marshalling complex forces. By contrast to the Western perspective, however, they tend to pay more attention to the non-military ingredients of power, placing greater emphasis on ideological and political strength.

When examining the Soviet view of the United States, however, American officials are also aware of the manipulative nature of the Soviet image due to domestic concerns. They suppose that the Soviet image of the West sometimes varies not as a function of changes in Western policies but as a consequence of domestic shifts of emphasis. This is deemed to be of particular importance with regard to the assessment of the "United States threat". The Soviet image of the enemy up to the early 1980s was never so dramatic as to stir up fear among the Soviet population. The Soviet leadership carefully avoided overrating the "United States threat" up to a point where the Soviet population would have felt directly menaced and probably also doubted the wisdom of the CPSU leadership. In all circumstances, the main conclusion offered was that despite "imperialist aggression and war-mongering", the Soviet people could sleep calmly and be confident of being fully protected by the Soviet Army. As one American expert argues, this approach to the "United States threat" may also have had something to do with the unwillingness of the civilian party leaders to increase the role of the military by creating an atmosphere of militant hysteria.

Yet this approach thoroughly changed in the early 1980s when the Soviet Union launched an unprecedented propaganda effort aimed at Western European public opinion to abort NATO's plans for deployment of Pershing-2 and cruise missiles in Western Europe. According to a leading American expert the Soviet media thus inadvertently involved the whole Soviet population in this campaign, scaring it by detailed descriptions of the frightening military potential of the United States enemy and even suggesting that American military power was greater than the corresponding Soviet potential, and offering descriptions of the capacity of Western weaponry to destroy Moscow and other Soviet cities. To some American observers it seems that the Soviet authorities unwillingly overdid things a little when picturing the danger of the "United States threat", and they expect a certain moderation soon for purely domestic reasons because the CPSU leadership feels uncomfortable with the present mood, widespread among the Soviet population, that even the infallible leadership and its scientifically based policies are no longer able to cope with that "threat".

On the other hand, American officials also acknowledge that the intrinsic nature of the Soviet system always and necessarily leads to a kind of paranoia with regard to the United States: they assume that for the Soviet leaders, the United States - as any state or party outside their control - constitutes a threat, owing to the shaky legitimatory basis of the Soviet regime. In this connection a distinguished United States official approvingly quotes George F.

Kennan, who said that "they hate us - not for what we do, but for what we are", thus indicating that the United States, as a democracy, represents a constant challenge to any communist regime and therefore is automatically perceived as a threat. Hence, there is no kind of friendly behaviour towards the Soviet Union that might lead to a more benign Soviet image of the United States.

Assessment of information about the adversary: no words - deeds only

American observers of the Soviet Union concede that assessing the adversary represents no easy task. In the last resort, "only a handful of people in the Soviet Politbureau can claim with any confidence to know the Soviet Union's real motives and plans, what constitutes their 'grand design', or indeed whether they have a 'grand design'" (Brown 1981:14). American officials point to the high degree of secrecy which surrounds Soviet society and politics, and to the closed nature of the Soviet political system. The most dismal consequence of authoritarian centralism, however, is seen in the peculiar Leninist attitude to truth and information. As one American expert puts it:

"The Soviet Union is a country in which official policy is not only to keep its own citizens... ignorant of some of the things that happen in the world outside but in which policy dictates going to enormous and expensive lengths to keep the outside world from knowing what is happening internally... In tsarist and Leninist Russia, reality is understood officially as that which is planned by the supreme authority." (Bathurst 1979:1)

In addition, American officials question the ability of any "Westerner" adequately to grasp information available on the East, for there are two different "mindsets" and hence the possibility of misunderstandings arises. They therefore assume that whatever is thought or said about the Soviet Union and its leaders is mere guesswork. Similarly, American officials warn against taking Soviet statements at face value. It is surmised that "to rely on what they say would be - to put it mildly - unwise". Hence, in order to give a proper assessment of the Soviet Union and its strategy, one must concentrate on what can actually be observed, despite the impediments created in this respect by that closed society. In addition it is recommended that inferences should be drawn from what is observed (Brown 1981:14). It is quite interesting to note that American official analysts often tend to mistrust and dismiss declaratory statements available from Soviet sources and are not willing to see any significance in the coherent structure of Soviet political and military thinking.

Among those responsible in the American Administration for the assessment of information about the Soviet Union it is therefore generally held that one should rely on and investigate capabilities and not inferred intentions. A sober analysis of Soviet capabilities is said to be far preferable to any speculation and anticipation of Soviet moves.

Among the methods available for analysing observable Soviet data official American institutions have a marked preference for quantitative analyses based mainly on Soviet defence expenditure. Although the shortcomings of this approach are acknowledged, it is nevertheless held to provide a rough, but useful measure (cf. Weinberger 1982:II-4f.; Brown 1981:15). More refined approaches also include special analyses of military investment, i.e. that portion of spending allocated to weapons system procurement, facility construction, and research, development, test and evaluation (RDT&E) (United States Military Posture for FY 1983:15).

Despite the basic distrust of verbal Soviet sources, Soviet strategic thought is nevertheless not considered completely misleading or irrelevant. According to Admiral Nitze, the Soviet system is not wholly silent because "the word must be gotten down to the cadres and to the troops". In view of the high degree of continuity and persistence in the Soviet strategic approach, "it therefore is not a useless exercise to try to judge what the main elements of that approach may be" (Nitze 1980:87).

American observers also believe that the Marxist-Leninist ideology ought to be taken seriously as a real determinant of Soviet behaviour. The laws of dialectic "cannot be rejected because if they were, any possible basis for legitimacy of the Soviet Government and the power of the Communist Party would disappear" (Bathurst 1979:29).

It is felt that the Soviet leaders are quite explicit about their intentions and that the nature of Marxist-Leninist ideology seems to offer some potential for prediction, although Soviet leaders are not assumed to actively believe in dialectical materialism. But American observers think that ideology affects Soviet perceptions; once one is able to grasp this "mind-set", including its cultural and historical elements, one may to a certain extent predict the way the Soviet system reacts. An intimate knowledge of the Soviet power structure and awareness of the fact that there is a hierarchy of authority in Soviet statements is also considered helpful for a proper understanding of Soviet sources. Even "old" and seemingly "outdated" written sources may be of some value given the Marxist-Leninist ability to make use of elastic dialectics.

Yet, while conceding some limited utility to the use of Soviet written sources, the attitude among leading American officials nevertheless prevails that in the last resort one should concentrate on capabilities, even if this may seem simplistic. The ultimate rationale given for preferring capabilities as the prime indicator for Soviet behaviour again points to one of the crucial assumptions regarding Soviet motives: as the Soviet leadership cynically exploit any opportunities offered to them, it is their capability which counts for them when deciding whether or not to push forward - and hence prudent Western observers have no other choice than to closely monitor the capabilities at the disposal of the Soviet Union.

THE UNITED STATES VIEW OF ITS OWN ROLE AND CHOICES

The principal aim: preserving freedom and containing the adversary

In their most general form, the principal aims underlying American politics and strategy can be summed up in the following four priorities mentioned in the 1983 Annual Report of the Department of Defense:

"- To preserve our freedom, our political identity, and the institutions that are their foundation -- the Constitution and the rule of law.
 - To protect the territory of the United States, its citizens, and its vital interests abroad from armed attack.
 - To foster an international order supportive of the interests of the United States through alliances and cooperative relationship with friendly nations; and by encouraging democratic institutions, economic development, and self-determination throughout the world.
 - To protect access to foreign markets and overseas resources in order to maintain the strength of the United States' industrial, agricultural, and technological base and the nation's economic well-being." (Weinberger 1983:15)

As indicated by this statement, the international implications of America's principal political aims are twofold: they express themselves in the interest in promoting a favourable, i.e. democratic international environment, on the one hand, and in the determination to defend the United States specific economic interests abroad.

In more practical terms, this means protecting these interests from being opposed or denied by the Soviet Union as the principal opponent. The basic objectives of the United States Armed Forces are therefore said to be "to help preserve the United States as a free nation, with its fundamental institutions and values intact", on the one hand, and "to contribute to the shaping of an international environment in which United States interests are protected" (United States Military Posture for FY 1985:1), on the other hand.

As a consequence, the principal aims are translated into a set of politico-military imperatives considered to constitute the main rationale of United States armed strength:

"- To deter military attack by the USSR and its allies against the United States, its allies, and other friendly countries; and to deter, or to counter, use of Soviet military power to coerce or intimidate our friends and allies.

 - In the event of an attack to deny the enemy his objectives and

159

bring a rapid end to the conflict on terms favorable to our interests; and to maintain the political and territorial integrity of the United States and its allies ...
- To promote meaningful and verifiable mutual reductions in nuclear and conventional forces through negotiations...
- To inhibit further expansion of Soviet control and military presence, and to induce the Soviet Union to withdraw from those countries, such as Afghanistan, where it has imposed and maintains its presence and control by force of arms.
- To foster a reduction in the Soviet Union's overall capability to sustain a military buildup by preventing, in concert with our allies, the flow of militarily significant technologies and material to the Soviet Union, and by refraining from actions that serve to subsidize the Soviet economy." (Weinberger 1983:16)

Although the first aims are status-quo-oriented and express a commitment to deterring Soviet attack and to opposing the exploitation of Soviet force for political aims, it is interesting to note that this set of aims also includes a dynamic component: it is reflected in the reference to the need "to induce the Soviet Union to withdraw from those countries... where it has imposed and maintains its presence and control by force of arms". By contrast to the Soviet aims, which envisage an inevitable overall change of the international situation culminating in the ultimate "triumph of socialism", this dynamic component seems much more limited and does not in principle deny the opponent the right to exist. Rather, it results in a policy of containment both strategically and politically.

This is sometimes felt to constitute a disadvantage. Some American officials argue that by not promoting an international mission, American political culture forgoes the opportunity to project an idealistic vision. In terms of justification of United States aims, American sources often simply refer to people's basic needs. Meeting these needs is considered to constitute the purpose and duty of any government. As ultimately the needs of people are defined by the demands felt and expressed by the people, the need for defence must be evaluated in the context of the overall configuration of needs, i.e. in comparison with other needs. Yet, as Secretary of Defense Weinberger reminds the public, priority ought to be given to defence needs. Quoting British Air Marshal Sir John Slessor, he holds:

"It is customary in democratic countries to deplore expenditure on armaments as conflicting with the requirements of social service. There is a tendency to forget that the most important social service that a government can do for its people is to keep them alive and free." (Weinberger 1982:I-9)

This relative sense of mission also implies an international scope; Secretary of the Navy John F. Lehman, in this context, talks about the need "to restore stability to the international environment, to return to an environment in which freedom can flourish and totalitarianism is once again put on the defensive" (Hearings HASC

1982, part 1:553). Again, the emphasis is on restoration rather than revolution or change.

The United States' assumptions regarding its own capabilities: a collage of optimism and pessimism

Western defence planners are faced with a dilemma when juxtaposing the justification of defence efforts - the needs expressed by their people - and the realities of Western politics. They often find reasons to deplore the perceptions held by the public for giving too little attention to the external threat jeopardizing freedom and welfare. They regret that "the Western democracies have been far less willing to demand economic sacrifice in peacetime" (United States Military Posture for FY 1983:3), that "other voices have been more persuasive in declaring the risks acceptable" (ibid. 1982:i). This calamity is mainly ascribed to the fact that a threat remote from the homeland is less apparent than a threat from armour massed on a territorial border (ibid.:iii). Insufficient rational consensus in support of resolute defence efforts appropriate to the nature and magnitude of the threat is seen to prevail not only in the United States but in the allied countries of Europe as well. Official United States Government sources therefore often complain about allies failing to provide adequately for real growth in defence spending due to competing social demands, economic difficulties, and vocal minority opposition (ibid. 1983:5).

Another structural feature of the West said to be prejudicial to defence requirements is the inability "to concert fully our defence efforts", resulting in duplication, lack of interoperability, and inability to achieve certain economies of scale". These deficiencies are held to be the price paid for the fact that NATO is an "alliance of independent nations" (Weinberger 1982:II-7; United States Military Posture for FY 1982:6).

On the other hand, the United States Government feels that the voluntary nature of the Alliance also has considerable advantages. By contrast to non-Soviet members of the Warsaw Pact, the loyalty of the NATO members is assumed not to be subject to question. The task at hand, therefore, is "drawing strength from diversity" (United States Military Posture for FY 1983:3). As Secretary of Defense Brown put it:

"In any reasonable likely European or Japanese war scenario, our allies would be fighting to defend their homeland and their own freedom, an intangible factor, but one that could make a decisive difference in the outcome of a war." (Brown 1981:28)

The West's strength, however, is ultimately held to depend on the ability of the Western allies to co-operate "the more unified we are", the more successful the alliance will be on the strategic level (cf. General Bernard F. Rogers, in: Hearings HASC 1982, part 1:951).

161

When analysing official United States statements about American capability, one has to bear in mind that they are addressed to a specific audience and serve a specific purpose: to raise public support for convincing the Congress that additional efforts are required. This fact is of the utmost importance because it implies a certain bias to be found in practically all documents dealing with this aspect of the American view. The bias expresses itself in a general propensity to portray American capabilities in a way tinged with pessimism. Propositions such as "trends in the military balance are unfavorable" and the claim that there exists a "mismatch between announced national strategy and available forces" (United States Military Posture for FY 1982:i) are quite typical of this attitude.

American leaders are of course aware that by painting too gloomy a picture of United States capabilities they risk creating a feeling of resignation which may undermine the political will for self-defence. Therefore official statements about United States military capabilities usually reflect an infinitely subtle effort not to come down prematurely on either side of the fence - neither instigating fatalistic pessimism nor giving grounds for careless optimism. The following paragraph from the United States Military Posture Statement for FY 1982 (p.VIII) may serve as an indication of this position:

> "In summary, my view of the United States military posture and prospects is a blend of mixed judgements and a collage of pessi- mism and optimism. Our capability remains formidable in most key areas and is better than some people believe. However, measured against the challenges and imperatives of the 1980s, there are many critical improvements to be made. I am pessimistic in the near term because the risks are here now and will grow in the years ahead, while the remedies will take time even under the best of circumstances. I am more optimistic over the longer term because I detect a reversal of public attitude and a greater determination to correct the consequences of our long slide down the slippery slope of wishful thinking, lost momentum, and aging capability".

General statements about the United States own capabilities are thus usually quite ambiguous and inconclusive. Hence preference should be given to more specific reflections on military capabilities relating to specific aspects of the military balance.

As far as the overall strategic balance is concerned, a consensus seems to prevail that the United States and the Soviet Union remain "essentially equivalent" (United States Military Posture for FY 1981:5). Maintaining a balance of forces and preventing superiority for any side is held to be of crucial importance. In the words of Secretary of Defense Weinberger:

> "History has shown us all too often that conflicts occur when one state believes it has a sufficiently greater military capability than another and attempts to exploit that superior strength

through intimidation or conflict with the weaker State" (Wein-berger 1983:19).

Judgements differ, however, with respect to the future perspective of the strategic balance; here a strong tendency to express warnings about the declining United States posture can be observed. Of course, everything depends on how the overall strategic balance is measured and on what terms it is evaluated. Former Secretary of Defense Brown offered a set of four criteria to be used for assessing the strategic nuclear balance:

"1. Soviet strategic nuclear forces do not become usable instruments of political leverage, diplomatic coercion, or military advantage;
2. Nuclear stability, especially in a crisis, is maintained;
3. Any advantages in strategic force characteristics enjoyed by the Soviets are offset by United States advantages in other characteristics; and
4. The United States strategic posture is not in fact, and is not seen as, inferior in performance to that of the Soviet Union." (Brown 1981:44)

On the basis of these four conditions, American officials conclude that the strategic nuclear forces of the two countries remain essentially equivalent although the American forces are constantly being challenged in all four respects by Soviet moves. The most serious challenge is perceived in the field of "ICBM vulnerability and declining effectiveness against hard Soviet targets, SLBM limitation against hard targets, and decreasing ability of United States manned bombers to penetrate Soviet defences" (United States Military Posture for FY 1983:21). A "window of vulnerability" is seen to have been opened as "analyses project that a Soviet strike against United States missile fields could destroy a major portion of the United States ICBM force if the United States choose to ride out the attack before responding" (ibid.:21). Nevertheless it is held that the Soviet Union would still have to contend with the United States SLBM force, secure and survivable at sea, and the manned bombers that had been launched for survival at the first confirmed warning of attack (ibid.). A more recent comparative evaluation of Soviet and American strategic systems lists ASAT, BMD and SAM systems as being superior in the Soviet Union, while Soviet and American ICBMs are assessed as equal and the United States is said to have superiority in all remaining categories (United States Military Posture for FY 1985:17).

In at least two conventional fields United States sources claim superiority and also emphasize the determination to maintain it: air superiority (Brown 1981:29) and maritime superiority (Weinberger 1982:II-12). There are some doubts, however, as to the maritime or naval balance, "depending on where the action would take place; the amount of strategic warning available on both sides; the amount of pre-deployment of forces; and whether one side allowed the other to get the first blow in" (Admiral M. Staser Holcomb, Director, Navy

Program Planning Office, in: Hearings HASC 1981, part 3:117). Concern is also expressed with regard to the credibility of a conventional defense of Western Europe, which rests on the capability to move reinforcements rapidly across Atlantic lines of communications. NATO's reinforcement capability is seen as being jeopardized by "the loss of a clear margin of maritime superiority over the Warsaw Pact" and limitations and shortfalls of airlift and sealift capabilities needed to transport personnel and equipment to Europe (United States Military Posture for FY 1983:6).

Yet in the most recent comparative force assessment Soviet superiority in the conventional field is acknowledged with reference to chemical weapons only; most other categories of conventional power are said to be characterized by United States - USSR equality or indicate a diminishing American lead (United States Military Posture for FY 1985:17).

In the American view, however, the United States is facing a dilemma because its capabilities may not be sufficient to honour all its commitments. This dilemma has to be solved by flexibility and concentration on the essentials:

> "With regard to these global responsibilities, United States forces are obviously not available to defend everywhere against every threat at all times. United States military strategy does not envision that approach. At the same time, the United States must make it clear that its interests will be defended and its obligations to all allies will be met. War must be deterred, but if conflict occurs, the United States will seek to limit the scope of that conflict and the involvement of the USSR. US force employment planning considers the fundamental tasks which must be carried out, as well as the flexibility to meet circumstances which may arise under an almost infinite range of contingencies which can threaten US security interests" (United States Military Posture for FY 1984:5).

Another source of weakness perceived in the context of American capability assessment has to do with the vulnerability of the sophisticated industrial economy of the West. For instance, American officials are concerned about the possibility of the Soviet Union gaining control of vital sources of energy. In such a contingency, "much of the industrialized world would be brought to its knees without a single enemy soldier crossing a Western frontier" (United States Military Posture for FY 1982:iii).

When addressing the question of United States capability, American sources never fail to refer to the "technological edge". It is considered evident that "technology has made us strong economically, agriculturally, and, of course, militarily" (Verne Orr, Secretary of the Air Force, in: Hearings HASC, 1981, part 1:1390). Technological superiority, however, is not believed to constitute a guarantee for incessantly maintaining military superiority or essential equivalence, as the Soviet Union too has been establishing a technology base rivalling the one developed by the United States (ibid.; United States Military Posture for FY 1983:51). But on the whole, as Secretary of Defense Weinberger put it, the United States still has a chance not to lose equivalence provided that America continues to exploit two of its "greatest potential resources - our technological genius and our industrial prowess" (Hearings HASC 1981, part 1:1001).

These statements, however, do not mean that the official view in the United States is based on a purely technological or technocratic perspective. American leaders are fully aware of the fact that the ultimate strength of the United States resides in "the patriotism and conviction, in the skills and courage of each of us" (Weinberger 1982:1-3).

American spokesmen emphasize that United States strategy is designed "to capitalize on the enduring strength of the United States - its political and social values, diversified economy, advanced technology, and ingenuity of its people" (United States Military Posture for FY 1985:9). In this respect they cannot but trust confidently in the capability of their nation.

The principal political-military strategies for shaping relations with the adversary: creating leverage and being aware of global responsibilities

The American view of the political strategies to be employed in dealing with the Soviet Union starts from the assumption that the adversary has a propensity to exploit opportunities wherever and whenever he has a chance to do so. Hence, in order to cope with this challenge, appropriate counter-pressure is required:

"History teaches us that the refusal to respond to a major challenge invites conflict, or invites at least another major challenge." (Secretary of Defense Caspar Weinberger, in: Hearing HASC 1981, part 1:1977)

This assumption implies a clear rejection of any isolationist withdrawal from global responsibilities:

"In an interdependent world system, any United States reversion toward isolationism could have serious implications for the internal prosperity and stability and the mutually supporting relationships of the United States and its allies. Moreover, such a change in international relations would present the Soviet Union with an unprecedented opportunity to expand its influence to the detriment of our interests and responsibilities." (Statement on United States Military Posture for FY 1984:2)

In more general terms, American sources indicate the premise that "we still live in a world in which the use and potential use of military power can influence policies, alignments and actions" (ibid.

1982:iii). Power is seen to constitute an indispensable element of statecraft. This requires a mobilization of America's power in the broad sense, encompassing non-military elements as well as military force.

Viewed in this perspective, however, the ultimate objective of power is not to be obliged to use it. Power primarily serves the purpose of demonstration, and only if this function fails will force actually be employed in the interest of the United States and the West. The Chairman of the Joint Chiefs of Staff characterized this order of priority as follows:

> "I do not suggest that the only, or even the first, response to threatened Soviet penetration should be the United States military intervention. However, a key imperative for the 1980s will be to demonstrate that we have the power, the will, and the wisdom to prevent these interests from being undermined by hostile forces." (United States Military Posture for FY 1982:iii)

In order to convince the Soviet leaders "that further investments in military power can provide no net and lasting advantage" (United States Military Posture for FY 1983:3), the United States must generate leverage by embarking "energetically on the rebuilding of its own military capabilities" (ibid.:14).

In more specific terms this comprises five general underlying objectives and requirements:

> "- build greater military strength -- we must continue the pattern, begun five years ago, of steady and sustained increases in defense spending as an index of increased efforts to build that strength;
> - revitalize collective security -- we must persuade our allies to assume their fair share of the total, common, and growing burden of defense;
> - employ flexibility -- we must be able to respond to threats both within the NATO theater and outside it, including particularly the Southwest Asia-Persian Gulf-Indian Ocean areas and the Northeast Asia area;
> - pursue arms control -- we should use such equitable and verifiable agreements as can be negotiated, to reduce the military threats arrayed against us and to enhance stability; and
> - exploit United States advantages -- we must take advantage of our geography, the inherent appeal and strength of our political and economic system, the contributions of our allies, and our technological process." (Brown 1981:4)

When thinking about power and leverage, American officials are aware that together with its allies, the United States has a sufficient "economic and technological potential to frustrate the Soviet drive for superiority" - yet this potential is held to "count for little unless it is converted into actual military strength evident

to the Soviets and all others as well" (United States Military Posture for FY 1982:54). That is why American sources put strong emphasis on "collective security" by which, in American terminology, they
understand combined commitment, planning, and operations, based on an
appropriate burden-sharing (ibid. 1983:6 and 14). This strategy is
recommended mainly for the Atlantic region and with regard to America's European partners.

Thus, the United States' political and military strategy is fully
committed to alliance co-operation. This principle is held to be
deeply embedded in American historical experience:

"Twice in this century, the United States sought, and failed, to
stand aloof from conflicts across the seas. From this experience
we learned that maintaining a system of defensive alliances is
necessary both to deter attacks... and to share the burden of
defending freedom." (Weinberger 1984:17)

As far as other regions are concerned, the American conception
focuses on security assistance as a vital component of United States
national security and foreign policy. It incorporates the following
elements: transfer of military equipment and services, provision of
low-cost training, friendly force development, and influencing future
military leaders by professional military training. Security assistance is seen to serve both a complementary role in the case of the
friendly nations concerned and to enhance the availability of overseas facilities which United States forces need (ibid.:66; Weinberger
1982:I-15). In a more systematic listing of security assistance
objectives, the following primary objectives are mentioned:

"...assist countries in preserving their independence; promote
regional security, help obtain access, overflight, transit, and
forward basing rights; contribute to interoperability among military forces; ensure access to critical raw materials; and provide
a medium for increasing United States influence". (United States
Military Posture for FY 1985:82)

American diplomacy, economic policy and cultural values too, are
considered as means that "can help develop 'antibodies' against the
appeal of Soviet 'assistance' to those nations" (United States Military Posture for Fiscal Year 1982:ii).

The policy of security assistance is held to be increasingly
important in areas such as Southwest Asia (United States Military
Posture for FY 1982:21) with the aim of being "capable of deterring
or defeating Soviet aggression in the area" (ibid. 1983:8). In Africa, emphasis is put on other elements as well in order to achieve "a
careful blending of security assistance with economic, political, and
technical support". The rationale behind this approach is described
as follows:

"United States efforts to promote internal stability and economic

167

self-sufficiency will help to limit Soviet influence by reducing African dependence on Soviet aid. The United States must work in concert with friends and allies to develop consistent and mutually supporting policies designed to weaken incentives for cooperation with the Soviet Union and other hostile nations, create more effective support of United States security objectives, and promote Africa's economic and social development." (United States Military Posture for FY 1983:9)

The United States intends to apply similar strategies to Latin America, where in addition to demonstrating that it is a "reliable and capable security partner", it wishes to assist "efforts to improve socio-economic conditions as an essential contribution to stability and progress" (ibid.:13).

The backbone of all the efforts to prevent the adversary from exploiting opportunities is said to be the capability of power projection. According to Secretary of the Navy Lehman, power projection serves a threefold purpose: (1) to sustain a peacetime forward deployment posture at levels and locations appropriate to United States needs, (2) to meet crisis control or contingency requirements flexibly and effectively, and (3) to engage any adversary at times and places of the United States' choosing with a high probability of success, while denying that adversary a like opportunity (in: Hearings HASC 1981, part 3:574). American sources assert that the posture of power projection "should not be interpreted as advocacy for either automatic and unrestrained intervention by United States troops in every bushfire or a United States role as the world's policeman" (Military Posture for FY 1983:vi). In addition, it is hoped that the availability of American power and the knowledge that the United States is willing to use it may be sufficient to provide an opportunity for the peaceful resolution of problems (ibid.:21), or as Vice Admiral Sylvester R. Foley, Deputy Chief of Naval Operations, put it with reference to the dispatch of navy units, naval ships' visits serve "as a presence, as an impact, in that particular area, and a force for stability, for stabilizing, calming, and soothing in a visible manifestation of our real interest in that particular area" (in: Hearings HASC 1981, part 3:39).

In sum, the Navy and Marine Corps are viewed as "the vital implements of sea power and, as such, serve as instruments for diplomacy and for deterrence" (General Robert A. Barrow, Commandant of the Marine Corps, in: Hearings HASC 1982, part 1:629). Peacetime deployments of the United States Navy serve "to deter aggression by potential adversaries while providing tangible evidence of our commitment to protect the safety and security of our allies and friends" (Weinberger 1984:133).

Another crucial instrument serving this purpose is the continuous evolution of the Rapid Deployment Joint Task Force (RDJTF) established in 1981 and capable of deploying and employing a balanced and flexible United States projection force that combines the unique capabilities of each of the services (United States Military Posture for FY 1983:8). In addition to the mobility capability, American sources point to the need to complement the RDJTF with factors which go beyond military forces and equipment, chief among them treaties of alliance and friendship, overseas military presence, rights of passage and overflight, base, port, and other facility use agreements, prepositioning equipment and supplies, the willingness of friends to co-operate, and correct perceptions of the United States' resolve to protect its interests (Weinberger 1982:II-16; Brown 1981:6). The rapid deployment capability is said to constitute an important element of a credible posture of deterrence (Weinberger 1984:173).

On the whole, by using a policy of power projection the United States Administration envisages two purposes:

"First, we must have a capability rapidly to deploy enough force to hold key positions, and we must be able to interdict and blunt a Soviet attack. It is the purpose of this capability to convince enemy planners that they cannot count on seizing control of a vital area before our forces are in place, and that they cannot therefore confront us with an accomplished fact which would deter our intervention. Second, this strategy recognizes that we have options for fighting on other fronts and for building up allied strength that would lead to consequences unacceptable to the Soviet Union." (Weinberger 1982:I-14)

American officials are aware that "as a result of... Soviet gains, the demands on our projection forces are greater today than ever before", especially with regard to the simultaneous dispatch of forces to any number of regions around the world (Weinberger 1984:173). In the American conception, the strategy of power projection necessitates naval superiority or at least "an essential margin of clear maritime superiority" (United States Military Posture for FY 1983:49f.; Hearings HASC 1981, part 1:1344).

In Secretary of Navy Lehman's terms and restating this issue quite bluntly:

"America must regain that condition which through history has been seen as indispensable to any maritime nation's survival: command of the seas, an uncomplex term." (Hearings HASC 1982, part 1:553)

Finally, and going beyond a purely force-oriented approach, American officials increasingly draw attention to the ideological dimension of the struggle between East and West. As one of them suggested, it is not only power that impresses the Soviet leaders; in addition, one should also engage in ideological battle. Some speeches by President Reagan also point in this direction. Ultimately, therefore, American officials perceive the United States strategy to cope with the Soviet challenge as both a test of force and a test of legitimacy.

169

Elements of nuclear policy and strategy: deterring any attack and warfighting in case deterrence fails

The conception of nuclear forces in American security policy clearly centers around the idea of deterrence. Again and again, American sources emphasize that United States nuclear forces serve first and foremost to deter a Soviet nuclear attack. While stressing that in this context the United States is not interested in achieving nuclear superiority, it is said that it will make every necessary effort to prevent the Soviet Union from acquiring such superiority and to "insure the margin of safety necessary for our security" (Weinberger 1982:I-17).

Yet they also conceive of this simple deterrence posture being increased by the threat of escalation. American nuclear weapons also serve the purpose of signalling to the potential adversary "that there is a good chance that, if they <the Soviets> attack the West, it may escalate to theater and then to strategic nuclear weapons". In other words, the United States wants to keep the Soviet leaders uncertain as to the type and degree of escalation (General David C. Jones, Chairman, Joint Chiefs of Staff, in: Hearings HASC 1981, part 1:230). The American Government wishes to have the options available to escalate any conflict by its own choosing - and through this very prospect deterring any Soviet attack (United States Military Posture for FY 1982:vi). Such a reinforced deterrent is held to be particularly enhanced by coupling conventional forces to Theater Nuclear Forces (TNF), which contribute to deterrence by creating uncertainty for the aggressor concerning United States and allied responses (United States Military Posture for FY 1983:27). This philosophy of "escalation dominance" constitutes the essence of NATO's strategic doctrine of "flexible response". It also implies the first-use of nuclear weapons should Western conventional defence be unable to withstand a massive attack by the Warsaw Pact forces.

However, official American strategists are aware that the loss of United States strategic nuclear superiority has led to increased uncertainty about United States capabilities to deter both nuclear and non-nuclear conflict. In this connection the Statement on US Military Posture for FY 1983 (p. 26) concludes:

"The relative decline in US strategic and theater nuclear capabilities has reduced the ability of the United States to deter or control lower level conflicts by the threat of nuclear escalation. To enhance the deterrence of both non-nuclear and nuclear conflict, the United States must modernize the strategic TRIAD and associated C^3 systems and upgrade homeland defense capabilities. A sustained commitment is required to correct asymmetries in the strategic balance and create a more stable and secure deterrent."

The American "TRIAD" concept comprises a set of forces that is assumed to be capable of withstanding and responding to a wide range of threats and uncertainties; it consists of submarine-launched ballistic missiles (SLBMs), land-based intercontinental ballistic missiles (ICBMs) and the "bomber leg" which includes cruise missiles and supporting tankers. These three "legs" of the strategic TRIAD are designed to be capable of surviving a pre-emptive first strike with a credible counterstrike capability of such magnitude as to deny the Soviets a favourable strategic outcome (General Kelly H. Burke, Deputy Chief of Staff, United States Air Force, in: Hearings HASC 1981, part 4:375). The diversity offered by the TRIAD serves five objectives: it prevents concentration of Soviet resources, complicates Soviet attack planning, hedges against system failure, compensates for Soviet technology breakthrough and is mutually reinforcing (Weinberger 1984:30).

American sources suggest "stability" to be the key criterion for assessing the state of nuclear deterrence. Stability, first of all, requires survivability and endurance of United States strategic forces and C3I systems. As far as ICBMs are concerned, the invulnerability of the land-based "leg" of the American deterrent is felt to be declining. Therefore, the modernization of the bomber element of the strategic TRIAD is held necessary for making the deterrent more secure and stable (FY 1983 Arms Control Impact Statements:XV; Weinberger 1984:56). A similar impact is also expected from the development and deployment of the new MX missiles; as these missiles will primarily threaten Soviet SS-18 and SS-19 ICBMs, which are charged with being mainly responsible for the imbalance in prompt hard-target-kill capability, MX deployment is hoped to provide incentive for the Soviet effort to lessen the vulnerability of their land-based ICBMs (ibid.:XII). Also air-launched cruise missiles (ALCMs) are thought to be conducive to the cause of stability and invulnerability, since the bombers and ALCMs take at least several hours after take-off to deliver their weapons on target and hence are not perceived as a first strike threat against the Soviet Union while still enhancing deterrence by their considerable retaliatory capacity (ibid.:XV). Accordingly, the SLBM systems are also assessed to be very helpful for the further stabilization of the United States deterrent because, while at sea, they are highly survivable (ibid.:XIV). An identical impact is also ascribed to sea-launched cruise missiles (SLCMs) because the variety and number of potential available launch platforms complicate Soviet targeting problems (ibid.:XVIIIf.; Weinberger 1984:56f.). In summary, as Secretary of Defense Weinberger pointed out, the objective of nuclear forces is to survive and, if necessary, to be effectively employed - thus deterring any enemy attack:

"Survivability of our Intercontinental Ballistic Missile (ICBM) force and the readiness and responsiveness of the sea- and air-based legs of the TRIAD are critical to the maintenance of an adequate deterrent posture in the near term. The objective is to survive and, subsequently, to be effectively employed through all phases of a conflict." (Weinberger 1982:III-127)

171

The last point - effectively employing nuclear forces in case deterrence fails - is much more than a marginal afterthought about the unthinkable. American sources indicate quite explicitly that the United States leaders have clear ideas about and pay a lot of attention to the contingency of nuclear war-fighting. This is, in Secretary of Defense Weinberger's terms, the offensive tactical element in an otherwise strictly defensive United States policy (Weinberger 1982:I-11). Weinberger therefore prefers the notion of "counteroffensive":

"Strategic planning for counteroffensive is not provocative. It is likely to increase the caution of the Soviet leaders in deciding on aggression, because they will understand that if they unleash a conventional war, they are placing a wide range of their assets - both military and political at risk." (Weinberger 1982:I-16)

In more systematic terms, therefore, American strategy incorporates three main principles as summed up by Secretary of Defense Weinberger:

"- First, our strategy is defensive. It excludes the possibility that the United States would initiate a war or launch a pre-emptive strike against the forces or territories of other nations.
- Second, our strategy is to deter war. The deterrent nature of our strategy is closely related to our defensive stance. We maintain a nuclear and conventional force posture designed to convince any potential adversary that the cost of aggression would be too high to justify an attack.
- Third, should deterrence fail, our strategy is to restore peace on favorable terms. In responding to an enemy attack, we must defeat the attack and achieve our national objectives while limiting - to the extent possible and practicable - the scope of the conflict. We would seek to deny the enemy his political and military goals and to counterattack with sufficient strength to terminate hostilities at the lowest possible level of damage to the United States and its allies." (Weinberger 1983:33).

In other words, the United States leadership views nuclear weapons first as a deterrent and second as a means of controlling escalation (Sollinger 1983:7). According to American sources, limiting a nuclear conflict implies three principles: firstly, it means limiting the scope of a conflict, i.e. "to deter the Soviets from exploiting their global capability"; secondly, it requires limitation of the duration of a conflict; and thirdly, the United States wants to limit the intensity of a conflict by "employing forces that do not require escalating the conflict to new dimensions of warfare" (Weinberger 1984:38).

In more operational terms, American nuclear war-fighting strategy is outlined in Presidential Directive No. 59 signed by President Carter on 25 July 1980, which continues to be valid. The essentials of this document, although classified, have been made public in several authoritative statements and testimonies. It codifies the movement away from a primarily countervalue, assured destruction policy towards one of greater flexibility, combining countervalue and counterforce capability into what is now called a "countervailing" strategy, i.e. a kind of nuclear tit-for-tat strategy that would make any attack against the United States and its interests clearly incompatible with any expectable gains:

> "The fundamental objective of the countervailing strategy outlined in Presidential Directive 59 remains deterrence. But it is deterrence achieved through a flexible and enduring force capable of responding appropriately to every level of violence. We must insure that any potential adversary understands fully that no plausible outcome of a nuclear exchange would represent victory by any reasonable definition of that term. If deterrence fails we want to preserve the possibility of bargaining effectively to terminate the war on acceptable terms that are as favorable as practicable with minimum damage to the United States and her allies. To that end PD-59 requires that we be capable of fighting successfully so that an enemy would not achieve his war aims, and would consistently lose more than he would gain from initiating a nuclear attack. It is felt that the ability to deny an enemy his objectives, underpinned by a survivable and enduring capability to execute the ultimate response of punishment by large scale destruction of his urban and economic structure, constitute a more credible deterrent strategy than an assured destruction strategy alone." (Rear Admiral Powell Carter, Director, Strategic and Nuclear Warfare Division, in: Hearings HASC 1981, part 3:127f.)

Indications are also available regarding the types of targets which the American political and military leaders have in mind when they refer to the option for more selective, lesser retaliatory attacks: it is envisaged, in such a case, to attack those things which "the Soviet leadership prizes most - political and military control, nuclear and conventional military force, and the economic base needed to sustain a war" (Brown 1980:40). However, the meaning of countervailing strategy is not merely punishment or revenge; again, emphasis is put on deterrence - even if deterrence had failed. In this latter contingency, it is intended to deter the adversary from further pursuing his goals and to create leverage that induces him to compromise and to seek a cessation of the armed conflict (ibid.:40).

In this context, United States sources increasingly emphasize the need to lessen dependence on nuclear weapons (Weinberger 1983:53) which, should war break out, would also limit the intensity of conflict. This is the rationale behind the present exploration, together with NATO allies, of ways to take full advantage of new techniques and technologies to improve conventional defence (ibid.:35).

In more general terms, this approach means that any "simplistic concept of deterrence" would be futile because, if it fails, the consequence would be catastrophic. The actual United States deterrence posture is aptly called "a multiple-barrier deterrent" aimed at limiting damage in case deterrence fails (Donald H. Latham, Deputy Under-Secretary for C3I, Department of Defense, in: Hearings HASC 1982, part 5:1107). This also implies a rejection of what Secretary of Defense Weinberger calls the "short-war assumption" (ibid.: part 1:7).

Thinking along these lines leads American strategists to examine, in addition, scenarios of nuclear blackmail to which the United States might be exposed. The scenario (which is sometimes called the scenario of "self-deterrence") is described in the following terms:

"Soviet military writings demonstrate a belief that nuclear conflict could begin with a series of limited strikes and counterstrikes against military targets, such as missile silos or command bunkers, most of which are heavily hardened against nuclear attack. Those advocating a strengthening of United States capabilities to wage a nuclear war of this type argue that a president faced with a limited strike against a few military targets might not be willing to unleash a massive US counterattack knowing that it would call forth a similar massive response from the Soviets. If the Soviets were to believe that the United States would be so paralyzed, they might not be deterred from launching a limited strike." (Congressional Budget Office 1983:14f.)

In order to cope with this risk, American nuclear doctrine emphasizes the need for a choice of ways to respond to a limited strike while also maintaining the capability for a massive strike, such as the increase of the number of targets in the Soviet Union (at present over 40,000) and the creation of new attack strategies that have the capability of being employed over a protracted period of time in many and highly selective attack options (ibid.:15).

American strategic doctrine always stresses the crucial importance of perceptions held by the adversary. As former Secretary of Defense Brown puts it, "the countervailing strategy is designed with the Soviets in mind" (Brown 1981:38). However, it is clear that any conjecture about these perceptions ultimately rests on assumptions and insoluble judgement. This has been expressed by Brown in words that could not characterize better the very issue of the present study:

"Because it is designed to deter the Soviets, our strategic doctrine must take account of what we know about Soviet perspectives on these issues, for, by definition, deterrence requires shaping Soviet assessments about the risks of war-assessments they will make using their models, not ours. We must confront these views and take them into account in our planning. We may, and we do, think our models are more accurate, but theirs are the reality deterrence drives us to consider." (Brown 1981:38)

This statement precisely and pointedly establishes a linkage between one's own assumptions and guesses about the adversary's views, on the one hand, and the evolution of strategic doctrine and deployment of strategic forces suitable for dealing with this adversary, on the other hand. It lucidly reveals the dilemma of conflictive cognition.

Summing up the main elements of American nuclear strategy, one might envisage four major functions which, according to Secretary of Defense Weinberger, United States strategic forces have to fulfil:

"(1) to deter nuclear attack on the United States or its allies; (2) to help deter major conventional attack against United States forces and our allies, especially in NATO; (3) to impose termination of a major war - on terms favorable to the United States and our allies - even if nuclear weapons have been used - and in particular to deter escalation in the level of hostilities; and (4) to negate possible Soviet nuclear blackmail against the United States or our allies." (Weinberger 1982:I-18)

Again and again, American officials emphasize that, in their view:

"There is no contradiction between deterrence of war and planning to employ nuclear weapons to deny victory to the Soviets if deterrence fails... It should be apparent that, if our forces cannot be used effectively, if necessary, neither can they credibly deter." (Weinberger/Draper 1983, letter of 20 May 1983)

This is how United States nuclear doctrine is expected to be perceived by the adversary as the primary addressee. Hence it is up to the adversary to decide whether or not the assumptions underlying this fourfold strategy are correct. Such considerations obviously imply a degree of uncertainty. It is increasingly felt that the whole policy and strategy of deterrence may not be as satisfactory in the long run as one might have wished. After all, ultimately deterrence means threatening to revenge an attack by retaliation; however, as one might argue, once deterrence fails it may not seem rational to kill the attacker's population and destroy his cities, for that will no longer alter one's own fate. On the basis of these very fundamental second-thoughts about the meaning of deterrence, President Reagan, in March 1983, suggested that a completely different approach should be studied:

"Would it not be better to save lives than to avenge them? Are we not capable of demonstrating our peaceful intentions by applying all our abilities and all our ingenuity to achieving a truly lasting stability?... It is that we embark on a program to counter the awesome Soviet missile threat with measures that are defensive." (Reagan, quoted in Weinberger 1983a:4)

He suggested a defence against ballistic missiles that eliminate the danger of a disarming first strike, i.e. a reliable strategic defence based on a multi-layered system which would not have to be nuclear, but which could detect and destroy thousands of incoming Soviet missiles and "would lift the cloud of terror which has hung over us since the beginning of the nuclear age" (ibid.). If this project were to become reality, this would mean that "the United States concept of deterrence could shift toward the ability to defend against attack and away from total reliance on the ability to retaliate" (United States Military Posture for FY 1985:33). However, the American Administration realizes that major research efforts will be required because numerous complex technical problems must be overcome. Nevertheless an effective defence against ballistic missiles is held to be potentially feasible (Weinberger 1984:193).

Promoting arms control by leverage

When talking about arms control policies, American sources never fail to emphasize that arms control is not an end in itself but serves United States security by redressing the military imbalance while simultaneously reducing costs (United States Military Posture for FY 1983:68).

Arms control is therefore conceived as one element of a comprehensive security policy. There seems to be a shift, at least in nuances, of the rationale of arms control from the Carter Administration to the Reagan Administration. While statements made by spokesmen of the Reagan Administration start from the intention to "reduce the imbalance", the Carter Administration felt satisfied with the principle of "maintaining essential equivalence in the future" (Brown 1981:5). However, both Administrations agree that arms control must not be considered as a substitute for force modernization and military power (ibid.:27f.; United States Military Posture for FY 1983:68). Still, to both Administrations arms control does seem to be a suitable means for diminishing the risks of war and for helping to reduce the threat to American security (Weinberger 1982:1-21) by limiting the Soviet threat and making it more predictable (Brown 1981:V).

Another criterion used for assessing the suitability of arms control policies is, not surprisingly, the issue of stability. Secretary of Defense Brown (1981:59) suggested that arms control agreements "can contribute to stability by foreclosing competition in certain potentially destabilizing areas and by channeling competition into less destabilizing directions". When talking about stability, it is clear to American spokesmen that what counts in arms control is "to create a more stable nuclear balance at lower levels of armament" (United States Military Posture for FY 1985:8).

When thinking about strategic stability, the issue of perceived vulnerability is held to be absolutely central as "the existence of survivable, secure United States retaliatory capabilities will enhance strategic stability" (FY 1983 Arms Control Impact Statements:VII). In more general terms American sources also talk about "crisis stability" which is also said to be a function of the survivability of retaliatory systems (ibid.:IX). American officials are aware that their preference for stability is not shared by their Soviet adversary, who prefers the concept of parity to be the key issue in arms control. They are also aware that there is little hope of "teaching" the Soviet Union the merits of stability; the latter would always reject this idea.

Apart from enhancing security and stability, arms control, according to American official sources, must also serve the objective of limiting the horrors of war should war break out, lessening political tensions, and reducing the economic burden of armaments (Security and Arms Control 1983:13f.). For arms control to meet the four objectives, agreements must be based on four criteria:

> "Security. Arms control agreements cannot be considered in isolation as ends in themselves. Their priority objective is to enhance the security of all parties. Although such agreements may contribute to reduce tension and greater international understanding, those effects, desirable as they may be, should not replace enhanced security as the benchmark for judging arms control... Arms control should achieve a significant lowering of the level of current forces.
>
> Equality. Arms control agreements should bring about mutual reductions to equal levels in the important measures of military capability...
>
> Militarily Significant Reductions. To enhance security, arms control agreements should actually constrain the military capability or potential of the parties. Agreements providing only promises or statements of intent, without constraining the parties' ability to undertake military action, are of illusory benefit and can be destabilizing...
>
> Verifiability and Compliance. Since arms control agreements are directly related to the security of participants, it is vital that they incorporate measures to permit effective verification and ensure compliance by all parties. Without such provisions, agreements can be circumvented and endanger the security of participants. Experience has shown that accords lacking adequate provisions for verification and compliance become a source of suspicion, tension and distrust, rather than reinforcing the prospects for peace." (Security and Arms Control 1983:13f.)

In this context the problem arises how the Soviet Union has to be approached and how negotiations have to be conducted in order to achieve agreements corresponding to these four criteria. American officials stress the importance of a sober approach; this in turn implies first of all, a clear statement of principles of what one wishes to achieve and what one wants to preserve in terms of essential arms systems.

Secondly, they hold that the Soviets must by prevented from influencing or controlling the public debate in the West. American negotiators are aware that this is no easy task in a democracy where the government must constantly spend energy in order to maintain public support.

Most importantly, however, American officials start from the assumption that their Soviet counterparts in arms control negotiations are skilled professionals and smart and tough negotiators who cannot be fooled and from whom nothing can be extorted. This means that, according to American officials, an agreement is feasible only if the situation is favourable, i.e. balanced. Speculating on "Russian psychology" is considered to be an idle task. Yet they think that one should make efforts to demonstrate to Soviet negotiators that the solution offered fits into the overall structure of their approach - only if this condition is fulfilled (provided of course it also corresponds to the American national interest), can they be expected to be comfortable with the solution, and then they will become co-operative.

Finally, a high degree of prudence and thoroughness is recommended in order to arrive at an agreement that is really meaningful, concrete and verifiable - which means one without any loopholes. This aspect is believed to be important also with regard to the American public and Congress, which will scrutinize carefully any agreement before ratification and will no longer accept any agreement raising the slightest doubt about its fulfilling the basic requirements to be expected from substantive arms control. Increasingly, American officials draw attention to the need to strive for greater specificity of the provisions to be agreed upon.

The main problem is seen in the necessity of offering the Soviet Union the proper incentives to enter into meaningful negotiations on arms control treaties. In this respect the concern about creating incentives by going ahead with new American arms projects can be said to constitute a kind of standard theme in official American statements on this subject (cf. for instance FY 1984 Arms Control Impact Statements: XI, XIV, XV, XVIII). To United States decision-makers it is clear that the adversary would not be willing to make any moves towards progress in the field of arms control unless forced to do so by appropriate United States leverage; this has been amply demonstrated above in connection with the American perception of Soviet arms control policy.

Most fundamentally, this means denying the Soviet Union any advantage through the use of force - "only through demonstrated commitment on one part to denying the Soviet Union such advantage may we hope to bring them to the negotiating table for serious arms reductions" (Soviet Military Power 1984:136). According to Secretary of State Shultz, "it is the fact that we are strong that gives us a chance to deal effectively with the Soviet Union" (Shultz 1984) - or simply "peace through strength", as President Reagan put it (Reagan 1983b). The precise operational implication to be deduced from those perceptions and assumptions can be found in a combination of the negotiation process taking place on the diplomatic level with more or less substantive hints regarding the possible use of the "stick". That is why, for instance, the impact of the new "Tomahawk" cruise missile is assessed with the explicit idea in mind of creating leverage:

"The cruise missile represents a potent nuclear system which is highly mobile and difficult to detect. From the Soviet perspective, the problem is compounded by the fact that Tomahawk cruise missiles will be deployed on many different platforms, thereby making it difficult to negate United States retaliatory capabilities. Thus, the Soviets could become more willing to engage in substantive arms control negotiations which could limit such systems." (FY 1984 Arms Control Impact Statements:XIX)

The assumption expressed here seems to constitute a continuing element of the United States negotiation posture equally applicable to any field of arms control, including negotiations on intermediate-range nuclear forces in Europe; this has been summed up already in 1979 by Secretary of State Cyrus Vance:

"The West must demonstrate its seriousness about modernization - or the Soviets will have no visible incentive to negotiate reductions in forces." (Vance, quoted in Vigeveno 1983:93)

The least that has to be done in this connection is not to engage in a unilateral freeze at current levels of weapons that would "remove any incentives for the Soviets to negotiate seriously in Geneva" (Reagan 1983b:56).

Similarly, the idea of creating leverage for reaching arms control agreements is made explicit in the context of negotiations on banning chemical weapons (CW). According to President Ronald Reagan, "the production of lethal binary chemical munitions is essential to the national interest" because "this step will provide strong leverage towards negotiating a verifiable agreement" (letter of 8 February 1982, in: Hearings HASC 1982, part 5:845; United States Military Posture for 1985:63).

The same line of reasoning also applies to the post-agreement phase: once an agreement on arms control has been signed, it is supposed that the Soviet Union will respect it only to the extent that it feels discouraged from break-out (ibid.:XVII). Verification measures alone are not held to ensure that treaties are respected

(Weinberger 1984:34). The best hedge reinsuring against such break-out is again leverage - or more precisely the threat of retaliation. Such is the rationale underlying United States declaratory policy in the field of chemical weapons:

> "Our CW programs are designed to provide a credible deterrent to the use of chemicals by a potential enemy. The purpose is to make it less likely that the Soviet Union would initiate first use of chemical weapons in violation of the long-standing international treaty." (Weinberger 1982:III-148)

In more general terms, American decision-makers assume that "success in arms reduction depends on a sustained commitment to improving our force posture" (Weinberger 1983:40). Still, they insist on not confusing this will to persevere with policies of "bargaining chips", which is outrightly rejected as an "absurd procedure":

> "We need to emphasize that this Administration is not developing the Peacekeeper (MX) or any other weapon as a 'bargaining chip'. In its current loose usage, the term 'bargaining chip' weapon has come to mean a weapon that is developed - often at great cost - for the sole purpose of then negotiating away that very weapon. That, obviously, would be an absurd procedure.

> What is true, however, is that arms control negotiations must reflect the balance of power, including the forthcoming power obtainable from weapons under development. To the extent that we do make progress in modernizing our forces, the Soviet Union has a stronger incentive to negotiate in good faith, and we thus have a better opportunity to reach agreement on the control of arms." (Weinberger 1983:57f.)

Of course, in this connection a question may arise as to how much is enough, for too much emphasis on strength may lead Soviet negotiators to believe that the United States is not really interested in serious negotiations. American officials are aware of this problem; yet they trust that the Soviet leaders will always have a precise idea to what extent the United States really wants to negotiate. But American negotiators do concede that one has to find a "middle line" in dealing with Soviet partners - i.e. neither acknowledging too much, which may be misunderstood as a concession of weakness, nor humiliating and insulting them with careless use of strength, and the attempt to outbid them, which would simply lead them to vigorous withdrawal given their extreme sensitivity regarding status.

CHAPTER IV

THE AMERICAN VIEW
A SURVEY OF THE ACADEMIC LITERATURE

REMARKS ON THE WESTERN ACADEMIC DEBATE
ON THE SOVIET UNION

The literature published by American and other Western students of the Soviet Union, not surprisingly, offers an overwhelming variety of views and assessments. As a "cast of thousands" participates in the strategic and political debate (Carter 1978:21), there is virtually no conceivable point of view that does not occur somewhere. An American author inquiring into appraisals of American images of Soviet foreign policy (Welch 1970) and thereby examining a sample of 22 leading works written by academic experts suggests a two-dimensional typology for grasping the variety of use: in the first dimension it is possible to distinguish the various views according to the "hardness" they ascribe to the Soviet conduct of foreign affairs, while the second dimension refers to the perceived consistency in this conduct over time. Thus the views identified range from "infinitely expansion-minded" to "moderately hegemonic" with images suggesting the Soviet Union to be "driven by ambition tinged with fear" somewhere in between (ibid: 56).

Given this variety of images it goes without saying that Western literature on the Soviet Union is highly controversial, featuring diverse "schools of thought" with more or less irreconcilable views. Sometimes, these different approaches are confronted in rather radical terms. One author even talks about "quotation mongering", i.e. "selectively quoting Soviet sources to bolster an interpretation based upon prior conceptions of Soviet behaviour" (Dallin, quoted in Potter 1980:71). Undoubtedly, one of the decisive reasons for disagreement in the assessment of Soviet policies can be seen in basic assumptions held by the respective authors. This was demonstrated by the CIA's "Team B" exercise: in 1976, the CIA appointed a "Team B" of private analysts known for their pessimistic views of Soviet intentions and capabilities to review the same raw intelligence data used by the CIA's "Team A"; not surprisingly, "Team B" took a much darker view of the Soviet Union (Wells 1981:66).

"Liberal" American authors do not hesitate to argue that "US perceptions of hostile Soviet intentions have increased, not when the Russians have become more aggressive or militaristic, but when certain constellations of political forces have come together within the United States to force the question of the Soviet threat onto the American political agenda" (Wolfe 1979:2) - i.e. for purely domestic reasons. Irrespective of whether or not this contention can really be corroborated in any case, it might of course as well be argued that such "liberal" positions are probably not less determined by domestic considerations than the "conservative" views they accuse of being inaccurate. More often than not they seem to be shaped by the desire to avoid any association with right-wing movements and by the difficulty of combining domestic social criticism with a critical stand toward the shortcomings of other societies (cf. Hollander, quoted in Anschel 1978:348f.).

Ultimately perceptions of the Soviet Union are not shaped only by the amount of information available but also by the conceptual frameworks used. As one American analyst notes, "Western scholars gather a plethora of detail into their analytical baskets while the synthesizing insight seems to be lacking to put detail about the current Soviet social forces comprehensively together" (Dunham in: Perceptions 1979:43). One feels tempted to add: more often than not such "synthesizing insights" are fully present, but in a too overwhelming and prepotent fashion.

Apart from basic attitudes shaping Western views of the Soviet Union, the instability of these views constitutes another reason for the high degree of variation to be discerned in the debate among Western academic analysts. The very nature of the Western academic debate calls for innovation, and this means that the views never cease to be in flux. One Western expert even argues that while Soviet objectives have always remained constant, Western attitudes have only alternated by varying between overemphasis and underemphasis on the threatening nature of Soviet objectives (Nye 1982:225). Still, one might object to this thesis by pointing to the tendency towards repetitions of previous views and theories, as an analyst put it with regard to the debate about the policy of containment which he finds "little more than reruns of those between George Kennan and Paul Nitze three decades ago" (Gaddis 1982:354).

As it is not the purpose of the present study to present a full picture of American, and more generally, Western "Sovietology" or "Kremlinology", the following sections refer only to those aspects of the academic debate which have an immediate relevance for the specific problems listed under heading 2 in the "checklist" in chapter I (see above p. 15). In other words, the present chapter will not be dealing comprehensively with the various issues of conflictive cognition but will concentrate on the assumptions regarding the potential adversary more restrictively, thereby trying to expound the diverging views to be identified in the literature. As pointed out above, the rationale for this chapter must be seen in the potential influence these views exert on the official view(s) held in Washington.

It is quite another matter, however, to determine the relative weight these academic contributions have in shaping the official attitude; no attempt will be made therefore to make conjectures on this relationship. Some doubts are certainly appropriate, considering the fact that, as an American observer laments, "American national security policy tends typically to be dominated by people who truly are experts only in inappropriate American domestic matters" and "the 'best and the brightest' of the American educational process tend to be almost heroically ill-equipped to cope with the Soviet Union" (Gray 1981:46).

Yet the various views expressed in the academic debate in the West do deserve examination because they are constantly at the disposal of the decision-makers for whose attention they compete. Whatever their impact, they are there. It would be quite presumptuous to surmise that their influence is negligible or nil - it certainly is greater than that.

Furthermore, it must not be forgotten that Soviet experts, in particular the more than 700 persons working at the Moscow USA-Institute, carefully and critically study the Western debate, and they are very familiar with the various views published in the West. Hence these views may be said also to condition - although in a manner different from the United States and to a limited extent only - the views and assumptions held by Soviet experts and policy advisers, and implicitly, the views of Soviet authorities.

THE NATURE OF SOVIET AIMS IN WORLD POLITICS: STRUGGLE FOR VICTORY?

In search of a typology

When inquiring into the American perception of the Soviet Union and the ultimate aims underlying its foreign policy and strategy one has to bear in mind that in any culture there is a tendency to perceive things in terms of prior experience. As suggested by Bialer (1981:434) "the terminology applied and the imagery evoked in the American discourse on Soviet foreign policy more often than not duplicate the terminology and imagery of the Nazi expansion in the pre-World War II period". Of course, such an approach must be said to be quite misleading. It seems appropriate therefore to concentrate upon those approaches which do not propose any single predominant aim to determine Soviet policy but which perceive a multitude of trends and tendencies.

That implies some reservations with regard to those analyses of Soviet aims that are ultimately rooted in American domestic political preferences and lead to either "left of the centre views" or "views to the right of the political spectrum": According to the first, the Soviet Union is a status quo Power decreasingly motivated by a revolutionary or missionary ideology and committed to détente; according to the second view it is an expansionist, imperial Power (Foster 1979). Most American experts can in fact be said to adhere to views that fall between these two extreme images or combine aspects of both (ibid.; Hyland 1982a: 52), while it seems that the American mass media disseminate the view that the Soviet Union is an inherently "mature" industrial society, motivated by "post-revolutionary" values and primarily interested in providing more freedoms and more material satisfaction to its citizens (Hollander, quoted in Anschel 1978: 351f.).

An interesting typology of Soviet aims has been suggested by Strode/Strode (1983:107), who distinguish two divergent policy tendencies or national security approaches competing in the Soviet Union; they might be characterized as "diplomacist" and "unilateralist":

"Diplomacists' believe that, in the nuclear age, the USSR cannot secure its national security and foreign policy objectives without some degree of cooperation with the West. 'Unilateralists', on the other hand, believe that détente has run its course, and that Soviet diplomatic and arms control efforts can no longer hope to secure US acquiescence in Soviet attempts to shift the correlation of forces further to the Soviet advantage." (Strode/Strode 1983: 107f.)

According to these authors the utility of diplomacist or unilateralist policies in the estimation of the Soviet leadership is enhanced or reduced by the global political and strategic environment.

Another author prefers to distinguish four main tendencies, calling them "sectarian, activist, reformative and properly reformist" (Bialer 1981: 41), which he sees to coexist uneasily in Soviet foreign conduct. Depending on the external environment and developments within the USSR, these four tendencies are assumed to produce changes in inflection and sometimes mark shifts of emphasis and mood in Soviet behaviour, thus producing a Soviet foreign policy which is not unilinear as far as its underlying aims are concerned (ibid.: 41).

These and other sophisticated approaches seem increasingly to replace the more "unidimensional" approaches which, for example, start from the assumption that the Soviet Union is envisaging an attack on Western Europe, thus bringing about a total change in the 1945 settlement and in the global balance of power (Huntington 1983).

The Soviet claim for "world revolution"

However, in this connection the question arises as to the existence of any more stable aims determining Soviet foreign policy. Assumptions regarding the existence of a Soviet master plan in the sense of a step-by-step blueprint for world conquest are no longer held valid (Mitchell 1982:118). According to MccGwire (1981a: 218) the Soviet Union's behaviour is constantly shaped by two sets of objectives. The first focuses on "extirpating the capitalist system", the second on "preserving the socialist system". Of course, the first objective is made relative and restricted by the second, which, in turn, calls for caution irrespective of the paramount importance of the primary goal.

As far as the first objective is concerned, it is surmised that "the Soviets apparently consider themselves increasingly at liberty to pursue an active foreign policy supportive of the inevitable 're-volutionary process'" (Payne 1981: 6). The Soviet Union is criticized for allowing itself a "dynamic licence potential" for interventions abroad whenever an opportunity arises which seems to be fit for such a practical pursuit of its primary objective (Jacobsen 1979: 31-34). Stability in major Power relationships, let alone any form of "hope for cooperative US/Soviet condominium of a stable world order" (Payne 1981: 20; Ermarth 1981: 58f.) is therefore not believed to be acceptable to Soviet leadership. Some Western experts conclude that the Soviet "game... is by definition a zero-sum game, to be won without fighting and preferably through 'negotiations'" (Young/Young 1980: 16; cf. also Mitchell 1982: 131).

This also means that neither a true and lasting coexistence of the two social systems is feasible from a Soviet point of view, nor can mutual tolerance be desirable. The ultimate aim always was and continues to be victory - Western observers like to refer to Lenin's dictum "Kto-kogo? Who Whom?" (Dirnecker 1981: 11). Of course such a world view also implies that there are no "neutral areas", i.e. the world being a zero-sum world is perceived as a purely dichotomous structure (Deane 1978: 76f.). The Soviet view of the world as a continual situation of conflict and war determines the broad framework or "prism" through which the Soviet leaders identify foreign policy objectives (Shultz/Godson 1984: 9).

This view is assumed to have two practical implications: the first is the claim to ensure the "irreversibility of Soviet authority defined as 'socialist gains' in its own sphere" (Gelman 1981: 11); the second is "the legitimacy of the Politbureau's intention to make incremental use of emerging opportunities and capabilities" (ibid.: 12). Even in cases where there is no Soviet victory but only an American mishap or loss or defeat - such as the fall of Emperor Haile Selassie and the Shah of Iran, the loss of Vietnam, problems due to OPEC's policies after 1973 and the like - even then the zero-sum perspective leads Soviet obervers to a positive evaluation of any such event, due to its assessment within the framework of the correlation of forces theory (Gelman 1982:92f.). As one American analyst puts it:

"Every loss by the capitalist side is seen as a positive gain from the communist side, and every capitalist achievement is considered a net loss for communism." (Deane 1978: 75).

Western European students of the Soviet system tend to highlight the Soviet claim for a world-wide, global change, i.e. "world revolution". At the same time, however, they express doubts as to the seriousness with which the CPSU leadership still believes in the feasibility of this ultimate aim. Yet they suggest that at least world hegemony, i.e. a global predominance of the Soviet Union, is still considered to be a viable and realistic goal pursued by Soviet leaders (Meissner 1982: 8). That means that the ultimate aims underlying Soviet foreign policy and strategy are not simply a continuation of Tsarist traditions (ibid.).

In this connection, Western analysts sometimes also refer to a (non-identified) confidential source according to which General Secretary Brezhnev is supposed to have defined "peaceful coexistence" as "a ruse to enable the Soviet Union to increase its military and economic power to such an extent as to achieve a decisive change in the correlation of forces by 1985 and to have its intentions implemented whenever she might wish to do so" (Gray/Brennan 1982: 519). As Hosmer/Wolfe (1983: 161) argue, the practical implications of this new constellation may materialize soon in the third world; as it seems that the Soviet leaders find the benefits of the Afghanistan invasion worth the costs, they will probably be less dipsosed than before to stand by until coups materialize spontaneously and rather more tempted to stimulate them artificially whitin the geographic range of effective Soviet power-projection capabilities.

Changing the "correlation of forces"

Irrespective of these and other interpretations and extrapolations, Western academics specializing in Soviet affairs seem to be generally aware of the specific meaning of the Soviet concept of the "correlation of forces". In particular, they express full knowledge of the fact that this concept is not identical with the Western concept of "balance of power" (Gibert 1977: 23). They are cognizant also of the multidimensional nature of this concept, which comprises military, economic and other elements - the "military factor", however, being the decisive one (Deane 1978: 75f.; Millet 1981:4f). Soviet sources are quoted which propose that the progress of socialism has been feasible thanks to the military might of the Soviet Union, which allegedly has also been the decisive factor in the success of "national liberation" movements (Deane 1978: 78f.). As far as the non-military factors of the "correlation of forces" are concerned, Western authors are aware of their importance, especially with regard to their promotion by Soviet "active measures" such as propaganda and other types of political warfare, e.g. disinformation, the use of front organizations, the sponsorship of clandestine radio broadcasts, and the conduct of agent-of-influence operations (Shultz/Godson 1984: 10-17).

Western analysts also point to the Soviet emphasis on the necessity of a constant shift in the "correlation of forces" in favour of socialism (cf. Lider 1981: 212-218; Mitchell 1982: 119; Becker 1982: 55). A crucial element in Soviet theory to which Western scholars explicitly refer is the view that "the object of Soviet policy is to further the movement of the correlation of forces towards socialism, not to maintain a balance of power between socialism and capitalism" (Holloway 1983: 82). In other words, the concept of "correlation of forces" is interpreted as a voluntaristic concept (Osadczuk-Korab 1983: 171), ultimately aimed at military superiority, not parity with the United States. Similarly, "essential equivalence" may not constitute a desirable purpose, and any idea of "equilibrium" in the Western sense seems to rank very low on the Soviet agenda and may not even be taken into consideration at all (Erickson, quoted by Gray/Brennan 1982: 518). Moreover, the attempt made by the United States "to reverse the correlation of forces" is vigorously condemned by Soviet spokesmen - American analysts are also acquainted with this variation of the theme (Gelman 1982: 89f.).

Similar thoughts are offered about the Soviet assumption that the

188

"imperialist camp" has to restrain its aggressive drive because the change of the correlation of forces compelled the "ruling circles" in the United States to revise their foreign policy and military concepts and accept the "sobering influence" of the newly achieved parity (Deane 1978: 76f.). Western analysts draw attention to the close causal relationship that exists, in the Soviet view, between the concepts of "change of the correlation of forces" and "peaceful coexistence", and they warn the Western public of not rejecting as a paradox what in Marxist-Leninist thought simply represents flawless logic: "As peaceful coexistence comes to be the accepted norm of superpower competition, so it becomes even more necessary to increase the strengh of Soviet military forces". (Gibert 1977: 125)

Comparing Western academic reflections on the Soviet Union with the views expressed by official Soviet sources (see chapter II), one cannot but conclude that, in the West, there is a broad area of correct understanding of the Soviet views despite a considerable amount of diverging interpretations and evaluations. Dissenting opinions do emerge as soon as efforts have to be made to assess the relative weight of the various aspects stressed in Soviet behaviour. This is of particular importance with respect to the analysis of motives underlying Soviet aims.

THE ULTIMATE MOTIVES UNDERLYING SOVIET AIMS: IDEOLOGY AND OBSESSION WITH SECURITY

The discussion about the ultimate Soviet motives basically concentrates on two supposedly motivating forces: ideology and the sense of security (or insecurity). The view emphasizing the first points at Soviet power-maximization as the overriding objective of the Soviet system, while the view emphasizing the latter holds that Soviet preoccupation with defence primarily grows out of Russian history and culture (Wolf 1983:149). The manifold positions expressed by Western specialists generally reflect variations in assigning relative importance to these two motives and hence represent variations of these two basic views.

The role of ideology

Many Western scholars tend to rate the role of ideology rather low, or they diagnose a gradual yet constant decline of the ideological factor in the shaping of Soviet policy, suggesting that a pragmatic or "technocratic" approach is gaining strength in Soviet behaviour (Adomeit 1982: 382f.). Some Western authors reach the same conclusion by pointing in the opposite direction: the Soviet ideological belief system, they argue, has become so generalized and loose that in substance it now sanctions the view that anything is possible - "revolutions may or may not take place; force may or may not be needed" (Dallin, quoted in: Bialer 1981: 423). Seen from this angle, the extent to which ideology actually functions in Soviet decision-making, according to Western analysts, must be assumed to vary not only from time to time but also from individual to indi-

189

vidual; hence it would be futile to offer an abstract discussion of the role of ideology (Dallin 1983: 30).

Proponents of the theory de-emphasizing the role of ideology usually draw attention to the importance of the tradition of Russia being an imperial nation (Luttwak 1983: 116), which is said to constitute a far more important factor than mere ideology. It is also deemed that "Marxism-Leninism could be compared to an official religion which is no longer believed in"; at best, Party leaders use Marxism-Leninism as an analytical tool for analysing certain political and economic phenomena at home and abroad. Essentially, however, "to paraphrase an American industrialist's statement of some years ago, they feel what is good for the class and national interests must be good for world Communism" (Ulam, in: Perceptions 1979: 132). In this view, ideology serves as a cynical justification for preserving the power and privileges of the Party's ruling class.

The opposite theory comes out far more directly: here, the basic assumption is that the Soviet leadership feels itself driven by a sense of mission to promote the course of history and hence acts obstinately to fulfil this claim (Lüder 1981: 113). According to two British authors:

> "Marxism-Leninism is not only the public religion of the Soviet Union, it is the public philosophy which at all levels and in all contexts defines and directs knowledge and science and language; it is the political theory that explicates world history and world affairs; it is the criterion for the administration of justice and the logic of the arms build-up; it underpins the relations with allies and with the various capitalist and other foreign countries and governments." (Young/Young 1980: 7)

In a more detailed analysis, several distinct functions of ideology may be discerned. This has been amply outlined by Adomeit (1982: 330-334), who suggests five particular functions: the analytical function of ideology shapes the way the Soviet leadership perceives the structure of the international system, the sources of conflict, and the factors accounting for stability or change. Secondly, the operational function means that the ideology defines the main line of a particular era in world affairs and arrives from there at the main tasks to be pursued. Thirdly, ideology has an utopian, revolutionary or missionary function - which is often but incorrectly taken to be the only one that matters and seems to underlie some simplifying ideology vs. national interest dichotomies. Fourthly, ideology has an important legitimizing function because the rule of the Communist Party of the Soviet Union is based on and legitimized by Marxism-Leninism; any negligence with regard to this very basis of political power in the USSR would destroy the ground on which the leadership is operating. The fifth function, the "socializing function", according to Adomeit, rests in the interplay between ideology and the education, upbringing, and career patterns of the top leadership.

Given the combined impact of these five functions, one may pertinently conclude that it would be a fallacy to argue that ideology represents nothing but an ex post facto rationalization of actions shrewdly chosen on grounds of national interest and national power (cf. also other analyses of the role of ideology by Ulam 1980: 141). There are at least two central aims which are ultimately rooted in ideology: "the irreducible, minimum goal of survival of the regime (that is avoidance of bourgeois restoration) and the assumption of the ultimate unification under Soviet leadership" (Mitchell 1982: 118).

The most important impact of ideology on Soviet politics is its role as a unifying factor. As Lenczowski (1982: 266) in his study on "traditionalists" and "realists" in Soviet policy points out, all groups, whatever their position on the traditionalist-realist continuum, tend to agree on a wide array of basics, and they do so because ideology serves them as a framework for orientation. Thus, according to Lenczowski, there seems to be consensus "(1) on the nature of the fundamental reality of contemporary international relations - the struggle between the two social systems; (2) on almost all the elements essential to capitalism and imperialism; (3) on most of the elements that constitute the ideological means of American foreign policy; (4) on the nature of American foreign economic methods; (5) on American foreign policy's basic inclination to pursue the arms race and to use force as an instrument of policy; (6) on the anti-Soviet, imperialist nature of the NATO alliance; (7) on the nature of the ends and means of American alliance policy; (8) on the nature of American participation in and use of international organizations; (9) on the general ends and means of American policy toward the Third World; and even (10) on the notion that a favorable shift has occured in the world correlation of forces."

The same author concludes:

> "What we see, therefore, is the unifying dynamic of Soviet politics, reconciling disparate views in policies that conform to the basic tenets of the Marxist/Leninist ideology. We must emphasize that the views shared by the realists and traditionalists far outweigh their differences... The differences that remain concern the means rather the ends of policy..." (Lenczowski 1982: 259)

To sum up the conclusion reached by Western experts, in the Soviet Union ideology serves as a kind of common denominator in an ongoing debate among groups with partially differing interests and outlooks. It represents a strong unifying concept determining the range for discussion and at the same time guaranteeing a certain stability of the Soviet views held about the outside world and the proper approach to deal with it. Ideology is therefore held to be central to the process of socialization, thus conditioning the Soviets' approach to all questions of their relations with the outside world (cf. von Beyme 1982: 22). It should not be juxtaposed to national interest; ideology and national interest do not form a dichotomy - rather, they are inseparable (Gibert 1977: 19).

Implications for Western analyses

This constitutes another reason why, to Western experts, it definitely makes sense to study the officially expressed views with great care and sober attention. Nothing would be more wrong than to discard the information conveyed by Soviet sources as amounting to sheer irrelevant orthodox formalism or outright disinformation. Even if Soviet statements on the whole do not tell much about what Western observers would like to know, they nevertheless, by their intrinsically ideological orientation, reveal a great deal about "the general mind-set of the Soviet leadership" (Lambeth 1981: 108).

As the beginning and during the period of détente many Western experts believed that ideology, the "miles and miles of Leninology and Leninography" in Soviet texts, is not what really counts. They assumed that it represents merely the medium in which the true messages are buried, so to speak, the "neutral cotton-wool" required to wrap up these messages safely (Young/Young 1980: 8). Typically, in an article published first in 1970, Zimmerman (1980: 21) scorned Western analysts among whom "the belief was widespread that ideology would retain its significance in explaining Soviet foreign policy long after it had ceased to play a significant role domestically". Even to Dallin (1981: 358) "it seems sensible... to accept the notion of a gradual, uneven, and unacknowledged erosion, decline, or 'relativization' of the unique elements of the faith" that has become "increasingly fuzzy and irrelevant to day-to-day decision-making in Moscow".

Therefore it seems conceivable "that the Soviet leaders do not believe in their publicly cherished values" (ibid.: 268). Dallin (1981: 359) assumes "a learning process that has led to growing sophistication and 'emancipation' from doctrinal stereotypes on the part of a relatively small number of members of the intellectual and political elites, but that has not yet been explicitly acknowledged nor affected the reiteration of orthodox clichés in and by the mass media and routine propagandists". In addition, "the official style requires, whitin limits, continued adherence to the conventional formulae and jargon (though experienced Soviet officials and scholars know how to ignore, manipulate, or circumvent these when necessary or when possible)" (ibid.).

But this does not necessarily imply that adherence to ideological principles in Soviet thinking represents nothing more than cynical lip service or precaution in the struggle for political survival. The particular structure of the Soviet political system may indeed further the internalization of those values that "secure public approval for (the ruling élite's) policies and the party's monopoly over power" (Lenczowski 1982: 268). On the one hand, there is still a "deeply engrained animus against the capitalist world" (Dallin 1981: 359); on the other, it is quite natural that one part or the other of the ideological reiterations "rubs off and becomes part of the diffuse body of assumptions accepted in the dominant culture" (ibid.).

As pointed out before, most Western analysts are convinced that ideology is a crucial factor in maintaining internal stability in the Soviet Union, and "the Soviet élite constantly feels obliged to prove the legitimacy of its rule, both abroad and to the Russian empire's own citizens" (Sime 1980/81: 81; see also Labedz 1978: 38). Furthermore, the "internal dynamics of the Soviet political system place a high premium on doctrinal orthodoxy and continuity" (Schwarz 1978: 148). In addition, "bureaucratic inertia reinforces ideological proclivity" (Kissinger 1982: 13).

In sum, the publicly cherished values are generally surmised to prove valuable or in fact invaluable for the élite. This tends to lead to a situation in which "the mere existence of this set of values becomes a value in itself" (Lenczowski 1982: 269). Lenczowski concludes: "Given this situation it would not be surprising if the Soviets actually began to believe in these values, and perhaps they already do." It is further argued that "to present this ideology as a species of opium with which the Soviet leaders contrive to lull the people while taking care never to indulge in it themselves is to attribute to them an ability to dissociate themselves from the logic of their system - an ability which it is unlikely they possess" (Hunt 1980: 107).

Therefore some Western authors argue that the biggest mistake that can be made with regard to the interpretation of Soviet sources is naive underestimation of what they actually convey (Gibert 1977: ii). In this perspective, responsible American statesmen and Government officials are sometimes criticized by their fellow countrymen specializing in academic analysis of Soviet thought for failing to perceive Soviet statements as indicative of a totally different world view, thus becoming victims of their ethnocentric projection of their own values based on more or less complete cultural or psychological block (Bathurst 1981: 40). The most salient feature of this kind of erroneous approach must be seen in the inclination to assume that the Soviet leadership thinks in a similar way as the United States leadership or at least is converging (Ermarth 1981: 52). Ideology seems to preclude any such possibility. Western European students of the Soviet Union especially warn against confusing Soviet concepts with seemingly similar Western concepts; they emphasize, for example, that the Soviet concept of "peaceful coexistence" is not compatible with the Western concept of "détente" (Dirnecker 1981: 11).

Similar observations are also expressed with regard to the prospects of "drawing the Soviet Union into the 'world community' via the establishment of an increasingly complex 'web of entanglement' with the West" (Payne 1982: 82). This and other forms of "convergence" are said to constitute mere illusions as the Soviet Union is no status quo Power and not interested in maintaining the current order of world community (ibid.: 91-111). The ultimate foundation of this attitude must be seen in what Payne calls "a Hobbesian view of international politics" perceiving conflict as an inevitable and natural process of international relations (ibid.: 140).

The meaning of "security" to Soviet authorities

Many Western analysts discern a link between ideological motives and the motive of national security: the feeling of being surrounded by enemies - primarily (and by definition) ideological enemies. As one observer notes, "enemies are inherent in the language of Soviet politics and are one of the dynamics of Soviet society" (Bathurst 1981: 29). In fact, as long as the Soviet leadership sees the Soviet Union surrounded by capitalist States, it also perceives a challenge and a threat to its own legitimacy, since the presence of any alternative cannot but be qualified as a kind of challenge. More generally, and without going into such far-reaching interpretations, one may say that the Soviets are suffering from a "sense of loneliness". They have no real allies; partnerships are forced and unreliable - the Soviets are powerful but friendless, and on every horizon they see some threat, as Whelan (1983: 518) puts it.

This feeling of insecurity can be attributed to a long tradition - ultimately to "the sense of territorial insecurity on the part of the system's Great Russian national core" (Brzezinski 1983: 1). The sense of insecurity was produced by invasions of Mongols, Swedes, French, and Germans (Kime 1980: 20; Strode 1982: 321), leaving behind a traumatic feeling of being vulnerable to foreign attacks, and at the same time giving rise to a powerful desire to draw the "lessons from the past" (Dallin 1981: 382), i.e. to avert any further repetition of this fate. In fact, insecurity is held to be a standard feature of Russian history and obsession with security a Russian tradition (Legvold 1978). As Western experts would readily admit, this concern is "deeply embedded in Russian and Soviet history" (Holloway 1980: 67):

> "For most of the 55 years of its existence, the Soviet Union has been, both objectively and in the eyes of its leaders, in a chronic state of relative military weakness... Military vulnerability, in fact, has been a characteristic feature of Russian history". (Booth 1981: 75-76).

Therefore, "one can never have enough security to protect oneself" (Alexander 1984:20).

This experience may explain what some Western experts call an "obsession with physical security" (Leebaert 1981: 21; Jacobsen 1983: 6f.) or a "drive towards sécurité totale" (Gray/Brennan 1982:523). In more operational terms this may mean that the Soviet leaders are simply "insatiably defensive", as Singer (1983: 177) puts it:

> "The term insatiable implies that no concessions we make, no victory they achieve, no guarantee or promises we give them, nor any policies that we might adopt, could allow them to conclude a satisfactory and stable peace... They profoundly and correctly understand that their ultimate safety cannot be achieved without ending either the independence or the potential power of the United States". (Singer 1983: 177f).

The notion of "overinsurance" seems to be alien to Soviet thinking (Alexander 1984: 20). This implies that defensive interests become offensive (Gelman 1982: 96), particularly also with regard to the third world (Hosmer/Wolfe 1983: 127).

Russian and Soviet obsession with security became reinforced by Bolshevism and the fear of anti-Bolshevist intervention (Jacobsen 1983: 6-8). Since the "early days of the Revolution" the Soviet Union "perceives the West as hostile" (Segal/Baylis 1981: 21), and quite pertinently so. The emerging Soviet State found itself in a hostile environment in the post-First World War international system. The tremendous Soviet losses in the Second World War (Lambeth 1981: 116; Arnett 1981: 65) were an especially traumatic experience which is very well remembered by the current Soviet leadership, who still have vivid memories of that period. The Soviet concern with respect to first-strike capabilities, the bitter lesson learnt that "it pays to strike first" (Lambeth 1981: 112f.), must be seen to some extent as an additional conclusion drawn from this experience, as the "German invasion of 22 June 1941 took Stalin by surprise, and found the Red Army in a State of unpreparedness" (Holloway 1980: 67). The Cuban missile crisis, finally, has been another "lesson in strategic inferiority" for the Soviet Union (Booth 1981: 95). As some Western experts argue, this interpretation of the Cuban missile crisis as seen in Soviet perspective has been widely neglected in the West; it should, however, be taken seriously in view of its practical implications for the future course of the Soviet Union's policy vis-à-vis its main adversary (Young/Young 1980: 13; Lambeth 1981: 119).

Yet in the end it does not matter what particular motive accounts for Soviet behaviour as it can be observed. As American analysts note, it would be nothing but a waste of time and energy to argue about whether Soviet imperialism is radical-expansionist by nature or, rather, conservative-defensive-expansionist; what counts is the fact that the Soviet Union is expansive (Gray/Brennan 1982: 523).

The search for absolute security by armed force

The Soviet "perception of the world through a lens of military insecurity" (Segal/Baylis 1981: 19) has not only induced a massive build-up of forces beyond what is deemed to be sufficient in Western eyes. According to Western experts the "deeply felt commitment to achieve what amounts to almost absolute security" (Simes 1980/81: 81) leads to serious distortions in the evaluation of the West, its policies, and views. In particular, Western experts are critical about the Soviet inability to recognize that "absolute security for the USSR means very little security for everybody else" (Simes 1980/81: 81). One might even argue (e.g. Whelan 1983: 517) that the Soviet obsession with security has fed upon itself in a circular fashion: "Even when 'equal security' was recognized as a central principle in Soviet/American relations, these fears have not subsided but rather have magnified in the interacting cycle of escalation." (Whelan 1983: 517)

For practically all Western experts the incompatibility of Soviet and Western concepts of security is quite obvious: while in Western thinking military security is perceived as a "public good" of an international system or a collective attribute of that system, and hence to be regarded as "common security", security in Soviet terms has the connotation of "equality" and "equal strength". Hence, comparing the Soviet capabilities (military and other) with those of the United States, the stakes for the Soviet Union are said to be still high despite changes in the correlation of forces that are admitted and often boasted about (Hyland 1979).

Therefore, security for the Soviet Union means continued efforts in all fields (including the military) to catch up (Sonnenfeld/Hyland 1979: 16), a tendency viewed in the West as overinsurance and disregard of the security of everybody else. In the Soviet view, security also implies equality with the United States regarding influence in third countries (Haselkorn 1978: 91f.). Finally, the notion of "equality" that is referred to when Soviet authors talk about security claims equal chances for the Soviet Union to defend herself. Hence, the Soviet Union feels entitled to greater force levels in order to compensate for geography and other unique geopolitical burdens (Gelman 1981: 17). In this respect Soviet military strength might indeed be understood as a function of weakness in other spheres (Windsor 1979: 2 and 10), i.e. the outcome of what might be called the "dialectics of weakness".

In the last resort one may also take the linguistic bases of military thinking into consideration; this is of particular importance with respect to the Soviet (or Russian) understanding of the notion of "security". As Miller points out:

> "If one accepts that a people's language reflects their political culture, historical experience, and the way they view themselves and the world, then the Russian word for security, bezopasnost - literally, without danger - has profound implications for Soviet foreign and military policy. Bezopasnost connotates a state of absolute security. Its psychological genesis is a basic intolerance of, and hostility towards, any alien culture that poses even the remotest threat, military or otherwise, to the established socio-political order in Russia. Marxism-Leninism, by dint of its emphasis on the innate aggressiveness and hostility of imperialism toward socialism, serves to reinforce and calcify this peculiar psychology."(Miller 1982: 205)

Much has been written by Western authors about the geopolitical situation of a land Power with limited access to the open oceans. In particular, Soviet naval policy is perceived to be fashioned in accordance with the century-old Russian aspiration to create an open ocean navy (Understanding Soviet Naval Developments 1981: 79). Western experts concede that the Soviet Union has difficult security problems that accrue from geographical peculiarities. However, it is maintained that the Soviet Union not only overcompensates but to some

196

extent has made things even worse with attempts to achieve a geopoli-
tically more favourable situation, for example by establishing, after
the Second World War, a <u>cordon sanitaire</u> of dependent countries at
her Western borders. Consequently, all efforts in these countries to
lessen dependence on the Soviet Union are opposed as a direct threat
to Soviet security even if those tendencies are active in the local
communist parties. In this connection Kissinger has argued that "the
Soviet Union is the only country in the world entirely surrounded by
hostile communist states" (Kissinger 1982: 13).

VIEWS ABOUT THE SOVIET INTERNAL STRUCTURE

Totalitarian unity or competing factions?

The debate about the unity or diversity of the Soviet domestic
power structure constitutes one of the central themes in the writings
of Western experts on the Soviet Union. Views on this question tend
to vary considerably, especially with regard to the foreign policy
implications of the assumed internal structure (cf. Alexander 1984:
11; Meyer 1984c: 257-268).

For instance, Dallin (1981: 345f.) talks about a "left-right"
dichotomy, the "left" centring on transformation, mobilization,
militancy, partisanship, and, if needed, violence, the "right" opting
for stabilization, consensus-building, incrementalism and priority of
economics. Thus, the left-right cleavage can also be seen to be identical in substance with the "red versus expert" cleavage. Others
prefer to call it the cleavage between "reform-minded elements" and
"conservative elements" (Bjorkman/Zamostny 1984). Other interpretations to be found in the Western literature (as listed by Lenczowski 1982: 239-245) distinguish between "hawks" and "doves",
"orthodox" and "revisionists", "neo-Stalinists" and "détenters".

According to Dallin, it is only toward the outside world that the
Soviet élite has continued to present a united front while internally
an "unreconciled diversity of approaches and cognitions in Soviet
outlook and utterances" does exist (Dallin 1983: 27f.). Yet the
relationship among the various special groups, lobbies, vested
interests, regional and ethnic rivalries, power struggles, technical
disputes and a number of other antagonisms is held to be variable and
hence makes it difficult to provide a simple analytical formula for
the inputs into Soviet policy-making (Dallin 1983: 30; Juviler/
Zawadska 1978: 165f.). The "interest-group approach" as applied by
Western "Kremlinology" focuses on the top-level power struggle,
suggesting a bargaining synthesis (Joensson 1979: 136f.).

Western experts, even those believing in the existence of a
fierce competition among domestic factions in the Soviet Union,
emphasize, however, that Soviet "pluralism" must not be confused with
its Western counterpart; in particular, the various groups involved
in the power struggle in the Soviet Union lack public support, as the
Soviet citizens, in the mass, expect to be governed, not to be left

197

free to pursue any path they might choose. Therefore, "the factions are alone in their self-proclaimed participant orientation to politics" (Connor 1981: 167). In addition, as Richelson (1982: 33) notes, it should also be borne in mind that even if there are various factors determining preferences, these factors can be manipulated by those who control information and are entitled to present the alternatives and to set the agenda - in other words the General Secretary's personal secretariat and the Departments of the CPSU Central Committee Secretariat. Furthermore, it is noted that even if there is something like a "pluralistic" competition among different interest groups or opinion groups, its impact will be minimal or almost non-existent in the field of foreign policy (von Beyme 1983: 40); here, unanimity prevails.

Generalizing about the relationship between internal structural characteristics and the shaping of foreign policy, most Western experts would probably agree with Joensson (1979: 214f.) that one should avoid exclusive emphasis on either external or internal factors and start from the assumption of a complex interplay between the two. In terms of the typology developed by the American political scientist Allison (1971), this means that there are grounds for utilizing each of the various approaches - the rational strategic actor approach, the pluralistic approach, the national leadership role approach (Spielman 1978: 68) and other approaches as well (cf. Meyer 1982). In other words, one must be careful not to superimpose specific standard assumptions about Western policy on each and every manifestation of Soviet policy (Adomeit 1982: 342f.). In more operational terms this conclusion implies that there are several foreign policy alternatives which, to some extent, all depend on domestic factors: creating an external crisis to distract attention from the internal one or other forms of international confrontationism, isolationism coupled with domestic repression and an active policy of greater collaboration with the West - yet "none of these policies is preordained" (Juviler/Zawadska 1978: 166f.).

"Realists" and "traditionalists"

In the Western academic debate about the relative weight of various internal factors to be discerned in Soviet politics, increasing attention is being paid to what some Western analysts call the divergence between "traditionalists" and "realists" (e.g. Lenczowski 1982, ch. 7). The latter are usually identified as representatives of the two leading Soviet academic institutions in charge of studying the United States and other Western countries, namely the USA-Canada Institute (Institut Soyedinennykh Shtatov Ameriki i Kanady) and the Institute for World Economy and International Relations (Institut Mirovoy Ekonomiki i Mezhdunarodnykh Otnosheny/ IMEMO). To some Western experts, these specialists have acquired a new - and more objective and hence more realistic - assessment of the West, particularly those concerned with the study of the United States, i.e. the new generation of Soviet "amerikanisti". They are said to have an "intellectual stake in détente" thus virtually being "salesmen of détente" (Schwartz 1978: 161).

On the other hand, what Western experts call the "traditionalists" are said to be less sanguine about détente because they represent a more conservative outlook, mainly that of the military and related interests. "Traditionalists" and "realists" may also differ with regard to a wide variety of other issues, particularly with respect to (1) the predisposition to make different assessments of the correlation of forces; (2) the tendency to link certain readings of reality to other, seemingly unrelated, policy positions; (3) the course of Soviet strategy toward the non-communist world, with positions ranging from offensive revolution to détente, bluff, and compromise; (4) the question of whether one can do business at all with capitalism; (5) the debate over the nature of international tensions; and (6) the question of what constitutes the wisest alliance policy (Dallin 1980, summarized by Lenczowski 1982: 242-243).

Another dichotomy, also suggested by Dallin (in: Perceptions 1979: 73f.) simply refers to the generation gap: it seems that the younger leadership is likely to resent "unnecessary" constraints and overcentralization. It will be more jingoistic and assertive abroad, and of course better trained.

The consensual basis of Soviet politics

Despite all visible and invisible differences in views, "traditionalists" and "realists" may agree on a wide variety of basics; their similitaries are more significant than their differences (Lenczowski 1982: 266). Western analysts also observe that, particularly in recent years, "the distance between military and institute analysis continued to narrow" (Jackson 1981: 635), and they even conclude that in Soviet politics something like a system of "bipartisanship" is emerging (Pedill 1980). More importantly, as some Western experts argue, there is basic harmony of interest between "realists" and "traditionalists" deeply embedded in ideological convictions which remain completely intact and untouched. As Lenczowski concludes:

"There is, after all, no evidence to exclude the possibility that all of these policies are part of one comprehensive strategy pursued by a single, dominant, and unopposed coalition in the Kremlin." (Lenczowski 1982: 259)

This may also explain why even throughout the period of détente, high levels of military spending were maintained despite decreasing economic growth, apparently with the consent of "realists" among Soviet decision-makers (Becker 1981: 44). As a matter of fact, the Western academic literature on the Soviet Union exhibits a growing tendency to agree on the assumption that Soviet policies are made on a much more consensual and centralized basis than Western observers, preoccupied with the nature of their own system, were inclined to perceive.

One of the fallacies realized in this context refers to the supposed conflict between "doves" and "hawks" which allegedly exists in Soviet ruling circles and which, in fact, artificially projects the image of United States divisiveness on to the Soviet Union. Therefore it is appropriate to avoid "mirror-imaging which attributes the American tradition of civil-military division to Soviet society" (Simes 1980/81: 81-85). As Jacobsen put it:

> "It is futile to speculate about hidden motivations and conjectured split loyalties... We must rid ourselves of our fascination for possible group antagonisms, personalized jealousies and the like... Rather than focusing on discord, the past history of which is strewn with fallacious or futile inferences, it is time to focus on the extraordinary wealth of evidence of unity of basic conceptual outlooks." (Jacobsen 1979: 145; cf. Jacobsen 1983: 27).

Emphasis is being put on the "consensual power base" and the Soviet principle of the primacy of politics (Volten 1982: 145), and the "common outlook" shared by the Soviet élite (Whelan 1983: 421). The ultimate reason for this powerful trend active in Soviet society can be seen in the specific historical tradition of political rule in Russia, especially the traditional methods of determining truth: "Truth is what has been declared to be true by a sound authority: first the Church and the Tsars, now the party leaders." (Young/Young 1982: 27)

Even apart from the commonly shared ultimate beliefs and profound convictions, one has to assume that on the operational level there is full "cooperation in employing mutually acceptable and efficacious foreign policy means in the struggle against capitalism" (Lenczowski 1982: 260). Western observers diagnose a shared preoccupation with security, and, most importantly, what might be called "fierce patriotism" and a view "that the Soviet Union leads the world-wide struggle against the fundamentally hostile West" (Petrov, quoted in Simes 1980/81: 98). In other words, even if the assumption regarding the alleged "absolute likemindedness" of all members of the Soviet élite may be going too far, there exists at least "a shared image of the basic challenge confronting the Soviet Union and of the main international objectives the USSR should pursue" (Simes 1980/81: 98).

Is there militarism in the Soviet Union?

The most important and continuous bone of contention in the Western academic debate about the domestic determinants of Soviet foreign and military policy concerns the role of the military and hence the importance of militarism in Soviet politics. Obviously, ever since Peter the Great began to modernize Russia, the role of the military has been predominant in Russian society (cf. Kime 1980: 207).

Obsessions with Russian security, the build-up of the armed forces with extended influence in society, and socio-economic and political change depended upon each other in Russian and Soviet history (Holloway 1981: 268).

The term "militarism" may have several different meanings. It generally describes an aggressive foreign policy, based on a readiness to resort to war. A further meaning of militarism stresses the preponderance of the military in the State, with military rule as the extreme case. Another interpretation conceives militarism as the subservience of the whole society to the needs of the army, and this may also involve a recasting of social life in accordance with the patterns of military organization. For instance, the "Bolshevik predilection for a command economy is clearly optimal from a military viewpoint" (Jacobsen 1979: 147). Finally, militarism is thought of as an ideology propagating military ideals (Holloway 1981: 62-63). The entire Soviet society seems to be shaped in accordance with military needs. Soviet industry is closely linked to military needs (Dziak 1981: 6f.).

Early Soviet leaders, including Lenin himself, were apparently fully aware of the possible societal effects of military and related heavy industry considerations being given permanent top priority. "Trotsky was afraid that both economy and society would become militarized. Such, to him, was the essence of 'Bonapartism'..." (Dziak 1981: 7). Some Western experts believe that Trotsky's worst fears have materialized in the Soviet Union, given the similarities of contemporary socialism and the garrison State on the one hand (Holloway 1981: 63), and the emergence of a powerful "military-industrial-scientific complex" (ibid.: 62) on the other hand. Particularly after the removal of Khrushchev, the influence of the military is seen to have vastly increased (Holloway 1971: 11). Simes (1981/82: 123f.) perceives Soviet society as being completely penetrated by the military. Another indication of the influence of the military in Soviet politics is their role in the recruitment of top officials. Most high-ranking Soviet political administrators also hold military titles, at least that of an army general (Erickson 1979: 33). On the other hand, it has been noted that the military is underrepresented in the various Party organs (von Beyme 1983: 41): the defence establishment has about 45 representatives (i.e., 12 per cent) on the Central Committee of the CPSU (Kolkowicz, in: Perceptions 1979: 82).

As far as the assumption of Bonapartism is concerned, among others, Kissinger refers to one of Trotsky's arguments:

"The irony of communist systems is that they contain the seeds of Bonapartism, for the sole organization outside the Communist Party with autonomous command structures are the armed forces and the paramilitary units - some 200,000 men strong - of the KGB... Since no one can achieve eminence - much less the top spot - without military or paramilitary support, these forces are in a position to exact constantly increasing resources. The

growth of Soviet military power is built into the system..."
(Kissinger 1982: 13)

Since, according to Western analysts, militance and permanent alert is a structural principle of Soviet society (Wagenlehner 1981: 32), an alarmist image of the outside world is thought to constitute a basic requirement to maintain the influence of the military in Soviet society. Above all, as Gelman (1981: 23) puts it, "the prestige of the Soviet military establishment and its leaders, already greatly enhanced by the political effects of growing Soviet strategic strength, rose further with successive demonstrations of Soviet power projection capabilities".

Institutionally, as analysts of the Soviet decision-making process argue, the Defence Ministry has considerable influence in national security and foreign policy matters (Whelan 1983: 424; Holloway 1979). Military representation and involvement in government and administration as well as in the defence industry may be "on a tremendous scale" (Volten 1982: 155).

The most interesting and relevant question in this connection refers to the fundamental relationship between the military and the Party: is it a "party-military amalgam", as proposed by Dziak (1981b: 7f.), characterized by communality of interests centred on party political concerns and shaded by a fusion of institutions which leaves uncertain boundaries (ibid.:14)? Or is it conflict-prone and thus presenting a perennial threat to the political stability of the Soviet State, as suggested by Kolkowicz (quoted by Colton 1981: 120)? Is the Party traditionally fearful and suspicious of the armed forces (Holloway 1971: 11) in terms of the "anti-Bonapartist" tradition (Dallin, in: Perceptions 1979: 76)? Or is there a "demilitarizing tendency", i.e. a decline of the centrality of the military (Holloway 1981)?

Here again, simplistic notions must be avoided, because there exist more subtle linkages between the Soviet military and Soviet civilians. First of all, and again, one has to reiterate that the High Command has no policy objectives that are different from those of the Politburo (Holloway 1979: 30). As Colton puts it, "the army is an important focus for political socialization, but this is principally due to civilian acceptance of many of the ideals it embodies" (Colton 1981: 135). It seems that there is no evidence that the marshals and admirals can dictate to the civilian leadership, nor that they would want to do so (Dallin, in: Perceptions 1979: 75). On the contrary, as Blacker (1983:148) concludes, the military has never challenged the authority of the political leadership to direct the affairs of the state, and never has the military taken a position opposed to that of the Party on any critical policy issue.

Secondly, one may argue that the extensive identity of values, views, interests and policies of the various groups within the Soviet Union, including the military, ultimately amounts to a more or less complete virtual identity of these groups. This hypothesis can be summed up in the conclusion that "the US has a military industrial complex and the USSR is a military industrial complex" (Baylis/Segal 1981: 29), or, as Brzezinski puts it, there is a "symbiotic relationship" based on an institutionalized fusion of views and interests (quoted in Becker 1982: 66). This relationship is characterized by a high degree of interdependency, i.e. the military and the current Party leadership have established a modus vivendi that suits both partners (Kolkowicz, in: Perceptions 1979: 84). It rests on the firm grounds of commonly accepted and cherished values, mainly the unquestionable priority of assuring the security of the Soviet political system, the intense feeling of patriotism making protection of the Soviet "motherland" not just a matter of national security, but a sacred cause, and the unwillingness to renounce the sacred international liberationist mission (Simes, in: Perceptions 1979: 93f.).

In conclusion, Western experts' views seem to converge on the general assumption that, rather than envisaging a multitude of rival factions allegedly fighting for influence over Soviet policy, one has to start from the assumption that the Soviet decision-makers decide about foreign affairs and strategies in a widely consensual and coherent way, irrespective of whether or not one prefers to call that cohesiveness "totalitarianism".

Views about Soviet trustworthiness and predictability

The assumptions regarding the nature of Soviet aims and the Soviet decision-making structure have an immediate practical and operational significance when it comes to evaluating Soviet trustworthiness and predictability. The approaches and methods to be chosen for dealing with the adversary depend to a large extent on this fundamental evaluation. The academic experts' views on this crucial aspect are highly controversial.

Many observers refer to what they perceive as incongruity between words and deeds, suggesting that the Soviet leadership is engaged in a deliberate "disinformation" campaign designed to mislead Western public opinion (Strode/Strode 1983: 94, quoting Dziak 1981: 66f. and others). One cannot deny that, historically, the congruence of the Soviet leadership's public statements with actual Soviet stategy has differed over time (ibid.: 96). Yet today, and especially with respect to the fact that some dissenting statements are being published in widely circulated Soviet newspapers and journals, inclung army journals, differences in words and deeds may rather indidcate conflict or confusion in the USSR's propaganda efforts themselves (ibid.: 98).

However, many experts raise a question far more fundamental than the suspicion that there is disinformation: is the Soviet Union not a Power which, in accordance with its principles of Marxism-Leninism, operates with the deliberate intent of acting with infidelity whenever this seems profitable to her, a Power that does not believe in the sanctity of international treaties, and enters into such with no intention of honouring them, but only to lull opponents to sleep while preparing their undoing (Welch 1970: 211)? While indeed some authors bluntly charge the Soviet Union and any Marxist-Leninist regime with being faithless, others tend to adopt a more moderate position, supposing a Soviet record that is neither outstandingly good nor outstandingly bad (Welch 1970: 217). In an empirical study examining the actual Soviet record of pledge fulfilment, one author draws the conclusion that "fidelity, not infidelity is the norm" (ibid.: 261). The Soviet Union did in fact commit gross violations of pledges, he says, and some of them have been spectacular and unambiguous, carried out brutally and rationalized in patently absurd terms, yet they seem to be the exception rather than the rule. With respect to this issue, there seems to be some discrepancy between the findings produced by academic experts, on the one hand, and the assumptions held by responsible Government officials, on the other hand.

Related to the issue of faithfulness is the issue of predictability. To many observers in the West, the Soviet system, due to its peculiar attitude towards information and other characteristics, appears quite enigmatic, and predictability is thus seen to be very limited. Yet, against this the argument is advanced that the Soviet leadership, due to the co-optation procedures employed for determining its succession, does not allow for many "grand or horrific alternatives" (Connor 1981: 171). As far as Soviet foreign policy more specifically is concerned, experts note a growing degree of institutionalization and regularization (Bialer 1981a: 414); this fact, too, can be said to be supportive of an increasing stabilization and hence conducive to predictability of Soviet external behaviour.

VIEWS ABOUT SOVIET CAPABILITIES: DRAWING AN UNEVEN BALANCE

Pitfalls of perception

Western analyses of Soviet military power rarely argue about sheer numbers, which are usually beyond doubt. But they do argue about how the numbers of soldiers and weapons are to be evaluated. In practice, however, more often than not capabilities, and implicitly, the East-West military balance are assessed in terms of very simple numerical indicators such as the number of divisions or the number of battle-tanks deployed. The utilization of such simple indicators sometimes leads to a perception of Soviet superiority. This may have dire political consequenses, as Luttwak points out:

"In the absence of conflict, the political shadow cast by European perceptions of Soviet superiority on the ground sufficed to induce Western governments to make important concessions to the Soviet Union, accommodating Soviet demands that would otherwise have been rejected out of hand or... ignored." (Luttwak 1978: 24)

By this process, the argument runs, the delusion by false images of Soviet superiority gave the Soviet Union some political leverage, or in other words: via perceptions force was transformed into power (ibid.: 28).

The question must be raised, however, whether such perceptions of Soviet capabilities are the result of a deliberate Soviet strategy of deception or simply the product of illusions generated and cherished independently by American decision-makers. As Jervis points out, the latter may ultimately lead to self-deterrence. If American decision-makers, for instance, believe that United States Minuteman silos are vulnerable to Soviet attack, they may draw frightening inferences from it, leading to inaction and political setbacks (Jervis 1982: 11-17). By paying too much attention to calculations about United States vulnerability, the American decision-makers "may act more hesitantly, become less confident, refuse new commitments or retract old ones, and may even encourage the Soviets to believe that it is safe to undertake actions they previously shunned" (ibid.: 17). It seems that both "liberal" and "conservative" Western observers converge in finding this argument convincing. As a "liberal" commentator contends, "ones can only conclude that the constant bellowing about 'Soviet superiority'... may do more harm to the image of American strength of the eyes in the world than all the throw-weight of all the heavy Soviet missiles combined" (Kaplan 1980: 73f.).

Hence when trying to avoid the pitfalls of naive perception, several aspects have to be taken into consideration.

The argument about the standards of Soviet technology

The first issue for debate refers to the standard of Soviet military technology as compared with Western technology. Western analysts admit that in past decades the Soviet Union had problems with modern technology and its application in the military field, and, given matched numbers, one might easily have made a finding of United States superiority and Soviet inferiority due to the differing technological quality of the military hardware.

Yet today, and especially with regard to strategic weaponry, it seems "that US complacency over qualitative deficiencies of the Soviet command economy, one that has to buy an entire truck plant from the West, will no longer compensate for quantitative shifts in the military balance" (Leebaert 1981: 9). Only weapons of air combat are said to constitute an exception; Western fighter aircraft are still held to be clearly superior to their Soviet counterparts (Luttwak 1983: 43f.). For the rest, the Western advantage in research and development is usually offset by faster Soviet production cycles (ibid.: 44; Albert 1979: 150).

While many Western analysts and especially official United States Government spokesmen tend to highlight the rapid growth of Soviet might and often diagnose superior Soviet capabilities, others emphasize that all the talk about perceptions of American inferiority is of Western provenance and should not easily be believed. In addition, the question is also asked what "superiority" really means in the nuclear age; in the absence of any satisfactory objective definition of this notion it is argued that worring about alleged "inferiority" may really be beside the point (cf. Hanson 1982/83; Kaplan 1980: 52-54).

Deficiencies and liabilities

As far as the economic infrastructure of Soviet military power is concerned, the inadequacies of the Soviet system are obvious to all observers. Western observers note with respect to the modernization process that has helped to make the USSR one of the two most powerful nations (e.g. Granick, in: Perceptions 1979: 55; Katsenelinbogen, in: ibid.: 59f.). Today the so-called "sicientific-technical revolution" is continuing this line of development (Starr, in: ibid.: 68).

On the other hand, Western analysts draw attention to growing difficulties not overcome by the Soviet economic system, and a steady decline of the growth rate of GNP (Thornton, in: ibid.: 69). There are shortcomings of all kinds, and some major factors for economic growth are reported to be declining (Jamgotch 1983a: 7). Bialer concludes that (1) the level of Soviet economic development and Soviet achievement in the last decade still provides a sufficient base for the maintenance of a strong military posture, both strategic and conventional, and (2) for the foreseeable future the Soviet Union can continue to increase the level of its military expenditures without incurring additional major difficulties in its economic programmes; but (3) increasing military expenditure would be difficult (Bialer 1981: 413). This means that the gap between the universalist quest for power and the economic potential required for its implementation is nevertheless constantly widening (Meissner 1982: 44).

Western experts also draw attention to other liabilities. Scott/Scott (1983: 135f.) point to the force required by Soviet rulers in order to keep in line Soviet nationality groups, many of which are still hostile to Soviet rule; demographic changes in the Soviet population involving a continuing decrease in the percentage of Soviet people who are Slavs may soon aggravate this problem. In addition, the USSR is surrounded by hostile neighbours; major Soviet forces are deployed opposite China, and the nations of Eastern Europe would probably quickly seek to throw off Soviet rule should the Soviet Union be weakened (ibid: 136). Generally, one might argue that the "reliability factor" is increasingly affecting the military capability of the Warsaw Pact forces and that the dependability of the Soviet Union's proximate allies is becoming uncertain (Jamgotch 1983b: 1). Some Western experts even argue that the USSR's security buffer in Eastern Europe is disintegrating (Hyland 1982/83: 8). Other problems affecting Soviet strength are held to emerge from conflicts growing out of efforts to reform the top (Singer 1983: 175).

Implications for future Soviet policy

What are the implications of this state of affairs for the future course of action chosen by Soviet leaders? Fewtrell (1983: 39) argues that what is perhaps most likely to emerge is a "policy of muddling through" by minor adjustments in the economic system and a conservative and unadventurous policy in the years ahead. However, many Western experts seem inclined to assume a different conclusion drawn by Soviet leaders in face of the growing constraints: while the Soviet Union feels very strong and formidable in terms of military power, Soviet capabilities in all other respects are felt to be dwindling - hence it "may well take risks while the moment is optimal" (Hyland 1982a: 59: Lebow 1981: 223-233).

The latter inference has obvious relevance with regard to policy consequences, as assessed by Western experts. The rapid growth of Soviet capabilities, especially the acquisition of powerful military projection capabilities (Jacobsen 1979: 51ff.), is seen to have a decisive impact on Soviet attitudes: Luttwak (1983: 60) believes that "it is natural that a more confident and far less prudent external policy should also be in evidence". One development frequently mentioned by Western specialists is the possibility of rescuing the problem-ridden Party rule by external success. As the economic difficulties grow and as the fundamental internal contradictions continue to become more pronounced without any process available for adjusting them, an external victory may seem preferable to watching the problems getting out of hand. As Singer puts it:

> "In brief, one reasonable way to look at the Soviet prospect is as a race between internal collapse and external victory. Either one can happen and the one which comes first may prevent the other." (Singer 1983: 175)

In addition, many Western experts indicate that the Soviet Union, by most usual standards, is a true major Power, but at the same time by other standards a developing country. The "traditional economic, industrial, and general developmental inferiority to the West has very likely bred a natural inclination to overcompensate and overinsure on security matters" (Ross 1981: 126). Hence it is psychologically quite understandable that there is a Russian-Soviet tendency to regard "bigness as a symbol of goodness or greater effectiveness <that> has seemingly maintained a persistent influence over Soviet approaches to weaponry,... <for example> the psychological inclination to favor super-sized missilry" (Ross 1981: 125-126). Strode (1982: 336) affirms a predilection for quantity, as a substitute for quality to be one of the major elements of Soviet strategic style. Hence, in the Soviet style of war, the emphasis is on the massive application of all available means (Leites 1981: 185). What is believed to count in Soviet military thinking are sheer numbers;

sophisticated approaches are not cherished. The likely impact on the psychology of the smaller Western European countries of trying to compensate for the Western lead in technology by sheer size and sheer numbers does not seem to be appreciated very much.

The discrepancy existing between geopolitical status and economic strength may also have a more serious implication, as Luttwak argues. While, on the one hand, the Soviet leadership can hardly view the economic future with optimism and hence may also feel sceptical about the long-term future of their regime, they have good reasons to have operational confidence in their armed forces:

> "But when leaders are pessimistic about the longterm future of their regimes and at the same time have high confidence in the strength and ability of their armed forces, then all they know and all they fear will conspire to induce them to use their military power while it still retains its presumed superiority." (Luttwak 1983: 40)

A similar line of reasoning can be developed with regard to the growing discrepancy between the domestic legitimacy of the Party's rule and the military capability at its disposal. In this connection, some authors ask whether the Soviet leadership, faced with the risk of losing the Party's control over Soviet society and the empire, would not resort to behaviour in extremis, i.e. for instance by launching a pre-emptive attack against the American enemy (Miller 1982: 217). Even without sharing such far-reaching conclusions some observers maintain that Soviet risk-taking behaviour may change as a function of the growing gap between the internal situation and the available power capability. This gap may stimulate the search for "solutions" by an adventurous, bold foreign policy and exploitation of all kinds of opportunities such as situations of a power vacuum existing in many parts of the world (Dirnecker 1981: 118-120).

These are quite far-reaching implications of assumptions held about Soviet capabilities. They refer to peculiar operative consequences determining Soviet external behaviour. Thus, the analyses and opinions proposed by academic authors, even more clearly than the views expressed by officials, indicate the crucial importance such assumptions regarding capabilities have for the shaping of what one expects from the adversary.

SOVIET STRATEGY IN PERSPECTIVE

The nature of Soviet military thought

Soviet military strategy, for obvious reasons, attracts a considerable amount of attention from Western commentators. Yet the picture conveyed by Western academic literature is far from coherent.

The evaluation of Soviet strategic doctrine tends to oscillate between the view that this doctrine is lagging behind American doctrine and the opinion that one should pay more attention to what Soviet sources say and overcome one's own "dogma" (Hanson 1982/83: 61-63).

In fact, many Western observers seem to be quite confused by what they read and hear from Soviet sources. There may be many reasons for this state of affairs.

The first reason has to do with the fact that Soviet authorities do not publicize their strategic views. They prefer a high degree of discretion and secrecy as far as military matters are concerned. There is no public in the Soviet Union that would demand information about alternative strategic options. This also means that a public strategic debate does not take place. As, according to Marxism-Leninism, any policy is scientifically correct or false, policy choice is a matter of scientific knowledge and does not need any debate (Beukel 1979: 235). One may also assume that the notion of public debate generally is totally alien to the Russian tradition (ibid.).

Secondly, Soviet declaratory strategy is most of all concerned with one possible war scenario, namely the all-out nuclear exchange. Even though one may assume that Soviet planners in fact envisage other scenarios as well, the concentration, in declaratory strategy, on the nightmare of general nuclear war is suitable for scaring the Western public (Stratmann 1981: 173-181).

Thirdly, Soviet military thinking is reacting in a very sensitive way to new technological developments. Hence it has a strongly dynamic character, altering swiftly within rather short intervals. Therefore the Soviet sources used in the current Western analyses are "increasingly older ones and perhaps outmoded" (Hyland 1982b: 60).

Fourthly, the overall logical structure of Soviet military thinking differs from the Western approach, thus giving rise to all kinds of misunderstandings on the part of Western analysts thinking in terms of Western concepts. One may even argue that the Soviet approach intentionally refuses to adopt the terminology of American strategic thinking; some Western authors point to the warnings expressed by Soviet sources that the Soviet Union would not "play" in accordance with the American "rules of the game" (Segal/Baylis 1981: 36; Lambeth 1981: 118; Lenczowski 1982: 165-166). According to Gray (1982: 92-97) "the fog of culture has interfered with the theory and practice of strategy" in the United States when dealing with Soviet military thought. The surprise of Soviet strategic behaviour as experienced by many Americans may in fact be due to a lack of attention and sensitivity to the distinctly different roots of Soviet theory and practice, i.e. to the failure to consider "how American words and deeds will likely be assayed by a distinctive, and indeed in many important respects alien, Soviet strategic culture" (ibid.).

Fifthly, there are various terminological asymmetries. Russian words more often than not are not identical with their apparent counterparts in English strategic terminology. In this connection, von Beyme draws attention to the fact that while "defence" ("oborona") constitutes the central term in describing Soviet strategy, Soviet authors refer to Western "deterrence" by using the Russian word "ustrasheniye" ("intimidation"), "davleniye" ("pressure") or "prinuzhdeniye" ("blackmailing") (von Beyme 1983: 63), while the Soviet policy of deterrence is called "sderzhivaniye" ("keeping out") (Miller 1982: 186).

As far as the latter point is concerned, only recently a clarification of the structure of Soviet military thinking has been offered by the British expert Holloway who, starting from definitions given in the Soviet Military Encyclopaedia, suggests a strict distinction between military doctrine and military science. Doctrine, according to Holloway (1981: 260; 1983: 29f.) and his Soviet sources, "embodies the fixed positions of the state on questions of war and military policy", it is "likely to be stable for some time, being revised only in response to major political and military developments". By contrast, military science is defined as "the system of knowledge about the character and laws of war, the preparation of the armed forces and the country for war, and methods of waging it"; as such, it is constantly advancing as it tackles new problems". In addition, Holloway draws attention to the notion of "military art", which comprise "the theory and practice of preparing and conducting military operations and thus embraces strategy, operational art and tactics". The theory of military art, and hence strategic and tactical theory, form part of military science. Western experts also seem to be sufficiently acquainted with the official nature and hierarchical structure of Soviet military thought which represents "a single system of views and directions free from private views and evaluations" (Rose 1980: 23, quoting a Soviet author).

Those Western observers who are really familiar with the structure and contents of Soviet military thinking explicitly warn against underestimating it as being "backward"; they conclude that any such view is ultimately rooted in Western "ethnocentrism" (Baylis/Segal 1981: 16). Particular emphasis is also being put on what might be called the Soviet "style" in strategy, such as the inclination to cherish "bigness as a symbol of goodness" (Ross 1981: 125), the preference for mass in both manpower and equipment, the reliance on quantity over quality (Strode 1982: 328), and other features characteristic of Soviet military thinking (Ross 1981: 126; Strode 1982: 330f.).

The meaning of the Clausewitzian tradition

When it comes to discussing more specific aspects of Soviet strategy, there is considerable controversy regarding the ultimate meaning of war in Soviet political thinking. Many Western commentators point to the Clausewitzian tradition prevailing in Marxism-

210

Leninism (Sonnenfeldt/Hyland 1979: 24). According to this line of argument the Soviet leaders are supposed to regard the dictum of "war as a continuation of politics" to be tantamount to war serving as a practical instrument of policy (Arnett 1981: 56). Yet, as Arnett concludes from a careful study of authoritative Soviet sources, the second assumption does not necessarily follow from the first. Of course, Marxism-Leninism proposes that no war can be properly understood without analysing its political causes and "class content", i.e. it emphasizes the political primacy over military professionalism (cf. Kolkowicz 1981b: 5). But this by no means implies that Marxism- Leninism recommends war, and nuclear war in particular, to be unleashed and used as an instrument of policy (Arnett 1981: 57f.; Kaplan 1980: 15-24). Soviet leaders are therefore held to no longer consider war as a rational choice (Garthoff 1981b: 96f.). Soviet spokesmen advocating the continuing validity of the classical Clausewitzian dictum seem to be more and more criticized by those endorsing the view that any nuclear war would be foolish and impossible to win (Bjorkman/Zamostny 1984: 198-207; Lange 1984).

On the other hand, Western observers frequently point to the growing Soviet assertiveness of military power. Dallin (1981: 339) argues that the growing military forces at the disposal of the USSR are "likely to have heightened the disposition to pursue such opportunities". The awareness of the "shift of the correlation of forces in favor of socialism" is supposed to foster pressures in Moscow to move forward unilaterally in the international arena.

Nevertheless, there seems to be agreement among Western experts that Soviet military thinking puts emphasis on deterrence as the best means for preventing war. This also implies that the best deterrent is an effective war-fighting capability (Lambeth 1981: 109). With certain restrictions this also means that the Soviet leaders assume victory to be possible, that it pays to strike first, that restraint is foolhardy and that numbers matter (Lambeth 1981: 109-117). The restrictions are determined by what, in Soviet theory, is defined as the functions of military power. According to Holloway, military power, as seen through Soviet eyes, clearly serves a threefold purpose: (1) to deter a nuclear attack, (2) to defend the socialist community, and (3) to aid national liberation movements (Holloway 1983: 81f.).

Soviet risk-taking behaviour

Of course, all this has to be seen within the confines of Soviet risk-taking behaviour. Quite a number of Western experts stress the fundamental preference for risk-aversion prevailing in Soviet conduct (Leites 1982: 380; Ross 1984: 237). The Western discussion of Soviet attitudes in world politics hinges to a considerable extent on whether or not the Soviet Union behaves in a reckless or cautious manner (Adomeit 1982: 51), and several theories have been evolved in order to provide answers to this question (ibid.: 55-62). Examining Soviet behaviour in a number of actual international crises, Adomeit concludes that there are possibly four principles or axioms guiding Soviet risk-taking behaviour:

"(1) Do not embark on forward operations against an opponent which are not carefully calculated in advance and move forward only after careful preparation...

(2) Push to the limit. Engage in pursuit of an opponent who begins to retreat or make concessions, but know where to stop...

(3) Before engaging in forward operations carefully construct a fall-back position...

(4) Never lose sight of the political objectives to be achieved, and in pursuing them do not let yourself be diverted by false notions of bourgeois morality..." (Adomeit 1982: 315-327; cf. also Adomeit 1981a: 53-63)

Additional "basic rules of the game" presumed to be observed by the Soviet leaders are suggested by Kolkowicz (1981: 339), who draws attention to the Soviet inclination to avoid both direct confrontation with the other super-Power and the commitment of Soviet forces or presence in an irrevocable either-or position in areas of limited Soviet control. Furthermore, the high degree of caution does not rule out decisive action if Soviet leaders perceive high costs of inaction (Ross 1984: 237). When considering these and other hypotheses about Soviet risk-taking behaviour, it should be borne in mind that no universally valid generalization can be offered; rather, everything depends on the global balance in conjunction with the local and regional balance (Adomeit 1982: 339). Soviet behaviour is therefore determined by an amalgam of various factors (Gelman 1982: 104): the sense of attractive opportunities due to American mishaps and the changing "correlation of forces", the Leninist urge to cash in potential benefits, the feeling of having acquired new and powerful power-projection capabilities, and the fear of missing future opportunities if opportunities today are not quickly exploited.

Therefore, as Gibert (1977: 152f.) puts it, future Soviet risk-taking behaviour must not only be assessed on the basis of past experience. By contrast to previous episodes of crisis confrontation, the Soviet Union has now achieved parity and more with the United States; Moscow's future conduct may thus be quite different from its former behaviour.

Does the Soviet Union envisage nuclear war-fighting?

As far as nuclear strategy more specifically is concerned, Western academic literature exhibits considerable disagreement about how Soviet leadership perceives the role of nuclear war-fighting. There is much speculative argument about whether or not the Soviet Union really accepts the principle of mutual deterrence or prepares for nuclear-war fighting. Openly accessible Soviet sources tend to keep largely silent about it (Leites 1982: 379). However, the rapid deployment of new strategic forces has led many Western observers to conclude that the Soviet Union is acquiring a capability "which would enable them to fight, survive and win a nuclear war" (Lord Chalfont, quoted in Suddaby 1982a: 8). Other capabilities acquired by the Soviet Union are equally held to reflect a well-conceived nuclear war-fighting doctrine; in this perspective, the high-accuracy MIRVs, antisatellite systems, antisubmarine warfare preparations, civil defence efforts, antiballistic missile defence technology and comprehensive air defence seem to be particularly ominous (Friel 1981: 99). Similarly, the deployment of new intermediate-range nuclear weapons in Europe (SS-20) may be supposed "to fit into a broader process of force modernization designed to provide an enhanced warfighting capacity" (Holst 1981: 40), especially due to their range, accuracy, number of warheads and state of readiness.

Some Western experts therefore tend to assume that, in Soviet strategic thought, there is substantial evidence of a concept evoking the aim of victory rather than pointing at the suicidal futility of any use of nuclear weapons (Strode/Strode 1983: 92). They assert that the Soviet objective in any war, and especially in a global nuclear war , is victory (Douglass/Hoeber 1979: 14). Soviet sources are quoted which clearly propose that if a nuclear war breaks out it has to be won and will be won (Arnett 1981: 61; Lambeth 1981: 113; Holloway 1982: 54; Jamgotch 1983a: 4; Ermarth 1981: 51). Other Western experts point to the importance of long-standing traditions of Soviet military thinking and conclude that the "Soviets have not abandoned their long-established views on war and the possibility of victory even in a general nuclear conflict" (Miller 1982: 193; cf. also Vigeveno 1983: 27f).

They refer to Soviet military writings which, according to their interpretation, clearly indicate that Soviet strategists have "worked out a war-fighting and winning doctrine - on both the tactical-battlefield and strategic-exchange levels" (Rose 1980: 33, quoting Cohen, Van Cleave, Pipes and others). Additional evidence for this assumption is seen in the fact that Soviet ground forces and military planners envisage the conduct of military operations in a future war in a nuclear environment, as outlined by Rose:

"Their doctrinal literature focuses on it; their training is oriented around it; their organization and equipment is able to fight and survive in it; they have developed, tested, and deployed a variety of nuclear capable weapons systems... Soviet writers on military affairs appear, generally, to see nuclear weapons and nuclear armed forces as central to all phases of Soviet military power." (Rose 1980: 150)

There are, in fact, ambiguities. However, as some experts argue, the "war-fighting" assumption may be related to an earlier stage of Soviet thought, while growing emphasis is being put on strategies to prevent nuclear war and on the absolute necessity to avoid the disastrous consequences of a nuclear conflagration (Jamgotch 1983a: 5; Holloway 1983: 55). By contrast to Western strategic thinking, Soviet writings on war in general and nuclear war in particular are the exclusive domain of the military - hence the heavy imprint of classical military thinking (Vigeveno 1983: 27).

It should also be noted that it is one thing to think about how to survive and win a nuclear war, should such a war break out, but quite another to deduce from such arguments the intention to voluntarily unleash a nuclear war in order to achieve a victory (Legvold 1982: 196f.). In this connection one has to recall what has been argued with regard to the Clausewitzian tradition in Soviet military thought; the dictum of "war as a continuation of politics by other means" must always be interpreted in two ways and it would be a mistake to confuse the two interpretations. Another explanation of what seems to be a contradiction between political rhetoric (declaring the attempt to count on victory in a nuclear war as "dangerous madness") and military theory (advocating preparation for fighting and winning a nuclear war) may be seen in the distinction between deciding in advance whether the outcome of a nuclear war would meet some theoretical standard of victory, on the one hand, and preparing to wage a nuclear war which continues to be a legitimate and indeed mandatory enterprise, on the other hand (Hyland 1982b: 58).

Furthermore, it must not be overlooked that "deterrence and warfighting per se are hardly incompatible in principle" for the ability to fight a war has traditionally been considered one of the more reliable ways to deter aggression (Simes 1980: 82; Kaplan 1980: 23f.). After all, deterrence by denial, based on the doctrine of war-fighting, naturally implies provision for the failure of deterrence (Leebaert 1981a: 17). Obviously Soviet military doctrine does not separate the idea of "nuclear deterrence" from the general concept of defence - "deterrence equals defense" (MccGwire 1980: 108; 1981a: 217). After all, this idea is not completely alien to Western strategic doctrine either, where a credible deterrent has always been linked with the demand to be underpinned by a capability to deal with various levels of possible conflict (Shulman 1982: 88). Western experts seem to converge on this theory, which Lockwood sums up in the following concise phrase:

"The assumption underlying this doctrine is that the better prepared the Soviet armed forces are to fight and win a nuclear war, the more effective they will be as a deterrent to an attack on the Soviet Union as well as an 'umbrella' under which the Soviets can pursue a more aggressive foreign policy." (Lockwood 1983: 36)

But some confusion or misunderstanding seems to be unavoidable, as outlined by Erickson:

"Yet another contradiction was that certain American attitudes professed war-avoidance and the 'unthinkability' of nuclear war, while the Soviet Union determined on war-prevention coupled with the acceptance of the possibility of nuclear war, an admixture

214

which produced no small degree of confusion, acrimony and accusation in Western circles, certain of which insisted on the implacability of Soviet intentions in a quest for unchallenged military superiority - thus demolishing deterrence and undermining any mutuality." (Erickson 1982: 249)

Some Western authors think that the Soviet concept of war and Soviet strategic doctrine are ultimately based on the conviction that a major nuclear war between East and West is inevitable. Due to the antagonistic nature of the two social systems, capitalism and socialism, the likelihood that the former would resort to violent means in case peaceful means fail, and the fact that these means are doomed to fail according to Marxism-Leninism, war may indeed be perceived to be inevitable (Lambeth 1981: 109; Backerra 1983: 46f.). Any Soviet pronouncements on nuclear war-fighting must be seen in this context. If Soviet strategist envisage victory in a nuclear war, they think in terms of the "end of a long road of incalculable chances and immense suffering" (Dyson 1984: 190).

Related to this is the issue of limited nuclear war. As Segal/ Baylis point out, "it is clear that Moscow's declaratory policy rejects the notion of limited war" because it is an American invention for overcoming NATO's conventional weakness in Europe and would be bound to involve the territory of the USSR and not that of the United States (Segal/Baylis 1981: 36; Lenczowski 1982: 166). Western experts are aware that in this respect NATO's strategy may seem untenable to the extent that it permits the United States to wage nuclear war against the Soviet citadel while the American territory is allowed to remain a sanctuary (Miller 1982: 221). Soviet thinking about the use of theatre nuclear forces is evolving and changing rapidly. Meyer concludes that the Soviet leadership assumes that a war in Europe would probably begin by conventional operations. In this contingency, Soviet air and ground forces using conventional munitions would launch preventive strikes against NATO's theatre nuclear forces (TNF), while at the same time their use of these forces would be deterred by Soviet TNF. Should NATO escalate to employing its TNF capability, Soviet TNF would strike at targets in Western Europe, primarily at Western nuclear weapons bases and C^3 facilities (Meyer 1984: 34; cf. also Douglass/Hoeber 1981: 6).

As far as the problem of limited war elsewhere, as in Afghanistan, is concerned, from the Soviet point of view, such events are of course not a limited war (Hart 1982: 61-67) but an internal affair of world socialism. Other authors point to the growing Soviet willingness to fight limited wars in the third world. There may be an intrinsic relationship between Soviet engagements of this kind and the neutralization of American nuclear weapons by Soviet armaments (Kolkowicz 1981b: 77-81).

Mutual deterrence - acceptable or unacceptable?

While some Western authors tend to emphasize the similarity and symmetry of Soviet and American views on nuclear war-fighting and deterrence, there are others who question the meaningfulness of any comparison of Soviet and American strategies (e.g. Legvold 1979). In particular, they wonder whether the idea of mutual deterrence is really acceptable to the Soviet leadership. As the basic idea underlying "mutual assured destruction" is punishment of the attacker, one might doubt whether this idea really fits into the overall patterns of Soviet military thinking. As Kime (1980: 212) argues, for the USSR the crucial question is "Who controls post-war Eurasia?, while punishing the enemy is not seen as a useful end in itself; he holds that "the Russian mind understands 'mutual assured destruction' for its political utility: it is simply not good military strategy". In fact, it seems that for the Soviet strategists deterrence constitutes "the first, but not the only, and not the last, objective of strategy" (Ermarth 1981: 58). They rather tend to stress the importance of deterrence not only for war prevention but also for the protection of prior political gains (ibid.). Hence one may assume the Soviet concept to correspond to what in Western terminology might be called "extended deterrence (Soviet style)" and aimed at deterring the American deterrent in order to provide opportunities for operations elsewhere, mainly in the third world (Payne 1982: 130 and 162ff.).

At any rate, it seems highly improbable that Soviet strategists share the American preference for "mutual vulnerability" - they are much more interested in what Lambeth calls "unilaterally assured survivability", providing at least the rudiments of a plausible war-waging posture (Lambeth 1979: 27). Furthermore, as has already been noted above, the English term "deterrence" has no Russian equivalent properly conveying the same meaning; rather, it has the connection of "politico-psychological pressure" (Lenczowski 1982: 160) or even blackmail and intimidation (Ross 1981: 124f.; Shulman 1982: 91; cf. also Lider 1979: 194). Soviet "traditionalists" are therefore said to be anxious not to signal any acceptance of the principle of deterrence since, from their point of view, this could be misread as yielding to American pressure which in turn is dangerous.

But on the whole, Western experts generally agree that, notwithstanding the fundamental incompatability of Marxist-Leninist expectations of the "ultimate victory of the progressive forces of socialism" and the idea of being caught in a mutual hostage situation, in practice the Soviet Union fully accepts the principle of mutual deterrence. This assumption is supported by the acute Soviet awareness of the destructive capabilities of the American nuclear arsenal (Arnett 1981: 66f.; Ross 1981: 138; Garthoff 1981a: 180), on the one hand, and the frequent reference to be found in Soviet sources to the principle of retaliating in order to frustrate aggression, on the other hand. These references can be said to express implicit acceptance of the principle of deterrence (Vincent 1975: 5; Lenczowski 1982: 160; Garthoff 1984). Soviet military doctrine favours what might be called "deterrence by denial" (Segal/Baylis 1981: 22; Dibb 1982: 159). By contrast to the American idea that deterrence can be guaranteed by assuring the capacity to punish, the Soviet view is that right from the beginning the aggressor must be denied any possibility of profiting from an assault on the Soviet Union. In order to fulfil this task, the capability of "guaranteed annihilation of the enemy state" (Lenczowski 1982: 166, quoting a Soviet source) is considered to be a necessary prerequisite.

Parity or superiority?

Western experts also ask whether the Soviet Union really accepts the principles of parity and stability which, for obvious reasons, are intrinsically interconnected with the principle of mutual deterrence. Here again, the Western literature is characterized by disagreement. Although Soviet leaders have repeatedly and explicitly disavowed any intention to strive for superiority - a fact which is carefully noted by Western experts (cf. Garthoff 1981b: 106f.; Garthoff 1981a: 180; Sonnenfeldt 1980: 724; Hyland 1982b: 62f.) -this attitude may seem less conclusive if seen within the framework of the Marxist-Leninist theory of the "correlation of forces": if this correlation, by the very essence of the law of history, is bound to continuously shift in favour of socialism up to the point where capitalism or "imperialism" is doomed to final extinction, it may be hard to accept the renunciation of superiority. That is why one observer concludes that "the question of whether Soviet military growth has the specific purpose of securing 'superiority' in accordance with some systematic schedule and with specified criteria cannot, in fact, be definitively answered" (Sonnenfeldt 1980: 724). The identical premises as offered by the Soviet theory of the "shift of the correlation of forces", however, lead another expert to a more pessimistic conclusion: according to Gibert (1977: 152), "the Soviets ... are not intending merely parity but are attempting to acquire meaningful military superiority over the United States" (cf. also ibid.: 125f.).

The ambiguity is increased by the fact that the respective authoritative statements by Soviet leaders and other spokesmen for the Warsaw Pact member States have tended to change in the course of the past one or two decades (cf. Miller 1982: 195-208). As one Western expert argues, the Soviet Union originally affirmed the intention of seeking military superiority and constantly called superiority a good and necessary thing as long as it felt inferior; having finally reached parity, it no longer propagates these views, which might be counterproductive at the present stage, provoking additional defence spending on the part of the United States and irritating the peace movement active in the West" (Wagenlehner 1982: 12f.). Hence, as another author asks, "would it not be far more effective to sedate than to intimidate the West?" (Miller 1982: 201). If this assumption is correct, the non-use and denial of any claim for superiority would simply represent a disinformation technique to deceive the capitalist adversary (ibid.). Those believing in a Soviet intention to achieve strategic superiority are afraid that the Soviet leaders might become emboldened towards a more adventuresome foreign policy (Lambeth 1979: 22). Other Western analysts, however, while taking due note of the tactical reasons which Soviet leaders have to disclaim their intention to strive for strategic superiority, nevertheless acknowledge that - in addition - there may in fact also have been a "deeper reappraisal of the risks" brought about by such a policy (Hyland 1982b: 62).

As far as the Western concept of "strategic stability" more specifically is concerned, Soviet strategists are said to be very reticent in this respect. As Rubinstein puts it, stability "was never the Soviet goal" (Rubinstein 1981: 286), and the Soviet negotiators to SALT therefore never accepted it as the guiding principle. This also means that the Western concept of "mutual vulnerability" is clearly incompatible with Soviet strategic thought (Payne 1982: 138).

In addition, some Western experts also question the philosophical acceptability of "stability" by Soviet political thinking in general. Perhaps in the Marxist-Leninist perspective social, political, and economic processes cannot be deliberately frozen (Ermarth 1981: 59). Concepts like "equivalence" and "balance" may therefore seem unnatural to the Soviet authorities because they imply an enshrinement of the status quo (Lambeth 1979: 25). Efforts to stop what Marxism-Leninism regards as the natural course of history (that is, in particular, the increasing influence of socialism in all parts of the world) will only deepen existing contradictions and lead to increasingly dangerous crises. On the basis of this assumption, Western experts conclude that "the Soviets have had little use for such abstract Western notions for shoring up deterrence as improving communication between adversaries, strategic equilibrium, force symmetries, and the credibility of the threat of assured destruction" (Miller 1982: 186). Similarly, the favourite Soviet concept of "equality and equal security", which has never been defined in precises quantitative terms, is suspected to be "but one more manifestation of the Soviet penchant for overinsurance against the failure to engage one enemy at a time" (Miller 1982: 103).

Whatever concept of Soviet foreign policy is being examined, one should always recall the fundamental overall framework within which Soviet authorities operate when using such terms. According to Gray/Brennan, this fundamental assumption includes for instance the following elements: (1) For objective and scientific reasons the West is an enemy. (2) The struggle between communism and capitalism must be fought until the end, and this end will of course be the victory of the first. (3) Situations where restraint by the other side provides damage-limitation for the Soviet Union do not represent real stability; Soviet leaders trust only what they are able to control. (Gray/Brennan 1982: 526).

Finally, one should distinguish between what the Soviet Union would prefer - which is, no doubt, superiority - and what it perceives to be attainable in the foreseeable future - which is pursuing a policy of mutual deterrence (Garthoff 1984: 310).

The probability of a Soviet surprise attack

When discussing the principles of Soviet strategy, Western experts regularly end up by expressing their concern about what might be called the nightmare of nuclear confrontation: the possibility of a Soviet surprise attack, i.e. nuclear pre-emption or (used synonymously) a nuclear first-strike. The documentary background of such fears is the abundant reference, in Soviet literature, to the desirability of taking the initiative, using speed and shock, mastering deception and "maskirova" techniques, exploiting secrecy and surprise and striking first and fast whenever possible in order to demoralize the enemy (cf. Betts 1982: 202ff. and 231-238; Vigeveno 1983: 31; Freedman 1984: 12f.). Obviously, surprise constitutes a dominating aspect of Soviet stategy, probably as a result of the massive trauma inflicted on the Soviet Union by the German invasion of 1941. The lesson drawn from that shocking experience is that any successful attack must surprise the enemy by employing superior forces and proceeding with correct timing (Erickson 1981: 49-70). This assumption constitutes a familiar line of reasoning in Western literature.

Yet Vigor, who has written the most comprehensive and up-to-date study on what he calls "Soviet blitzkrieg theory", explicitly denies the existence of such a threat although he suggests that the Soviet political and military leadership has a very clear view of the utility of surprise attack at the strategic level. However, "so long as neither of the super-powers acquires a first-strike capability", it can hardly be considered to be a serious option (Vigor 1983: 145). The Soviet leaders, probably planning a launch-under-attack response in case of a nuclear war, would also expect the United States to launch under attack - thus they are not apt to attribute to themselves, for the time being, the advantage of launching a surprise attack and escaping with impunity (Leites 1982: 376). Both sides are aware of the virtual impossibility of a disarming attack (Erickson 1981: 55). Furthermore, as one expert observes one should not forget that the leaders of the Soviet Union "are cautious and rather fearful men" (Howard 1981: 8). That is why, as another Western expert notes, Soviet spokesmen caution against the hypothesis of what they call an "adventurist strategy", implying unacceptable and uncontrollable risk (Erickson 1982: 246).

Any imaginable reasons for launching a first-strike with nuclear weapons do not seem to be very realistic; as Betts (1982: 237f.) points outs, a Soviet briefer would have to convince his superiors that the Soviet Union has a disarming capability sufficient to preclude retaliation and/or that the logic of self-deterrence working on the American side paralyses United States decision-makers, who then abstain from retaliation. Neither the first nor the second condition can be fulfilled in the foreseeable future.

Still, in this connection one might argue that this conditional explanation does not bring much comfort because it "does not sufficiently take into account the extreme subjectivity inherent in a psychology of preemption" (Miller 1982: 213). More specifically: how would Soviet leaders decide if they were convinced that an American nuclear attack is imminent? A Soviet nuclear first-strike is said to be in fact thinkable if it reflects the "conviction that the least miserable option at the brink of a hopelessly unavoidable nuclear catastrophe would be to strike first and decisively and to do so as to secure a measure of initiative and control" (Lambeth 1981: 114). Indeed there remains at the centre of Soviet doctrine an ominous proposition that has never been alleviated or repudiated: the proposition that any nuclear war would be decided in its initial phase - therefore the side attacking first would have a decisive advantage (Hyland 1982b: 59). Two situations may be envisaged where this doctrine would be applicable: either if, to Soviet leaders, an American nuclear attack seems imminent, or if they feel an impending dramatic negative shift in the balance of power, coupled with dire internal problems and domestic competition for power (Lebow 1981: 223-233). By contrast to the Western tactical concept of first-use, this would amount to a virtual strategic first-strike doctrine for a situation "if the worst comes to the worst" (Dyson 1984: 250f.). One possible scenario would then be a situation in which the Soviet Union believes in the inevitability of a war and pre-empts either because NATO alerts its forces or because NATO does not respond and thus offers an opportunity to be beaten before it is too late (Betts 1981: 129f.; 1982: 162f.). And even if a surprise attack "out of the blue" can be ruled out as completely unfeasible because the attacker would hardly be capable of eliminating all warning signs, one might argue that these signs could be blurred by a period of military manoeuvres coupled with additional deception measures including "whispering campaigns" and "diplomatic noise" (Erickson 1981: 55f; Betts 1982: 164f.). It has been noted that Warsaw Pact troops, during their annual military exercises, regularly adopt attack positions without provoking any impact on the state of Western readiness. Such exercises might be used as the first stage of a real attack which would then be quickly executed provided that Western intelligence did not react in time by identifying the first move as a signal triggering alert status (Hermann 1982: 307f.). Also Soviet indications of having adopted a launch-on-warning posture (Blechman/Luttwak 1984: 43) are often viewed in this perspective. At any rate, as Western experts argue, the basic Soviet aversion to the risk of launching a strategic nuclear first strike does not necessarily exclude the possibility of initiating a pre-emptive strike on a regional scale such as against NATO forces in Europe (Understanding Soviet Military Developments 1977: 55; Douglass/Hoeber 1981: ch. V; Valenta 1982: 60; Vigor 1983: ch. 14).

As far as the risk of a surprise attack by purely conventional means is concerned, success would be achieved only under very special circumstances. Stratmann reports that a very short warning time is sufficient to remove NATO's tactical nuclear weapons from their vulnerable storage sites; hence the main purpose of Soviet surprise attack - denying NATO the capability of responding by the first-use of nuclear weapons - would not be met (Stratmann 1981: 122f.). Also, a

220

pre-emptive strike against NATO's command, control and communication (C3) systems would hardly put the West in a situation of complete helplessness, due to redundancy in the C^3 structure (ibid.: 151). From a purely military point of view the Soviet Union does have a sufficient capability to launch a conventional surprise attack against NATO's key positions in Western Europe (Meyer 1984: 27) in order to take as hostage some NATO territory and thus acquire an important bargaining chip and undermine Western Alliance cohesion; still, the risks of thereby triggering a limited nuclear response by NATO are much too serious as long as NATO's commitment to the first-use of nuclear weapons remains credible (Stratmann 1981: 19-37, 157-164). Nevertheless, as one expert cautions, although conceding that NATO's threat to use nuclear weapons makes the risks of a Soviet attack on Western Europe astronomical, one must not foster "the illusion of permanence about post-1945 European stability". At the least the emergence of Soviet parity in nuclear arms did not enhance the credibility of escalatory American nuclear threats (Betts 1981: 121; Meyer 1984: 53).

Still, most Western experts agree that whatever the risks of "limited" Soviet surprise actions, at least the nightmare of a large-scale strategic "bolt from the blue" counterforce strike can be excluded (Lockwood 1983: 175). They point to the low state of readiness of Soviet strategic forces and, most importantly, to the fact that the Soviet strategic posture of balanced strategic offensive and defensive capabilities "is designed to restrain as much as possible the US threat to use its military power in response to Soviet-sponsored 'national-liberation movements' in areas vital to Western and US interests and security" (ibid.: 176).

The political uses of military power

Western students of Soviet military strategy increasingly tend to focus not only on nuclear strategy in terms of contingencies and responses the Soviet Union might choose; they also give growing attention to the significance of military power in peacetime or in acute international crises short of the actual use of military force. According to Hyland, a consensus is emerging in the West that "Soviet policymakers in any case see a close linkage between military power and political influence" (Hyland 1982a: 58; cf. also Mason 1984: 174).

In this context Western analysts inquire into the intervention capabilities available to the Soviet Union and its allies. They point to the Soviets' claim now to have the right to exercise their power on a global scale (Holloway 1983: 91). There seems to be wide agreement among Western experts that the most immediate utility of the Soviet effort to build up military power and to change the "correlation of forces" has to be seen in the context of foreign policy, i.e. in terms of "power projection" into distant crisis areas (Marshall 1979: 12f.; Haselkorn 1978: 91f.; Baylis/Segal 1981: 40; Kolkowicz 1981c: 30f.; Meissner 1983b: 151-162). This is said to be logically in line with the Marxist-Leninist premise that the role of military force depends on the general politico-military condition (Lider 1981: 191-193). Also the use of military power, according to the Marxist-Leninist view, must always be evaluated in the political context. One Western expert cites the Soviet diplomat Falin who said that "a weapon has an impact even if it is still in the depot" (Backerra 1983: 51). Western analysts seem to agree that - by contrast to some confusion prevailing in American strategic doctrine - for the Soviet Union the relationship between military policy and foreign policy has always been clear. According to Rubinstein, "Moscow ...is a firm believer in the ability to provide additional foreign-policy options and political advantages" (Rubinstein 1981: 187). Or, as Miller puts it:

> "The Soviets are perhaps todays's most diligent practitioners of the classical dictum that the purpose of strategy is to achieve one's objectives without recourse to armed force." (Miller 1982: 205)

In fact Western analysts refer to dozens of Soviet statements indicating unambiguously and coherently that the growing military strength of the Soviet Union has a healthy influence on the evolution of international politics and that the shift of the "correlation of forces" in favour of socialism is increasingly constraining "imperialism" (cf. Deane 1978: 88f.; Legvold 1982: 199-201). Of course they know that the Soviet term "correlation of forces", encompassing a variety of elements, must not be equated with the Western concepts of "balance of power" or "military equilibrium" (Legvold 1982: 200f.).

More specifically, it is argued that the rapid build-up of Soviet forces made some options previously available to the United States highly questionable by undermining and paralysing them (Backerra 1983: 50). First and foremost among the instrument serving this purpose is deterrence by nuclear weapons. As Simes puts it:

> "...members of the Soviet ruling group approach nuclear deterrence not as a way to preclude use of military force, but on the contrary, as a means of allowing greater operational flexibility below the nuclear threshold. When Moscow talks about strategic stability, it does not mean stability on all levels of military competition; rather it seeks stability that deters action only on the highest (holocaust) level of superpower confrontation to create more favorable conditions to exploit its conventional military advantages." (Simes 1981: 95)

In more operational terms, the Soviet Union is assumed to attain the capability to win a nuclear war and survive it; in this case the United States would feel the "pressure of constraint" and thus, in every important clash of insterests, be "the one pressed by the necessity to make concessions and to propitiate" (Nitze 1978: 11).

This line of reasoning is also held to be particularly relevant with regard to the Soviet "modernization programme" for intermediate-range nuclear weapons systems in Europe; as Holst put it, the deployment of SS-20 missiles "raised several basic questions with respect to Soviet long-range intentions in Europe about the purposes of the Soviet Union's continued investment in special capabilities for holding Europe as a nuclear hostage" (Holst 1983). More generally, one might argue that in the minds of the Soviet leaders their investment in strategic forces has "yielded handsome political dividends" (Lambeth 1979: 32). In this connection, American analysts quote Soviet references to "the unalterable truth that the balance of forces... has changed radically and continues to change to the detriment of imperialism"; such references seem to reflect a mood of self-assurance, conducive to an assumption of licence to meddle in troubled third world areas (ibid.: 33).

Yet the same analysts warn against projecting simplistic concepts for employing strategic threats for political gains (i.e. "compellence" in Western strategic terminology). The Soviet leadership probably does not aim at predictable pay-offs in crisis diplomacy but perceives strategic power as a means for supporting Soviet participation in global diplomacy. This assumption is aptly summed up by Lambeth:

"It is almost impossible to isolate any systematic Soviet 'theory' concerning the political exploitability of strategic muscle. The best that can be said here is that the Soviet leaders harbor unforgettable memories of what it means to be on the short end of the strick in superpower showdown." (Lambeth 1979: 38)

While this conclusion may be somewhat fuzzy and leave too many uncertainties, another American author suggests that distinctions should be drawn between six different Soviet theories about the political uses of military power: (1) between the unlimited Soviet preoccupation with military power and unlimited Soviet reliance on military power, (2) between the Soviet attitude to military power developed on the basis of Soviet reception of Western concepts, and the view that Soviet military policy is exclusively a product of domestic factors, (3) between a military policy aimed at making historical changes safe, and a military policy aimed at bringing about such changes, (4) between a military strategy aimed at precluding certain options should war in Europe break out, and a strategy aimed at precluding options already in peacetime, (5) between wishful thinking and safe expectations, and (6) between a foreign policy where military power plays a central role without being employed systematically, and a foreign policy in which military power is right from the beginning carefully and systematically integrated. Neglecting these differentiations would lead to either overestimation or underestimation of Soviet intentions (Legvold 1982: 232f.).

Apart from nuclear weapons, the classical military instrument to exert political pressure in peacetime is perceived to be Soviet seapower. Analysing the increasing readiness to use a "Soviet military presence" in support of foreign policy objectives several kinds of operations are identified, ranking from positioning ships in certain regions to the full establishment of strategic infrastructure for naval support of war-related missions (MccGwire 1981a: 251). At any rate, there is hardly any disagreement about the fact that the Soviet Union has become a global Power with corresponding power projection capabilities (Ermarth 1982: 116) and about the credibility of the Soviet naval threat (Miller 1978: 55). Higher levels of military activity outside the European and Chinese border theatres seem inevitable (Jukes 1981b: 73; Kolkowicz 1981b: 84). And as the Soviet Union is at least as powerful as the United States, it must be expected to no longer practice the traditional confrontation avoidance whenever a direct clash with the other super-Power appears to be inevitable. As Kolkowicz concludes, "the Soviets are not likely to blink first in an eyeball-to-eyeball confrontation" - the two super-Powers are on a potential collision course (Kolkowicz 1981c: 35).

However, it should be noted that the interpretation of specific developments in terms of the power projection theory necessarily implies elements of subjective speculation. In addition, as one author notes, one should not forget that the efficacy of the political use of Soviet naval forces is quite relative; it depends to a large extent on the nature of the West's response to Soviet initiatives of this type, and even more so as the peacetime role of Soviet naval forces is still in its formative stages (MccGwire 1981a: 250f.). Furthermore, one should not forget that the growing Soviet power projection capabilities have had and will have a sobering impact on the image of the Soviet Union in the third world (Ayoob 1981: 115).

More generally, one might argue that ultimately the political impact of military force depends on the perceptions held by those who are at the "gunpoint" of such power. Such perceptions, in turn, can be and in fact are being influenced by Soviet propaganda. As a result it seems to some Western European politicians and statesmen that the idea "beware of provoking the Soviet Union" has become the very essence of political wisdom for shaping relations with the Soviet Union (Ruehl 1982: 306). As Ruehl points out, the psychological effects of Soviet power, coupled with subtle Soviet insinuations, have led to a growing readiness for adaptation to Soviet interests. In this connection it seems that Soviet propaganda is particularly successful in playing on Western sensitivity with regard to the risk of war; this development might ultimately paralyse Western decision-making (ibid.: 307).

Another issue in this context is the choice of adequate strategies available to the West to cope with the Soviet challenge. In this respect Western analysts offer a bewildering variety of propositions and suggestions - all of course depending on the basic assumptions held about what causes the Soviet leadership to accommodate and how it will react to the various positive and negative incentives offered. The suggested responses embrace the entire continuum ranging from unilateral restraint to bellicosity. Any such proposal is explicitly or implicitly linked to hypothetical premises in terms of an "if-then" clause; for instance, Shulman argues:

224

"It is sometimes argued that the only language the Soviets understand is force and that therefore we must confront them with a
tough policy in order to encourage restraint or a willingness to
negotiate. This is to confuse firmness with bellicosity. A quiet
and civil firmness, which is the mark of true strength, may be
productive, but a bellicose challenge or ultimatum is more likely
to evoke a belligerent response... Evident weakness would also
evoke Soviet aggressiveness..." (Shulman 1982: 97f.)

This type of reasoning clearly exhibits both the importance of
the basic assumptions held about the adversary and the inherently
hypothetical nature of all of this thinking. Ultimately the policy
advice offered by these experts rests on insoluble matters of judgement expressed in simple, axiomatic propositions such as: "If American toughness, then Soviet restraint = wrong"; "if American bellicosity, then belligerent Soviet response = correct"; "if unilateral
American weakness, then Soviet aggressiveness = correct", and so on.
Such propositions may or may not be true; at any rate they are difficult to prove or disprove. There is no need, at this point, to detail
the enormous number of policy implications and operational consequences they carry.

ASSESSMENTS OF SOVIET ARMS CONTROL POLICY

The motive of Soviet arms control policy

Assessing Soviet behaviour in the field of disarmament and arms
control means first and foremost assessing Soviet aims and motives in
this specific field. It is clear that this can only be done by speculation. Therefore, a variety of theories regarding Soviet motives for
arms control can be found, some of which are mutually compatible
while others are downright contradictory, accusing each other of
starting from erroneous premises regarding Soviet intentions. This,
in turn, gives rise to heated debates. Thus, a considerable part of
the Western debate about Soviet arms control policies is highly
polemic in both tone and content.

One of the most controversial arguments concerns nothing less
than the very basic assumption that arms control negotiations indicate the existence of some minimum common interest and consensus. For
instance Gray/Brennan dismiss this view as representing nothing but a
myth rooted in a completely inappropriate understanding of the Soviet
concept of war and peace. They argue that it is futile to hope for a
beneficial education process continuously bringing Soviet negotiators close to the concepts and philosophy of their Western counterparts (Gray/Brennan 1982: 515). Another of the illusions scorned by
American experts is the assumption widely held by American
decision-makers that in arms control negotiations "we have sought to
change facts via negotiations - it cannot be done" (Gray, in:

225

Perceptions 1979: 348). It may certainly not be useless to discuss these and other naive assumptions critically before engaging in any further theorizing about Soviet aims and motives.

Why does the Soviet Union engage in arms control negotiations, and why has it signed several agreements? In searching for an answer, most Western experts start from an interpretation of the overall political strategy presumed to guide Soviet leadership. Thus they assume a fundamental unwillingness, on the part of the Soviet negotiators, to agree to fair and equal arrangements, suspecting them of aiming at unilateral advantages only. It is in fact difficult to find many American expert opinions expressing the conviction that the Soviet Union has definitely accepted the condition of strategic equivalence and parity and will not launch major efforts to gain advantage (an exception is Wells, in: Perceptions 1979: 367f.). Lambeth (1980: 33) goes so far as to suggest that the Soviet leadership did not even look at SALT as an alternative means of addressing the problem of Soviet security, but from the very outset approached the negotiations "as a direct adjunct to her military planning." Western analysts also point to statements made by Soviet spokesmen who have explicitly claimed that any progress in the field of arms control is due to the shift of the "correlation of forces" in favour of socialism, which thus has been able to force the agreement on the United States (Deane 1978: 82f.).

Of course it is conceded by many Western authors that some sense of economic difficulties may also have led the Soviet leadership to a preoccupation with domestic concerns and thus the desire to stabilize the international environment (Caldwell 1971: 20). Yet theories about alleged economic motives for arms control are very critically examined; in a careful analysis based on the totality of statistical material available Becker concludes that it is virtually impossible to discern the slightest move towards political restraint generated by economic weakness or technological dependency (Becker 1982: 58f.). Soviet military expenditure continued to grow irrespective of SALT, and Soviet leaders clearly expressed their intention not to slacken their efforts to improve the strength of Soviet armed forces (ibid.: 57). Therefore, any hopes regarding growing pressures by Soviet "consumers" to shift priorities from the military sector to welfare and improvements of the standard of living are inevitably futile (ibid.: 80f.). After all, priorities and preferences are definitely different in East and West; ever since Lenin, Soviet leadership has primarily emphasized the creation of an economic base for developing future military programmes (Hardt 1978: 123).

Similar reservations are expressed by analysts of the Soviet decision-making process for arms procurement. According to Hyland (1982b: 55f.) Soviet force policy tends to be shaped mainly by three factors: (1) by five-year economic planning increments, (2) by actual implementation of strategic weapons programmes in a rather mechanical and almost routine process, and (3) by technical considerations. Actual changes brought about by SALT and other arms control agreements have been marginal.

Hence, Western experts overwhelmingly tend to emphasize the less benign intentions supposedly underlying Soviet arms control policies. Summarizing the respective hypotheses, Rubinstein concludes that Moscow has exploited the theme of arms control:

"as a means for compensating for military and technological inferiority trying to induce the rival to offer unilateral concessions and limit its military programs, and gaining support internationally and among pacifist-minded groups whose domestic lobbying might affect their own government's policies." (Rubinstein 1981: 177)

The first aim is repeatedly stressed in Western literature. According to this view, the Soviet Union "saw the negotiating route a possible way of curtailing Western programs and dispositions that tended to offset the gains the USSR had herself been making in bringing about a more satisfactory military balance" (Sonnenfeldt/Hyland 1979: 22). At best Soviet behaviour is viewed as being motivated by intentions to "buy time for the Soviet Union to complete the process of overhauling, and in some respect surpassing, the United States in strategic capability" (Gelman 1981: 44). "Catching up" in strategic high technology is often quoted as being one of the crucial motives for the Soviet interest in arms control negotiations (Gray, in: Perceptions 1979: 348).

This line of reasoning again fits into the overall Soviet conception of the "correlation of forces" which, according to the fundamental assumptions of Marxism-Leninism, is bound to shift constantly in favour of socialism. That is why President Carter's "deep cuts" proposal regarding reductions of up to 50 per cent of the nuclear arsenal was so quickly and vigorously rejected (Young/Young 1980: 23). The most damaging consequence of the "correlation of forces" approach to Soviet-American relations, according to Gibert (1977: 142), is the Soviet refusal to engage in a process of reciprocity:

"The Soviet leaders do not perceive the attempts of the American government to negotiate issues, to ameliorate the arms race,... as indicating any genuine desire for peace. On the contrary, these are involuntary acts forced on a still hostile and aggressive America. Accordingly, indications that the United States really would like to improve superpower relations do not induce reciprocal feelings on the part of the Soviet leaders." (ibid.: 142f.)

On a more general level of explanation, Western authors note that nothing "can induce the Soviets to scrap their fundamental approach to the inevitable conflict of systems"; as arms control negotiations are no exception to this rule, they are also definitely subject to Soviet perceptions of a zero-sum conflict (Mitchell 1982: 131). Therefore, it is assumed that "to a Marxist theorist, the basic premise of arms control - that weapons in themselves contribute to the risk of war - is sophistry" because in the Soviet perspective "conflict results from the necessary clash of opposing social forces" (Blechman 1980: 106f.).

When discussing the aims underlying Soviet arms control policy, one may wish to differentiate according to the regional or global framework within which arms control negotiations take place. As far as Europe is concerned, the Soviet Union is held to envisage a more or less fundamental change of the existing web of political relation-ships, first 'by defusing the previously disputed Soviet presence in Eastern Europe, secondly by promoting its version of political "nor-malization" on the European continent (van Oudenaren 1982: 238-244), thirdly by the attempt to split the unity of the Western alliance by exaggerating the threat emanating from the American armed forces and simultaneously offering "military détente" to Western Europe (ibid.: 257f.; Sharp 1984: 239). Other long-term objectives supposed to underlie Soviet arms control policies with regard to Western Europe are the will to maintain Eastern Europe as an ideological and mili-tary buffer, and to limit foreign and military bases around the Soviet perimeter, most especially American forward-based nuclear weapons in West Germany (Sharp, loc. cit.).

As far as arms exports to the third world are concerned the Soviet Union is assumed to give priority to its policy of support for "wars of national liberation" - hence it has little interest in conventional arms control negotiations (Luck 1978: 64).

In spite of all these rather pessimistic analyses of the Soviet motives underlying arms control policies the overall picture of future prospects for arms control is not necessarily a gloomy one. Even if one fully and realistically accepts that "arms control cannot change the Soviet view of history" and "cannot transform the relationship" (Nye 1982: 243), it may still provide communication that enhances crisis stability (ibid.).

Even with regard to the suspected motives underlying Soviet arms control policies, some American experts think that one should not adopt a cynical attitude but, rather, try to leave open the question as to whether the Soviet leaders are using the arms control nego-tiations to conceal an aggressive strategic programme or whether they envisage a programme for political accommodation. The latter possibi-lity should not be excluded from serious consideration; according to Steinbruner (in: Perceptions 1979: 365) "the error of spurning a constructive lead is as serious as that of being gulled by cynical propaganda."

Furthermore, as Bjorkman/Zamostny (1984: 198) argue, one should also bear in mind the possibility that there are differing views prevailing in the Soviet Union, such as those that "question the wisdom of viewing East and West as two irreconcilable hostile camps in an age of potential global destruction", on the one hand, versus those that advocate security "to be achieved solely through unilateral increments in military power" (ibid.). Therefore, it may not be appropriate to offer generalizations about motives determining Soviet arms control policies without paying due attention to considerable variations within the Soviet political élite. It is clear, however, that the merits or demerits of this argument again depend on the pertinence of the assumptions regarding the internal structure of the Soviet political system and its degree of unity or diversity.

Conclusions about Soviet negotiation techniques

According to a more radical version of the theories about Soviet aims and motives, the Soviet conduct of negotiations is ultimately designed to lull the West into complacency and thus forms part of a "carefully orchestrated deception campaign" aimed at strengthening those elements in the United States that favour arms control as an alternative to higher military expenditure (Miller 1982: 202). The decisive element of Soviet strategic deception in the field of arms control is said to be the shift from advocating superiority to advocating parity because "the Soviets have learnt... that bragging when the US felt weak would precipitate massive US rearmament while a low profile would institutionalize Soviet superiority" (Mihalka 1982: 90).

Another particularly obnoxious effect of Soviet deception technique is seen in "causing fissures in the Western alliance structure" (Miller 1982: 202) as well as within each Western country splitting the "ruling circles" committed to further armaments from the "peace-loving masses" motivated by "political realism." So strategic deception goes hand in hand with propagandistic efforts to influence the public (Joensson 1979: 51). The insight that the American "ruling class" is not a monolith but is open to influences of all kinds, even foreign, is one of the major findings of the Soviet "amerikanisti" (Schwartz 1978: 157). From a Marxist-Leninist point of view these cracks in the monolith are undoubtedly "signs of American weakness" (Lenczowski 1982: 262). Likewise, the protracted struggle within the American administration over "guns versus butter" questions is of course interpreted as a "symptom of the demoralization of a large segment of the American ruling class" (ibid.). Since "communist ideology has no rationale for not exploiting a favorable power balance" (Kissinger 1982: 13), Western experts are afraid of the temptation to profit from what to Soviet decision-makers appears an unprecedented chance to interfere in Western affairs.

To Western analysts the Soviet tactics in the case of the INF problem in Europe provide ample evidence of a more refined but likewise misleading perception of the West and particularly of the role of the "antimilitaristic trend" in Western Europe. As Gelman points out, Soviet authorities increasingly borrow political and public relations techniques in the United States, thereby mainly encouraging the American public to project aspects of United States life on Soviet society and suggesting the necessity to help "moderate groups" in the Soviet Union by adopting co-operative policies (Gelman 1981: 51).

Soviet negotiation and bargaining tactics in a more restricted sense are viewed in the same context. Western experts analysing the Soviet conduct of arms control negotiations seem to largely agree on some crucial characteristics. First and foremost, they emphasize the Soviet inclination to negotiate from strength, a policy to be seen in connection with the general Soviet approach to power as an instrument of diplomacy - "the conviction that matchless military power is the most stable foundation on which to base both the security of the nation and the conduct of diplomacy" (Miller 1982: 283). In this connection it is interesting to note that Western analysts identify an explicit preoccupation with "position-of-strength" diplomacy by Soviet authors (Husband 1979).

Other features mentioned by Western analysts concern the unwillingness to make concessions (which, in the Soviet view, are interpreted as a sign of weakness), the use of "red herring" negotiation techniques (Joensson 1979: 61-78) and other typical patterns. One author draws particular attention to the Soviet search for ambiguous and generalized mutual pledges "each containing broad mutual promises so phrased as to fail to commit the Soviet Union to anything specifically defined, but having the potential for some constraining effect on the US public" (Gelman 1981: 46). Another - quite successful - negotiating technique is what might be called "preventive agenda-setting", i.e. defining certain basic problems in a way that does not offer any room for further compromise and commits the other side to negotiate on terms and within a frame of reference chosen by the Soviet Union. Such elements of a pre-set agenda in the current arms control negotiations are, for example, the theory that Afghanistan and Poland constitute issues belonging exclusively to the socialist community, the theory that the SS-20 missiles must not be compared with the American Pershing-2 missiles and cruise missiles because the latter are said to be far more dangerous, the theory of necessarily including the Atlantic Ocean and North America in the area covered by confidence-building measures if the European part of the Soviet Union is to be included, etc. (van Oudenaren 1982: 273f.).

Finally, it has been noted that Soviet negotiators never supply hard data about Soviet capabilities, thereby avoiding the risk that they might tell their American counterparts something that the latter did not already know and obliging them to disclose what they know about the USSR. Hence, as Quester (1980: 205) observes, "the USSR has the best of both worlds, cashing in on a reputation around the world for having ever-more-accurate missiles, ever-more-powerful military forces, while choosing to deny having such capabilities, forcing the United States to accept the burden of proof that the West has a need for matching weapons on its side."

American scholars tend to highlight the specific Soviet negotiating style even more distinctly when collating it with American
attitudes on negotiations. In a comparative perspective, the Soviet
leaders and negotiators, by contrast to their American counterparts,
are said to "consider negotiations competitive and barter-oriented;
conflict and crises normal, often incapable of peaceful resolution,
and often ripe for exploitation, and negotiating tactics obstruc-
tionary and designed to frustrate, confuse, and deceive" (Hulett
1982: 81). Since the Soviet approach to these negotiations reflects
the Soviet attitude to negotiations as a test of wills and as a form
of political struggle with offensives purposes, American analysts
diagnose an inherent incompatibility of United States and Soviet
expectations with regard to arms control negotiations (ibid.). Elaborating the comparative perspective further, one Western analyst
even doubts the capability of democracies altogether to deal with the
"hard-headed, clear-cut strategic ideas which shape Soviet foreign
policy in general and its arms control policy in particular",
especially when Western Governments are pushed about by the tides of
idealism (Towle 1983: 97).

In this way the image provided by Western analysts of Soviet arms
control policies and negotiation behaviour sketches an approach
comprehensively orchestrated and designed for promoting the cause of
socialism at all levels and by all means, at the expense of the capitalist adversary. The image conveyed by these analysts is obviously
inherently pessimistic, reflecting profound mistrust in the reliability of the Soviet Union as a partner for future arms control negotiations. Obviously, the assumptions underlying this image are hardly
conducive to energetic activity in the field of arms control negotiations.

THE META-IMAGE: ASSUMPTIONS REGARDING THE SOVIET VIEW
OF THE UNITED STATES

General characteristics of the Soviet view of the United States

The image of the United States held by Soviet authorities is of
great importance because it tends to influence behaviour. Generally
images may become self-fulfilling prophecies. In the Western academic
debate, however, there is widespread awareness not only of the general importance of images but also of the mismatch existing between
self-image and images held by others, especially in the East-West
context.

As many authors assume, the relationship between self-image and
image is characterized by the logic of the mirror-image: more specifically, the peaceful self-image of each major Power has, as its
corollary, the image of the potential adversary as threatening and
aggressive (Joensson 1979: 42f.). Hence each side's image of the
other side is "every bit as ideological, hegemonic, militaristic, and
polar" as is the other side's image of its own potential adversary

(Caldwell/Legvold 1983:6). This situation may become the origin of all kinds of misunderstandings, as Caldwell/Legvold argue with regard to the Soviet view of the United States:

> "It hardly needs to be said that this image is not the administration's self-image, nor more important, does it fit with a common US conviction that the Soviets understand US policy essentially as it is meant to be understood." (Caldwell/Legvold 1983: 6)

How, then do Soviet authorities perceive the United States, their potential adversary? What can be said about the Soviet image of the United States according to Western experts specializing in Soviet affairs and familiar with Soviet sources? For obvious reasons the United States is the country to which Soviet observers devote the most attention. In a content analysis of _Pravda_ monitoring the coverage of the United States, by taking the space devoted to reports and news on foreign countries as an indicator, the United States was found to be second to none regarding Soviet attention. The coverage of the United States in _Pravda_ during the period 1974-1976 was more than three times as great as the share of the country with the next biggest coverage (the German Democratic Republic with 11.4 per cent) (Katz 1978). In the West, those concerned with the nature of the Soviet threat are fully cognizant of this, and they are also fully aware of the importance the Soviet Union's image of its adversary has for shaping Soviet foreign policy and military strategy (Jackson 1981: 614). There are even several special studies written in the United States focusing on Soviet perceptions of the West and in particular the United States (e.g. Schwartz 1978; Jackson 1981; Lenczowski 1982; Lockwood 1983).

The nature and quality of the Soviet view of the United States is subject to controversy, even in the Soviet Union. It seems that attempts to generalize in this context are somewhat inappropriate because the respective views are constantly evolving. Some Soviet views about the United States can therefore no longer be held to be representative; even the leading Soviet "amerikanist", Academician Arbatov, has harshly criticized some of them, condemning the "vulgaristic work" by authors who "marked their own dogmatism, laziness of thought or simply lack of knowledge with lofty ideological considerations and with concern for the purity of Marxist-Leninist theory" (Arbatov, quoted in Schwartz 1978: 156f.).

While originally Western scholars tended to be "shocked" by what one of them termed the "quality of caricature" of Soviet studies like one by Anatoly Gromyko on the Kennedy Administration (Morgenthau, quoted in Schwartz 1978: 147), more recently Western experts concede that the nature and quality of the Soviet image of the West are improving rapidly. Lenczowski (1982: 261) notes a "tremendous growth of sophisticated Soviet analyses of American foreign policy and international politics in general." Jackson (1981: 638) also admits that "official Soviet analyses of US policies gained in sophistication during the SALT decade..., but remained tied in important respects to the myth structure of the cold war". Schwartz (1978: 163) confirms the existence of a "comparatively realistic assessment of the United States" and a "considerable broadening of views" (p. 158), and he holds that Soviet analysis of the United States has become "strikingly differentiated" (ibid.: 151). Such positive assessments are also shared by Western European observers (von Beyme 1983: 53). In this connection, account must be taken of the fact that American society is open and accessible to all kinds of information gathering; that is why "Soviet bloc intelligence officers sent to the United States are generally surprised since... they are able to obtain information for which they would have to pay a high price in a West European country" (Bittman 1981: 225). Hence one may assume Soviet authorities to be comprehensively and accurately informed about their potential adversary.

Nevertheless, many Western experts still seem puzzled by "incredibly low" Soviet scholarship and the lack of any feeling, in Soviet texts, for "what makes us <i.e. the US> tick"; as Byrnes (1983) points out, Soviet studies of the United States show "an inability to understand our culture", an inability that may be mutual since American and Soviet leaders "have little or no familiarity with each other's countries" (Blechman/Luttwak 1984: 11). To some authors, Soviet analyses of the West appear so strange that they ask themselves whether these analyses can be taken at face value at all. They argue that "there is reason to believe that Soviet public statements perform a variety of more specific mobilization, socialization, and legitimation functions" and that "statements may thus be made which bear little correspondence to actual Soviet perception" (Potter 1980: 71). One of the reasons for the highly ambivalent character of the Soviet view of the United States may be the fact that the Soviet attitude exhibits both fear and envy (Rositzke 1984: 74).

Obviously, the Soviet view has one particular feature that usually does not go unnoticed and is the subject of most critical remarks made by Western observers: this feature can be seen in the inclination visible in most Soviet statements about the West, to fit any information concerning the potential adversary into an all-embracing Marxist-Leninist framework with a rather high degree of rigidity and uniformity (cf. Schwartz 1978: 147). The "discovery" of this feature will, of course, be hardly surprising, as it originates in the very programmatic nature of the Soviet claim to have a "correct understanding" based on truly scientific knowledge. More particularly, Western experts tend to emphasize the following features of the Soviet view: (1) projection of the structure of one's own society on to that of the opponent (Lueders 1981: 112), (2) selection and filtering of those aspects with which Soviet observers feel more familiar, such as American bureaucracy, while neglecting the largely unpredictable legislative process (Schwartz 1978: 61), (3) the extensive use of the technique of discerning "contradictions" whenever inconsistencies observed cannot be explained otherwise (Lenczowski 1982: 75), and (4) the militant nature of many statements which leads

Soviet authors to castigate rather than analyse the policies of the American adversary (Carter 1978: 19).

Many Western experts are convinced that the peculiarities of Marxist epistemology deprive Soviet analysis of the West and the United States in particular of any clear criteria to distinguish reality from desire. The result is said to be wishful thinking at best, and distortion at worst. Western experts consequently find a clear tendency in Soviet analysis of the West to comment on only those aspects that happen to support the Soviet point of view while ignoring those that do not. Soviet "traditionalists" and "realists" may be distinguished by the extent to which they deliberately twist the facts, but "one can generalize that even the 'realists' among Soviet observers continue to tailor their analysis to the interests of the Soviet State" (Lenczowski 1982: 68). Western experts would admit that these tendencies are not necessarily malicious manipulations but, from the Marxist point of view, epistemologically fully justified and also a patriotic duty. But the "Soviet obsession with their own policy interest" (Schwartz 1978: 50) has favoured a rather selective view of the world, including the disregard of even vital aspects. So, for example, it strikes Western experts that "Watergate" was hardly noticed in the Soviet Union and resistance against Nixon was viewed not as a constitutional problem of the American political system but, rather, as an assault on détente.

Western experts are very critical of the methodological presumptions inherent in Soviet thinking on the United States and the insistence on discovering "contradictions", i.e. structurally incompatible tendencies, in the American system. According to Western analysts Marxist studies of the West and the United States confuse actual incompatible tendencies in the system under analysis with inconsistencies of the analysis itself. This has been elaborated by Lenczowski:

"The study of 'contradictions' is the primary method by which Soviet analysts rationalize and reconcile the inconsistencies of Marxism-Leninism and its misinterpretations of politics, economics, and society. 'Contradictions' include both the situations of social antagonisms postulated by Marx and Lenin and any inconsistency in the general theory brought on by new and unforeseen historical circumstances. The use of this 'technique' of 'contradictions' analysis is a tricky business, however, for while it allows a broader scope for the imaginations of 'creative' Marxist-Leninist analysis, it does not delineate the permissible limits of interpretation, a step beyond which would constitute 'revisionism' - a grave and punishable ideological sin. Nevertheless, this technique is indispensable to Soviet analysts, for without it, they would be hard-pressed to explain innumerable situations plausibly." (Lenczowski 1982: 75)

There is also a wide spread feeling among Western experts that the Soviet view is biased in favour of a "basically militant outlook"

(Schwartz 1978: 164) which has a distorting impact on the Soviet image of the West. Particularly disturbing for Western observers is the tendency of Soviet social scientists to use different language when on tour in the West and when at home among their colleagues. When campaining for "peaceful coexistence" abroad, the emphasis is definitely on "peace", while at home people like "Georgy Arbatov, the head of the Institute on the USA ... seek to persuade the hardliners that under the present circumstances 'peaceful coexistence' represents the most effective form of struggle against US imperialism" (Shulman, cited in: Dallin 1981: 376).

Western analysts offer at least two explanations of Soviet verbal militance: either Soviet militance is held to be only lip service for internal purposes, i.e. fulfilling propagandistic pro forma requirements and/or placating the military, or there is indeed a sense of mission in the Soviet Union, with militance as an indicator of militarism. In the latter case the more "realistic" tone of Soviet analysis since the initiation of détente is held to be mere public relations effort. Militance in Soviet analyses of the West, according to Western experts, can be ascribed to several causes, namely the Soviet "anti-capitalist ideology, traditional Russian suspicion of foreigners, the conservatism of the current Soviet leadership" (Schwartz 1978: 164) and, as some authors would maintain, creeping militarism (Colton 1981).

Unity or diversity in the Soviet view?

One of the dominant features of the Soviet view as identified in chapter II was the coherence and systematic nature of Soviet political thinking; emphasis was put on the highly unified character, i.e. mutual compatibility and absence of contradictions, of the set of texts analysed. Dallin describes this feature by pointing to the fact that:

"...in the Soviet case we encounter a special and important trait that might be called a psycho-ideological compulsion, rooted in the Leninist tradition, to provide a totalist, holistic, homogeneous analytical framework for the entire domain of public policy... due to a combination of (1) the notion of a 'general line'; (2) the operational assumption of the relatively high penetrability of foreign policies; (3) the claims to be engaged in 'scientific' analysis and the definition of strategy and tactics; (4) the predisposition to make entire societies the target of Soviet foreign policy behaviour; and (5) the axiom that there are no accidents." (Dallin 1981: 354)

Yet the "totalist, holistic, homogeneous" nature of Soviet political thinking is not always taken for granted. There are many experts in the West who tend to challenge this theory by assuming a certain diversity and partly conflicting views held by competing groups within the Soviet Union. This is of particular importance with regard to the Soviet views held on the West. The clarification of this point is of crucial importance for a proper understanding of the Soviet sources; depending on the pertinence of such assumptions, one either has to envisage the Soviet view or several Soviet views.

For instance, Griffiths (1972) prefers to distinguish at least two main groups having different images of the United States - a more moderate one and another one more inclined to hostile views. Hansen (1975) points out that what has changed is not the image of the West but the influence of each of the groups on the formulation of official doctrine and policy. Schwartz (1978), however, suggests the existence of changes in perceptions as well as in the policy vis-à-vis the United States, both manifest in the rise of a new group of "amerikanisti" in the Soviet Union, i.e. the specialists working at the major Academy institutes such as the Institute of the USA and Canada. According to Dallin (1978: 13) it makes sense to distinguish a "moderate-realistic, pragmatic" view from an "intransigent-hostile, dogmatic perspective." Other labels include, for example (as mentioned previously), the distinction of "realists" versus "traditionalists" (Lenczowski 1982: 261ff.) or "amerikanisti" and "institute scientists" versus "military analysts" and the "Stalinist tradition" (Schwartz 1978).

What is hardly contested among Western experts, however, is the variation of the Soviet view over time: Western experts distinguish four or five post-Second World War periods in Soviet political history: the Stalinist phase, the pre-détente and pre-SALT phase (with the period before and after Khrushchev left office), the phase of détente and finally the post-détente phase since 1976 (see, for example, Jackson 1981). It is assumed that all phases were also reflected in the Soviet image of the adversary: according to many experts, the "traditionalist" view of the United States dominated during the 1945-1953 period. The subsequent Khrushchev era was a time of upheaval not only in Soviet domestic politics but also in terms of images of the outside world. The era of détente and SALT was characterised by the rise of the new "class" of "amerikanisti" from the USA-Institute and the Institute for World Economy and International Relations (IMEMO) to influence and power (cf. Schwartz 1978). Still, according to the Western evaluation, the "traditionalists" maintained strong power positions in the armed forces and research institutes run by them. The post-détente phase with reorientations of United States attitudes toward the Soviet Union by the Carter and Reagan Administrations had "sobering" effects on the views held by the "realists" at the institutes, but basically their attitude remained unchanged. In the event that their theoretical advice might fail in practical Soviet foreign policy, another shift in favour of the traditionalists would come as no surprise.

Of course, consistency is a relative concept. Dallin points out that the "Soviet view of the United States is inherently ambiguous... The United States is the object of both envy and scorn; the enemy to fight, expose and pillory - and the model to emulate, catch up with and overtake" (Dallin 1978: 13). But apart from this ambiguity, "there has been a remarkable degree of consistency in the outlook and analysis which each cluster of images has helped define" (ibid.) since the Second World War. Lenczowski, too, points out that the differences among various views are perhaps less important than previously argued (particularly by Schwartz 1978). What he calls "realists" and "traditionalists" may differ with regard to tactics, but basically both groups are said to agree on questions of global and long-range strategy. Hence, the shifts in the view of the United States are held to be merely tactical in nature and do not represent a true change of mind by Soviet "amerikanisti", let alone Soviet decision-makers. It has also been pointed out that account must be taken of the context within which Soviet statements are made, because public pronouncements can play a plural role (Potter 1980: 71).

The Soviet interpretation of American aims and motives

In analyses of official Soviet statements on United States aims and their underlying motives, a striking feature observed by many Western experts is the absence, in the Soviet view, of attention to, let alone appreciation of, the values, aims and motives usually assumed to be central and dear to American society. According to Schwartz, Soviet spokesmen:

"...do not seem able to understand, for example, the principle of limited government, the rule of law, the separation of powers and majority rule. They have difficulty even conceptualizing the value we place on individual liberty, freedom of speech and press, or the concern we have regarding the morality of our public leaders." (Schwartz 1978: 46-47)

This may also explain the Soviet reluctance to understand the American concern for human rights abroad and particularly in social-ist countries. Soviet sources portray these human rights efforts as "anti-communist propaganda" and "hypocritical" efforts to cloak the true motives of these campaigns in arguments about the freedom of the individual (Lenczowski 1982: 122). In particular, Soviet sources allege that the human rights campaign initiated by the Carter Administration served merely as a pretext to depart from the paths of East-West détente (ibid.: 191).

From the point of view of Western analysts this evaluation of the deep concern of United States Governments for questions of human rights is paradigmatic for the general Soviet perception of ideas and values such as personal liberties, freedom of speech, etc., and their function in and impact on American foreign policy. Western experts note that there is hardly any debate in the Soviet literature on the function of these ideas and values, which are portrayed as mere tools in the hands of the American ruling class, serving for cynical manipulation of the people (ibid.: 100).

On the other hand, it is noted to what extent Soviet analysts emphasize the American aim of halting the spread of communism. According to Western analysts' stressing this aspect at the expense of recognizing other aims can be attributed either to inherent ideological preconceptions or to propaganda purposes (cf. ibid.: 1978: 102-193). Yet one may as well argue that all these elements simply reflect the intrinsically ideological nature of Soviet political thinking in general.

Whatever the rationale of the argument, the Soviet leaders, as one Western analyst puts it, "must and do see the United States as a potentially deadly enemy" (Singer 1983: 176). They cannot but perceive the existence of a society founded on a legitimacy other than Marxism-Leninism as a challenge, a threat to their safety. Consequently, as Bialer and Afferica note, President Reagan's concentration on the communist danger as the fundamental issue in world politics has greatly contributed to a Soviet view interpreting United States policy as "a clear menace to its stability and international authority" (Bialer/Afferica 1982/83: 250). In this perspective, Soviet authors are particularly disquieted by five key elements of President Reagan's policy towards their country: (1) the attempt to alter the balance of military power, (2) the efforts to shape an effective campaign of economic warfare, (3) the effort to redefine the very atmosphere of Soviet-Western relations in terms of anti-Soviet rhetoric, (4) the utilization of "sticks" first in any negotiations, (5) the treatment of third world issues primarily through the prism of American-Soviet relations (ibid.: 250-253). Another American analyst draws attention to a very indicative feature of Soviet perceptions expressed by Kirilenko who complained about the United States launching a "counter-attack" against the Soviet Union (Gelman 1982: 83). As the notion of "counter-attack" logically implies an attack, one might ask how Soviet leaders view this context. Obviously, the meaning of the term "counter-attack" as a reaction refers to what in Soviet perspective constitutes the objective process of the progressive change of the correlations of forces based on the law of history (ibid.: 83f).

Western analysts of the Soviet Union, when inquiring into the perceived roots of American motives as pictured by Soviet sources, draw attention to the general Soviet preference for discerning all kinds of "contradictions." They note that a considerable part of the Soviet effort to understand American aims is devoted to the "general crisis of capitalism" expressing itself in an intensified "class-struggle" between "progressive" and "reactionary" forces in United States society (cf. Gibert 1977:29f. and 63-72). The crisis of American capitalism is ascribed to the irreconcilable conflict between the social classes, and hence weakens the United States socio-political system (ibid.: 85). This approach seems to lead Soviet observers to a somewhat ambiguous conclusion with regard to the shaping of Soviet-American relations. As Gibert puts it:

"Soviet spokesmen contend that internal conflict, irrationality and exploitation will eventually cause a revolutionary change in

the American system, but for the near future they seem to anticipate continuing Soviet competition with a viable imperialist
government." (Gibert 1977: 85)

The Soviet interpretation of American politics

Western analysts are aware that the American political system
seems to be quite puzzling and difficult to understand from a Soviet
viewpoint. The usual juxtaposition of "ruling circles" and "masses",
although frequently referred to in Soviet statements, exhibits some
variations in its practical application: during the 1950s, the "ruling circles" were pictured as a monolithic bloc or unitary actor,
while during the 1960s certain changes were admitted. Soviet commentators perceived "increasing realism" in the ruling circles, most of
all a tendency to acknowledge the increasing power of the socialist
countries, that is, shifts in the "correlation of forces." In the era
of détente Soviet spokesmen believed that in the ongoing struggle
between "sober-thinking elements" on the one hand and "extremely aggressive circles" on the other hand, the latter were in trouble and
consequently forced to make concessions. The post-détente era finally
brought about a growing influence of "reactionary forces" on matters
of foreign policy (cf. Jackson 1981: 615-636). Most Western analysts
are convinced that these changes in view reflect shifts in the internal power balance in the Soviet Union rather than genuine learning
processes, since, by contrast to the newly emerging group of "amerikanisti", which is itself a by-product of détente, military analysts
have always remained sceptical about the influence of "sober-thinking
elements" in American politics.

As far as the social composition of the "ruling circles" is
concerned , both Soviet "traditionalists" and "realists" include the
"monopoly families", directors of large companies, military leaders,
and top political administrators. However, one finds striking
disagreements among Soviet experts when they attempt to describe the
nature and the influence of the American "ruling class." According to
Lenczowski (1982: 262) "traditionalists" and "realists" disagree
about the degree of internal cohesion in the American "ruling class."
Another bone of contention or, to use the proper expression, "unre-
solved contradiction", pertains to the influence that other individuals, groups , agencies, and organizations might exert on the
"ruling circles". Western experts such as Schwartz, Hough and others
draw the following conclusion with regard to the Soviet view of
domestic factors in United States policies: public opinion, according
to the "traditionalists" among Soviet spokesmen is either manipulated
completely by the ruling circles or negligible whenever public views
are critical of the policies of these ruling circles. On the other
hand, "realists" maintain that public opinion has some influence on
American politics and particularly foreign policy, at least since the
"crisis of imperialism" aggravated during the United States
engagement in Vietnam. In their view the "popular masses" are
becoming an increasingly important factor in American politics,

although still remaining instruments in the hands of opposing factions within the ruling circles.

As far as elections and the United States Congress are concerned "traditionalists" would maintain that elections in the United States are a mere ritual, a pro forma affair, a "sham." The crucial question according to "traditionalists" is who finances the campaigns of candidates. "Realists" at least admit that a real struggle is in fact occurring, but they assess it as a struggle among members of the ruling class and not as a genuine class struggle in the Marxist sense of the term. As Schwartz (1978: 47) points out, Soviet "amerikanisti" have made substantial efforts to understand the role of Congress in United States politics, particularly since the evidence is mounting that Congress indeed exerts considerable influence. Soviet analysts were especially astonished by the fact that a congressional majority organized by Senator Henry Jackson was capable of imposing severe constraints on the implementation of the 1974 Trade Reform Act, ignoring the President's warnings and in clear opposition to the interests of large parts of the United States economy. On the other hand, neither "traditionalists" nor "realists" see any difference between the two parties in American politics which is worthwhile mentioning.

The American press is treated in a similar way: according to the "traditionalists" the American press is completely remote-controlled by the ruling circles, and they cannot discern any true freedom of the press. "Realists", on the other hand, would admit that the press has some influence. "Watergate" and the publication of the "Pentagon Papers" provided some additional "contradictions" for Soviet analysts to contemplate. Again the common ground for "traditionalists" and "realists" is that these incidents reflect fissures within the ruling circles rather than a true autonomy of the press.

With regard to government and administration, "traditionalists" maintain that governmental institutions and the administration in the United States are agencies of "monopoly capital." In this perspective their members are seen to be loyal servants of the ruling class. "Realists" would admit some independence, particularly regarding the United States President; although acting fully in accordance with the interests of the ruling class as a whole, the President is held to be faced with difficult problems of mutually exclusive objectives envisaged by rival factions within the ruling circles, questions pertaining to different priorities, and so on. Bureaucratic inertia or even opposition is another problem. Western experts concede that bureaucratic politics is one of the very few facets of the American political system quite well understood in the Soviet Union (Schwartz 1982: 61ff.). The Department of State and the Department of Defense are both powerful in the "realistic" Soviet perspective, but hardly monolithic. Internal conflicts, particularly those between career officers and political appointees, are held to be the rule rather than the exception. Very much like all bureaucracies, both the Department of State and the Department of Defense are seen to have vested interests influencing American foreign policy. While the State Department, in the Soviet view, by and large favoured détente, the Pentagon is assumed to have a stake in the continued arms build-up.

From the Marxist-Leninist point of view, the entire political system of capitalist countries is a mere "agency" of economic interests and fully controlled by those who command the means of production. Soviet analysts have been particularly cautious in commenting on the crisis of Western economies during the 1970s and early 1980s. In the Soviet view, the United States is still the most advanced among the capitalist countries and the leader in terms of the most important indicators of economic performance. Among the reasons for continued economic prosperity in the United States, Soviet sources mention in the first place American technological capabilities and, interestingly, increased governmental interference in economic affairs, namely by the Keynesian practices of control - the "state-monopoly regulation of the economy" in Soviet terminology (Hough 1980: 517). "Traditionalists" and "realists" among Soviet experts to some extent disagree about the prospects of the United States and the West overcoming the current economic crisis. While "traditionalists" in fact see symptoms of capitalism approaching its final stage of decline and ultimate fall, "realists" recommend caution and still share "the grudging admiration that Marx and Engels express for the powers of economic growth under laissez-faire capitalism" (Lenczowski 1982: 79). The prevailing view among "realists" is that the current economic crisis is severe but that world capitalism is likely to recover.

The foreign policy interests of the economic actors are viewed as far from being homogeneous. While the alleged military-industrial complex is said to have a stance in continued arms production, it favours an aggressive foreign policy. Those sectors of the industry that are in search of new markets are assumed to favour an expansionist and risk-taking foreign policy, while groups with a vested interest in East-West trade, mainly the agrarian sector, are assumed to have a vested interest in détente. The conflicts within the "ruling circles" in the United States are to a large extent explained by mutually exclusive economic interests and their implications for the general orientation of American foreign policy.

On the whole, Soviet sources, whether "traditionalists" or "realists", perceive what they call a "deepening crisis" of American society. Among other symptoms are increasing crime rates, widespread drug addiction, racial tensions, a wave of pornography, and declining morale in general. While "traditionalists" among Soviet observers of the United States regard the alleged crisis of American society as just another indication of decline and decay due to the general crisis of capitalism, "realists" favour a somewhat differentiated view: Accordingly, irrational forms of protest (particularly crime, drug abuse, etc.) are distinguished from those that develop (from a Soviet perspective) a positive momentum. The latter include particularly the protest movements against the Vietnam war and the recent peace movement. A significant factor in the growth of mass protest has been, according to Soviet sources, the "increasingly organic interlacing" (Arbatov, cited in: Schwartz 1978: 25) of economic difficulties (decreasing growth rates, inflation, mass unemployment) with social problems (youth alienation) and discontent over American foreign policy (Vietnam).

According to the Soviet perception, as reported by Western experts, internal pressure in the United States was the crucial factor, besides the shift in the correlation of world forces, that led to a policy of détente during the Nixon Administration. The objective was allegedly a shift in the distribution of governmental resources from military expenditure to social programmes in order to placate the discontented population. As a prerequisite, a more favourable international climate was required - hence the better understanding with the Soviet Union. The discovery of the importance of the domestic crisis in the United States for the evolution of American-Soviet relations may in fact have been one of the major self-ascribed merits of the "amerikanisti" from the newly established institutes. As Schwartz (1978: 24) points out:

> "the importance attributed to the 'increasing aggravation of domestic contradictions' in American society reflects, in some measure, the enthusiasm with which the newly-formed USA Institute approached its task. Many of its leading analysts, never having been in the United States before..., could not but be fascinated by the 'conflicts' and 'tensions' of capitalist society, many of which were placed out before their very eyes. Their analyses, in some cases, were smug and self-satisfied." (Schwartz 1978: 24).

Katz (1978: 119), who made a content analysis of the coverage of the United States by Pravda, noticed that between 1974 and 1976 the coverage of domestic American subjects almost doubled, from 12 per cent to 23 per cent of the coverage devoted to the potential adversary. This represents a striking proof of the growing interest exhibited, by the Soviet leadership, in the "contradictions" within American politics.

With regard to the Reagan Administration, however, Soviet spokesmen seem to be particularly puzzled. As Bialer and Afferica (1982/83) note, two schools of thought can be discerned in Soviet publications: according to the first view, Reagan and his principal supporters constitute a specific tendency within American's "ruling circles" - by contrast to other, more "realistic" circles also present in American society. According to the second school of thought, "Reaganism" derives from changes in American politics and social policies, namely from the decline of American power resulting in frustration and hence anti-Sovietism. Both views have similar political implications leading to a pessimistic, reserved and suspicious attitude towards the main adversary.

Ultimately, however, Western analysts think that the Soviet perception of the United States is incapable of properly grasping the nature of Western pluralism (Barnet 1977:97f). As Gelman noticed, "the Soviet leaders were alternately incredulous, gratified, and appalled at the extent to which US leadership and the flow of US policy became buffetted and conditioned by elite pluralism and mercurial popular pressures" (Gelman 1981:44). Therefore, by contrast to the insights acquired by the Soviet "amerikanisti" the Soviet party leadership probably continues to underestimate the dispersion of authority in the United States (ibid.:45).

To Western observers it seems that in the ongoing argument between so-called "traditionalists" and "realists" the credibility and reliability of the West also constitutes a controversial issue. Dallin (1978:16) cites a statement by Foreign Minister Gromyko attacking certain comrades who see "any agreement with the capitalist states ... almost <as> a plot" against the right cause of socialism. The problem Soviet observers face when evaluating American trustworthiness and predictability is ultimately rooted in the Soviet assumption that in the United States system, domestic politics have a decisive influence in shaping United States foreign policy. Lenczowski (1982:76) argues that, as a consequence, Soviet observers perceive American foreign policy as part of a domestic struggle, "the result being the often incomprehensible 'zigzags' that mark American behaviour in international affairs." They then usually resort to rationalizing such "zigzags" as "contradictions." The question arises whether the constant references to "contradictions" may not in fact represent a kind of euphemism for the difficulties encountered by Soviet observers in explaining the key element in American politics.

Yet to the extent that they nevertheless succeeded in understanding Western pluralism, they began to exploit it by skillfully designed propaganda campaigns aimed at spreading dissension and fostering "friendly" groups having an influence on the shaping of American politics, as American analysts note with growing concern.

The Soviet assessment of United States capabilities

Western analysts are aware that Soviet efforts to assess American capabilities are constantly taking place in the context of the Soviet view of the "correlation of forces." Yet this concept, in Soviet usage, represents a much more comprehensive and ambiguous term than the Western concept of "balance of power" (Lenczowski 1982:51f.) comprising military strength, economic capability, political backing, and international support. In the process of assessing the comparative strength of the two countries on the basis of these four variables, a vast number of indicators are supposed to be taken into account (Gibert 1977:23f.). Hence, the procedure is complicated and the results may be "highly elastic and subjective" (Lenczowski 1982:52). It therefore comes as no surprise that the results of the Soviet "correlation of forces" analyses are sometimes subject to change, perhaps irrespective of actual changes in the relevant indicators, simply because the currently relevant "mix" of indicators or the relative weight attributed to them changed. Western experts are convinced that changing Soviet internal and foreign policy requirements have an impact on this approach to capability assessment.

In a study of selected statements by Soviet officials on the subject, Wagenlehner (1981) finds numerous statements claiming superiority of the socialist camp over the "imperialist" countries: however, in the military field Soviet analysts and officials perceive approximate parity. The official Soviet position in this respect is that the Soviet Union currently has a slight lead in the field of INF, while the United States have a minor edge in the field of strategic nuclear forces (Wagenlehner 1981:12). In the economic field the "imperialist camp" is said to be still leading, although the socialist countries are catching up. In the mid-1970s Arbatov warned that the economy of the United States remains very strong, while the late director of IMEMO, Inozemtsev, demanded at the end of the 1970s that the economic strength and possibilities of imperialism should not be exaggerated (cf. Schwartz 1978:17).

With respect to international support, the socialist countries are seen as clearly in the lead, backed by "progressive forces" all over the world while "imperialism" is on the retreat. Regarding internal political backing, however, "realists" and "traditionalists" among Soviet spokesmen may disagree. While "realists" note increasing difficulties for the "ruling circles" due to the worsening "crisis of bourgeois society", "traditionalists" apparently favour a perspective that sees the "ruling circles" still in full control of all aspects of American life. In sum, "realists" tend to see an increasingly advantageous shift in the correlation of forces, while "traditionalists" are less sanguine about the alleged turn of the tide in favour of socialism. Yet all groups increasingly tend to converge on the assumption that the American adversary's main weaknesses are social and economic decay, and waste of resources by "consumerism" - a development commented upon with open contempt by Soviet authors (Gelman 1982:93f). Crucial from the Western point of view is the fact that Soviet optimism with respect to the correlation of forces rests not so much on military capabilities as on an overall assessment of comparative strength. As far as military capabilities in the more restricted sense are concerned, Western experts are convinced that the Soviet Union has no illusions about the West's capability to punish any Soviet attack by a severe, devastating retaliatory strike (Arnett 1981:87f.). Soviet weapons development and deployment to a large extent occur in reaction to previous American moves in the respective sector; this fact is regarded by Western experts as a clear indication of Soviet respect for Western military strength. For example, United States navy officials would admit that Soviet naval policies during the 1950s and 1960s were largely anti-carrier in nature, obviously reflecting due respect for the American carrier force. The current emphasis on antisubmarine warfare (ASW) may indicate Soviet concern regarding American strategic missile submarines (Understanding Soviet Naval Developments 1981:4-5).

One should, however, be aware of the considerable uncertainty remaining with regard to the ways in which Soviet decision-makers perceive what they call the "American threat." As Becker (1981:25) argues, "we do not know whether Soviet images of US actions and intentions are influenced by this indicator <US defence spending> or others" - such as statements by congressional or administrative personalities (ibid.:26).

In sum, the Soviet approach to comparing capabilities takes into account a wide range of factors besides indicators of military strength; hence to Western experts it remains dubious. To them it is another indication of the Soviet tendency to provide a totalistic, holistic analysis of an extremely complicated phenomenon. From the perspective of Western analysts, this amounts to a quest for the impossible, and the result is fuzziness.

One practical conclusion stemming from Soviet reflections about the correlation of forces must not be neglected: as Dallin (1978: 18) notes, the Soviet leadership is starting from the assumption that the United States has acknowledged the Soviet claim for parity - hence "why, they ask, should the United States retain control of the seas as well as superiority in strategic weapons?" In other words: the principle of "correlation of forces" analysis underlying Soviet capability assessment is seen to be valid in all fields of United States-Soviet competition. If this assumption is correct, Soviet leaders must feel particularly disquieted by the Carter and Reagan Administrations' new arms procurement programmes which, in their view, clearly reflect an American drive to upset the military balance and to reacquire military superiority (Gelman 1982: 95f.; Garthoff 1983: 17). But it seems that when evaluating American capabilities, Soviet authorities tend to rely more on United States rhetoric than on facts, picking out what they view as the more ominous aspects of policy (Caldwell/Legvold 1983: 4).

Another, very important question is the incertainty of Western experts regarding the Soviet assessment of American capabilities. Some Western observers argue that the Soviet leaders may in fact underestimate Western resistance - a fatal miscalculation which might even set the Soviet Union on the road to war (Luttwak 1983: 116) or at least offer incentives to exploit "the current American weakness to change the correlation of forces so greatly that if a different community ever comes to power in the United States it will be too late" (Singer 1983: 176). In such a situation, deterrence might fail (ibid.: 192). That is why American analysts studying the Soviet image of the United States are sometimes worried about the possible underestimation of American capabilities by underestimating American intentions. Moscow may be "beginning to see this country as increasingly impotent" (Schwartz 1978: 165). Some experts even argue that Soviet leaders are deliberately playing on United States weakness and, whenever the United States feels reluctant to engage in global responsibilities, are adopting a low profile in order to ensure the acquiescense of the American public and avoid massive United States rearmament (Mihalka 1982: 90). In other words, Soviet strategic deception is assumed to be the direct consequence of a specific image of the United States held by the Soviet élite.

Nevertheless, it is argued, the Soviet Union continues to perceive the United States as adaptative, resourceful, flexible and forceful internationally. The Soviet estimate of American capabilities, according to the majority of Western analysts, is still characterized by respect and awareness of the realities of the strategic military balance. Still, in order to prevent Soviet misunderstandings, the practical consequence drawn from such elements of the meta-image is that efforts should be made "to stress the enduring elements of US strength rather than temporary areas of weakness" (Buchanan 1982: 42).

As far as the practical implications on the Soviet side are concerned, however, the image of American capabilities held by Soviet leaders point in the same direction: while the Soviet view of American military might seems to constitute a mixture of contempt and admiration, fear and confidence, Gibert concludes that "Moscow will continue to place the highest priority on further developing its already formidable military machinery" (Gibert 1977: 127).

The Soviet interpretation of American strategy

Since the end of the Second World War, American military strategy has changed several times. According to Western observers this has had a considerable impact on the way in which the Soviet leadership perceives its adversary. The essential feature of Soviet assumptions regarding American strategy can be seen in the suspicion that the United States may have adopted an attitude to deterrence which allows the utilization of military power for political purposes, i.e. for blackmailing the adversary from a "policy of strength" and exploiting strategic superiority (Legvold 1982: 199-213).

This view may simply constitute a mirror of the Soviet Union's own conception of nuclear warfare, as does the concept of "nuclear war-fighting" which Soviet sources discern to be an intrinsic element of American strategy. United States statements regarding deterrence and the essential unwinnability of nuclear war are dismissed by Soviet sources as propaganda, and they perceive the idea of victory in nuclear war as a primary consideration in United States strategic doctrine (Lockwood 1983: 171f.).

"Traditionalists" and "realists" among Soviet spokesmen differ considerably in their views of the evolution of American strategic doctrines. While "traditionalists" maintain that the present American doctrine is merely old wine in new bottles, "realists" see a real change in United States strategic doctrines to be attributed to the alleged shift in the correlation of forces in favour of world socialism (Jackson 1981: 615-619; Lenczowski 1982: 162).

246

Even "traditionalists" would admit that the United States is not currently in a position to successfully conduct a preventive strike. However, they still perceive an American quest for strategic superiority that could be exploited in different ways. To them "flexible response" does not have much advantage over "massive retaliation"; it merely reflects American flexibility in interpreting what constitutes a threat and how to cope with that challenge (Lenczowski 1982: 172). Likewise, "traditionalists" would not admit any difference between strategic superiority and strategic sufficiency, the latter being only the "diplomatic formula" (Lenczowski 1982: 162). Furthermore, "traditionalists" would simply not take seriously the notion of "mutual" in mutual assured destruction (MAD), while in their view selective and counterforce targeting in sum amount to a programme of "assured destruction" of the enemy, that is, the Soviet Union (cf. Lenczowski 1982: 166). Genuine mistrust characterizes the Soviet Union, mainly because of the assumption that the United States regards the qualitative edge as a means to go beyond a posture of deterrence against nuclear attack, i.e. seeking benefits from the manipulation of the threat of war (Legvold 1979: 12f).

"Realists", on the other hand, are said to maintain that the shift in American military strategy from massive retaliation to flexible response and finally to the strategy of realistic deterrence of the Nixon Administration represents a learning process. Implicitly Soviet "realists" are assumed to admit that a diplomacy of threatening the Soviet Union with nuclear weapons became increasingly impracticable in the 1960s and 1970s. As noted above, "realists" would attribute this favourable course of events to the changing overall correlation of forces.

This in fact seems to represent a recurrent theme in Soviet strategic thinking: any changes for the better which Soviet observers note in American strategy are ascribed to the restraint placed on United States "aggressive aspirations" by Soviet nuclear missile forces and not to any United States desire for peaceful relations (Lockwood 1983: 162).

Leaving aside these differences, however, one probably has to conclude that American strategic thinking is generally unacceptable to Soviet strategists. As Kolkowicz notes, "Soviet analysts find Western strategic sophistries objectionable and unacceptable" on several grounds: because of the apolitical nature of Western military doctrines, the status quo-supportive nature of deterrence and limited war theory, and the interdependent, controllable, mutually balanced, and self-constrained nature of Western doctrines of war (Kolkowicz 1981c: 8-11). These elements, which are taken for granted by American strategists, are questioned by Soviet military thinking for very fundamental ideological and other reasons. In particular, deterrence theory, as seen through Soviet eyes, is a uniquely American construct not understandable if evaluated by criteria applied in Soviet thinking (ibid.: 19).

It is even less understandable considering that, from a Soviet point of view, the American threat to make use of the nuclear component of the strategy of flexible response and more generally the American concept embodied in the PD-59 directive lacks credibility because the United States is felt to be more vulnerable to nuclear destruction at any level of nuclear war than the Soviet Union, no matter how limited United States strategy might try to make it. Since the United States has no significant civil defence provisions, and given the Soviet Union's marginal strategic superiority, any American plans to fight nuclear war are, from a Soviet view, mere "adventurism" and lack credibility- as does United States credibility to deter against Soviet-sponsored aggression (Lockwood 1983: 162-165).

As far as the problem of arms control is concerned, Western observers assume that the Soviet Union starts from an image of the United States favourable to arms control, probably also viewing a coalition of forces in the United States with which deals may be feasible (Jackson 1981: 637). On the other hand, the conviction may be widespread among Soviet leaders that the United States cannot restrain military expenditure because of the strength of the "military-industrial complex" (Hough, in: Perceptions 1979: 110). Based on this assumption, therefore, the Soviet side would be unwilling to believe in United States readiness to make real progress in the field of disarmament. This is merely one of the practical consequences of Marxist-Leninist analysis. Soviet authorities, orienting themselves within this framework, are therefore held to regard this assumption as being confirmed by what they presume about the United States economy's interest in further armaments and the United States Administration's alleged disbelief in arms control (Caldwell/Legvold 1983: 5). Soviet perceptions of the United States are therefore said to be basically characterized by the premise of suspicion and anticipated hostility determining any United States approach to arms control (Joensson 1979: 55-61).

This negative evaluation of United States arms control policies of course has negative implications for the Soviet willingness or unwillingness to negotiate. These implications are further reinforced by another element of the Soviet interpretation of American behaviour in this field. As Lockwood (1983: 175f.) points out, Soviet spokesmen conclude that increased Soviet strategic power has been mainly responsible for compelling the United States to seek arms control negotiations with the Soviet Union.

ASSESSMENT OF INFORMATION ABOUT SOVIET POLICY AND STRATEGY

As the preceding sections have amply shown, the American assessments of Soviet policies and strategies to a considerable extent rely on available written Soviet sources and their interpretation in the light of what is observed of Soviet behaviour and particularly force deployment. Another source are military exercises (Jones 1981), which are monitored by analysis of official reports, satellites, human intelligence and direct observer participation based on the CSCE Final Act. Although Soviet sources are distinguished by explicitness, coherence and a very systematic structure, it is widely felt that additional information and interpretation of the respective official statements would help to fill a real need for a better understanding of the Soviet view. Much has therefore been written about the meaning of official Soviet communications, and a variety of speculations are being offered about the motives and consequences implied by the published Soviet view. Many authors have also tried to infer, by interpolation, additional elements of the Soviet view that are not made explicit in the available sources. It is the purpose of this section to present the major lines of reasoning to be discerned in this context.

Must Soviet statements be taken at face value?

As pointed out in the introductory chapter, the central question raised whenever official source material has been examined, is whether the views expressed can be taken at face value or whether they rather reflect a specific propaganda or even deception purpose. Soviet sources seem to constitute a favourite subject of reservations of this kind. Not surprisingly, two completely opposite opinions are to be heard - one assuming that Soviet statements reflect a Potemkin facade at best and deliberate disinformation at worst, and another one assuming that the authors of Soviet statements really mean what they say and that credence can therefore be placed on published Soviet views (Gibert 1977: 8f.). Proponents of the first view often refer to Soviet statements about the meaning of verbal expression in politics, which seems to include concealment as an inherent part of its very nature:

> "As the Soviet political analyst, Alexander Bovin, has reminded us: 'The verbal expression of policy can play a dual role: it either reflects real political interests and intentions, or, conversely, is called upon to conceal these interests and intentions'." (Schwartz 1978: 6)

Soviet public statements may therefore conceal either particular strengths or particular weaknesses. In this connection, Jacobsen recalls that Stalin obscured the reality of Soviet weakness by promoting an image of exaggerated strength (Jacobson 1983: 8). Other Western experts assume that the same tendency is at work today, but with an inverse relationship: as Lange (1984: 184f.) suggests, Soviet behaviour is oriented by a "dialectical complementarity" of declaratory denial of power in favour of a purely defensive attitude, on the one hand, and determined, planned build-up of actual military power, on the other hand.

Nevertheless, according to a leading American scholar studying the Soviet view, "with the exception of precisely those distortions of recent historical facts, certain cynical and propagandistic criticisms, and the occasional concealment or omission of political intent, the Soviets do mean what they say" (Lenczowski 1982: 23). At least five arguments can be adduced in support of this hypothesis: (1) the evidence from archives captured in the Second World War, (2) the implausibility of the existence in the press of a constant deception divorced from reality, (3) the role of ideology in shaping the Soviet world view (ibid.: 23), (4) the fact that there is not much discrepancy between classified and public Soviet writings on strategic doctrine (Potter 1980: 71), and (5) as already mentioned in chapter I (with reference to a study by Zimmerman 1983) the empirical confirmation of a large coincidence of "words" and "deeds" in Soviet defense spending. These five arguments are self-explanatory. As far as the second argument is concerned, Meyer (1984: 6f.) points out that it would be hard to believe that the USSR can really doctor its military writings systematically, so as to mislead the West: "It would be a mistake to believe that the Soviet officer could quickly discern 'disinformation' from 'authentic' training information." (ibid.: 7)

Again, the key to a proper clarification of this issue probably has to be seen in the role of ideology as a motive force in Soviet political and military thinking and behaviour, as mentioned at the beginning of this chapter. Ideological claims are made "operational" by the CPSU's claim for unlimited leadership. As Schwartz (1978: 6) points out, "given the rigorous demands of a Party leadership highly intolerant of unorthodox formulation and views", it is a necessity for every author of a Soviet statement to keep in line with the official position. No statement published by Soviet sources can therefore be viewed as a politically insignificant expression of some individual attitude. On the other hand, as Gibert notes, "universalist goals, derived from ideology, are now so embedded in Soviet political culture that they impinge upon the entire Soviet foreign policy progress and especially the perceptual framework of Soviet officials" (Gibert 1977: 20). In addition, when considering the ideological nature of Soviet statements, it must be borne in mind that such statements, in a Soviet perspective, are much more than mere "descriptions" or "analyses": they represent programmes for the future as much as analyses of the present. Dziak recalls that:

"for years following the announcement of the new military doctrine in the early 1960s, Westerners were perplexed at the disparities between apparently heady goals of doctrine and yet meager capabilities available for their realization. The tendency was to dismiss doctrine and even strategy as mainly rhetorical exercises... The very nature of the Soviet structure, however, demands that capabilities will follow theory." (Dziak 1981a: 61).

Words can, and more often must, become deeds. As Elizabeth and Wayland Young have remarked:

"A great deal of Soviet activity is best understood in the double negative form as things that the Soviet Government cannot, for ideological reasons, not do. They cannot not support national liberation movements wherever they arise. They cannot not maintain supremacy within the 'Socialist Camp' or seek to extend it whenever opportunity ripens." (Young/Young 1980: 6)

In other words: verbal expressions of political and military strategy tend to have a momentum of "self-fulfilling prophecy." It therefore seems wise not to discard Soviet statements as mere products of propaganda and/or deception. It is precisely their intrinsically ideological character that relates them fully to the crucial principles deeply embedded in the Soviet political and social system. In this capacity they constitute an integral part of the dynamics of this system and they are far too important and too programmatic to be regarded as though they were nothing but a superficial veneer more or less unrelated to the reality of Soviet society and the way in which it is governed. It should, however, be borne in mind that the authors of Soviet source material increasingly pay attention to the foreign political reaction to their discussion; although this does not necessarily lead to deception, it has led to "some muffling of the more strident viewpoints", as Hyland (1982b: 57) puts it. As a consequence one may assume that, at least in the more sensitive areas of strategic doctrine and in recent years, public pronouncements have become a less reliable guide to what the Soviet leadership really thinks and intends.

There is increasing awareness, in the West, of the specific nature of Soviet political and military thinking - and also considerable self-criticism in this respect. A case in point is the occurrence of "gaps" (bomber gaps in the 1950s and missile gaps in the 1960s) where successive corrections had to be made to the earlier alarmist pictures presented by the intelligence community (Prados 1982: 89). Obviously, the interpretation of the information gathered about the Soviet Union is subject to considerable conceptual problems. For instance, Lambeth (1980: 27) criticizes those American officials who "until recently... tended to dismiss these <Soviet> views as merely parochial axe-grinding", while others castigate "Western analysts... fit to dismiss such articulations as propaganda and bombast or mere 'lip-service' to an ideology devoid of foreign policy relevance" (Richard Foster, in: Gibert 1977: ii). For this reason, a large part of the efforts made by Western experts is directed against naive and ethnocentric interpretations of Soviet thinking that do not sufficiently take into account the specific nature of the Soviet approach. Young/Young go so far as to claim that all official and quasi-official American interpretations of the Soviet system "show a profound unwillingness to accept the Soviet system at its own valuation" (Young/Young 1980: 9). It therefore seems that the Soviet sources are sometimes much more indicative than their interpretation by official American readers.

Other Western authors go even further and complain about "precon-ceived conceptual traps" which sometimes are not avoided when Western observers are faced with the dilemma of ambiguous information or lack of information. Such conceptual traps jeopardize perception when Western analysts impute their mentality and reasoning to the Soviet context (Rubinstein 1981: 286f.). One way of avoiding this type of conceptual trap may be increasing attention to historical insights and human understanding (Pipes 1981: 76), another the awareness of what Gray (1982: 92f.) calls the "fog of culture" interfering with American perceptions of Soviet theory and practice.

Ambiguity and the dynamic of Soviet terminology

There are other obstacles, however, to a proper understanding of Soviet sources: interpretation of Soviet texts tend to differ if these texts keep silent or remain ambiguous about certain aspects. Of course, it may be a futile exercise to argue about the meaning of what is not said by Soviet spokesmen. Still, it is quite pertinent to ask whether the ostentatious passing over in silence of certain important aspects of strategy amounts to deliberate concealment of hostile intentions or simply originates in a different evaluation of what is sufficiently important to deserve mentioning.

Yet other difficulties arise more regularly when interpreting Soviet texts: the dynamic evolution of Soviet terminology and the semantic incongruity between Russian terms and their ostensible Western equivalent. Soviet foreign policy terminology is subject to more or less regular shifts in the rules of practical use. Before the Khrushchev era, for example, the balance of power between the Soviet Union and the United States was referred to by the neutral term "dis-tribution of power" or "correlation of forces" (sootnosheniye sil). From 1959, the term "preponderance of power" or "favourable balance of power" (pereves sil) came into use, only to be subsituted by the expression "equilibrium" (ravnovesiye sil) in 1962, obviously taking the impact of the Cuban missile crisis into account. During the Brezhnev era, finally, the old expression of "correlation of forces" once again came into use (cf. Lenczowski 1982: 16; for the changes in the Khrushchev period see Zimmerman 1968: 165-179).

Soviet political language has its peculiar standards and style and it is difficult to follow for those not familiar with it (Vigor 1975a). Ideology "remains the language of analysis, although there was a growing tendency in the 1960s for specialists to adopt the vocabulary and tools of their Western counterparts" (Zimmerman 1980: 27f.). According to Dziak this language possesses:

"..an idiom and a hierarchy <of structure> which are character-ized by a certain degree of precision in usage and application; while the political flavorings are strong, they are mixed with a claim to scientific exactness and certitude. This idiom is not easy to render in clear English; it does not easily 'fit' Western

252

... concepts; it is frequently laced with tendentious claims; and it possesses a certain Aesopian quality" (Dziak 1981a: 17).

Hence, certain precautions are required when interpreting Soviet source material. As Dziak (1981a: 17) observes "Western analysts must approach it on Soviet terms and refrain either from substituting trendy Western strategic and arms control jargon, or dismissing the Soviet military idiom as propaganda or the untutored flummery of an archaic military caste".

Due attention must also be paid to the fact that some key notions important in the context of the politico-strategic relationship have a different - and even contradictory - meaning in East and West. Lenczowski argues:

"A constant feature of the official Soviet lexicon is the use of words with double meaning - each has a face value appropriate for Western consumption and a special meaning for the Soviet them-selves. Among such words are: 'peaceful coexistence', 'peace', 'progress', 'democracy', 'realism', 'security', 'normalization', and so on - all of which have foreign policy significance." (Lenczowski 1982: 270)

Hence it is correct to diagnose a certain ambiguity of many terms prevailing in Soviet theorizing about international affairs. Some Western authors tend to ascribe this fact to a deliberate intention to deceive the addressees by means of "semantic subversion" (Sleeper 1983: IX). However, the ambiguity may also simply constitute an inte-gral part of the whole Marxist-Leninist approach and thus fully conform with its logic. For a Western observer to reject all Soviet statements tinged with ideology for not conveying the "true" image as seen through Soviet eyes would indicate a lack of any proper understanding and an inability to "decode" Soviet ideological language.

If there are any serious restrictions affecting the interpre-tation of Soviet sources, they refer to what Bialer (1981a: 420f.) calls the ambiguity of the ideological influences in foreign policy. These influences "on the one hand make the Soviets extraordinarily conscious of their own security and hence hesitant to take risks; on the other hand they prompt them to see their global expansion in terms of a mission" (Bialer 1981a: 421). To the extent that the ambiguity in Soviet statements originates in a genuine ambiguity of the ideological underpinning itself, the ambiguity of course is hard to eliminate - and any attempt to do so is in fact futile and mistaken.

What do the Soviet sources really convey?

It is one thing to conclude that Soviet statements should and must be taken seriously, at least to the extent that they refer to ideological principles, and try to resolve ambiguities by improved familiarity with the reasoning and language of Soviet statements, but it is quite another matter to draw inferences from the best clues and try to "read" what is <u>not</u> spoken of in Soviet texts. This suggests another important reservation: Western experts have repeatedly drawn attention to the fact that openly accessible and published sources available in the Soviet Union cannot be expected to convey a full picture of Soviet strategic thinking, which in the Soviet view is a very sensitive matter. Jacobsen points out that "no topic is more sensitive to Moscow than that of security" (Jacobsen 1979: 143).

To American observers, published Soviet literature on military matters seems "oblique and cryptic", and the true Soviet military dogma can only be inferred (Millett 1981: 2). Western inferences and conclusions regarding internal Soviet "debates" have therefore been fraught with mistaken premises (Jacobsen 1979: 143):

> "Real strategic debates do occur, but they are in-house and as a rule not reflected in outward appearances. Even if they should sometimes be so reflected, there would be no way of knowing. The data for satisfactory comment is just not available." (<u>ibid.</u>)

It has been noted that for these reasons the structure of Soviet military doctrine is asymmetric - explicit, unequivocal exposure of the socio-political part yet much less clear information about the techno-military part (Lider 1983: 343); Soviet sources generally say little or nothing about numbers, characteristics or location of Soviet strategic weapons, and not even the names or designations of the various missiles and bombers are given (Carter 1978: 20).

In practice this means that the information available on Soviet politics and strategy in officially published material or in consultations with Soviet officials and "institutnichi" may represent just the tip of an iceberg - if it <u>is</u> really the tip of the iceberg and not of something else while the iceberg one is looking for remains completely submersed. There can be no absolute certainty in this regard.

At least one thing is certain, however, to Western analysts: even if the published material is not complete, and even if, at worst, what Soviet authorities publish is not in complete accord with what they really think, and even if to some extent what can be read is highly ambiguous, these statements are indicators "at least of what they find useful or necessary to have others believe in order to promote specific policies" (Jackson 1981: 614). In other words, they convey a message in terms of a desired image.

<u>Are American perceptions accurate? The self-assessment by Western analysts</u>

In 1978, the United States Senate Committee on Foreign Relations invited a large number of analysts specializing in Soviet and communist affairs to give their evaluation of the potential adversary. In addition, some of the analysts were also asked to evaluate to what extent the views provided by United States experts regarding the Soviet Union are accurate and whether the American public has an accurate perception of the Soviet Union, its people and its leaders (cf. Perceptions 1979: 311-325). Not surprisingly, the answer can neither be general nor homogeneous.

As one expert argues, experts' views "tend to become subjective, conditioned by personal experience or, regrettably, even by the anti-communist syndrome". Obviously there is the "Team A, Team B problem" - decide on policy, then pick the proper experts. The political demand for knowledge about Soviet Union may also have a seductive effect on the views expressed by academics - especially if, as Dallin (1982: 30) puts it, "primitive reductionism is politically far more rewarding than nuanced explication". Secondly, experts sometimes "know more and more about less and less" because an expertise useful in some situations may be irrelevant in another field (Marcy, in: Perceptions 1979: 314). This latter fact is also conceded by those who are more confident about the quality of Western expertise, suggesting that the "combining mind" can link the various sorts of comprehension (Tyroler, in: Perceptions 1979: 318). By contrast to the expert's view of the Soviet Union, the views held by the American public and also those conveyed by the American mass media are criticized for systematically highlighting negative features, using loaded language and lacking elementary knowledge about almost everything Soviet (Dallin 1982: 30; Cohen 1984).

As far as Western analyses of Soviet military writings are concerned, one may question the erroneous assumption that the theory of nuclear strategy is universal (Millett 1981: 2). However, American observers are increasingly aware of the intrinsic differences existing between American and Soviet assumptions and ways of thinking. Several American evaluations and hypotheses regarding Soviet policies are now, from an ex post perspective, being dismissed as having originated in cultural misunderstandings or a lack of empathy on the part of American observers. For instance, the current disillusionment with détente is now explained as "a consequence of earlier US ethnocentric perception rather than later Soviet 'bad faith' about détente" (Booth 1979: 48-51). Likewise, many "liberal" thinkers in the West may have tended "to underestimate the utility which groups in other countries attach to their own armed forces" (ibid.: 78f.).

As to the methods employed by Western experts, one may doubt the wisdom of drawing inferences about Soviet foreign policy objectives from Soviet military capabilities. As capabilities are ambiguous, quite different intentions can be inferred from them. American experts seem to be increasingly aware that it would be incorrect to base conclusions about a nation's intention primarily on an examination of its military capability (cf. Ferrari 1983: 63f.).

In conclusion, one cannot but take due note of the scope, depth and amount of self-criticism expressed by Western analysts of the Soviet Union. They are cognizant of all the epistemological problems involved in the process of assessing a political system such as that of the USSR, including also reflexions about the fallacies of inter-cultural perception as well as problems of inference known as "validity problems" in the methodology of the social sciences. This awareness of all the problems, pitfalls and cognitive traps intruding into the evolution of an image of the adversary can be expected, in principle, to yield an increasingly more solid view of the Soviet Union. However, to date, apart from some aspects on which all assessments seem to converge, no coherent body of assumptions and interpretations of the Soviet Union has emerged. The debate is still characterized by a considerable variety of approaches and opinions. Yet the rapid progress made in recent years in refining these approaches cannot go unnoticed. Its results, as extracted and summarized in this chapter, deserve serious consideration, and even more so as many of the authors quoted in the preceding sections were or are actively involved in the United States Government foreign policy decision--making process, and some of them (e.g. Pipes, Shulman, Lenczowski and others) even held or hold key positions.

CHAPTER V

CONFLICTIVE COGNITION
THE VIEW OF THE ADVERSARY AND ITS
CONSEQUENCES FOR DISARMAMENT

THE SOVIET AND AMERICAN VIEWS COMPARED

How do the Soviet and American views relate to each other? To what extent do they converge, and to what extent is their relationship characterized by mismatch or outright contradiction? In order to consider these questions the two views must be confronted and systematically compared. As the descriptive presentation of the two official views (chapters II and III) has been based on the identical "checklist" of relevant themes, the very same analytic tool can now be employed for summarizing and simultaneously juxtaposing them.

The two views in a nutshell: a synopsis of themes

The Soviet view	The American view

Views of the international system

Basic patterns of global politics

Two opposing classes	World of sovereign nations

Nature of international relations

International class struggle	Growing interdependence

General trend

The onward march of history= transition from capitalism to socialism on a world scale, irreversible shift of correlation of forces in favour of socialism	Decline of American strength, shift of balance of power in favour of USSR

259

Evaluation of the international system's structure

Actions for the sake of social progress = good and just, against value indifference	Cause of freedom and human rights = morally superior, USSR as an "outlaw", against value indifference

Views of the adversary

The adversary's aims

Liquidate communism, offensive aggressiveness, military superiority, resisting social progress by aiming at preservation of status quo, plundering nations	World domination, pushing towards superiority if unopposed

Motives underlying aims

Dogged resistance against inevitable decline, general crisis of capitalism, inter-imperialist rivalry and unemployment to be mitigated by war-mongering and more money for military-industrial complex	Genuine expansionism rooted in a combination of security obsession and ideological motives, cynicism combined with sense of mission

Internal structure

Contradiction between ruling circles and realists, instability, attempts by ruling class to re-establish discipline by propagating "Soviet threat" myth	Authoritarian centralism using force against own people and against rest of world

Trustworthiness

Predictably unreliable	Exploiting deception and surprise, lying, not to be trusted

Capabilities

Attempts to challenge existing equality for the sake of world supremacy and resisting historical progress	New capability to erode United States deterrence and for using coercive power, arming for superiority

Strategies

Ideological provocation, destabilizing socialism, policy of intimidation by power projection and nuclear blackmail, surprise attack - unless opposed by Soviet strength

Political and actual utilization of power projection, terrorism, disinformation, offensive "blitzkrieg" planning, preventive destruction of adversary's strategic weapons in crisis situation

Disarmament policies

Aimed at achieving military superiority, not interested in equality, not reciprocating Soviet goodwill gestures, negotiating for calming domestic pressure only, serving the interests of military-industrial complex, trying to blackmail USSR emphasizing verification and control as a pretext for interference or for shifting the blame for failure on USSR, nevertheless ultimately susceptible to shift of correlation of forces and thus compelled to accept agreements

Aimed at conducting negotiations for lulling West into complacency, dividing the West, affirming one's own "super-Power" status, constraining Western arms programmes, refusing effective verification, agreement to and compliance with treaties only if forced to do so by United States leverage, not living up to the spirit of agreement and "stretching" provisions, not to be trusted

Assessment of image held by adversary

Abusing "Soviet threat" lie for justifying arms expenditure instigated by big business, bourgeois view by definition incapable of understanding USSR, distortions caused by fears genuine to decaying society in decline

Mixture of sober realism and worst-case assumption, awareness of exploitable United States weaknesses, tendency to simultaneously overestimate and underestimate the West, paranoiac hatred of West due to democratic challenge to CPSU's shaky legitimacy

Assessment of information

Scientific grasp of American aims by applying Marxism-Leninism, no need to rely

Proper understanding of Soviet "mindset", no reliance on verbal statements -

| on verbal information, looking at concrete facts | looking at deeds and hardware only |

Views of one's own roles and choices

Principal aims

| Promoting world socialist revolution by consolidating own position and supporting struggle for national liberation | Preserving freedom, encouraging self-determination, deterring the USSR and inhibiting its future expansion |

Justification of aims

| Objective law of history, scientific methods employed by CPSU leadership | Superior value of freedom self-explanatory |

Own system

| Unanimity of leadership and masses due to absence of class cleavages, stable and predictable policy | Problems with Western concertation of defence efforts |

Own capabilities

| Sufficient to thwart any foreign aggression and to counter new United States steps in arms race | Still sufficient but challenged by Soviet quest for superiority, increasing number of windows of vulnerability, loss of prior margin of superiority |

Political strategies

| Peaceful coexistence = continuation of international class struggle by non-violent means, rejecting Western insistence on status quo, further change of the correlation of forces compelling imperialists to | Deterring Soviet expansion and maintaining stability by power projection, security assistance, economic aid, emphasizing ideological adversary relationship |

262

acquiesce, guaranteeing peace
by strengthening economic
and defence forces, helping
to fight counterrevolution,
protecting national
liberation movements by
naval power projection and
military assistance

Military strategy on nuclear level

"Holding back" (sderzhivaniye)
any United States attack by
threatening retaliation; preparing
for nuclear war-fighting in case
United States unleashes war, high
combat readiness, non-first
use posture, strictly
preserving parity

Deterring Soviet attack by
retaliatory capability and options
available for escalating conflict,
restoring peace on favourable
terms in case deterrence fails

Approaches to disarmament

Replacing "balance of terror"
by parity at lower level,
negotiating only in position
of equality and not
constrained by "position of
strength", verification as
far as necessary, inducing
United States to conclude
agreements by shifting the
correlation of forces

Aimed at enhancing United States
security by stabilizing the
international strategic system,
emphasis on verification and
specificity of agreements,
creating incentives to USSR by
leverage

Similarities and contrasts

The synoptic listing of the main themes touched upon in the Soviet and American views exhibits most striking similarities, even symmetries, as well as contrasts. In this respect the listing is self-explanatory. The mutual accusations seem to be largely identical - each side reproaches the other with aiming at world domination, being driven by incessant expansionism, being unworthy of trust, projecting and exploiting power, planning a nuclear pre-emptive attack, and misrepresenting and distorting the image of the respective adversary. Each side also criticizes the other for not being interested in really serious disarmament negotiations, not complying with the provisions of existing agreements, trying to obtain one-sided advantages of all kinds, and co-operating only if forced to do so by the changing "correlation of forces" or leverage-creating incentives. Symmetries can also be observed with respect to the assessment of information available about the respective adversary; it is generally held that "deeds" only, not "words", can be relied upon. A considerable proportion of conceptions related to appropriate political strategies also coincide, particularly the emphasis on employing military, especially naval, power projection for securing one's political goals abroad. As far as the basic rationale of military strategy is concerned, both sides stress the prime purpose of deterring the adversary and fighting a nuclear war in the event that the other side should nevertheless dare to unleash it. Most importantly, both sides start from the assumption that, in order to promote the cause of disarmament, negotiating from strength constitutes an indispensable approach.

There are, however, also some obvious dissimilarities reflecting a fundamental difference in orientation. The basic nature of the international system is perceived in a completely antithetical manner. The same must be said about the ultimate justification used by the two adversaries for legitimizing their evaluations and policies. Their overall frameworks for orientation are radically incongruous, and this fact has striking consequences for the way in which the two powers assess the nature of their political systems, their relations with third countries and their aims at the international level. In the field of disarmament negotiations, the two sides dissent with regard to the importance of verification. The most fundamental disagreement seems to relate to the desirability or undesirability of preserving the present global constellation; while the Soviet Union rejects the "balance of power" concept as a reactionary device to freeze the social status quo, the United States repudiates the dynamic Soviet concept of shifting the correlation of forces.

When further analysing the similarities and dissimilarities of the two views, it may be useful to make a formal distinction between two types of divergencies. On the one hand, the two views contain perceptions shaped by the pattern of an argument that can be summed up in the following general terms: "We are (or do) X; the adversary is (or

264

does) the opposite of X" - and vice-versa. For instance, either view implies that one's own side is inherently peaceful, having adopted a strictly defensive strategy, while the other side is basically aggressive, behaving in an offensive way. And either side professes to be interested in fair and equal steps towards disarmament while suspecting the adversary of aiming at one-sided advantages.

On the other hand, there are perceptions that reflect the very same, virtually identical view on the factual level but suggest a different evaluation of the respective facts, depending on whether they relate to one's own side or to the adversary. In general terms, the logic of this second pattern is: "We are (or do) X, and our X is positive; the adversary also is (or does) X, but his X is negative." The policies of naval power projection are seen in this way: according to the Soviet view, the dispatch of Soviet Navy units to distant regions is a good and just contribution to protecting national libe- ration forces against reactionary forces; the very same policy if adopted by the United States, however, is condemned as serving the purpose of subjugating liberated countries and supporting reactionary regimes. In the American perspective, Soviet naval deployments disclose a sinister design for military imperialism, while the dispatch of United States naval capabilities is justified as a necessary and constructive instrument to protect the security of America's allies and as a force for stabilizing and calming the situ- ation in the respective theatres. Likewise, the Soviet Union expresses optimism with regard to the United States future readiness to soberly accept the reality of the shifting correlation of forces, and hence expects the United States to acquiesce in the facts and to proceed to sign new agreements - which the United States criticizes as a cynical exploitation of opportunities by the Soviet Union. At the same time, however, United States sources speak of the necessity of creating leverage in order to induce the Soviet Union to engage in meaningful arms control negotiations - which the Soviet view in turn rejects as distasteful blackmail and a policy-of-strength attitude.

The first type of cognitive pattern is sometimes called "mirror image" (cf. White 1965: 255f.; Joensson 1979: 43); the second pattern reflects a kind of "double-think" or double standard. Both patterns seem to result from the conflicting situation itself, probably induced by some psychological factors existing in any human group. They represent just two of many typical cognitive patterns - although very salient ones - that can be identified on examining the views held by the two major Powers more closely.

THE STRUCTURE AND DYNAMICS OF CONFLICTIVE COGNITION

Some cognitive patterns inherent to the two views

A more thorough examination of the Soviet and American views with respect to cognitive structures and dynamics yields a surprising array of cognitive patterns. Many of these patterns have been discovered and analysed, in completely different contexts, by psychologists and sociologists, and they are well known in the respective research literature. Using the results of that literature as a guiding instrument, the following 28 patterns can be discerned in the two views:

Patterns of information gathering and processing:

(1) Process of inference or "anchoring": any new information is quickly adopted and integrated into a pre-existing image built on the principles of hierarchical organization of view, consistency, simplicity and stability (Steinbruner 1974: 71-109; Jervis 1982:24). As has been shown in chapters II and III, both the Soviet Union and the United States have evolved impressive belief structures performing this task and thus offering a framework for inferring the meaning of any new issue emerging in the field of disarmament and arms control by quick assimilation. This process of "anchoring" ties new perceptions in with already held beliefs; it generally leads to establishing and maintaining coherent connections among the different issues which are elements of one's view (McGuire 1969: 262f.; Hare 1976: 25). That is how the Soviet view explains an episode such as Watergate by assuming that the steps taken against President Nixon were ultimately instigated by the military-industrial complex which wanted to rid itself of a President who was too détente-oriented. And this is also the mechanism by which American sources quickly subsume a large part of new information about Soviet behaviour under the general heading of the goal of "world domination" ascribed to the Soviet Union.

(2) Incuriosity (cf. Booth 1979: 26f.) is another feature resulting from the propensity to rely on a hierarchical and stable pre-existing image. In the extreme, cognition may become an exclusively "internal" process no longer oriented to or interested in really watching the adversary but content with what one firmly and clearly "knows" about him - a kind of "autistic cognition" (Senghaas 1969: 156-161; 1972: 54-63). As has been repeatedly shown in chapters II and III, each side blames the other for not being interested in the "real" causes and consequences of their conflict.

(3) Overconfidence in one's cognitive abilities constitutes a frequent deficiency of perception (Jervis 1982: 18). The Soviet view of the adversary, claiming scientific qualification based on the tenets of Marxism-Leninism, is assumed to be perfectly adequate - and even superior- to the knowledge the adversary might have about himself. American sources express a similar, albeit not as far-reaching confidence. A prudent analysis of Soviet capabilities is held to be a sufficient basis for a reliable and realistic assessment of the adversary - no matter what the adversary actually intends.

(4) Selective perception, i.e. ignoring or rejecting information about the adversary which does not fit with existing beliefs, is (as Mitchell 1981: 77-80 points out) "a commonplace of psychology". Each side accuses the other of projecting a distorted and one-sided image. Soviet sources complain about the West's selective views and misuse of outdated works of Soviet military experts and treatises devoted to battlefield tactics - all with the aim of fabricating the "Soviet threat myth". The American view is very critical about how selectively the USSR proceeds when assessing the alleged "rough military equilibrium" in Europe, which appears to be identical irrespective of the actual evolution of weapons deployments since 1976. Often, selective perception not only ignores specific information but also excludes some possible alternative interpretations of existing information as being simply impossible (cf. Steinbruner 1974: 109-122), thus blocking off a whole range of alternative considerations and options. It is remarkable in this respect that both sides, in their statements about their policies of disarmament, usually focus on one single possibility only.

(5) Selective recall in historical analogies: in the same way as the present behaviour of the adversary is perceived selectively, the recollection of past events is also made to fit with the prior image (Mitchell 1981: 80). Soviet sources draw attention to the 1919 Allied intervention in the Russian Civil War, which is taken as a proof of traditionally hostile and anti-Soviet United States intentions, omitting, however, any reference to Soviet-American co-operation in the Second World War. American sources, on the other hand, argue that any historical instance of Soviet aggression may "turn around again" next time whenever the Soviet Union is faced with opportunities to push forward quickly. Generally, both views very often use historical analogies. For obvious reasons, preference seems to be given to recent history and events that happened early in the leading generation's adult life (Jervis 1976: 281). In the case of the Soviet Union, the memory of the Great Patriotic War (1941-1945) thus also has an important impact on the approach to disarmament: the memory of having been surprised by the German offensive, in June 1941, is not without significance for the current fears of becoming the victim of a nuclear surprise attack. In the American view, the memory of totalitarianism in both its National Socialist and Stalinist forms is of paramount importance; the present concern about Soviet secrecy and incalculability receives powerful support from this historical analogy.

(6) Emphasis on constant factors - neglecting factors of change (Jervis 1976: 271-273): both the Soviet and the American views frequently refer to regular features in the behaviour of the respective adversary. These features are held to exist independently of specific circumstances. The Soviet view, by the very nature of Marxist-Leninist philosophy, assumes the law of history to determine the course of events as well as United States behaviour in the field of disarmament negotiations: as, for fundamental reasons, any "imperialist" system desperately strives for superiority, and as the military-industrial complex sabotages any disarmament efforts, how

267

could anyone believe that the United States is seriously interested in disarmament, irrespective of its present problems with financing arms expenditure? The corollary American view is quite similar: as the Soviet Union, ever since the CPSU conquered power in Russia, aims at the ultimate triumph of socialism, and as Leninist morale explicitly rejects "bourgeois" rules of the game, how could anyone seriously advocate having confidence in their honestly concluding and not violating arms control agreements, irrespective of their interest in keeping down the costs of national defence? It is interesting to note that the American view also frequently refers to other constants determining Soviet behaviour, such as geography and the Russian national character.

(7) <u>Inferences of transformation</u> suggest that unfavourable immediate situations will succumb to a favourable trend over time (Steinbruner 1974: 109-122). Thus, any new issue emerging in connection with disarmament negotiations is immediately made relative by being integrated into a pre-established long-term evolution. In the Soviet view, nothing can upset the chances for disarmament because, in the long run, socialism will prevail over "imperialism" and through the shift in the correlation of forces accomplish disarmament. A similar optimism is expressed by American sources when arguing that the creativity, resilience, and economic strength of Western society will ultimately prevail and thus create the leverage necessary for inducing the Soviet Union to agree on arms control.

Patterns of perceiving the adversary:

(8) <u>Worst-case assumption</u> is a feature of any thinking related to security. (It may be recalled that, for instance also in civil engineering, the safety of a bridge is calculated by assuming the maximum stress plus a margin of safety.) However, in international politics emphasis on the worst case is identical to suspecting the adversary of being utterly dangerous and hostile (Booth 1979: 122-128; Buzan 1983: 228). There is pratically no way out of this perceptual security dilemma. It also affects cognitions in the field of disarmament and arms control: here, worst-case thinking leads to the assumption that the adversary does nothing else but devise plots to cheat and to gain one-sided advantages in order to prevail. The Soviet and American views offer ample evidence of this cognitive pattern.

(9) <u>Impossibility of falsifying assumptions</u> - the "bad faith model": even if the worst case clearly does not materialize as expected, the respective assumptions are not revised, because the cognitive pattern called "bad faith model" prevents the Governments from drawing such a conclusion. A striking feature that can be discerned in the Soviet view is the refusal to concede peaceful intentions to the adversary merely because he refrained from launching a pre-emptive nuclear attack when he still had the superiority to do so. It is argued that the only explanation for this behaviour must be the efficacy of

Soviet resistance. The American assumption about the Soviet Union's willingness to cynically exploit any opportunity unless its sinister designs are thwarted exhibits a similar logical structure. The respective adversary is given no chance to disprove his alleged aggressive aims (cf. Etzioni 1969: 547f.). If such a "bad faith model" (Hermann 1984: 32) is employed, the perception of the adversary becomes virtually independent from the latter's behaviour and thus invulnerable to empirical disconfirmation.

(10) Perceptions of greater coherence than is present (Jervis 1976: ch. VIII) leads .to assumptions of being confronted with an adversary acting in a fully centralized way and on the basis of a kind of master plan. That is how Soviet sources come to grips with the confusing pluralism of United States democracy - by pointing at the military-industrial complex as the ultimate villain controlling everybody else; the President, Congress, public opinion, etc. are perceived as mere puppets. American sources also reflect a view of an adversary where "authoritarian centralism" is at command, assuming the Soviet leadership to apply a strictly coherent modus operandi and also centrally remote-controlling its satellites.

(11) The black-top image of the adversary assumes an evil leadership and basically good followers (cf. Mitchell 1981: 105). This is the way in which Soviet sources distinguish between "warmongering ruling circles" and "realistic circles" in the United States. The American view of the Soviet Union perceives a cynical party dictatorship oppressing the Soviet people and also using force against the rest of the world. The corollary to the black-top image of the adversary is usually a view of one's own unity. That is how the Soviet view proudly highlights the unanimity of the Soviet leadership and masses. Likewise, the American view of United States society considers the freedom of expressing a plurality of opinions to be the very essence of a broad consensus underlying any free and democratic society.

(12) Assumption that the other shares one's view, i.e. overestimating the degree to which the other side understands what one is trying to say (cf. Jervis 1976: 115f.; 1982/83): the Soviet Union often feels taken aback by the fact that Americans accuse it of being aggressive, when it sees itself as clearly conveying the desire for peace; little attention is paid to the fact that this is due to American disagreement with the Soviet conception of "peace" rather than to American obstinacy. On the other hand, American spokesmen express concern about the West's debate concerning its own vulnerability and declining credibility of deterrence, pointing to the compromising impact this might have on the Soviet assessment of Western resolve - as though the Soviet view of the West's credibility would automatically be identical with Western self-assessment, which may at least be doubted.

(13) Projection of the understanding of one's own side on to the other side: it is often assumed that the adversary will think and act in an analoguous way to oneself (cf. Ra'anan 1981: 79; Pipes 1981).

269

An example is the way in which the Soviet Union perceives the American desire for ample verification which, in the Soviet understanding of how to deal with sensitive information, can only mean undue interference in internal affairs and legalized espionage. Similar mistaken projections occur when United States strategists assume their Soviet counterparts to draw the same distinction between "strategic" and "tactical" nuclear weapons as they do.

Patterns of perceiving the relationship with the adversary:

(14) Mirror images or "black and white pictures" ascribing positive qualities and/or behaviour to one's own side while attributing the very opposite to the adversary are one of the most salient features of conflictive cognition. They have already been amply dealt with and illustrated earlier in this chapter.

(15) "Double-think" or context hypothesis, i.e. the coexistence of logically contradictory beliefs (Rokeach 1960: 35f.; White 1965: 265), can be found whenever a major Power holds the view that the very same act is odious if done by the adversary but perfectly acceptable if done by oneself. Examples of such diverging evaluations or "double standards" have already been quoted above when touching upon similarities of the two views.

(16) The rejection of evaluative symmetry constitutes the logical corollary of "double-think". Not only do the two sides largely apply different standards when evaluating their own actions and those of the adversary, but they also explicitly repudiate the use of the same standards on both sides. Soviet sources criticize the Western anti-militarist and peace movement for its inability to distinguish between just and unjust causes or armaments serving progressive forces and armaments serving reactionary forces. Likewise, American spokesmen deplore growing value indifference as indicated by an attitude of "a plague on both your houses".

(17) Perception of irrelevance: both the Soviet Union and the United States accuse each other of bringing up irrelevant arguments (Rokeach 1960: 35-39). Proposals in the context of disarmament and arms control negotiations are typically denounced as an end in themselves, dishonest, frivolous, using arguments which have nothing to do with the subject matter and inconstant (according to Soviet sources), an end in themselves, propagandistic, evading clarification, and ambiguous (according to American sources). Each side also blames the other for not being honest in its communications. American officials feel that Soviet spokesmen use a different language at home and abroad, the latter serving the purpose of lulling the adversary into an attitude of credulity. On the other hand, Soviet sources frequently express reluctance to accept American statements, which are held merely to serve domestic politics and demagogy.

270

(18) Polarization: accentuation of differences and minimization of similarities (cf. Rokeach 1960: 35-39) can be observed, in the Soviet case, in the rejection of any world view other than the one based on the class cleavage. Soviet sources strongly emphasize that there is no such thing as a common interest, let alone common responsibility, of the "super-Powers" or the "rich North". Fundamental differences are also accentuated by American officials when talking about communism as the "focus of evil" and the necessity to "transcend communism". The propensity to perceive the world as a highly polarized system may be said to be particularly strong in strategic thinking because "strategists need enemies" and are most comfortable when relationships are polarizing or polarized (Booth 1979: 24). This also has an unavoidable impact on approaches to disarmament.

(19) Zero-sum thinking: The Soviet concept of the "shift of the correlation of forces" implies that any loss of "imperialism", even if the USSR does not directly benefit from it, ultimately means a gain for socialism, at least indirectly. American spokesmen use a similar cognitive structure when they assert that "whatever strengthens the Soviet Union, weakens the cause of freedom in the world".

(20) The freedom-of-action differential (Mitchell 1981: 116) refers to the assumption that the range of alternatives open to the adversary is greater than the one perceived on one's own side. In this respect it is interesting to note that the same phenomenon - the extended Soviet border - is interpreted differently following this pattern: to the Soviet Union, the length of her borders and the fact of being surrounded by hostile States is perceived as putting the country into a "cornered" position while offering the adversary a variety of oppurtunities to harass and encircle the motherland of socialism. For American spokesmen, however, the same borders are far from United States shores and close to the Soviet Union and thus difficult to contain for the first but easy to expand for the latter. In disarmament and arms control negotiations it is typically the adversary who is held to be responsible for any failure of negotiations because he enjoys a free choice while one's own side feels confronted with dire necessity.

(21) Explaining negative actions by the disposition of the adversary and one's own situational constraints (cf. Hart 1978): according to the Soviet view, the United States is constantly fuelling the arms race because of a disposition to overpower socialism and because of the class nature of capitalist society, in which the military-industrial complex exerts incessant pressure for more arms expenditure; the Soviet Union, for its part, is only reacting to this situation. Likewise, according to the American view, the Soviet Union continuously and resolutely goes on building up military strength, obsessed with the mission of securing the triumph of socialism, while United States armaments are perceived to be a merely transitory response to this threatening situation. A corollary pattern can be

observed as to the explanation of positive actions:

(22) Explaining positive actions by situational constraints of the other side and one's own positive disposition (cf. ibid.): the Soviet view assumes that the United States has so far agreed to sign some arms limitation treaties only because it has been compelled to do so by the shift of the correlation of forces in favour of socialism; by contrast, the Soviet policy of disarmament is an expression of a genuine disposition to struggle for peaceful coexistence. On the other hand, the American view holds that the Soviet Union co-operates in arms control only if faced with appropriate leverage, while United States arms control policies originate in a genuine American commitment to global stability and détente.

Patterns of drawing conclusions about how to deal with the adversary:

(23) Fixation on chosen policy - reluctance to examine alternatives: sometimes, cognitive processes prevent decision-makers from seeing value trade-offs between alternative policies (Jervis 1982: 21). As has already been mentioned with regard to selective perception, it occurs that in both the Soviet and the American views the respective policy of disarmament is usually closely associated with one single specific course of action. Little attention is given to other policies, and they are commented upon in a negative way as impossible, illusory and based on the wrong premises.

(24) Reaction to failure - doing the opposite from last time (cf. Jervis 1976: 275-278): prior negative experiences affect the way similar problems are handled today. For the Soviet Union (or, more precisely, Russia) military weakness has repeatedly been the cause of traumatic experiences. The frequent reference to the many invasions by Mongols, Swedes, French, and Germans have some relevance for the contemporary Soviet attitude towards armaments and disarmament: namely that priority must be given to being ready for any eventuality. The United States view includes lessons from the more recent past: if the Soviet Union did not refrain from developing and deploying new weapons systems precisely at a time when détente reached its zenith, the agreements must never again be based on trust but only on iron-clad guarantees, i.e. full verifiability and the threat of retaliation deterring any Soviet break-out.

(25) Reaction to success - doing the same again (cf. Jervis 1976: 278f.): once a policy has had success, it is applied to later situations, irrespective of whether or not the circumstances are the same. In the Soviet view, it is evident that the shift in the correlation of forces convinced the "ruling circles" of the United States of the necessity to sign agreements - hence the obligation to proceed to work for a further shifting of this correlation. In the American view it is undeniable that only if the Soviet leaders have seen the West as determined to modernize its own forces have they seen an incentive to negotiate arms control agreements - hence it is wise to continue to rely on creating incentives.

(26) Impossible reciprocity (cf. Lebow 1984; Richter 1982: 121f.): neither the Soviet nor the American view acknowledges any goodwill gestures made by the other side. Rather, unilateral gestures are automatically interpreted as either a sign of weakness and decay or a consequence of one's own firm posture, thus confirming that a "tough" approach is indeed successful. Hence there is no reason to respond by a reciprocal measure - for there is nothing to respond to. Although the idea of reacting on the basis of reciprocity and equity is, in principle, recognized by both sides, neither sees any occasion to implement it because it cannot perceive the value of gestures initiated by the adversary. On the contrary, both Soviet and American sources frequently complain about the futility of their own gestures, which the adversary constantly and malignantly ignores.

(27) Images of extended self: in conflictive situations, the perception of global politics tends to include disputed areas as parts of oneself, involving concomitant exclusive rights to do what one chooses (Mitchell 1981: 100). The Soviet claim for irreversibility of the achievements of social progress in newly liberated countries may be seen in this context, as may the American claim for hemispheric spheres of interest and, in a larger context, the call for "command of the seas".

(28) A tough self-image is associated with the feeling that, facing the adversary, a demonstration of firmness and resolution is a necessity (Mitchell 1981: 101f.). This attitude seems to constitute a central theme in both Soviet and American attitudes and can be detected in a large number of statements, mainly by military spokesmen. In the Soviet Union, the emphasis on mass, bigness, alertness, "keeping one's powder dry" and heroism, if required, constitute elements of systematic "military-patriotic education". In the United States, where the Administration has the constant task of convincing Congress of the need for higher defence expenditure, a similar self-image is projected as desirable, although regret is expressed that it has not yet been achieved.

Consequences of cognitive patterns for disarmament

It should be noted that this list of 28 major cognitive patterns includes only those patterns that can be discerned in both the Soviet and American views. In addition, there are many more patterns to be found specifically in either the Soviet or the American view; they have been mentioned in chapters II and III.

These patterns amount to a powerful mechanism affecting the views which each side has about the adversary, the international environment and itself. They may even lead to more or less distorted images. In the academic literature, much attention has been devoted to these cognitive processes. It is felt that to a large extent they constitute an inherent element of cognition as such, since any acquisition of knowledge involves categorization (Edelmann 1977: 23-42) and the use of organizing schemata (Thorndyke/Hayes-Roth 1979) or analogies that make the novel seem familiar by relating it to prior knowledge (Gick/Holyoak 1983; Heradstveit 1980). Generally, it seems that human cognitive capacity is "bounded" and therefore constructs simplified models of the real world (Shaklee 1979) such as the views described in this study.

There is much speculation as to the factors determining the specific structure of such cognitive schemes or views. Ingrained anthropological dispositions have been suggested to be at their origin; such dispositions would generate a kind of "psycho-logic" operating independently from "real" logic and inevitably producing those cognitive patterns (Jervis 1972: 272-274; Booth 1979: 161-166; Mitchell 1981:111f.). There is also evidence that the relative importance and intensity of such patterns depends on personality traits (Mitchell 1981: 76; Jervis 1981: 58; Hermann 1983), cultural factors (Booth 1979: 17f.; Taifel 1969: 359-370; Hare 1976: 25), and organizational dynamics such as group solidarity (Fagen 1967: 13f.). Other theories point to generic difficulties of acquiring information in situations characterized by limited availability of data, signals embedded in a great deal of noise, the possibility of deception and the existence of ambiguous and multiple possible interpretations and options (Betts 1978: 69ff.; Knorr 1979: 74 ff.; Clarkson 1981: 32f.); therefore the situation of the environment itself is supposed to activate those cognitive patterns.

Among these situational theories one particular hypothesis seems to be of paramount relevance in the context of this study, namely the theory that the existence of conflict generates specific cognitive patterns (White 1965; Finley/Holsti/Fagan 1967; Mandel 1979; Zajonc 1968). In other words, the situation of enmity has its own "psycho-logic". That indeed is precisely what the preceding chapters have amply shown.

The main problem to be dealt with, however, is not determining the causes and dynamics shaping cognitive processes. Rather, one has to raise the question of their consequences for disarmament. According to a familiar dictum, what is "real" is what men perceive to be real. There can be no doubt that this also applies to the problem of armament and disarmament. The arms race owes substantial momentum to this "self-fulfilling prophecy" (cf. Keys 1981: 18; Freedman 1984: 17), and the hostile views which each side holds about the adversary impede disarmament and may prevent it altogether. Those holding these views perceive only one choice left when facing such a dangerous, aggressive and powerful adversary - be prepared and acquire more arms! And they envisage only one response to any moves by such an unreliable, tricky partner - be cautious when engaging in arms control negotiations!

When assessing the impact of conflictive cognitive patterns on the prospects for disarmament, however, it would be misleading to assume that disarmament has so far failed solely because of distorted perception or "misperception". It is generally inappropriate simply to distinguish "perceptions" from so-called "misperceptions" and to blame statesmen for becoming victims of the latter. As has been pointed out by Levy (1983), the concept of misperception is meaningful only "if there exists in principle a correct perception", which in turn presupposes the extremely difficult task of determining what is "reality" and "objective truth" in each case (cf. also Lippert/Wakenhut 1983: 328; Boulding 1956: 164-175).

First of all, the hostile views of the adversary result from the fact that there is conflict and not vice-versa. Conflictive views therefore constitute an intrinsic expression of that very conflict. They reflect a real clash of interest. Unfortunately, mutual conflictive cognition is more than mere mutual misunderstanding. Just as the arms race originates in the political conflict, and just as arms cannot be banned without prior solution of the underlying political conflict, the irreconcilable, hostile views cannot simply be done away with by better mutual information and goodwill unless the underlying political conflict is settled first.

But in either field - armaments and conflicting views - the conflict, jointly with a variety of additional causes, triggers secondary factors that subsequently reinforce the consequences of the original conflict situation. Just as the arms race is constantly heated up by escalatory dynamics and additional secondary factors (such as technological drift, domestic group interests, inertia of bureaucracies responsible for arms procurement, etc.), the hostile views are reinforced by the patterns of cognitive dynamics and other factors (such as personality traits, cultural factors, organizational dynamics, situational logic).

In the end, the reinforced hostile views offer powerful incentives to procure more arms to cope with the perceived threat. "Overperceived" threats fashion responses with a "margin of safety" (Caldwell 1971: 23). This reaction in turn frightens the adversary and confirms and reinforces his view on the threat emanating from the other side (cf. Jervis 1976: 373ff.), and even more so if he infers the other side's intentions from its capabilities. There seems to be no way out of this dilemma.

In sum, by activating a number of specific patterns of perception, the original, real conflict stirs up a whole sequence of reinforcing mechanisms which end up by inadvertently aggravating and perpetuating the conflict and rendering any meaningful steps towards disarmament almost unthinkable and perhaps unfeasible. The following graph sums up this web of causes and effects and mutually reinforcing mechanisms and expresses this vicious circle in visual form:

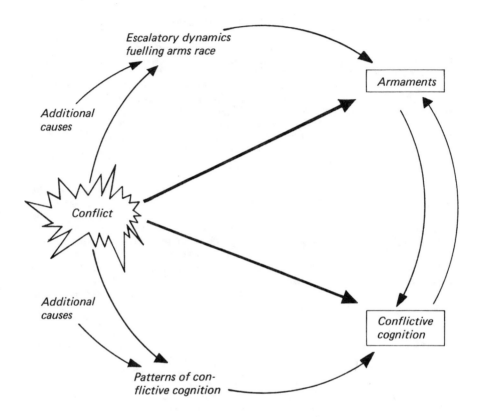

It is important clearly to distinguish the primary cause-effect relationship originating in a real and serious conflict between East and West (symbolized by the two boldface arrows) from the secondary consequences brought about by reinforcing processes (symbolized by the other arrows). It would be nothing but wishful thinking to hope for a general settlement of the conflict if only the mutual views were "rectified".

ASSESSING THE POTENTIAL FOR UNDERSTANDING

Perceptions as persistent beliefs

As has been shown in the preceding paragraphs, some aspects of the views held by the two major Powers about each other may originate in perceptual patterns characteristic of any conflict situation. Such reinforcing mechanisms are amenable to change. To the extent that cognitive dynamics are at work, mutually held views can in fact be improved. Some of the inadvertent cognitive obstacles to disarmament will thereby be removed or reduced to lesser importance.

However, there are other themes to be discerned in the two views that reflect the conflict in its genuine intensity. They evince a fundamental divergence of political and philosophical orientations and are thus an expression of a real conflict of interests. The ensuing contrasting evaluations are largely determined by irreconcilable positions that characterize the deep conflict dividing the two major Powers. Being persistent beliefs, they continue to impede disarmament and arms control negotiations. The crucial question therefore is to what extent the views relevant for disarmament and arms control negotiations also belong to this category of unalterable and persistent beliefs, i.e. to what extent they reflect a "real" incompatibility rather than an "illusory" incompatibility (cf. Jervis 1982/83). A criterion for distinction can be found by checking whether or not a specific perception is stringently linked to the basic tenets of the two positions.

As far as the Soviet view is concerned, the following assumptions are logically connected with the fundamentals of the official Soviet Party and State doctrine, Marxism-Leninism:
Reliance on the changing correlation of forces as the main determinant for progress in disarmament and compliance with agreements;

The principle of equality and equal security, and its specific Soviet definition;

Priority for disarmament measures, followed by verification and rejection of some forms of verification as interference;

Assuming the United States to be uninterested in true disarmament and only aiming at military superiority;

Assuming United States conduct of negotiations to serve the purpose of domestic propaganda and/or disguising real intentions;

Assuming the United States Government's disarmament policy to be obstructed by the military-industrial complex;

Assuming that the United States seeks to blackmail USSR into one-sided agreements.

This set of essential assumptions seems to be absolutely indispensable to Soviet leaders and negotiators. It would be futile to ignore them or to treat them as "misperceptions" to be revised by goodwill and patient dialogue. They have to be taken seriously.

277

The American view, too, comprises a set of assumptions that are to be considered rather firm, even though the American approach to disarmament and politics in general is not derived from a single, unified body of State doctrine. However, the following assumptions are obviously closely linked with the fundamental beliefs determining the nature of the American political system and its self-identification with regard to the potential adversary:

Inducing the USSR to agree to and abide by agreements by using leverage and the threat of retaliation;

Serving United States security by reducing imbalance, stabilizing the strategic system and lowering the level of armaments;

Importance of verifiability and compliance;

Assuming the USSR to be aiming at military superiority;

Assuming the USSR to be lying and cynically exploiting opportunities and hence not to be trusted.

Either set of fundamental assumptions is deeply embedded in the philosophical beliefs cherished by each side. In this respect, the discord between the two views cannot be ascribed to "misunderstandings" or "misperceptions". Quite the opposite is true: each side either absolutely resists, for reasons of its very political identity and basic goals, any suggestion that it should modify its views, or it is quite aware of the mismatch yet tries to deliberately manipulate and change the other side's view. Therefore the mutual views can neither be "rectified" nor be expected simply to be abandoned.

The two sets of fundamental assumptions define the room for manoeuvre available, in principle, in disarmament negotiations. As they are almost mutually exclusive, the potential left for a common understanding seems at first glance to be rather small.

Nevertheless, they establish a minimum of stability. By their tenacious nature they create predictable patterns among the two major Powers. As Frank/Weisband (1972: 132) have argued, "even a stable pattern of hostility among nuclear powers is likely to be more psychologically tolerable than one in which the interaction is entirely idiosyncratic". In the context of disarmament this means that each side can at least count on the other side thinking and acting within the confines of a stable and clearly defined framework of assumptions. Hence it is correct to say that even the most discrepant and unalterable elements of the two views contain some constituents conducive to mutual understanding. In order to activate this understanding, however, a proper grasp of each other's persistent beliefs is required. This presupposes a minimum degree of empathy, as will be shown below.

Assessing the accuracy of perceptions: measuring empathy

If inadvertent reinforcements of hostile views and persistent beliefs are supposed to impede the dialogue in the field of disarma-

278

ment and arms control, the question has to be asked to what extent the views held by each major Power about its adversary are accurate. More specifically, one may ask (1) to what extent the perception of the adversary corresponds to the adversary's self-perception and (2) to what extent the perception of the adversary's image of oneself (i.e. one's meta-image) corresponds to that adversary's actual image of oneself.

Again, it must be emphasized that in this highly subjective realm of perceptions the question is not to evaluate to what extent the perceptions are matched by objective evidence from the real world. Hence no attempt will be made to identify misperceptions; as has been said above, such an endeavour would be largely futile anyway. When labelling some perceptions as "accurate" and others as "inaccurate", "accuracy" is meant in a restricted sense only. It refers to the degree of match or mismatch to be observed when juxtaposing perceptions, self-perceptions and meta-images.

To the extent that perceptions are "inaccurate", they are bound to impede negotiations and perhaps prevent them from producing substantive agreements. On the other hand, to the extent that they are "accurate", a dialogue may be fruitful and lead to concrete results. In other words, the problem to be dealt with is the problem of empathy, i.e. the ability to intellectually grasp the foundations, patterns and contents of the respective adversary's thoughts and actions. It then remains to be seen whether all "inaccuracies" and instances of lack of empathy are inevitable for reasons of the fundamental difference in orientation adopted by the two opponents, or whether there are some opportunities left for facilitating negotiations by furthering a better match between perceptions and by generally activating empathy. This problem will be addressed at the end of the present chapter.

To what extent does the Soviet view of the United States match the American perceptions? When comparing the Soviet view of the American adversary with the United States view of its own role and choices, one has to begin with the perception and conception of American aims. According to the Soviet view, the United States has been intrinsically committed to aggressive anti-communism ever since the Soviet State was established in 1917. This principal goal is seen to be deeply embedded in the social nature of any capitalist society, as is "resistance to progress" as defined in Soviet terms. The American aim of preserving the status quo is also perceived as an expression of capitalist society; it is held to point in much the same direction as the other principal United States aim, namely weakening or liquidating socialism by striving for superiority. The nature of capitalism is said also to lead to the aim of plundering nations and robbing other peoples in the interest of American monopolies. This overall view held by the Soviet leadership to a considerable extent corresponds to how the United States sees itself, although of course a completely different evaluative emphasis is placed on identical issues. United States Administrations do in fact consider the Soviet

Union as the main threat - a threat, however, to be deterred and contained rather than effaced. The primary aim, in American eyes, is to preserve the freedom of the United States, its allies and friends, which means resisting Soviet attempts to encroach upon that freedom. In principle, this is accurately realized although naturally not liked by the Soviet Union. The two views, however, differ completely with regard to what they perceive to be the ultimate vision of the American concern for a global order: while the Soviet view holds that American capitalism simply fights for its profit and survival in an epoch of crisis and decline, the Americans feel themselves committed to fostering an international order supportive of democracy and self-determination throughout the world.

As far as the assessment of the overall power balance is concerned, the Soviet and American views agree on the fact that it has shifted from United States superiority to equality. However, with regard to the present time, the American view assumes that the balance is further deteriorating due to rising Soviet strength and increasing "windows of vulnerability". Soviet observers see the matter quite differently accusing the United States of striving for superiority. The two views again match almost completely with regard to the United States policy of power projection, although of course again evaluating this issue differently. Furthermore, the Soviet view expresses concern about the American strategy of destabilizing socialism, while the United States view of itself indicates the intention to stabilize the status quo without necessarily changing it at the expense of socialism. A total mismatch can also be found with regard to the perception of American nuclear strategy: Soviet sources accuse it of being designed to launch a pre-emptive strike against the Soviet Union; by contrast, American sources emphasize the exclusively defensive nature of the United States strategic deterrent, which is aimed at preventing any war, i.e. both conventional and nuclear wars.

Soviet assumptions about American disarmament and arms control policies are permeated with the fear that the United States will abuse negotiations in order to achieve military superiority, rejecting the principle of equality and inducing the Soviet Union to make one-sided concessions. This strongly contrasts to the United States view of its own disarmament and arms control policies, which are seen to be oriented towards establishing and securing strategic stability at a lower level of armaments. The views regarding the American approach to verification do not match either: for the Soviets, American insistence on verification is nothing but a pretext for torpedoing talks or spying on the Soviet Union, while in the American perspective verification is vital and indispensable given the mistrust felt towards the USSR. The Soviet view holds that the shift of the correlation of forces in favour of socialism has induced and is further inducing the United States leadership to become more soberminded and realistic and hence to agree to progressive steps in the field of arms limitation. Yet the United States maintains that it is not reacting to compulsion but is acting with the intention in mind of promoting strategic stability at a lower level.

If one tries to juxtapose the Soviet view of how the United States perceives the Soviet Union (i.e. the meta-image held by the Soviet Union) and the actual American view of the Soviet Union, one once more finds a mixture of correspondence and mismatch, with the latter prevailing. From the Soviet viewpoint, almost nothing in the American perception of the Soviet Union seems to be correct and almost everything is said to be distorted and slanderous. This primarily applies to the image of the "Soviet threat", which is seen to constitute a mere lie fabricated by the sinister forces of the military-industrial complex. To Soviet observers this also implies that the whole United States policy of deterrence rests on mistaken premises, because there is nobody to deter - an argument that hardly harmonizes with the American view of the Soviet adversary. At most, to Soviet observers the American assessement of the Soviet threat is understandable and acceptable inasmuch as it reflects the genuine fear of a decadent society in decline and facing its historic ruin. For the rest, Soviet leaders feel completely misunderstood with regard to their policy of "world revolution" and Soviet strategic doctrine; they see the American interpretation of either as being determined by the spirit of aggressiveness, which arouses their indignation. Yet on the whole Soviet observers are not very resentful of the mismatch they notice when comparing their self-image with what they see and hear about the United States perception of the Soviet Union; they think that, owing to their Marxist-Leninist analysis, they know better than anyone else why the United States image of the Soviet Union is wrong: namely for the simple reason that it once more reflects "bourgeois" inability to grasp the essence of history, capitalist contradictions and pressures by monopolies whose business interests quite naturally necessitate "smearing the Soviet people". Again, the American point of view strongly disagrees with such a critique as well as with the praise offered to "realistic circles" in United States society having a more benign image of the USSR.

To what extent does the American view of the Soviet Union match Soviet perception? As in the preceding section, the corollary question of whether the American view of the Soviet adversary corresponds to what Soviet spokesmen think of themselves has to focus first on the perception of fundamental aims and motives. The American view pays much attention to what is perceived to be an insatiable Soviet drive for expansion and ultimately world domination. In this connection, American sources often quote the Soviet concept of "shifting the correlation of forces". They also point to the sense of mission emanating from Marxist-Leninist ideology; the latter is held to be relevant at least as a conditioning factor of the Soviet "mindset". As a result, the Soviet Union is assumed to aim at exploiting any opportunities offered by Western weakness in order to push forward. Although the moral and political evaluation of these issues by Soviet observers is different, on a purely factual level the Soviet Union's view of its own aims and motives roughly corresponds to this American perception. The Marxist-Leninist assumptions of the law of history, the task of promoting the correlation of forces are all genuine elements of the Soviet view, and they seem to have been grasped properly by American analysts.

Differences arise with respect to views regarding Soviet military strategies. According to the American view, the Soviet Union wants to utilize military power projection for political purposes - an apprehension to which Soviet spokesmen, albeit using a different terminology to describe it, would still basically agree, pointing to the necessity to guarantee peace by strengthening economic and military forces, helping to fight counterrevolution and protecting national liberation movements by naval activities and military assistance. However, when it comes to American suppositions about Soviet "blitz-krieg" planning, offensive conventional postures and pre-emptive strikes against American nuclear forces, the Soviet view clearly diverges: from a Soviet viewpoint, high combat-readiness only serves the purpose of deterring an attack, while the pre-emptive strike accusation is assumed to be wholly disproved by the Soviet Union's pledge not to be the first to use nuclear weapons. Similarly, the American accusation that the Soviet Union is striving for strategic superiority is refuted by the latter's assertion that it strictly adheres to the principle of equality and parity on the level of nuclear armament.

In the field of disarmament and arms limitation, the American view holds that the Soviet Union is not really interested in substantive agreements but, rather, aims at lulling the West into complacency, exploiting Western public opinion, dividing the West, abusing existing treaties, refusing efficient verification and generally diverting attention from the incessant efforts to achieve strategic superiority. Again, this view is - in its factual substance and once more expressed in a different terminology - partly shared by the Soviet Union's own conception of disarmament, which counts on "realistic circles" and "forces of peace" in Western public opinion and which also encourages Western Europeans to become aware of their own security interests, allegedly different from those of the United States. The American view and the respective Soviet self-perception do not match, however, with regard to verification which, according to the Soviet conception, represents an important but not outstanding element for its own sake and must not exceed the necessary minimum; still, the American and the Soviet views agree that, in the Soviet approach to disarmament, verification plays a lesser role than in the American approach. United States sources also explicitly recommend the creation of "leverage" by preparing new arms programmes as an indispensable prerequisite for the successful conduct of negotiations with the Soviet Union; from the Soviet point of view this fact is properly perceived, although of course criticized and rejected as "blackmail".

To what extent do American observers perceive correctly the way in which Soviet sources view the United States? The relationship between the meta-image and the actual image held by the adversary is a crucial determinant of the potential for mutual understanding or

282

misunderstanding. The main feature to be observed in this relationship refers to the Soviet assessment of American strength and weaknesses: generally, while Soviet sources constantly stress the dangerous nature of American capabilities, American sources are not sure
whether the Soviet Union does not perceive United States capabilities
in a different way: they are afraid that Soviet observers very accurately realize and exploit all kinds United States weaknesses, such
as the West's growing vulnerability due to global economic
interdependence and the problems faced by democracies in rallying
public support for defence and co-ordinating the defence efforts of
the allies. While Soviet spokesmen accuse the United States of
struggling for frightening superiority, United States officials are
concerned about the future effectiveness of United States deterrence,
which of course depends on the perceptions held by the Soviet
adversary to be deterred. On the other hand, the American meta-image
reflects awareness of how Soviet sources analyse at length the internal crisis and ultimate decay of capitalist society; yet it is
surmised that the Soviet Union may grossly underestimate Western
vitality and resilience. Still, American spokesmen conceive the
possibility that Soviet observers may be somewhat confused by the
complex and fluid nature of pluralist Western society. Finally, there
is one important issue on which both the Soviet view of the United
States and the American meta-image held about this Soviet view are in
full accordance: the issue of the "United States threat". The Soviet
fixation on this threat is duly appreciated by American observers,
who think that the challenge posed to a Marxist-Leninist system by a
democracy must necessarily, and correctly so, be assessed as a
threat.

Drawing a balance: When the two views are compared on the basis of
the preceding analysis, the conclusion suggests itself that the
mismatch existing between the Soviet view and its corresponding
American self-perceptions is larger than the mismatch to be observed
between that American view and its corollary Soviet self-perceptions.
(In numerical terms, 11 themes were identified where the Soviet view
diverged from the American perception, while there were four themes
characterized by mismatch in the inverse relationship.*)

- - - - - - - - -

*) The 11 diverging Soviet views are: (1) the United States is fight-
ing for profit and survival only, (2) the United States is striving
for superiority, (3) the United States wants to destabilize social-
ism, (4) the United States plans a pre-emptive nuclear strike, (5)
United States disarmament policy serves military superiority, (6)
United States insistence on verification is a pretext, (7) the United
States agrees only if compelled to do so, (8) United States capabili-
ties are extremely dangerous - United States weaknesses ignored, (9)
United States deterrence far exceeds necessary size, (10) United
States moves determined by decline of decaying capitalism, (11)
United States image of "Soviet threat" is slanderous.
The four diverging American views are: (1) the USSR plans for a

In the context of the present study, however, the question which of the two major Powers has a stronger ability to empathize is of lesser importance than the significance of empathy for the task of disarmament as such. Negotiations in the field of disarmament and arms control are highly reflexive by their very nature. As Goffmann (1970: 101) has pointed out, in a situation of strategic interaction "courses of action or moves will be made in the light of one's thoughts about the other's thoughts about oneself", on the basis of "mutual assessed mutual assessment" (cf. also Schelling 1963: 92f.). The better one understands how threatened the adversary feels and how oneself appears to the adversary, i.e the higher the degree of empathy on both sides, the more constructive negotiations will become. As has been shown above, the degree of empathy can be ascertained by juxtaposing images and meta-images with corresponding self-images and examining them for their match. In the absence of a minimum correspondence, it will be very difficult to reach agreements in the field of disarmament. Or if in these circumstances an agreement is signed, it will sooner or later collapse and make the situation more tense than it was previously: Governments may then feel betrayed by the adversary's "infidelity", which more often than not is just due to a mere difference in outlook and usage of terms and concepts - a difference that unfortunately went unnoticed in the course of negotiations. Empathy and thus a realistic mutual assess-

- - - - - - - - -

blitzkrieg offensive and pre-emptive strike, (2) verification is crucial, (3) the USSR reacts to leverage only, (4) the USSR may be misled by a mistaken image of Western weakness.

Although this cursory analysis does not claim the signifiance of a stringent quantitative analysis, the proportions observed (roughly 11: 4) are still indicative. In the other words, the American view seems to be more suitable, although not absolutely perfect, for grasping the situation in a way which is also acceptable to the adversary. The degree of empathy available to Americans for understanding the Soviet view and understanding how one appears to the adversary is therefore larger than Soviet empathy for the American view. A possible explanation of this fact may be that the Americans devote more attention to their adversary than do Soviet observers to theirs. Psychological research has shown that low level of contact more likely leads to mirror-images on both descriptive and evaluative dimensions while closer contact leads to a mirror-image merely in evaluative aspects (Mitchell 1981: 115) i.e. to the type of perception that has been referred to above as "double-standard". Instances of mismatch due to such "double-standard" approaches clearly prevail in both the Soviet and the American views. Other authors have referred to different cultural legacies, arguing that Russian tradition has always been less evidence-oriented than the American tradition (White 1965: 256) and probably imbued with a more normative, principle-oriented approach to reality in general. This tendency has been reinforced by Marxism, which always intended to change the world rather than to explain it.

ment represents a prerequisite for any productive steps in the field of disarmament and arms control.

However, empathy can be promoted, at least to the extent that it does not touch upon fundamental beliefs. In the views analysed in this study, the latter interfere only marginally with the ability to understand each other's "mindsets". As has been shown, the majority of instances of mismatch identified when comparing images, self-images, and meta-images take place on the evaluative level (i.e. in terms of irreconcilable mirror-images and double-standard assessments) while· on the factual level there is far-reaching agreement. In this respect, additional progress seems quite feasible. The further fostering of empathy - perhaps by the process of negotiation itself - therefore represents an important contribution to progress in disarmament. Such is also the rationale of the attempt made by the present study to provide a sincere and detailed account of the two views.

PRACTICAL CONCLUSIONS AND RECOMMENDATIONS

The analysis of the world views of the Soviet Union and the United States and their assumptions about each other indicates that the general "climate" is not favourable for disarmament and arms control, at least for the time being. Ironically, the analysis provides ample and satisfactory explanations for the failure or near-failure of disarmament rather than showing how to put negotiations on the right track, which is no easy task.

This can certainly not be done by wishful thinking such as pleading for overcoming "misperceptions" and learning to perceive each other "realistically" in order to establish harmony. Any such approach - which is ubiquitous in the literature on perceptions - must be said to be naive, to put it mildly. On the other hand, adopting an attitude of "cultural and ideological relativism" (White 1965: 239) by indulging in all kinds of "pseudocorollaries" (Booth 1979: 175f.) discovered in the two conflicting views is also of little help for defusing an irreconcilable confrontation, and it diverts attention from the harsh realities of international politics. One should also beware of cognitive processes activated in periods of détente. The image of the "friend" may be no less illusiory than the image of the "enemy". It seems preferable to have no illusions at all.

The background and complexity of the two conflicting views require a subtle approach to draw the kind of practical conclusions and recommendations that are relevant to the real world of the politics of disarmament. With due consideration of this reservation, the following practical implications emerge from the foregoing analysis:

(1) The fundamental incompatibility between the Soviet and American views must be taken seriously to the extent that it reflects a real conflict of interest and world outlook. Attempts to play it

285

down for the sake of harmony are not helpful for a proper mutual assessment. Rather, its appreciation must become the starting point for any further steps towards disarmament.

(2) While the leaders and negotiators representing the two nations are largely cognizant of the fundamental incompatibilities, the general public and a large part of the media, especially in the West, very often underestimate the weight of that fundamental incompatibility and hence tend to become impatient. Its proper understanding helps to rally the political support required for the continuous and steady conduct of disarmament negotiations.

(3) Empathy is needed for acquiring thorough mutual knowledge about the adversary's indispensable values and beliefs, irrespective of whether they are compatible or incompatible with one's own views. Empathy is of course not the same as sympathy. Empathy may and should also include an understanding of the adversary's less benign and more threatening traits.

(4) Therefore special attention ought to be given to each side's ability to understand how it appears to the other side, i.e. the meta-image. Awareness to what extent, how and why the adversary perceives itself to be threatened by oneself constitutes a crucial element of empathy.

(5) The more contacts there are between the Soviet Union and the United States, the more opportunities there will be to promote empathy. Ongoing disarmament and arms control negotiations, even if they do not produce rapid and substantive results, constitute a good means to this end. Nothing would be more wrong, therefore, than to belittle them as "negotiations for the sake of negotiations". So called "ineffective" negotiating forums deserve to be reassessed in the light of this specific contribution, likewise, the political relevance of limited steps and marginal agreements must not be underestimated.

(6) It may be desirable to open new and additional bilateral and multilateral forums for negotiations in order to multiply the number of opportunities to foster the growth of empathy.

(7) With regard to the evolution of a proper mutual assessment, even the diplomatic "drama" of walkouts, refusal to negotiate, and public declarations and accusations can be said to be meaningful to some extent. At any rate, it is to be preferred to intellectual and diplomatic neglect of certain disarmament issues.

(8) An attitude of empathy should not only be adopted but also be signalled to the other side. This aspect has been mentioned by Keys (1981: 19), who argues that "steps which portray one side to the other as the first really wishes to be seen will finally reap the reward of a change in perception or attitude on the part of the adversary".

(9) It should also be borne in mind that meta-images of one side can be influenced by appropriate communications by the other side. The examination of the adversary's meta-image should lead to a communicative strategy designed to bring that meta-image closer to one's own self-perception.

(10) Since stimulating empathy on the part of the adversary requires communicating one's view to the other side, this in turn presupposes that assumptions are made explicit. When negotiating disarmament, the fundamental rationale for one's proposals and responses to the other side's proposals should therefore be made plain to the maximum extent possible, even if that may seem repetitive.

(11) While negotiators of the Soviet Union and the United States frequently interact, there are very few contacts between military experts of the two sides and almost no contacts between those responsible for shaping the strategies of their countries. Since their views and assumptions are absolutely crucial for the future of Soviet-American relations it seems desirable that they should be given opportunities to come to a full understanding of the respective adversary's views. To this end, seminars and other opportunities for dialogue among military experts may be organized. The purpose of such discussions of course is not the illusory hope of overcoming conflicting strategic concepts but the aim of increasing the degree of empathy of the institutions involved.

(12) Discussions among experts may also be held about the assumptions regarding the adversary to be found in published, non-classified textbooks and manuals used in military education. (The successful German-Polish exchange of views held about textbooks for the teaching of history may serve as a model for such talks.)

(13) Appreciation of the fundamental incompatibility of views held by the two sides must not lead attention to be focused exclusively on these incompatibilities. Rather, they should be seen as a relatively stable framework within which the search for commonly accepted disarmament measures has to take place. The intellectual energies available for this task deserve to be directed to what lies beyond the irreconcilable conflict.

(14) This also means that either side should strictly refrain from presenting proposals in disarmament negotiations that may touch on the essentials of the beliefs held by the other side and even call for concessions of a fundamental nature. Although since the 1950s the "style" prevailing in disarmament negotiations has clearly shifted from a propagandistic orientation towards a to-the-point approach, there is still room for improvement in this respect.

(15) Generally, critical attention ought to be given to those elements of perception that are the inadvertent, secondary consequences of reinforcement mechanisms generated by specific cognitive patterns

of conflict situations. In practical terms, this means first of all greater awareness of the working of these mechanisms in one's own cognition and avoiding over-confidence in one's own cognitive abilities.

(16) Another useful step in this direction is the periodic review of the images held of the adversary and the systematic examination of alternative views in the light of new information. Envisaging alternative explanations seems particularly important with reference to assumed intentions that may motivate the adversary's capabilities.

(17) Likewise, critical attention must be given to the way in which the adversary's hostile views may be affected by one's own behaviour and one's own verbal communications. Acts and words that may reinforce the adversary's hostile perceptions ought to be avoided or at least restricted to what is absolutely necessary for defending one's own interests.

(18) It is clear that the persons responsible for the security of their nation, including policy-makers and negotiators in the field of disarmament, have no choice but to assume the worst case, i.e. perceiving their adversary by allowing themselves a "margin of safety" and thus perceiving him to be a little more dangerous than he possibly is. (As Jervis 1976: 424, aptly put it: "If it is disastrous to mistake an enemy for a friend but not so costly to take a friend for an enemy, then decision-makers are well-advised to suffer the latter misperception rather than run high risks of the former.") This logic of the situation too must be taken seriously. However, the "margin of safety" in perceiving the adversary should be constantly monitored and reduced to the minimum tolerable range.

(19) Reducing the degree of secrecy surrounding military capabilities and intentions may offer incentives to resort to less massive worst-case assumptions, as such assumptions are often evolved for want of reliable information about the adversary's capabilities and intentions.

(20) As far as the agenda of arms control negotiations is concerned, it would seem useful for a large variety of confidence-building measures covering both the conventional and nuclear field to be urgently studied and negotiated. They can be assumed to affect not only the existing military situation but also perceptions, given the paramount role of mutual suspicions rarding offensive conventional postures, "blitzkrieg"-type planning, and nuclear pre-emption.

(21) Finally, it should constantly be remembered that conflictive perceptions impeding disarmament, like the arms race itself, are ultimately caused by the political conflict dividing the two major Powers. The overriding task of our time therefore is to find appropriate political methods for containing and, in the long run, solving this fundamental conflict. Only then will the cognitive processes cease to sway and poison relations between the Soviet Union and the United States.

REFERENCES

1. Soviet source material (and official publications from other socialist countries) (used for chapter II)

Abarenko, V., L. Semeĭko, and R. Timerbaĭev (1983): Problèmes du désarmement nucléaire. Moscow: Nauka Publishers.

Afanasyev, Victor G. (1977): Osnovy nauchnogo kommunizma. Moscow: Politizdat.

--- Fundamentals of Scientific Communism. Moscow: Progress Publishers.

Agayan, Ts. P. (1982): "Leninskaya politika mirnogo sosushchestvovaniya i klassovaya borba''. In: Leninskaya politika mira i bezopasnosti narodov. Moscow: Nauka Publishers. pp. 34-42.

Akhromeyev (1983): " Yadernaya voina - prestupleniye protiv chelovechestva. Vsesonaya konferentsia vtehenykh". In: Pravda, 18 May 1983.

Akhtamzian, A. (1979): "Sovechanie po bezopasnosti i sotrudnichestvu v Evrope novyi etap reuradki v mezhdunarodnykh otnosheniakh". In: Problemy bezopasnosti i sotrudnichestvo v Europe. Moscow: Moscowsky Gosudarstvenny Institut Mezhdunarodnykh Otnochenii. pp. 3-13.

Alexandrov, Anatoly (1982): "Science and the Struggle for Peace". In: Peace and Disarmament: Academic Studies 1982. Moscow: Progress Publishers. pp. 15-23.

Alexandrov, V.V. (1982): "Sovetsko-amerikanskiye otnoshenia voyvtoroy polovine 70-kh godov''. In: Leninskaya politika mira i bezopasnosti narodov. Moscow: Nauka Publishers. pp. 248-257.

Amelko, Nikolai (1984): "La marine de guerre soviétique: Défense ou Attaque?" In: Les Nouvelles de Moscou, No. 11.

Andropov, Yuri V. (1982): Report at a Jubilee Meeting of the Central Committee of the CPSU, the Supreme Soviet of the USSR... to Mark the Sixtieth Anniversary of the Formation of the USSR, December 21, 1982. Moscow: Novosti Press Agency.

--- (1983a): Our Aim is to Preserve Peace. A Collection of Speeches. Moscow: Novosti Press Agency.

--- (1983b): Statement of September 28, 1983. Moscow: Novosti Press Agency.

--- (1983c): To Preserve Peace for Present and Future Generations. Moscow: Novosti Press Agency.

--- (1983d): Who Wrecked the Geneva Talks and Why? Moscow: Novosti Press Agency.

--- (1983e): Statement at the Plenary Meeting of the CPSU Central Committee, 26 December 1983. Moscow: Novosti Press Agency.

--- (1984): "Interview Given on 24 January 1984''. In: Disarmament, Vol. 7, No. 1, pp. 135-147.

Arbatov, Georgy A. (1973): The War of Ideas in Contemporary International Relations. The Imperialist Doctrine, Methods and Organization of Foreign Political Propaganda. Moscow: Progress Publishers.

--- (1980): "Vneshnyaya politika SShA na poroge 80-kh godov". In: Mir i razoruzheniye. Nauchnye issledovaniye. Moscow: Nauka Publishers.

--- (1981a): "Strategiya yadernogo bezrassudstva". In: Kommunist, No. 6, pp. 102-111.

---, and Willem Oltmans (1981b): Der sowjetische Standpunkt. Ueber die Westpolitik der UdSSR. München: Rogner & Bernhard.

--- , and Willem Oltmans (1981c): The Soviet Viewpoint. New York: Dodd, Mead, and Co.

Arms Control - Disarmament (1983). Moscow: Novosti Press Agency.

Batsanov, Sergei (Ed.) (1982): How the Soviet Union is Working for Disarmament. Selected Documents. Moscow: Novosti Press Agency.

Belov, V. I., A. A. Karenin, and B. C. Petrov (1979): Socialist Policy of Peace; Theory and Practice. Moscow: Progress Publishers.

Bovin, Alexander (1982): "Politics and War". In: Peace and Disarmament. Academic Studies 1982. Moscow: Progress Publishers. pp. 95-111.

Brezhnev, Leonid I. (1976): Report of the CPSU Central Committee and the Immediate Tasks of the Party in Home and Foreign Policy, 25th Congress of the CPSU. Moscow: Novosti Press Agency.

--- (1978): To Stop the Arms Race. Moscow: Novosti Press Agency.

--- (1981): Report of the Central Committee of the CPSU to the 26th Congress of the Communist Party of the Soviet Union and the Immediate Tasks of the Party in Home and Foreign Policy. Moscow: Novosti Press Agency.

--- (1982): To Uphold the Ideal of Helsinki. Moscow: Novosti Press Agency.

--- (s.d.), Leninskim kursom, Vol. 5. Moscow: Politizdat.

Bunkina, M. K. (1979): USA versus Western Europe: New Trends. Moscow: Progress Publishers.

Burlatsky, Fyodor M. (1982): "The Philosophy of Peace versus the Apocalypse". In: Moscow News, No. 31.

--- (1983a): "Philosophie des Friedens". In: Sowjetwissenschaft - Gesellschaftswissenschaftliche Beiträge, Vol. 36, No. 3. pp. 321-334.

--- (1983b): "USSR-USA: Partners, Rivals, Enemies?" In: Moscow News, No 23.

--- (1984): "Einige Fragen der Theorie der Internationalen Beziehungen". In: Sowjetwissenschaft, Gesellschaftswissenschaftliche Beiträge, Vol. 37, No. 2. pp. 120-129.

Bykov, Oleg (1980): "Imperativy voennoi razriadki". In: Mir i razoruzheniye.
Nauchnye issledovaniye. Moscow: Nauka Publishers. p. 135.

--- (1982): "Any Alternative to Military Equilibrium?" In: Peace and Disarmament: Academic Studies 1982. Moscow: Progress Publishers. pp. 77-94.

"Byt ili ne byt novomu vitku gonki vooruzheny". In: Pravda, 10 February 1982.

Chernenko, Konstantin U. (1984a): Safeguard Peace and Ensure the People's Wellbeing. Moscow: Novosti Press Agency.

--- (1984b): "Intervention". In: Matériaux de la Session plénique extraordinaire du CC du PCUS, 13 février 1984. Moscow: Novosti Press Agency.

--- (1984c): In the Central Committee of the CPSU. Moscow: OKPOVO (mimeo).

Diatchenko, Evgéni (1978): Les forces armées soviétiques. Moscow: Novosti Press Agency.

Dictionary of Basic Military Terms (1965). A Soviet View (Slovar osnovnych voyennych terminov 1965). Washington, DC: US Government Printing Office.

Diligensky, Gherman, and Yevgeny Yaropolov (1982): "The Working-Class Movement in Developed Capitalist Countries Fights for Peace". In: Peace and Disarmament Academic Studies 1982. Moscow: Progress Publishers. pp. 130-138.

Disarmament: Who's against? (1983). Moscow: Military Publishing House.

Documents and Resolutions (1981): The 26th Congress of the Communist Party of the Soviet Union. Moscow: Novosti Press Agency.

Falin, Valentin (1982): "Détente's Difficult Paths". In: Peace and Disarmament. Academic Studies 1982. Moscow: Progress Publishers. pp. 59-76.

Fedoseyev, Pyotr N. (1981): "Technoloy, Peace, and Contemporary Marxism". In: John Somerville (Ed.): Soviet Marxism and Nuclear War. London: Aldwych Press. pp. 17-52.

--- (1983): "Preventing Nuclear War is the First and Foremost Task of Humanity". In: Responsibility for the Future of Our Planet. Conference of Soviet Scientists for Ridding Humanity of the Nuclear War Threat and for Disarmament and Peace. Moscow: Novosti Press Agency.

Frolov, I.T. (Ed.) (1980): Filosofsky Slovar, 4th Edition. Moscow: Politizdat.

The Fundamentals of Marxist-Leninist Philosophy (1982). Moscow: Progress Publishers.

Golubnichy, Mikhail (1978): Détente: The Soviet Viewpoint. Moscow: Novosti Press Agency.

Gorshkov, Sergei G. (1979): The Sea Power of the State. Annapolis: Naval Institute Press. (translated from the 2nd edition, Moscow 1976: Voyenizdat)

--- (1983): "Basy agressy". In: Pravda, 15 April 1983.

Great Soviet Encyclopaedia (1976/1980). A Translation of the Third Edition. Moscow: Sovetskaya Entsiklopediya Publishing House/New York: Collier- Macmillan.

Grechko, A. A. (1977): The Armed Forces of the Soviet State. Moscow: Progress Publishers.

Gromyko, Anatoly (1982): "Razvitiye sotrudnichestva SSSR s osvobodivshimisya stranami". In: Leninskaya politika mira i bezopasnosti narodov. Moscow. Nauka Publishers. pp. 118-129.

Gromyko, Andrei (1980): Lenin and the Soviet Peace Policy. Articles and Speeches, 1944-1980. Moscow: Progress Publishers.

--- (1983a): Press Conference Given on April 2, 1983. Moscow: Novosti Press.

--- (1983b): Report of the Session of the USSR Supreme Soviet, June 16, 1983. Moscow: Novosti Press Agency.

--- (1984): "V.I. Lenin and the Foreign Policy of the Soviet State". In: Coexistence, Vol. 21. pp. 59-82.

Henri, Ernst (1983): Derrière la porte de la Maison-Blanche. Moscow: Novosti Press Agency.

Hoffmann, Heinz (1974): Sozialistische Landesverteidigung. Berlin: Militärverlag der DDR.

How to Avert the Threat to Europe (1983). Moscow: Progress Publishers.

How to Strenghten Peace and Security in Europe: Soviet Proposals (1983). Moscow: Novosti Press Agency.

Inozemtsev, Nikolai (1982): "The 26th CPSU Congress and Soviet Foreign Policy". In: Peace and Disarmament. Academic Studies 1982. Moscow: Progress Publishers. pp. 24-33.

Issraelyan, Victor (1982): "Disarmament and the Foes of the Dialogue". In: Peace and Disarmament. Academic Studies 1982. Moscow: Progress Publishers. pp. 112-119.

Iwanow, I. (1983): "Die Konzeption von den 'armen' und den 'reichen' Ländern". In: Sowjetwissenschaft, Gesellschaftswissenschaftliche Beiträge, Vol. 36, No. 6 (November/December). pp. 778-786.

Kalyadin, A.N., O.V. Bogdanov, and G.A. Vorontsov (1983): Prevention of Nuclear War. Soviet Scientists' Viewpoints. New York: United Nations Institute for Training and Research (UNITAR).

Kaltakhchyan, S. T. (1983): Marksistsko-Leniniskaya teoriya natsii i sovremennost. Moscow: Izdatelstvo politicheskoy literatury.

Kapchenko, N. (1983): "The Problem of Preserving Peace and the Ideological Struggle". In: International Affairs, No. 7, (July), pp. 3-13.

Kashlev, Y. (1984): "Ideological and Propaganda Subversion against Socialist Countries - A Weapon of Imperialism". In: International Affairs, No. 1 (January). pp. 93-98.

Klaus, Georg (1971): Sprache der Politik. Berlin, GDR: VEB Deutscher Verlag der Wissenschaften.

Kortunov, Andrei, and Nikolai Sokov (Eds.) (1984): Who is Violating International Agreements? Moscow: Novosti Press Agency.

Kortunov, Vadim (1979): The Battle of Ideas in the Modern World. Moscow: Progress Publishers.

---(1982): "Ideological Battles and World Politics". In: International Affairs, No. 12 (December). pp. 83-91.

--- (1983): "The Ideology of Peace versus the Ideology of War". In: International Affairs, No. 11 (November). pp. 7-15.

Kubalkova, V., and A.A. Cruickshank (1980): Marxism-Leninism and the Theory of International Relations. London: Routledge & Kegan Paul.

Kulish, V.M. (1982): "Koordinirovannaya vneshnyaya politika stran sotsialisticheskogo sodruzhestva v borbe za mir, bezopasnost i sotsialnyy progress". In: Leninskaya politika mira i bezopasnosti narodov. Moscow: Nauka Publishers. pp. 82-91.

Kuznetsov, Vladimir I. (1983): Truth about Intermediate Range Nuclear Missiles. Moscow: Novosti Press Agency.

--- (1984): Evropa: Bezyadernaya ili sverkhyadernaya. Moscow: Politizdat.

Lebedev, Nikolai (1982): The USSR in World Politics. Moscow: Progress Publishers.

Lenin, Vladimir I. (1977): "Materialism and Empirio-criticism ("Collected Works, Vol. 14). Moscow: Progress Publishers.

--- (s.d.): Polnoiye Sobraniye Sochineny, 55 Vols. Moscow: Politizdat.

Leninskaya politika mira i bezopasnosti narodov (1982). A. L. Narochnitsky (Ed.). Moscow: Nauka Publishers.

Lokshin, G., and V. Oryol (1984): "The Athens Anti-War Conference". In: The New Times (Moscow), No. 11 (March). p. 21 f.

Lomeiko, V. (1984): "Mutual Security in Europe: An Alternative to the Arms Race". In: International Affairs, No. 3 (March). pp. 128-136.

Lukov, Vadim B. (1979): "Politiko-ideologichesky aspekt novoi kontseptsy 'interesov bezopasnosti' SShA, Podkhod administratsy Kartera k problemam evropeiskoi bezopasnosti". In: Problemy bezopasnosti i sotrudnichestvo v Evrope. Moscow: Moskovsky Gosudarstvenny Institut Mezhdunarodnikh Otnochenii. pp. 40-58.

--- , and Victor M. Sergeyev (1982): "Paterns of Crisis Thinking. An Analysis of Governing Circles in Germany". In: Daniel Frei (Ed.): Managing International Crises. Beverly Hills: Sage Publications. pp. 47-60.

Luzin, Nikolai (1981): Nuclear Strategy and Common Sense. Moscow: Progress Publishers.

Mamontov, Vassili (1979): Disarmament - The Command of the Times. Moscow: Progress Publishers.

Marksistsko-Leninskoye ucheniye o voyne i army (1984). Moscow: Voyennoye Izdatelstvo.

Marxism-Leninism on Proletarian Internationalism (1972). Moscow: Progress Publishers.

Marxism-Leninism on War and Army (1972). Moscow: Progress Publishers.

Matveyev, V. (1984): "Ideology of Aggression: The Essence of Washington's Diplomacy". In: International Affairs, No. 1 (January). pp. 75-78.

Nalin, Y. (1982): "The Big Lie of the Century: 'Soviet Threat' Myth and Imperialist Propaganda". In: International Affairs, No. 11 (November). pp. 72-80.

Narochnitsky, A. L. (1982): "Istorichesky opyt borby SSSR za osushchestvleniye vneshnepoliticheskoy programmy KPSS". In: Leninskaya politika mira i bezopasnosti narodov. Moscow: Nauka Publishers. pp. 7-25.

Nauchnye osnovy sovetskoy vneshney politiki (1982). Edited by N.I. Lebedev. Moscow: Mezhdunarodnye otnoshenya.

Novopashin, Yu. S.: (1982): "Razvitiye internatsionalisyticheskikh otnosheny mezhdu stranami sotsializma - Glavnoye napravlenye vneshney politiki KPSS". In: Leninskaya politika mira i bezopasnosti narodov. Moscow: Nauka Publishers. pp. 62-72.

Obchestvennost i problemy voiny i mira (1978). Moscow: Mezhdunarodnye otnoshenya.

The Officier's Handbook (1971) (S.N. Kozlov, Ed.). Soviet Military

Thought Series, No 13. Washington, DC: US Government Printing Office.
Ogarkov, Nikolai B. (1981): "Na strazhe mirnogo truda". In: Kommunist, No. 10. pp. 80-91.
--- (1982): Vsegda v gotovnosti k zashchite otechestva. Moscow: Voyennoye Izdatelstvo.
Ovinnikov, R. (1981): "Za kulisami agressivnoi politiki Washingtona". In: Kommunist, No. 14. pp. 76-87.
Peace and Disarmament. Academic Studies 1980 (1980). Moscow: Progress Publishers.
Peace and Disarmament. Academic Studies 1982 (1982). Moscow: Progress Publishers.
Petit Dictionnaire Politique (1982). Moscow: Progress Publishers.
Petrovsky, V. F. (1980): "Topical Problems of Disarmament". In: Peace and Disarmament. Academic Studies 1980. Moscow: Progress Publishers. pp. 146-159.
--- (1982a): Dialogue for Peace. Moscow: Progress Publishers.
---(1982b): Razoruzheniye kontseptsiya, problemy, mekhanizm. Moscow: Izdatelstvo politicheskoy literatury.
---(1984a): "Disarmament and the Political and Ideological Struggle". In: International Affairs, No. 1 (January). pp. 79-84.
---(1984b): "Reason vs. Nuclear Insanity". In: International Affairs, No. 3 (March). pp. 29-38.
Political Terms: A Short Guide (1982). Moscow: Novosti Press Agency.
Ponomarev, Boris N. (1979): The Living and Effective Teaching of Marxism-Leninism. Moscow: Progress Publishers.
---(1983): "The Role of Scientists in Strengthening International Security". In: Responsibility for the Future of Our Planet. Moscow: Novosti Press Agency. pp. 7-17.
Primakov, E.M. (1980): "Gonka vooruzheny i regionalnye konflíkty". In: Mir i razoruzheniye. Nauchnye issledovaniya. Moscow: Nauka Publishers. pp. 81-95.
Problemy voyennoy razriadky (1981). Moscow: Nauka Publishers.
Proektor, Daniel M., et al. (1978): European Security and Co-operation: Premises, Problems, Prospectus. Moscow: Progress Publishers.
--- (1983): Osnovy mira v Evrope. Moscow: Nauka Publishers.
Proletarian Internationalism - Our Banner, Our Strength! (1980). Moscow: Novosti Press Agency.
Pumpyansky, Alexander (1983): Cannon Shell and the Parthenon. Moscow: Novosti Press Agency.
The Race against Reason (1983). Moscow: Novosti Press Agency.
Razryadka mezhdunarodnoy napriazhennosty i ideologicheskaya borba (1981). Moscow: Akademia Nauk.
Razryadka protiv antirazryadki (1982). Edited by G. A. Deborin, J. J. Gaglov, and L. N. Kornev. Moscow: Politizdat.
Responsibility for the Future of Our Planet (1983). Conference of Soviet Scientists for Ridding Humanity of the Nuclear War Threat and for Disarmament and Peace. Moscow: Novosti Press Agency.
Rybkin, Yevgeny, Ivan Tyulin, and Vadim Kortunov (1982): "Anatomia odnogo burgeoissnogo mitha". In: Mirovaya Ekonomika i Mezhdunarodniye Otnosheniya, No. 8. pp. 136-147.

Schachnasarow Georgii Ch. (1982): Die Zukunft der Menschheit: Prozesse, Probleme, Prognosen. Leipzig: Urania Verlag.

Schwarz, Siegfried, Gerhard Basler, and Martin Winter (1981): Imperialistische Aussenpolitik am Beginn der 80er Jahre. Berlin, GDR: Institut für International Politik und Wirtschaft der DDR.

Schmidt, Max (1982): "Der militärische Faktor in den internationalen Beziehungen". In: Daniel Frei (Ed.): Sicherheit durch Gleichgewicht? Zürich: Schulthess Polygraphischer Verlag. pp. 35-61.

Scientific-Technical Progress and the Revolution in Military Affairs (1975). (Nauchno-tekhnichesky progress i revolyutsiya v voyennom dele, 1973). Washington, DC: US Government Printing Office.

Selected Readings from Military Thought, 1963-1973, 2 parts (s.d.) (Soviet Military Thought, Vol. 5). Washington, DC: US Government Printing Office.

Semyonov, Vladimir S. (1979): Nations and Internationalism. Moscow: Progress Publishers.

Shakhnazarov, Georgy Ch. (1979): The Destiny of the World. Moscow: Progress Publishers.

--- (1983): Sotsialism i budushcheye. Moscow: Nauka Publishers.

Shebchuk, B. N. (1983): Provodaniye voyennye termini v angliskom yazyke. Moscow: Voyennoiye Izdatelstvo.

Shishkin, G. (1984): "Nuclear War Propaganda in the USA and Washington's Imperial Ambitions". In: International Affairs, No. 1 (January). pp. 89-93.

Siegmund, Werner, and Joachim Kleine (1982): "Die gegenwärtige Militärdoktrin der USA." In: Deutsche Aussenpolitik, Vol. 27, No. 9. pp. 72-92.

Sivachev, Nikolai V., and Nikolai N. Yakovlev (1979): Russia and the United States. Chicago: University of Chicago Press.

Sovetov, A. (1984): "'Peace Built on Strenth' - A Doctrine of International Terrorism". In: International Affairs, No. 2 (February). pp. 52-62.

Soviet Committee for European Security and Co-operation, Scientific Research Council on Peace and Disarmament (1981): The Threat to Europe. Moscow: Progress Publishers.

--- (1983a): How to Avert the Threat to Europe. Moscow: Progress Publishers.

--- (1983b): December is Near: Europe Must Choose. Moscow: Progress Publishers.

Sowjetische Militärenzyklopädie, Auswahl (1980). Berlin: Militär-verlag der Deutschen Demokratischen Republik, 28 Volumes.

Sredin, G., D. A. Volkogonov, and M. P. Korobeynikov (1981): Chelovek v sovremennoy voyne. Moscow: Voyennoiye Izdatelstvo.

Strategiya mira protiv strategy konfrontatsy (1982): Moscow: Politizdat.

A Study of Soviet Foreign Policy (1975). Moscow: Progress Publishers.

Tolkunov, L. (1984): "Ideological Struggle and Peaceful Coexistence Today". In: International Affairs, No. 1 (January). pp. 64-70.

Trofimenko, G. A. (1982): "Osnovnye postulaty vneshney politiki

SShA". In: Leninskaya politika mira i bezopasnosti narodov. Moscow: Nauka Publishers. pp. 313-326.

--- (1983): "The Role of the Soviet Union in the Struggle for Disarmament". In: Co-existence, Vol. 20, No. 1. pp. 13-26.

Ustinov, Dimitry (1981): Against the Arms Race and the Threat of War. Moscow: Novosti Press Agency.

--- (1982): The Existing Parity Must Not be Destroyed (Pravda, 7 December 1982). Moscow: Novosti Press Agency.

--- (1983): "An Immortal Feat" Daily Review, Novosti Press Agency (APN), Vol.XXIX, No. 89 (72/9), 10 May 1983.

Vasilyev, B. A. (1972): Long-Range Missile-Equipped (Soviet Military Thought, Vol. 15). Washington, DC: US Government Printing Office.

Vidyasova, L. (1984): "Militant Anticommunism: The Basis of Washington's Reckless Course". In: International Affairs, No. 1 (January). pp. 70-75.

Volkogonov, Dimitri (1982): Ideologiya-ostreyshy front klassovoy borby. Moscow: Znaniye.

--- (1983): Psikologicheskaya voina. Moscow: Voyennoie Izdatelstvo.

Whence the Threat to Peace, Second Edition (1982): Moscow: Military Publishing House.

Yefremov, A. Y. (1979): Nuclear Disarmament. Moscow: Progress Publishers.

Yegorov, P. T., I. A. Shlyakhov, and N. I. Alabin (1970): Civil Defense (Soviet Military Thought, Vol. 10). Washington, DC: US Government Printing Office.

Zagladin, Vadim V. (1981): La conception soviétique de la paix. Moscow: Novosti Press Agency.

--- (1982): "Peace and Human Progress". In: Peace and Disarmament: Academic Studies 1982. Moscow: Progress Publishers. pp. 34-50.

--- (1983): "La conception soviétique de la sécurité". In: Bulletin d'information, Comité soviétique pour la sécurité et la coopération européennes, No. 37 (Décembre). pp. 26-32.

Zavizion, G. T., and Yu. Kirshin (1972): "Sovetskaya voyennaya nauka: Sotsialnaya roli funktsy". In: Kommunist vooruzhennykh sil. No. 17, September 1972. pp. 9-16 (transl. 1975 in: Selected Soviet Military Writings, 1970-1975, Vol. 11). Washington, DC: US Government Printing Office. pp. 76-85.

Zhukov, Yuri (1984): Interview, in: Newsweek, 16 April 1984. p. 60.

Zukunft, Hans (1982): "Aktuelle Aspekte der imperialistischen Bedrohungslüge". In: Deutsche Aussenpolitik, Vol. 27, No. 9. pp. 31-42.

2. American source material (United States Government publications and publications by Gouvernment officials currently or formerly in office; used mainly for chapter III)

Abshire, David M. (1984): "Some Prescriptions for Europe's Present Danger". In: International Herald Tribune, 28 February 1984.
Arms Control (1984). Washington, DC: US Arms Control and Disarmament Agency.
Arms Control Impact Statements, Fiscal Year 1981. Washington, DC: US Government Printing Office.
Arms Control Impact Statements, Fiscal Year 1982. Washington, DC: US Government Printing Office.
Arms Control Impact Statements, Fiscal Year 1983. Washington, DC: US Government Printing Office.
Arms Control Impact Statements, Fiscal Year 1984. Washington, DC: US Government Printing Office.
Bathurst, Robert A. (1979): Understanding the Soviet Navy: A Hand Book. Newport: Naval War College Press.
Baxter, William P. (1981): "Soviet Perceptions of the Laws of War". In: Graham D. Vernon (Ed.): Soviet Perceptions of War and Peace. Washington, DC: National Defense University Press. pp. 17-26.
Brown, Harold (1981): Department of Defense Annual Report, Fiscal Year 1982. Washington, DC: US Government Printing Office.
---(1983a): Thinking About National Security. Boulder: Westview Press.
---(1983b): "Domestic Consensus and Nuclear Deterrence". In: Adelphi Paper No. 183. London: International Institute for Strategic Studies. pp. 19-27.
Brzezinski, Zbigniew (1983): The Conduct of East-West Relations in the 1980s. (mimeo, Paper presented to the Annual Conference of the International Institute for Strategic Studies, London).
Chaney, Otto P. (1983): The Soviet Threat to Europe: Prospects for the 1980s. Carlisle Barracks: Strategic Studies Institute, US Army War College.
Eccles, Henry E. (1979): Military Power in a Free Society. Newport: Naval War College Press.
Ford, Gerald R. (1983): Text of Interview. In: USA Today, 6 September 1983.
Giffen, Robert B. (1982): US Space System Survivability: Strategic Alternatives for the 1990s. Washington, DC: National Defense University Press.
Grayson, Benson Lee (1982): Soviet Intentions and American Options in the Middle East. Washington, DC: National Defense University Press.
Hearings on Military Posture, House Armed Services Committee (1981), Parts 1-6. Washington, DC: US Government Printing Office.
---(1982), Parts 1 and 5. Washington, DC: US Government Printing Office.
Heans, Terry L. (Ed.) (1983): Understanding US Strategy: A Reader. Washington, DC: National Defense University Press.
Hibbits, John G. (1978): "Admiral Gorshkov's Writings: Twenty Years

of Naval Thought". In: Paul J. Murphy (Ed.): Naval Power in Soviet Policy. Washington, DC: US Air Force. pp. 1-22.

Kissinger, Henry A. (1982): "How to Deal with Moscow". In: Newsweek, 29 November 1982.pp. 12-15.

Lee, William T. (1981): "Soviet Perceptions of the Threat and Soviet Military Capabilities". In: Graham D. Vernon (Ed.): Soviet Perceptions of War and Peace. Washington, DC: National Defense University Press. pp. 67-96.

Murphy, Paul J. (Ed.) (1978): Naval Power in Soviet Policy. Washington, DC: US Air Force.

National Security Management (1983): International Issues and Perspectives. Washington, DC: National Defense University Press.

NATO Special Consultative Group (SCG) (1983): Progress Report to Ministers. Bruxelles: NATO (mimeo).

Nitze, Paul H. (1978): "The Global Military Balance". In: Grayson Kirk and Nils Wessell (Eds.): The Soviet Threat: Myths and Realities. New York: Praeger. pp. 4-14.

--- (1980): "Strategy in the Decade of the 1980s". In: Foreign Affairs, Vol. 59, No. 1 (Fall). pp. 82-101.

Nuechterlein, Donald E. (1983): "National Interests and National Strategy: The Need for Priority". In: Terry L. Heyns (Ed.): Understanding US Strategy: A Reader. Washington, DC: National Defense University Press. pp. 35-63.

Perceptions: Relations Between the United States and the Soviet Union (1979) Ed. by United States Senate Committee on Foreign. Relations. Washington, DC: US Government Printing Office.

Perle, Richard (1981): "SALT II: Who is Deceiving Whom?" In: Robert L. Pfaltzgraff, Jr., Uri Ra'anan and Warren Milberg (Eds.): Intelligence Policy and National Security. London: Macmillan. pp. 148-160.

Petersen, Philip A. (1980): Soviet Air Power and the Pursuit of New Military Options. Washington, DC: US Air Force.

Pipes, Richard (1977): "Why the Soviet Union Thinks it Could Fight and Win a Nuclear War". In: Commentary, July.

-- (1981): "American Perception and Misperception of Soviet Military Intentions and Capabilities". In: Robert L. Pfaltzgraff, Jr., Uri Ra'anan and Warren Milberg (Eds.): Intelligence Policy and National Security. London: Macmillan. pp. 74-81.

Reagan, Ronald (1983a): Text of Television Address. In: Washington Post, 6 September 1983.

--- (1983b): "Communism is the Form of Evil in the Modern World". In: Coexistence, Vol. 21. pp. 7-21.

Scott, William F., and Harriet F. Scott (1981): "Soviet Perceptions of US Military Strategies and Forces". In: Graham D. Vernon (Ed.): Soviet Perceptions of War and Peace. Washington, DC: National Defense University Press. pp. 97-112.

Security and Arms Control: The Search for a More Stable Peace (1983). Washington, DC: Department of State.

Shulsky, Abram N. (1978): "Gorshkov on Naval Arms Limitations: Kto Kogo?". In: Paul J. Murphy (Ed.): Naval Power in Soviet Policy. Washington, DC: US Air Force. pp. 247-258.

Shultz, George P. (1984): Transcript of Interview "Meet the Press". Department of State Press Release No. 108, 9 April 1984 (mimeo).

Sollinger, Jerry M. (1983): Improving US Theater Nuclear Doctrine. Washington, DC: National Defense University Press.

Sonnenfeldt, Helmut, and William G. Hyland (1979): Soviet Perspectives on Security (Adelphi Paper No. 150). London: International Institute for Strategic Studies.

Sorrels, Charles A. (1983): Soviet Propaganda Campaign against NATO. Washington DC: US Arms Control and Disarmament Agency.

Soviet Military Power (1984), Third Edition. Washington, DC: US Government Printing Office.

Taylor, Maxwell D. (1978): "The Reality of the Soviet Threat". In: Grayson Kirk and Nils Wessell (Eds.): The Soviet Threat: Myths and Realities. New York: Praeger. pp. 168-178.

Thomas, Walter R. (1981): Essays on War. Washington, DC: National Defense University Press.

Understanding Soviet Military Developments (1977). Background Material for Addressing Soviet Military Development by US Army Personnel. Prepared at the Direction of the Assistant Chief of Staff for Intelligence. Washington, DC: Department of the Army.

Understanding Soviet Naval Developments (1981). Report Prepared at the Direction of the Chief of Naval Operations by the Director of Naval Intelligence and the Chief of Information. Washington, DC: US Government Printing Office.

United States Military Posture for Fiscal Year 1982. Washington, DC: US Government Printing Office.

United States Military Posture for Fiscal Year 1983. Washington, DC: US Government Printing Office

United States Military Posture for Fiscal Year 1984. Washington, DC: US Government Printing Office.

United States Military Posture for Fiscal Year 1985. Washington, DC: US Government Printing Office.

Vernon, Graham D. (1981a): "Controlling Conflict: Soviet Perceptions of Peaceful Coexistence". In: Graham D. Vernon (Ed.): Soviet Perceptions of War and Peace. Washington, DC: National Defense University Press. pp. 113-142.

--- (Ed.) (1981b): Soviet Perceptions of War and Peace. Washington, DC: National Defense University Press.

Weinberger, Caspar W. (1982): Department of Defense. Annual Report to the Congress, Fiscal Year 1983. Washington, DC: US Government Printing Office.

--- (1983a): Department of Defense Annual Report to the Congress, Fiscal Year 1984. Washington, DC: US Government Printing Office.

--- (1983b): Remarks before the Atlantic Institute. Paris (mimeo).

--- (1984): Department of Defense Annual Report to the Congress, Fiscal Year 1985. Washington, DC: US Government Printing Office.

--- , and Theodore Draper (1983): "On Nuclear War: An Exchange with the Secretary of Defense". In: The New York Review, 12 August 1983.

Zurhellen, J. Owen, Jr. (1981): "Arms Control: The Record of the 1970s and the Outlook of the 1980s". In: Robert O'Neill and D.M. Horner (Eds.): New Directions in Strategic Thinking. London: George Allen & Unwin. pp. 246-260.

3. Academic reference material (used for chapters I, IV and V)

Adomeit, Hannes (1981): "Soviet Risk Taking and Crisis Behavior". In: John Baylis and Gerald Segal (Eds.): Soviet Strategy. London: Croom Helm. pp. 185-209.
--- (1981a): "Consensus versus Conflict: The Dimension of Foreign Policy". In: Seweryn Bialer (Ed.): The Domestic Context of Soviet Foreign Policy. Boulder, CO: Westview Press/London: Croom Helm. pp. 49-83
--- (1982): Soviet Risk-Taking and Crisis Behavior. A Theoretical and Empirical Analysis. London: George Allen & Unwin.
--- (1983): Die Sowjetmacht in internationalen Krisen und Konflikten. Verhaltensmuster, Handlungsprinzipien, Bestimmungsfaktoren. Baden-Baden: Nomos.
Albert, Bernard S. (1979): "The Strategic Competition with the USSR". In: Comparative Strategy, Vol. 1, No.3. pp. 139-167.
Alexander Arthur J. (1984): "Modeling Soviet Defense Decisionmaking". In: Jiri Valenta and William Potter (Eds.): Soviet Decisionmaking for Defense. London: George Allen & Unwin. pp. 9-22.
Allison, Graham T. (1971): Essence of Decision: Explaining the Cuban Missile Crisis. Boston: Little, Brown.
Anschel, Eugene (1978): American Appraisals of Soviet Russia, 1917-1977. London: Scarecrow Press.
Arkin, William M. (1981): Research Guide to Current Military and Strategic Affairs. Washington, DC: Institute for Policy Studies.
Arnett, Robert L. (1981): "Soviet Attitudes Toward Nuclear War: Do They Really Think They Can Win?" In: John Baylis and Gerald Segal (Eds.): Soviet Strategy. London: Croom Helm. pp. 55-74. (a shorter version in: The Journal of Strategic Studies, Vol. 2, No.2 (1979). pp. 172-191)
Aspaturian Vernon V. (1981): "US Perceptions of Soviet Behaviour". In: Robert E. Osgood (Ed): Containment, Soviet Behavior, and Grand Strategy, Berkeley: Institute of International Studies. pp. 19-28.
Axelrod, Robert (Ed.) (1976a): Structure of Decision: The Cognitive Maps of Political Elites. Princeton University Press.
--- (1976b): "The Cognitive Mapping Approach to Decision Making". In: Robert Axelrod (Ed.): Structure of Decision: The Cognitive Maps of Political Elites. Princeton: Princeton University Press. pp. 3-17.

--- (1976c): "The Analysis of Cognitive Maps". In: Robert Axelrod (Ed.): Structure of Decision: The Cognitive Maps of Political Elites. Princeton: Princeton University Press. pp. 55-76.

Ayoob, Mohammed (1981): "Autonomy and Intervention". In: Robert O'Neill and D. M. Horner (Eds.): New Directions in Strategic Thinking. London: George Allen & Unwin. pp. 104-116.

Azrael, Jeremy (1981): "The 'Nationality Problem' in the USSR: Domestique Pressures and Foreign Policy Constraints". In: Seweryn Bialer (Ed.): The Domestic Context of Soviet Foreign Policy. Boulder: Westview Press/ London: Croom Helm. pp. 139-151.

Backerra, Manfred (1983): "Zur sowjetischen Militärdoktrin seit 1945". In: Beiträge zur Konfliktforschung, Vol. 13, No. 1. pp. 35-55.

Ball, Desmond (1983): Targeting for Strategic Deterrence (Adelphi Paper No.185). London: International Institute for Strategic Studies.

Barnet, Richard J. (1977): the Giants: Russia and America. New York: Simon and Schuster.

Bathurst, Robert A. (1981): "Two Languages of War". In: Derek Leebaert (Ed.): Soviet Military Thinking. London: George Allen & Unwin. pp. 28-49.

Baylis, John, and Gerald Segal (Eds.) (1981): Soviet Strategy. London: Croom Helm.

Becker, Abraham S. (1981): The Burden of Soviet Defense. A Political-Economic Essay. Santa Monica: Rand Corporation. (Report No. R-2752-AF)

--- (1982): "Der Vorrang militärischer Anstrengungen der Sowjetunion unter den politisch-ökonomischen Bedingungen der 80er Jahre". In: Uwe Nerlich (Ed.): Die Einhegung sowjetischer Macht. Baden-Baden: Nomos Verlagsgesellschaft. pp. 39-82.

Bennett, W. Lance (1981): "Perception and Cognition". In: Samuel L. Long (Ed.): The Handbook of Political Behavior, Vol. 1. New York /London: Plenum Press. pp. 69-193.

Betts, Richard K. (1978): "Analysis, War, and Decision". In: World Politics, Vol. 31, No.1. pp. 61-89.

--- (1981): "Surprise Attack: NATO's Political Vulnerability". In: International Security, Vol. 5, No.4 (Spring). pp. 117-149.

--- (1982): Surprise Attack. Washington, DC: Brookings Institution.

Beukel, Erik (1979): "Soviet Views on Strategic Nuclear Weapons: Orthodoxy and Modernism". In: Cooperation and Conflict, Vol. 14, No.4. pp. 223-237.

Beyme, Klaus von (1983): Die Sowjetunion in der Weltpolitik. München: Piper.

Bialer, Seweryn (Ed.) (1981): The Domestic Context of Soviet Foreign Policy. Boulder: Westview Press/London: Croom Helm.

--- (1981a): "Soviet Foreign Policy: Sources, Perceptions, Trends". In: Seweryn Bialer (Ed.): The Domestic Context of Soviet Foreign Policy. Boulder: Westview Press/London: Croom Helm. pp. 409-441.

--- (1982): "Das sowjetische System: Strukturelle Krisen und politisch-strategisches Aussenverhalten". In: Uwe Nerlich (Ed.): Die Einhegung sowjetischer Macht. Baden-Baden: Nomos Verlagsgesellschaft. pp. 13-38.

--- (1983): Andropov's Burden, Paper Presented to the Annual Conference of the International Institute for Strategic Studies, London (mimeo).

--- , and Joan Afferica (1982/83): "Reagan and Russia". In: Foreign Affairs, Vol. 61, No.2 (Winter). pp. 249-271.

Biedenkopf, Kurt (1983): "Domestic Consensus, Security and the Western Alliance". In: Adelphi Paper No.182. London: International Institute for Strategic Studies. pp. 6-13.

Bittman, Ladislav (1981): "Soviet Bloc 'Disinformation' and other 'Active Measures'". In: Robert L. Pfaltzgraff, Jr., Uri Ra'anan and Warren Milberg (Eds.): Intelligence Policy and National Security. London: Macmillan. pp. 212-228.

Bjorkman, Thomas N., and Thomas J. Zamostny (1984): "Soviet Politics and Strategy Toward the West". In: World Politics, Vol. 36, no2. pp. 189-214.

Blacker, Coit D. (1983): "Military Forces". In: Robert F. Byrnes: After Brezhnev: Sources of Soviet Conduct in the 1980s. Bloomington: Indiana University Press. pp. 125-185.

Blechman, Barry M. (1980): "Do Negotiated Arms Limitations Have a Future?" In: Foreign Affairs, Vol. 59, No.1 (Fall). pp. 102-125.

--- (Ed.) (1982): Rethinking the US Strategic Posture. Cambridge, MA: Ballinger.

--- and Edward N. Luttwak (Eds.) (1984): International Security Yearbook 1983/84. London: Macmillan.

Bonham, G. Matthew, and Michael J. Shapiro (Eds.) (1977): Thought and Action in Foreign Policy. Basel: Birkhäuser.

Booth, Ken (1979): Strategy and Ethnocentrism. London: Croom Helm.

--- (1981): "The Military Instrument in Soviet Foreign Policy". In: John Baylis and Gerald Segal (Eds.): Soviet Strategy. London: Croom Helm. pp. 75-101.

Bornstein, Morris (1981): "Soviet Economic Growth and Foreign Policy". In: Seweryn Bialer (Ed.): The Domestic Context of Soviet Foreign Policy. Boulder: Westview Press/London: Croom Helm. pp. 227-255.

Boulding, Kenneth N. (1956): The Image. Knowledge in Life and Society. Ann Arbor: University of Michigan Press.

--- (1969): "National Image and International System". In: James N. Rosenau (Ed.): International Politics and Foreign Policy. New York: Free Press. pp. 422-431.

Bretscher, Georges (1974): Das Erwartungskonzept in der Kommunikationsforschung. Ph. D. Thesis. Zurich: University of Zurich.

Bryder, Tom (1981): "Actor-Reliability: Some Methodological Problems". In: Karl E. Rosengren (Ed.): Advances in Content Analysis. Beverly Hills: Sage Publications. pp. 69-88.

Buchanan, Thompson R. (1982): "The Real Russia". In: Foreign Policy, No.47. pp. 26-45.

Buchholz, Arnold (Ed.) (1982): Soviet and East European Studies in the International Framework. New York: Transnational Publishers.

Bull, Hedley (1981): "Force in International Relations: The Experience of the 1970s and Prospects for the 1980s". In: Robert O'Neill and D. M. Horner (Eds.): New Directions in Strategic Thinking. London: George Allen & Unwin. pp. 17-33.

Buzan, Barry (1983): People, States, and Fear: The National Security Problem in International Relations. Chapel Hill: University of North Carolina Press.

Byrnes, Robert F. (1983): After Brezhnev: Sources of Soviet Conduct in the 1980s. Bloomington: Indiana University Press.

Caldwell, Lawrence T. (1971): Soviet Attitudes to SALT (Adelphi Papier No. 75). London: International Institute for Strategic Studies.

--- , and Robert LegVold (1983): "Reagan through Soviet Eyes". In: Foreign Policy, No. 52, Fall. pp. 3-21.

Calleo, David (1983): "Domestic Priorities and the Demands of Alliance: An American Perspective". In: Adelphi Paper No. 184. London: International Institute for Strategic Studies. pp. 2-11.

Carlsnaes, Walter (1981): "Can Perception Be Ideological?" In: Cooperation and Conflict, Vol. 16, No. 3. pp. 183-188.

Carnesale, Albert (1981): "The Adequacy of SALT Verification". In: Robert L. Pfaltzgraff, Jr., Uri Ra'anan and Warren Milberg (Eds.): Intelligence Policy and National Security. London: Macmillan. pp. 157-160.

Carter, Barry E. (1978): "The Strategic Debate in the United States". In: Grayson Kirk and Nils Wessell (Eds.): The Soviet Threat: Myths and Realities. New York: Praeger. pp. 15-29.

Clarkson, Albert (1981): Toward Effective Strategic Analysis. Boulder: Westview Press.

Cockburn, Andrew (1983): The Threat: Inside the Soviet Military Machine. New York: Random House.

Collins, John M. (1982): US Defense Planning: A Critique. Boulder: Westview Press.

Colton, Timothy (1981): "The Impact of the Military on Soviet Security". In: Seweryn Bialer (Ed.): The Domestic Context of Soviet Foreign Policy. Boulder: Westview Press/London: Croom Helm. pp. 119-138.

Connor, Walter D. (1981): "Mass Expectations and Regime Performance". In: Seweryn Bialer (Ed.): The Domestic Context of Soviet Foreign Policy. Boulder: Westview Press/London: Croom Helm. pp. 155-173.

Cooper Frank (1983): "The Management of Defense Expenditure". In: Adelphi Paper No. 182. London: International Institute for Strategic Studies. pp. 51-58.

Cottam, Richard W. (1977); Foreign Policy Motivation: A General Theory and a Case Study. Pittsburgh: University of Pittsburgh Press.

Dahlitz, Julie (1983): Nuclear Arms Control with Effective International Agreements. Melbourne: McPhee Gribble.

Dallin, Alexander (1978): "The United States in the Soviet Perspective". In: Adelphi Paper No. 151, London: International Institute for Strategic Studies. pp. 13-21.

305

--- (1980): "Soviet Foreign Policy and Domestic Politics: A Framework for Analysis". In: Erik P. Hoffmann and Frederic J. Fleron, Jr. (Eds.): The Conduct of Soviet Foreign Policy. New York: Aldine Publishing Co. pp. 36-49. (first published 1969 in the Journal of International Affairs)

--- (1981): "The Domestic Sources of Soviet Foreign Policy". In: Seweryn Bialer (Ed.): The Domestic Context of Soviet Foreign Policy. Boulder: Westview Press/London: Croom Helm. pp. 335-408.

--- (1982): "Soviet and East European Studies in the United States". In: Arnold Buchholz (Ed.): Soviet and East European Studies in the International Framework. New York: Transnational Books. pp. 11-31.

--- (1983): "The Making of Soviet Foreign Policy". In: Bulletin of the Atomic Scientists, August/September 1983. pp. 27-31.

--- , and Thomas B. Larson (Eds.) (1968): Soviet Politics since Khrushchev. Englewood Cliffs: Prentice-Hall.

Daniel, Donald C. (Ed.) (1978): International Perceptions of the Superpower Military Balance. New York: Praeger.

Davies, James Ch. (1980): "Biological Perspectives on Human Conflict". in: Ted Robert Gurr (Ed.): Handbook of Political Conflict: Theory and Research. New York: Free Press. pp. 19-68.

Deane, Michael J. (1978): "Soviet Perceptions of the Military Factor in the 'Correlation of World Forces'". In: Donald C. Daniel (Ed.): International Preceptions of the Superpower Military Balance. New York: Praeger. pp. 72-94.

De Vree, Johan K. (1982): Foundations of Social and Political Processes, Vol. I: Theory. Bilthoven: Prime Press.

Dibb, Paul (1982): "Soviet Capabilities, Interests and Strategies in East Asia in the 1980s". In: Survival, Vol. 24, No. 4. pp. 155-162.

Dirnecker, Rupert (1981): Sowjetische Weltpolitik unter Breschnew. Berlin: Duncker & Humblot.

Douglass, Joseph D., Jr., and Amoretta M. Hoeber (1979): Soviet Strategy for Nuclear War. Stanford: Hoover Institution Press.

--- , and Amoretta M. Hoeber (1981): Conventional War and Escalation: The Soviet View. New York: Crane, Russak.

Dyson, Freeman (1984). Weapons and Hope. New York: Harper & Row.

Dziak, John J. (1981a): Soviet Perceptions of Military Power: The Interaction of Theory and Practice. New York: Crane, Russak.

--- (1981b): "The Institutional Foundations of Soviet Military Doctrine". In: Graham D. Vernon (Ed.): Soviet Perceptions of War and Peace. Washington, DC: National Defense University Press. pp. 3-16.

Eason, Warren W. (1981): "Demographic Trends and Soviet Foreign Policy: The Underlying Imperatives of Labor Supply". In: Seweryn Bialer (Ed.): The Domestic Context of Soviet Foreign Policy. Boulder: Westview Press/London: Croom Helm. pp. 203-226.

Edelman, Murray (1977): Political Language. Words that Succeed and Politics that Fail. New York: Academic Press.

Erickson, John (1979): "Recruitment Patterns for the Leadership".

In: Adelphi Paper No. 152. London: International Institute for Strategic Studies. pp. 32-38.

--- (1981): "The Soviet Military Potential for Surprise Attack: Surprise, Superiority and Time". In: Robert L. Pfaltzgraff, Jr., Uri Ra'anan and Warren Milberg (Eds.): Intelligence Policy and National Security. London: Macmillan. pp. 49-73.

--- (1982): "The Soviet View of Deterrence: A General Survey": In: Survival, Vol. 24, No. 6. pp. 242-251.

Ermarth, Fritz W. (1981): "Contrasts in American and Soviet Strategie Thought". In: Derek Leebaert (Ed.): Soviet Military Thinking. London: George Allen & Unwin. pp. 50-69.

--- (1982): "Die Globale Projizierbarkeit sowjetischer Macht und die strategischen Erfordernisse ihrer Eindämmung". In: Uwe Nerlich (Ed.): Die Einhegung sowjetischer Macht. Baden-Baden: Nomos Verlagsgesellschaft. pp. 109-142.

Etzioni, Amitai (1969): "Social-Psychological Aspects of International Relations". In: Lindzey Gardner and Elliot Aronson (Eds.): The Handbook of Social Psychology, Second Edition, Vol. 5. Reading, MA: Addison-Wesley. pp. 538-601.

Ferrari, Paul L. (1983): "Soviet Military Power?" In: Arms Control, Vol. 4, No. 1. pp. 61-64.

Fewtrell, David (1983): The Soviet Economic Crisis: Prospects for the Military and the Consumer (Adelphi Papers, No. 186). London: International Institute for Strategic Studies.

Finlay, David J. (1967): "Some Theoretical Dimensions of the Idea of the Enemy". In: David J. Finaly et al. (Eds.): Enemies in Politics. Chicago: Rand McNally. pp. 1-24.

Fishbein, Martin, and Icek Ajzen (1975): Belief, Attitude, Intention, and Behavior. Reading,: MA Addison-Wesley.

Foster, Richard B. (1979): "Alternative Worldviews and Strategic Selection in US - Soviet Interaction". In: Comparative Strategy, Vol. 1, No. 3. pp. VII-XIV.

Frank, Thomas M., and Edward Weisband (1972): Word Politics. Verbal Strategy Among the Superpowers. London: Oxford University Press.

Freedman, Lawrence (1981): The Evolution of Nuclear Strategy. New York: St.Martin's Press.

--- (1984): "Strategic Superiority". In: Coexistence, Vol. 21. pp. 7-21.

Frei, Daniel (Ed.) (1977): Theorien der internationalen Beziehungen, Second Edition. Munich: Piper.

--- , Peter Gaupp, Hans-Martin Uehlinger, and Hans Vogel (1980): Weltbild und Aussenpolitik. Frauenfeld: Huber.

---, with the collaboration of Christian Catrina (1982): Risks of Unintentional Nuclear War. Geneva: United Nations Institute for Disarmament Research.

Friel, Patrick J. (1981): "United States and Soviet Strategic Technologies and Nuclear War Fighting: A Comparison". In: Robert L. Pfaltzgraff, Jr., Uri Ra'anan and Warren Milberg (Eds.): Intelligence Policy and National Security. London: Macmillan. pp. 98-128.

Fromm, Joseph (1983): "The Media and the Making of Defense Policy: The U.S. Example". In: Adelphi Paper No. 182. London: International Institute for Strategic Studies. pp. 29-35.

Gaddis, John L. (1982): Strategies of Containment. New York/Oxford: Oxford University Press.

Gäfgen, Gérard (1980): "Formale Theorie Strategischen Handelns". In: Hans Lenk (Ed.): Handlungstheorien interdisziplinär, Vol. 1. München: Fink. pp. 249-302.

Gardner, Lindzey, and Elliot Aronson (Eds.) (1968): The Handbook of Social Psychology, Second Edition, Vol. 1. Reading, MA: Addison-Wesley.

Garthoff, Raymond L. (1981a): "The Soviet Military and SALT". In: John Baylis and Gerald Segal (Eds.): Soviet Strategy. London: Croom Helm. pp. 154-182.

--- (1981b): "Mutual Deterrence, Parity and Strategic Arms Limitation in Soviet Policy". In: Derek Leebaert (Ed.): Soviet Military Thinking. London: George Allen & Unwin. pp. 92-124.

--- (1983): Perspectives on the Strategic Balance. Washington, DC: Brookings Institution.

--- (1984a): "The Debate About Soviet Strategy". In: Comparative Strategy, Vol. 4, No. 3 pp. 307-310.

--- (1984b): "The Soviet Military and SALT". In: Jiri Valenta and William Potter (Eds.): Soviet Decisionmaking for Defense. London: George Allen/Unwin. pp. 136-164.

Gati, Charles (1983): "The Soviet Stake in Eastern Europe". In: National Security Management: International Issues and Perspectives. Washington, DC: National Defense University Press. pp. 69-89.

Gelman, Harry (1981): The Politburo's Management of Its American Problem. Santa Monica, CA: Rand Corporation. (Report No. R-2707-NA)

--- (1982): "Eine amerikanische Herausforderung? Die Globalpolitik der USA in der Sicht der sowjetischen Führung". In: Uwe Nerlich (Ed.): Die Einhegung sowjetischer Macht. Baden-Baden: Nomos Verlagsgesellschaft. pp. 83-108.

George, Alexander L. (1975): "Towards a More Soundly Based Foreign Policy: Making Better Use of Information". In: Commission on the Organization of the Government for the Conduct of Foreign Policy, Vol. 2. Washington, DC: US Government Printing Office. pp. 7-143.

--- (1980): "The 'Operational Code': A Neglected Approach to the Study of Political Leaders and Decision-Making". In: Erik P. Hoffmann and Frederic J. Fleron, Jr. (Eds.): The Conduct of Soviet Foreign Policy. New York: Aldine Publishing Co. pp. 165-190. (first published 1969 in International Studies Quarterly)

Gibert, Stephen. P. (1977): Soviet Images of America. New York: Crane, Russak.

Gick, Mary L., and Keith J. Holyoak (1983): "Schema Induction and Analogical Transfer". In: Cognitive Psychology, Vol. 15. pp. 1-38.

Goffman, Erving (1970): Strategic Interaction. Oxford: Blackwell.

Golan, Galia (1979): "Soviet Power and Policies in the Third World:

The Middle East". In: Adelphi Paper No. 152. London: International Institute for Strategic Studies. pp. 47-52.

Goldhamer, Herbert (1978): "Perceptions of the US-Soviet Balance: Problems of Analysis and Research". In: Donald C. Daniel (Ed.): International Perceptions of the Superpower Military Balance. New York: Praeger. pp. 3-20.

Goodman, Walter (1984) "Emigré Novellists: Russian Exiles Worry About Perceptions of the Soviet Regime in the US". In: International Herald Tribune, 28 March 1984.

Gray, Colin S. (1980): "Strategic Forces and SALT: A Question of Strategy". In: Comparative Strategy, Vol. 2. pp. 113-128.

--- (1981): "National Style in Strategy: The American Example". In: International Security, Vol. 2, No. 2 (Fall). pp. 21-47.

--- (1982): Strategic Studies. A Critical Assessment. London: Aldwych Press.

--- , and Donald G. Brennan (1982): "Gemeinsame Interessen als Grundlage für Rüstungskontrolle?" In: Uwe Nerlich (Ed.): Sowjetische Macht und westliche Verhandlungspolitik im Wandel militärischer Kräfteverhältnisse. Baden-Baden: Nomos Verlagsgesellschaft. pp. 511-540.

Griffith, William (1979): "Soviet Power and Policies in the Third World: The Case of Africa". In: Adelphi Paper No. 152. London: International Institute for Strategic Studies. pp. 39-46.

Griffiths, Franklyn (1972): Image, Politics and Learning in Soviet Behavior Toward the United States. Ph.D. Thesis. Columbia University.

--- (1981): "Ideological Development and Foreign Policy". In: Seweryn Bialer (Ed.): The Domestic Context of Soviet Foreign Policy. Boulder: Westview Press/London: Croom Helm. pp. 19-48.

Gurr, Ted Robert (Ed.) (1980): Handbook of Political Conflict: Theory and Research. New York: Free Press. pp. 19-68.

Hansen, Robert W. (1975): Soviet Images of Foreign Policy, 1960-1972. Ph.D. Thesis. Princeton: Princeton University.

Hanson, Donald W. (1982/83): "Is Soviet Strategic Doctrine Superior?" In: International Security, Vol. 7, No. 3. pp. 61-83.

Hardt, John P. (1978): "Soviet Economic Capabilities and Defense Resources". In: Grayson Kirk and Nils Wessell (Eds.): The Soviet Threat: Myths and Realities. New York: Praeger. pp. 122-134.

Hare, A. Paul (1976): Handbook of Small Group Reseach, Second Edition. New York: Free Press.

Harkavy, Robert E., and Edward A. Kolodziej (Eds.) (1980): American Security Policy and Policy- Making. Lexington: D.C. Heath.

Hart, Douglas M. (1982): "Low-Intensive Conflict in Afghanistan: The Soviet View". In: Survival, Vol. 24. No. 2. pp. 61-67.

Hart, Jeffrey (1976: "Comparative Cognition: Politics of International Control". In: Robert Axelrod (Ed.): Structure of Decision. Princeton: Princeton University Press. pp. 180-220.

Hart, Thomas G. (1976): The Cognitive World of Swedish Security Elites. Stockholm: Esselte Studium.

--- (1978): "Cognitive Paradigms in the Arms Race". In: Cooperation and Conflict, Vol. 13. pp. 147-161.

--- (1979): The Spread of Extra-European Conflicts to Europe:

Concepts and Analysis. Stockholm: Utrikespolitiska Intitutet.

Hartmann, Frederick H. (1982): The Conservation of Enemies: A Study in Enmity. Westport: Greenwood Press.

Haselkorn, Avigdor (1978): The EVolution of Soviet Security Strategy, 1968-1975. New York: Crane, Russak.

Heintz, Peter (1982): "A Sociological Code for the Description of World Society". In: International Social Science Journal, No. 91. pp. 11-21.

Heradstveit, Daniel (1980): "An Information-Processing Approach to the Study of the Political Decision-Making". In: International Politik, No. 1B/Supplement. pp. 273-292.

--- , Narvesen, Ove (1978): "Psychological Constraints on Decision-Making: A Discussion of Cognitive Approaches; Operational Code and Cognitive Map". In: Cooperation and Conflict, Vol. 13. pp. 77-92.

Hermann, Margaret G. (1983): "Assessing Personality at a Distance". In: Mershon Center Quarterly Report, Vol. 7, No. 6, Spring. pp. 1-8.

Hermann, Robert (1982): "Die Sowjetische Fähigkeit zu Ueberraschungsangriffen und Mögliche Massnahmen zur Verlängerung der Warnzeit". In: Uwe Nerlich (Ed.): Die Einhegung sowjetischer Macht. Baden-Baden: Nomos. pp. 305-316.

Hermann, Richard K.(1984): Competitive Interference and Soviet Perceptions of the USA. Paper presented to the 25th Annual Convention of the International Studies Association, Atlanta (mimeo).

Heuer, Richard J. (1982): "Cognitive Factors in Deception and Counterdeception". In: Donald C. Daniel and Katherine L. Herbig (Eds.): Strategic Military Deception. New York: Pergamon Press. pp. 31-69.

Hodnett, Grey (1981): "The Patterns of Leadership Politics". In: Seweryn Bialer (Ed.): The Domestic Context of Soviet Foreign Policy. Boulder: Westview Press/London: Croom Helm. pp. 87-118.

Hoffmann, Erik P., and Frederic J. Fleron, Jr. (Eds.) (1980): The Conduct of Soviet Foreign Policy. New York: Aldine Publishing.

--- , and Robbin F. Laird (1982): The "Scientific-Technological ReVolution" and Soviet Foreign Policy. New York: Pergamon Press.

Holloway, David (1971): Technology, Management and the Soviet Military Establishment (Adelphi Paper No. 76). London: International Institute for Strategic Studies.

--- (1979): "Decision-Making in Soviet Defence Policies". In: Adelphi Paper No. 152. London: International Institute for Strategic Studies. pp. 24-31.

--- (1980): "War, Militarism and the Soviet State". In: Alternatives, Vol. VI. pp. 59-92.

--- (1981): "Doctrine and Technology in Soviet Armaments Policy". In: Derek Leebaert (Ed.): Soviet Military Thinking. London: George Allen & Unwin. pp. 259-291.

--- (1982): "Foreign and Defence Policy". In: Archie Brown and Michael Kaser (Eds.): Soviet Policy for the 1980s. Oxford: Macmillan. pp. 35-64.

--- (1983): The Soviet Union and the Arms Race. New Haven: Yale University Press.

Holst, Johan J. (1981): "Deterrence and Stability in the NATO-Warsaw Pact Relationship". In: Robert O'Neill and D.M. Horner (Eds.): New Directions in Strategic Thinking. London: George Allen & Unwin. pp. 89-103.

--- (1983): "Domestic Concerns and Nuclear Doctrines: How Should the Nuclear Posture be Shaped?" In: Adelphi Paper No. 183. London: International Institute for Strategic Studies. pp. 28-42.

Holsti, Ole R. (1962): "The Belief System and National Images: A Case Study". In: Journal of Conflict Resolution, Vol. 6, No. 3. pp. 244-252.

--- (1967): "Cognitive Dynamics and Image of the Enemy". In: David J. Finlay et al. (Eds.): Enemies in Politics. Chicago: Rand McNally. pp. 25-96.

--- (1975): "Operational Code, Belief System and Crisis Decisionmaking". In: Charles F. Hermann (Ed.): Research Tasks for International Crisis Avoidance and Management. Columbus: Mershon Center. pp. 92-109.

--- (1976): "Foreign Policy Formation Viewed Cognitively". In: Robert Axelrod (Ed.): Structure of Decision: The Cognitive Maps of Political Elites. Princeton: Princeton University Press. pp. 18-54.

--- (1977): "Foreign-Policy Decision-Makers Viewed Psychologically". In: G. Matthew Bonham and Michael J. Shapiro (Eds.): Thought and Action in Foreign Policy. Basel: Birkhäuser. pp. 9-74.

Hopple, Gerald W., and Paul J. Rossa (1981): "International Crisis Analysis". In: P. Terrence Hopmann, Dina A. Zinnes, and J. David Singer (Eds.): Cumulation in International Relations Research. Denver: Graduate School of International Studies. pp. 65-97.

Hosmer, Stephen T., and Thomas W. Wolfe (1983): Soviet Policy and Practice Toward Third World Conflicts. Lexington: Lexington Books.

Hough, Jerry F. (1980): "The EVolution in the Soviet World View". In: World Politics, Vol. 32, No. 4. pp. 509-530.

Howard, Michael E. (1981): "On Fighting a Nuclear War". In: International Security, Vol. 5, No. 4 (Spring). pp. 3-17.

--- (1983): "Deterrence, Consensus and Reassurance in the Defence of Europe". In: Adelphi Paper No. 184. London: International Institute for Strategic Studies. pp. 17-26.

Hulett, Louisa Sue (1982): Decade of Détente: Shifting Definitions and Denouement. Washington, DC: University Press of America.

Hunt, Kenneth (1981): "The Development of Concepts for Conventional Warfare in the 1970s and 1980s". In: Robert O'Neill and D. M. Horner (Eds.): New Directions in Strategic Thinking. London: George Allen & Unwin. pp. 183-201.

Hunt, R. N. Carew (1980): "The Importance of Doctrine". In: Erik P. Hoffmann and Frederic J. Fleron, Jr. (Eds.): The Conduct of Soviet Foreign Policy. New York: Aldine Publishing Co. pp. 101-108. (first published 1958, in: Problems of Communism).

Huntington, Samuel P. (1983): "Broadening the Strategic Focus:

Comments on Michael Howard's Paper". In: Adelphi Paper No. 184. London: International Institute for Strategic Studies. pp. 27-32.

Husband, William B. (1979): "Soviet Perceptions of US 'Positions-of-Strength' Diplomacy in the 1970s". In: World Politics, Vol. 31. No. 4. pp. 495-517.

Hveem, Helge (1972): International Relations and World Images. Oslo: Universitetsforlaget.

Hyland, William G. (1979): "Soviet Security Concerns in the 1980s". In: Adelphi Paper No. 152. London: International Institute for Strategic Studies. pp. 18-23.

--- (1982a): "The Soviet Union in the American Perspective: Perceptions and Realities". In: Adelphi Paper No. 174. London: International Institute for Strategic Studies. pp. 52-59.

--- (1982b): "The USSR and Nuclear War". In: Barry M. Blechman (Ed.): Rethinking the US Strategic Posture. Cambridge, MA: Ballinger. pp. 41-76.

--- (1982/83): "Clash with the Soviet Union". In: Foreign Policy, No. 49. pp. 3-19.

Jackson, William D. (1981): "Soviet Images of the US as Nuclear Adversary, 1969-1979". In: World Politics, Vol. 23, No. 4. pp. 614- 638.

Jacobson, Carl G. (1979): Soviet Strategic Initiatives. Challenge and Reponse. New York: Praeger.

--- (1983): Perceptions of the Soviet Union as a Threat. Miami: University of Miami/Graduate School of International Studies (mimeo).

Jamgotch, Nisch (1983a): Soviet Security in Flux. Muscatine: Stanley Foundation.

--- (1983b). "We are Exaggerating Soviet Power". In: International Studies Notes, Vol. 10, No. 2 (Summer). pp. 1-2.

Jervis, Robert (1970): The Logic of Images in International Relations. Princeton: Princeton University Press.

--- (1972): "Consistency in Foreign Policy Views". In Richard L. Merritt (Ed.): Communication in International Politics. Urbana-Chicago: University of Illinois Press. pp. 272-291.

--- (1976): Perception and Misperception in International Relations. Princeton: Princeton University Press

--- (1981): "Beliefs about Soviet Behavior". In: Robert E. Osgood (Ed.): Containment, Soviet Behavior, and Grand Strategy. Berkeley: Institute of International Studies. pp. 55-59.

--- (1982): Deterrence and Perception (Research Note No. 11). Los Angeles: Center for International and Strategic Affairs.

--- (1982/83): "Deterrence and Perception". In: International Security, Vol. 7, No. 3. pp. 3-28.

Jones, Christopher (1981): "Soviet Military Doctrine and Warsaw Pact Exercises". In: Derek Leebaert (Ed.): Soviet Military Thinking. London: George Allen & Unwin. pp. 225-258.

Jones, Reginald V. (1981): "Intelligence and Perception". In: Robert L. Pfaltzgraff, Uri Ra'anan, and Warren Milberg (Eds.): Intelligence Policy and National Security. London: Macmillan. pp. 3-22.

Jönsson, Christer (1979): Soviet Bargaining Behavior. The Nuclear Test Ban Case. New York: Columbia University Press.

--- (1983): "A Cognitive Approach to International Negotiation". In: European Journal of Political Research, Vol. 11. pp. 139-150.

Jukes, Geoffrey (1981): "Soviet Strategy 1965-1990". In: Robert O'Neill and D. M. Horner (Eds.): New Directions in Strategic Thinking. London: George Allen & Unwin. pp. 60-74.

Juviler, Peter H., and Hannah J. Zawadzka (1978): "Détente and Soviet Domestic Politics". In: Grayson Kirk and Nils Wessell (Eds.): The Soviet Threat: Myths and Realities. New York: Praeger. pp. 158-167.

Kaagan, Lawrence (1983): "Public Opinion and the Defence Effort: Trends and Lessons - The United States". In: Adelphi Paper No. 182. London: International Institute for Strategic Studies. pp. 14-23.

Kahan, Arcadius (1981): "Soviet Agriculture: Domestic and Foreign Policy Aspects". In: Seweryn Bialer (Ed.): The Domestic Context of Soviet Foreign Policy. Boulder: Westview Press/London: Croom Helm. pp. 257-268.

Kaplan, Fred M. (1980): Dubious Specter: A Skeptical Look at the Soviet Nuclear Threat. Washington, DC: Institute for Policy Studies.

Karber, Philipp A. (1982): "Mögliche Funktionen der Rüstungskontrolle bei der Stabilisierung der Rüstungskonkurrenz in Europa". In: Uwe Nerlich (Ed.): Die Einhegung sowjetischer Macht. Baden-Baden: Nomos Verlagsgesellschaft. pp. 455-468.

Katz, Aaron (1981): "Verification and SALT: A Different Line of Insight". In: Robert L. Pfaltzgraff, Jr., Uri Ra'anan and Warren Milberg (Eds.): Intelligence Policy and National Security. London: Macmillan. pp. 143-147.

Katz, Philipp P. (1978): "Détente and Pravda's View of the United States: A Quantitative Analysis". In: Conflict, Vol. 1, Nos. 1/2. pp. 113-130.

Kaufmann-Mall, Klaus (1981): "Grundzüge einer kognitiv-hedonistischen Theorie menschlichen Verhaltens". In: Hans Lenk (Ed.): Handlungstheorien interdisziplinär, Vol. 3/1. Munich: Fink. pp. 123-189.

Kelman, Herbert C. (Ed.) (1965): International Behavior. New York: Holt, Rinehart and Winston.

Keys, Donald (1981): "The Neglected 'Software' Aspects of Disarmament". In: Ervin Laszlo and Donald Keys (Eds.): Oxford: Pergamon Press. pp. 17-23.

Kime, Steve F. (1980): "The Soviet View of War". In: Comparative Strategy, Vol. 2, No. 3. pp. 205-221.

Kirk, Grayson, and Nils Wessell (Eds.) (1978): The Soviet Threat: Myths and Realities. New York: Praeger.

Kirkpatrick, Samuel A. (1975): "Psychological Views of Decision-Making". In: Cornelius P. Cotter (Ed.): Political Science Annual, Vol. 6. Indianapolis: Bobbs-Merrill. pp. 39-112.

Knorr, Klaus (1979): "Strategic Intelligence: Problems and Remedies". In: Laurence Martin (Ed.): Strategic Thought in the

Nuclear Age. Baltimore: Johns Hopkins University Press. pp. 69-89.

Kober, Stanley (1984): "Swapping the Empire". In Foreign Policy, No. 54. pp. 156-163.

Kolkowicz, Roman (1981a): The Military and Soviet Foreign Policy". In: The Journal of Strategic Studies, Vol. 4, No. 4. pp. 337-355.

--- (1981b): "On Limited War". In: Robert O'Neill and D. M. Horner (Eds.): New Directions in Strategic Thinking. London: George Allen & Unwin. pp. 75-88.

--- (1981c): Military Strategy and Political Interests: The Soviet Union and the United States (ACIS Working Paper No. 30). Los Angeles: Center for International and Strategic Affairs.

Korbonski, Andrzej (1981): "Eastern Europe as an Internal Determinant of Soviet Foreign Policy". In: Seweryn Bialer (Ed.): The Domestic Context of Soviet Foreign Policy. Boulder: Westview Press/London: Croom Helm. pp. 313-323.

Labedz, Leopold (1978): "Ideology and Soviet Foreign Policy". In: Adelphi Paper No. 151. London: International Institute for Strategic Studies. pp. 37-45.

Laloy, Jean (1978): "Western Europe in the Soviet Perspective". In: Adelphi Paper No. 151. London: International Institute for Strategic Studies. pp. 22-29.

Lambeth, Benjamin S. (1979): "The Political Potential of Soviet Equivalence". In: International Security, Vol. 4, No. 2 (Fall). pp. 22-39.

--- (1980): "Soviet Strategic Conduct and the Prospects for Stability". In: Adelphi Paper No. 161. London: International Institute for Strategic Studies. pp. 27-38.

--- (1981): "How to Think about Soviet Military Doctrine". In: John Baylis and Gerald Segal (Eds.): Soviet Strategy. London: Croom Helm. pp. 105-123.

Lange, Peer H. (1984): "Die sowjetische Militärdoktrin und der Westen". In: Europa-Archiv, Vol. 39, No. 6. pp. 179-186.

Lebow, Richard Ned (1981): "Clear and Future Danger: Managing Relations with the Soviet Union in the 1980s". In: Robert O'Neill and D. M. Horner (Eds.): New Directions in Strategic Thinking. London: George Allen & Unwin. pp. 222-245.

--- (1984): "The Paranoia of the Powerful: Thucydides on World War II". In: PS (Political Science), Vol. 17, No. 1. pp. 10-17.

Leebaert, Derek (Ed.) (1981): Soviet Military Thinking. London. George Allen & Unwin.

--- (1981a): The Context of Soviet Military Thinking". In: Derek Leebaert (Ed.): Soviet Military Thinking. London: George Allen & Unwin. pp. 3-27.

Legvold, Robert (1978): "The Concept of Power and Security in Soviet History". In: Adelphi Paper No. 151. London: International Institute for Strategic Studies. pp. 5-12.

--- (1979): "Strategic 'Doctrine' and SALT: Soviet and American Views". In: Survival, Vol. 21, No. 1. (January/February). pp. 8-13.

--- (1980): "The Nature of Soviet Power". In: Erik P. Hoffmann and Frederic J. Fleron, Jr. (Eds.): The Conduct of Soviet Foreign

Policy. New York: Aldine Publishing. pp. 673-693. (first published 1977 in: Foreign Affairs)

--- (1982): "Der politische Nutzen militärischer Macht in sowjetischer Perspektive". In: Uwe Nerlich (Ed.): Sowjetische Macht und westliche Verhandlungspolitik im Wandel militärischer Kräfteverhältnisse. Baden-Baden: Nomos Verlagsgesellschaft. pp. 187-236.

Leites, Nathan (1981): "The Soviet Style of War". In: Derek Leebaert (Ed.): Soviet Military Thinking. London: George Allen & Unwin. pp. 185-224.

--- (1982): The Soviet Style in War. New York: Crane, Russak.

Lenczowski, John (1982): Soviet Perception of US Foreign Policy. A Study of Ideology, Power, and Consensus. Ithaca/London: Cornell University Press.

Levine, Herbert S. (1981): "Soviet Economic Development, Technological Transfer, and Foreign Policy". In: Seweryn Bialer (Ed.): The Domestic Context of Soviet Foreign Policy. Boulder: Westview Press/London: Croom Helm. pp. 177-201.

Levy, Jack S. (1983): "Misperception and the Causes of War: Theoretical Linkages and Analytical Problems". In: World Politics, Vol. 36, No. 1 (October). pp. 76-99.

Lider, Julian (1979): The Political and Military Laws of War. Westmead: Saxon House.

--- (1981): Military Force. An Analysis of Marxist-Leninist Concepts. Westmead: Gower.

--- (1983): Military Theory. Aldershot: Gower.

Lifton, Robert Jay, and Richard Falk (1982): Indefensible Weapons: The Political and Psychological Case Against Nuclearism. New York: Basic Books.

Lippert, Ekkehard, and Roland Wakenhut (Eds.) (1983): Handwörterbuch der Politischen Psychologie. Opladen: Westdeutscher Verlag.

Lockwood, Jonathan Samuel (1983): The Soviet View of US Strategic Doctrine. New Brunswick: Transaction Books.

Lowenthal, Richard (1981): "The Logic of One-Party Rule". In: Erik P. Hoffman and Frederic J. Fleron, Jr. (Eds.): The Conduct of Soviet Foreign Policy. New York: Aldine Publishing. pp. 117-130.

Luck, Edward C. (1978): "The Soviet Union and Conventional Arms Control". In: Grayson Kirk and Nils Wessell (Eds.): The Soviet Threat: Myths and Realities. New York: Praeger. pp. 57-65.

Lüders, Carl H. (1981): Ideologie und Machtdenken in der Aussen- und Sicherheitspolitik der Sowjetunion. Baden-Baden: Nomos.

Luttwak, Edward N. (1978): "The Missing Dimension of US Defense Policy: Force, Perceptions, and Power". In: Donald C. Daniel (Ed.): International Perceptions of the Superpower Military Balance. New York: Praeger. pp. 21-39.

--- (1983): The Grand Strategy of the Soviet Union. London: Weidenfeld & Nicolson.

Mancke, Richard (1981): "Intelligence - The Economic Factor". In: Robert L. Pfaltzgraff, Jr., Uri Ra'anan and Warren Milberg (Eds.): Intelligence Policy and National Security. London: Macmillan. pp. 231-242.

Mandel, Robert (1979): Perception, Decision Making, and Conflict. Washington, DC: University Press of America.

Marerer, Paul (1981): "The Economics of Eastern Europe and Soviet Foreign Policy". In: Seweryn Bialer (Ed.): The Domestic Context of Soviet Foreign Policy. Boulder: Westview Press/London: Croom Helm. pp. 271-312.

Marshall, Andrew (1979): "The Sources of Soviet Power. The Military Potential in the 1980s". In: Adelphi Paper No. 152. London: International Institute for Strategic Studies. p. 11-17.

Mason R.A. (1984): "Military Strategy". In Moreton Edwina and Gerald Segal (Eds): Soviet Strategy Toward Europe. London: George Allen & Unwin. pp. 165- 203.

MccGwire, Michael (1980): "Soviet Military Doctrine: Contingency War Planning and the Reality of World War". In: Survival, Vol. 22, No. 3. pp. 107-113.

--- (1981a): "The Rationale for the Development of Soviet Seapower". In: John Baylis and Gerald Segal (Eds.): Soviet Strategy. London: Croom Helm. pp. 210-254.

--- (1981b): "Soviet Naval Doctrine and Strategy". In: Derek Leebaert (Ed.): Soviet Military Thinking. London: George Allen & Unwin. pp. 125-181.

--- , et al. (Eds.) (1975): Soviet Naval Policy: Objectives and Constraints. New York: Praeger.

McGinnis, Joseph S. (1978): The Belief Systems of Foreign Policy Decision-Makers: Values and Consistency. Ph. D. Thesis. Washington, DC: American University.

McGuire, William J. (1969): "The Nature of Attitude Change". In: Lindzey Gardner and Elliot Aronson (Eds.): The Handbook of Social Psychology, Second Edition, Vol. 3. Reading, MA: Addison-Wesley. pp. 136-314.

Meinefeld, Werner (1988): Einstellung und soziales Verhalten. Reinbek bei Hamburg: Rowohlt.

Meissner, Boris (1982): Weltmacht Sowjetunion. München: Bayerische Landeszentrale für Politische Bildungsarbeit.

--- (1983a): "Aussen- und sicherheitspolitische Entscheidungs- prozesse: Sowjetunion". In: Aus Politik und Zeitgeschichte, No. B 43, (October). pp. 31-45.

--- (1983b) "Die aussenpolitische Doppelstrategie der Sowjetunion". In: Moderne Welt, Jahrbuch für Ost-West-Fragen 1983. pp. 135-164.

Merritt, Richard L. (Ed.) (1972): Communication in International Politics. Urbana-Chicago: University of Illinois Press.

Meyer, Stephen M. (1982): Soviet Defense Decisionmaking (ACIS Working Paper No. 33). Los Angeles: Center for International and Strategic Affairs.

--- (1984): "Soviet National Security Decisionmaking: What Do We Know and What Do We Understand?" In: Jiri Valenta and William Potter (Eds.): Soviet Decisionmaking for Defense. London: George Allen & Unwin. pp. 255-291.

--- (1984a): Soviet Theatre Nuclear Forces. Part I: Development of Doctrine and Objectives (Adelphi Paper No. 187). London: International Institute for Strategic Studies.

--- (1984b): Soviet Theatre Nuclear Forces. Part II: Capabilities and Intentions (Adelphi Paper No. 188). London: International Institute for Strategic Studies.

Mihalka, Michael (1982): "Soviet Strategic Deception, 1955-1981". In: The Journal of Strategic Studies, Vol. 5, No. 1. pp. 40-93.

Millar, T.B. (1981): "Alliances in the 1970s and 1980s: Problems of Cohesion and Effectiveness." In: Robert O'Neill and D. M. Horner (Eds.): New Directions in Strategic Thinking. London: George Allen & Unwin. pp. 117-133.

Miller, G.E. (1978): "An Evaluation of the Soviet Navy". In: Grayson Kirk and Nils Wessell (Eds.): The Soviet Threat: Myths and Realities. New York: Praeger. pp. 47-56.

Miller, Mark E. (1982): Soviet Strategic Power and Doctrine: The Quest for Superiority. Miami: Advanced International Studies Institute.

Millett, Stephen M. (1981): Soviet Perceptions of Nuclear Strategy and Implications for US Deterrence (Occasional Papers No. 18). Columbus: Battelle.

Mitchell, C.R. (1981): The Structure of International Conflict. London: Macmillan.

Mitchell, R. Judson (1982): Ideology of a Superpower: Contemporary Soviet Doctrine on International Relations. Stanford, CA: Hoover Institution Press.

Moisi, Dominique (1983): "Domestic Priorities and the Demands of Alliance: A European Perspective". In: Adelphi Paper No. 184. London: International Institute for Strategic Studies. pp. 12-16.

Moreton, Edwina and Gerald Segal (Eds.) (1984): Soviet Strategy Toward Western Europe. London: George Allen & Unwin

Mouritzen, H. (1981): "Prediction on the Basis of Official Doctrine". In: Cooperation and Conflict, Vol. 16. pp. 25-38.

Münch, Richard (1976): Theorie sozialer Systeme. Opladen: Westdeutscher Verlag.

Nerlich, Uwe (Ed.) (1982a): Sowjetische Macht und westliche Verhandlungspolitik im Wandel militärischer Kräfteverhältnisse. Baden-Baden: Nomos Verlagsgesellschaft.

--- (Ed.) (1982b): Die Einhegung sowjetischer Macht. Baden-Baden: Nomos Verlagsgesellschaft.

Neubauer, Deane (1977): "Lying and the Stress for Cognitive Consistency". In: Matthew G. Bonham and Michael J. Shapiro (Eds.): Thought and Action in Foreign Policy. Basel: Birkhäuser. pp. 190-225.

Nishihara, Masashi (1983): "The Media and the Image of Defence Policy: Japan". In Adelphi Paper No. 182. London: International Institute for Strategic Studies. pp. 45-50.

Nye, Joseph S. (1982): "The Future of Arms Control". In: Barry M. Blechman (Ed.): Rethinking the US Strategic Posture. Cambridge, MA: Ballinger. pp. 223-246.

O'Neill, Robert, and D. M. Horner (Eds.) (1981): New Directions in Strategic Thinking. London: George Allen & Unwin.

Osadczuk-Korab, Bogdan A. (1983): "Das sowjetische Konzept des internationalen Kräfteverhältnisses". In: Moderne Welt, Jahrbuch für Ost-West-Fragen 1983. pp. 165-176.

Osgood, Charles E. (1981): "Psycho-social Dynamics and the Prospects for Mankind". In: Ervin Laszlo and Donald Keys (Eds.): Disarmament: The Human Factor. Oxford: Pergamon Press. pp. 73-91.

Ostermann, Anne, and Hans Nicklas (1976): Vorurteile und Feindbilder. München: Urban & Schwarzenberg.

Oudenaren, John van (1982): "Die sowjetische Politik in Europa und die Rolle von Rüstungskontrollverhandlungen". In: Uwe Nerlich (Ed.): Sowjetische Macht und westliche Verhandlungspolitik im Wandel militärischer Kräfteverhältnisse. Baden-Baden. Nomos Verlagsgesellschaft. pp. 237-274.

Payne, James L. (1983): "Foreign Policy for an Impulsive People". In: Aaron Wildavsky (Ed.): Beyond Containment: Alternative American Policies Toward the Soviet Union. San Francisco: Institute for Contemporary Studies. pp. 201-230.

Payne, Keith B. (1981): "Are They Interested in Stability? The Soviet View of Intervention". In: Comparative Strategy, Vol. 3, No. 1. pp. 1-24.

--- (1982): Nuclear Deterrence in US - Soviet Relations. Boulder: Westview Press.

Pedill, C. Grant, Jr. (1980): "'Bipartisanship' in Soviet foreign Policy-Making". In: Erik P. Hoffmann and Frederic J. Fleron, Jr. (Eds.): The Conduct of Soviet Foreign Policy. New York: Aldine Publishing. pp. 61-75.

Pfaltzgraff, Robert L., Jr., Uri Ra'anan, and Warren Milberg (Eds.) (1981): Intelligence Policy and National Security. London: Macmillan.

Pool, Ithiel de Sola (1981): "Approaches to Intelligence and Social Science". In: Robert L. Pfaltzgraff, Uri Ra'anan, and Warren Milberg (Eds.): Intelligence Policy and National Security. London: Macmillan. pp. 37-45.

Potter, William (1980): "Perception and Misperception in US-Soviet Relations". In: Problems of Communism, Vol. 29, No. 2, March/April. pp. 68-71.

Prados, John (1982): The Soviet Estimate: US Intelligence Analysis and Russian Military Strength. New York: Dial Press.

Pruitt, Dean G. (1965): "Definition of the Situation as a Determinant of International Action". In: Herbert C. Kelman (Ed.): International Behavior. New York: Holt, Rinehart and Winston. pp. 393-432.

Quester, George H. (1980): "Defining Strategic Issues: How to Avoid Isometric Exercises". In: Robert E. Harkavy and Edward A. Kolodziej (Eds.): American Security Policy and Policy-Making. Lexington, MA: D.C. Heath. pp. 195-207.

Ra'anan, Uri (1981): "'Static' and 'Dynamic' Intelligence Perceptions: The Soviet Union - Problems of Analysis and Evalutations". In: Robert L. Pfaltzgraff, Jr., Uri Ra'anan and Warren Milberg (Eds:): Intelligence Policy and National Security. London: Macmillan. pp. 82-90.

Reilly, Alayne P. (1971): America in Contemporary Soviet Literature. New York: New York University Press.

Reychler, Luc (1979): Patterns of Diplomatic Thinking. New York: Praeger.

Richelson, Jeffrey T. (1979): "Soviet Strategic Doctrine and Limited Nuclear Operations". In: Journal of Conflict Resolution, Vol. 23, No. 2. pp. 326-336.

318

--- (1982):Social Choice Theory and Soviet National Security Decisionmaking (ACIS Working Paper No. 37). Los Angeles: Center for International and Strategic Affairs.

Richter, Horst E. (1982): Zur Psychologie des Friedens. Reinbek bei Hamburg: Rowohlt.

Roberts, Adam (1983): "The Critique of Nuclear Deterrence". In: Adelphi Paper No. 183. London: International Institute for Strategic Studies. pp. 2-18.

Ropp, Theodore (1981): "Strategic Thinking Since 1945". In Robert O'Neill and D. M. Horner (Eds.): New Directions in Strategic Thinking. London: George Allen & Unwin. pp. 1-13.

Rose, John P. (1980): The EVolution of US Army Nuclear Doctrine, 1945-1980. Boulder: Westview Press.

Rosefielde, Steven (1982): False Science: Underestimating the Soviet Arms Buildup. New Brunswick: Transaction Books.

Rositzke, Harry (1984): Managing Moscow: Guns or Goods? New York: William Morrow & Co.

Ross, Dennis (1981): "Rethinking Soviet Strategic Policy. Impact and Implications". In: John Baylis and Gerald Segal (Eds.): Soviet Strategy. London: Croom Helm. pp. 124-153.

--- (1984): "Risk Aversion in Soviet Decisionmaking". In: Jiri Valenta and William Potter (Eds.): Soviet Decisonmaking for Defense. London: George Allen & Unwin. pp. 231-254.

Rubinstein, Alvin Z. (1983): Soviet Foreign Policy since World War II: Imperial and Global. Boston: Little, Brown.

Ruehl, Lothar (1982): "Die militärische Macht der Sowjetunion als Bedingung westeuropäischer Strukturentwicklung". In: Uwe Nerlich (Ed.) Sowjetische Macht und westliche Verhandlungspolitik im Wandel militärischer Kräfteverhältnisse. Baden-Baden: Nomos Verlagsgesellschaft. pp. 275-312.

--- (1983): "The Media and the Image of Defence Policy: Europe". In: Adelphi Paper No. 182. London: International Institute for Strategic Studies. pp. 36-44.

Ruf, Werner (1983): Bilder in der internationalen Politik. Saarbrücken: Sozialwissenschaftlicher Studienkreis für internationale Probleme.

Schelling, Thomas C. (1963): The Strategy of Conflict. New York: Oxford University Press.

Schilling, Warner (1981): "US Strategic Nuclear Concepts in the 1970s". In: Robert O'Neill and D. M. Horner (Eds.): New Directions in Strategic Thinking. London: George Allen & Unwin. pp. 34-59.

Schwartz, Morton (1978): Soviet Perceptions of the United States. Berkeley: University of California Press.

Scott, Harriet F., and William F. Scott (1982): "Soviet Strategic Thought" In: B. Thomas Trout and James E. Hart (Eds.): National Security Affairs: Theoretical Perspectives and Contemporary Issues. New Brunswick: Transaction Books. pp. 98-120.

-- , and William F. Scott (1983): The Soviet Control Structure: Capabilities for Wartime Survival. New York: Crane, Russak.

Segal, Gerald, and John Baylis (1981): "Soviet Strategy: An Introduction". In: John Baylis and Gerald Segal (Eds.): Soviet Strategy. London: Croom Helm. pp. 9-50.

Seiler, Bernhard (Ed.) (1973): Kognitive Strukturiertheit. Stuttgart: Kohlhammer Verlag.

Senghaas, Dieter (1969): Abschreckung und Frieden. Frankfurt am Main: Europäische Verlagsanstalt.

--- (1972): Rüstung und Militarismus. Frankfurt am Main: Suhrkamp Verlag.

Shaklee, Harriet (1979): "Bounded Rationality and Cognitive Development: Upper Limits to Growth?" In: Cognitive Psychology, Vol. 11, No. 3. pp. 327-345.

Sharp, Jane (1984): "Arms Control Strategies". in: Edwina Moreton, and Gerald Segal (Eds.): Soviet Strategy Toward Western Europe. London: George Allen & Unwin. pp. 235-284.

Sharp, Samuel L. (1980): "National Interest: Key to Soviet Politics". In: Erik P. Hoffmann and Frederic J. Fleron, Jr. (Eds.:) The Conduct of Soviet Foreign Policy. New York: Aldine Publishing Co. pp. 108-117.

Shulman, Marshall D. (1982): "US - Soviet Relations and the Control of Nuclear Weapons". In: Barry M. Blechman (Ed.): Rethinking the US Strategic Posture. Cambridge, MA: Ballinger. pp. 77-100.

Shultz, Richard H., and Roy Godson (1984): Dezinformatsia: Active Measures in Soviet Strategy. Washington, DC: Pergamon Press/Brassey's.

Sieber, Margaret (1978): Darstellen und Erkennen: "Maps", "Scripts", "Schema" und "Frames" (Kleine Studien zur Politischen Wissenschaft No. 125). Zurich: University of Zurich.

Sienkiewicz, Stanley (1979): "Observations on the Impact of Uncertainty in Strategic Analysis". In: World Politics, Vol. 32, No. 1. pp. 90-110.

--- (1981): "Soviet Nuclear Doctrine and Prospects for Strategic Arms Control". In: Derek Leebaert (Ed.): Soviet Military Thinking. London: George Allen & Unwin. pp. 73-91.

Simes, Dimitri K. (1980/81): "Deterrence and Coercion in Soviet Policy". In: International Security, Vol. 5, No. 3. pp. 80-103.

--- (1981/82): "The Military and Militarism in Soviet Society". In: International Security, Vol. 6, No. 3. pp. 123-143.

--- (1983): "Assessing Soviet National Security Strategy". In: Terry L. Heyns (Ed.) (1983): Understanding US Strategy: A Reader. Washington, DC: National Defense University Press. pp. 203-220.

Singer, Max (1983): "Dynamic Containment". In: Aaron Wildavsky (Ed.): Beyond Containment: Alternative American Policies Toward the Soviet Union. San Fransisco: Institute for Contemporary Studies. pp. 169-200.

Sitta, Horst (1980): "Zum strategischen Einsatz von Normverstössen". In: Dieter Cherubim (Ed.): Fehlerlinguistik. Tübingen: Niemeyer. pp. 209-223.

Sleeper, Raymond S. (Ed.) (1983): A Lexicon of Marxist-Leninist Semantics. Alexandria, VA: Western Goals.

Smoke, Richard (1984): National Security and the Nuclear Dilemma, Reading, MA: Addison-Wesley.

Snyder, Jack L. (1978). "Rationality at the Brink: The Role of Cognitive Processes in Failures of Deterrence". In: World Politics, Vol. 30, No. 3. pp. 344-365.

Sokoloff, Georges (1978): "Sources of Soviet Power: Economy, Population, Resources". In: Adelphi Paper No. 151. London: International Institute for Strategic Studies. pp. 30-36.

Solzhenitsyn, Aleksandr (1980): "Misconceptions about Russia are a Threat to America". In: Foreign Affairs, Vol. 58, No. 4. (Spring). pp. 797-834.

Spielmann, Karl F. (1978): Analyzing Soviet Strategic Arms Decisions. Boulder: Westview Press.

Stanley Foundation (1983): Strategy for Peace. Muscatine, Iowa.

Stein, Arthur (1982): "When Misperception Matters". In: World Politics, Vol. 34, No. 4. pp. 505-526.

Steinbruner, John D. (1974): The Cybernetic Theory of Decision. Princeton: Princeton University Press.

Steiner, Miriam (1983): "The Search for Order in a Disorderly World: World Views and Prescriptive Decision Paradigms". In: International Organization, Vol. 37, No. 3. (Summer 1983). pp. 373-413.

Stewart, Philip D. (1983): Informal Dialogue and the Prevention of Nuclear War. Columbus: Ohio State University (mimeo).

Stoessinger, John G. (1974) Why Nations Go to War. New York: St.Martin's Press.

Stratmann, K.-Peter (1981): NATO-Strategie in der Krise? Militärische Optionen von NATO und Warschauer Pakt in Mitteleuropa. Baden-Baden: Nomos Verlagsgesellschaft.

Strode, Dan L., and Rebecca V. Strode (1983): "Diplomacy and Defense in Soviet National Security Policy". In: International Security, Vol. 8, No. 2, Fall. pp. 91-116.

Strode, Rebecca V. (1982): "Soviet Strategic Style". In: Comparative Strategy, Vol. 3, No. 4. pp. 319-339.

Suddaby, Adam (1982a): Deterrence and Defence in Nuclear War. York: Longman.

--- (1982b): American Nuclear Issues. York: Longman.

--- (1982c): European Nuclear Issues. York: Longman.

--- (1982d): The Nuclear Arms Race II: Proliferation and Disarmament. York: Longman.

Taifel, Henri (1969): "Social and Cultural Factors in Perception". In: Lindzey Gardner and Elliot Aronson (Eds.): The Handbook of Social Psychology, Second Edition, Vol. 3. Reading, MA: Addison-Wesley. pp. 315-394.

Thorndyke, Perry W., and Barbara Hayes-Roth (1979): "The Use of Schemata in the Acquisition and Transfer of Knowledge". In: Cognitive Psychology, Vol. 11, No. 1. pp. 82-105.

Towle, Philip (1983): Arms Control and East-West Relations. London: Croom Helm.

Trout, B. Thomas (1975): "Rhetoric Revisited: Political Legitimation and the Cold War". In: International Studies Quarterly, Vol. 19. pp. 251-284.

--- , and James E. Hart (Eds.) (1982): National Security Affairs: Theoretical Perspectives and Contemporary Issues. New Brunswick: Transaction Books.

Ulam, Adam B. (1981): "Russian Nationalism". In: Seweryn Bialer (Ed.): The Domestic Context of Soviet Foreign Policy. Boulder: Wesview Press/London: Croom Helm. pp. 3-17.

--- (1983): "The World Outside". In: Robert F. Byrnes: After Brezhnev: Sources of Soviet Conduct in the 1980s. Bloomington: Indiana University Press. pp. 345-422.

US Defense Policy (1983), Third Edition. Washington, DC: Congressional Quarterly Inc.

Valenta, Jiri (1982): "Soviet Use of Surprise and Deception". In: Survival, Vol. 24, No. 2. pp. 50-60.

--- , and William Potter (Eds.) (1984): Soviet Decisionmaking for National Security. London: George Allen & Unwin.

Vertzberger, Yaacov (1982): "Misperception in International Politics: A Typological Framework for Analysis". In: International Interactions, Vol. 9, No. 3. pp. 207-234.

Vigeveno, Guido (1983): The Bomb and European Security. London: Hurst.

Vigor, Peter H. (1975a): "The Semantics of Deterrence and Defense" In: MccGwire et al. (Eds.): Soviet Naval Policy: Objectives and Constraints. New York: Praeger.

--- (1975b): The Soviet View of War, Peace and Neutrality. London: Routledge & Kegan Paul.

--- (1983): Soviet Blitzkrieg Theory. London: Macmillan.

Vincent, R. J. (1975): Military Power and Political Influence: The Soviet Union and Western Europe (Adelphi Paper No. 119). London: International Institute for Strategic Studies.

Volten, Peter M. E. (1982): Brezhnev's Peace Program. Boulder: Westview Press.

Wagenlehner, Günther (1981): "Militärische Ueberlegenheit, Gewalt und Krieg in den Aussagen der sowjetischen Führung". In: Beiträge zur Konfliktforschung, Vol. 11, No. 4. pp. 5-35.

Ward, Michael Don, and A.K. Mahajan (1983): Modelling Defense Expenditure in Light of Perceived Security (mimeo, Paper submitted to the Annual Convention of the American Political Science Association, Chicago).

Watzlawick, Paul (1976): Wie wirklich ist die Wirklichkeit? Munich: Piper.

Weigley, Russell F. (1973): The American Way of War. Bloomington: Indiana University Press.

Weinland, Robert G. (1984): "The Evolution of Soviet Requirements for Naval Forces". In: Survival, Vol. 26, No. 1 (January/February). pp. 16-25.

Welch, Jasper A. (1981): "Verification". In: Robert L. Pfaltzgraff, Jr., Uri Ra'anan and Warren Milberg (Eds.): Intelligence Policy and National Security. London: Macmillan. pp. 131-142.

Welch, William (1970): American Images of Soviet Foreign Policy: An Inquiry into Recent Appraisals from the Academic Community. New Haven: Yale University Press.

Wells, Samuel F. (1981): "The United States and the Present Danger". In: Journal of Strategic Studies, Vol. 1, No. 1 (March). pp. 60-70.

Whaley, B. (1982): "Toward a General Theory of Deception". In: Journal of Strategic Studies, Vol. 5. pp. 178-192.

Whelan, Joseph G. (1983): Soviet Diplomacy and Negotiating Behavior. Boulder: Westview Press.

White, Ralph K. (1965): "Images in the Context of International Conflict". In: Herbert C. Kelman (Ed.): International Behavior. New York: Holt, Rinehart and Winston. pp. 238-276.

White, Robert H. (1968): Nobody Wanted War. Garden City: Doubleday.

Wildavsky, Aaron (Ed.) (1983): Beyond Containment: Alternative American Policies Toward the Soviet Union. San Fransisco: Institute for Contemporary Studies.

Wildenmann, Rudolf (1983): "Public Opinion and the Defence Effort: Trends and Lessons - Europe". In: Adelphi Paper No. 182. London: International Institute for Strategic Studies. pp. 24-28.

Windsor, Philip (1979): "The Soviet Union in the International System of the 1980s". In: Adelphi Paper No. 152. London: International Institute for Strategic Studies. pp. 2-10.

Wolf, Charles (1983): "Extended Containment". In: Aaron Wildavsky (Ed.): Beyond Containment: Alternative American Policies Toward the Soviet Union. San Fransisco: Institute for Contemporary Studies. pp. 147-168.

Wolfe, Alan (1979): The Rise and Fall of the "Soviet Threat". Washington, DC: Institute for Policy Studies.

Wrightson, Margaret T. (1976): "The Documentary Coding Method". In: Robert Axelrod (Ed.): Structure of Decision: the Cognitive Maps of Political Elites. Princeton: Princeton University Press. pp. 291-332.

York, Herbert F. (1983): "Wettrüsten und amerikanisch-sowjetische Verhandlungen". In: Spektrum der Wissenschaft, Dezember. pp. 34-47.

Young, Elisabeth, and Wayland Young (1980): "Marxism-Leninism and Arms Control". In: Arms Control, Vol. 1, No. 1. pp. 3-29.

Young, Wayland, and Elisabeth Young (1982): "Disarmament Now". In. The Yearbook of World Affairs. pp. 25-37.

Zajonc, Robert B. (1968): "Cognitive Theories in Social Psychology". In: Lindzey Gardner and Elliot Aronson (Eds.): The Handbook of Social Psychology, Second Edition, Vol. 1. Reading, MA: Addison-Wesley. pp. 320-411.

Zimmerman, William (1968): "Soviet Perceptions of the United States". In: Alexander Dallin and Thomas B. Larson (Eds.): Soviet Politics since Khrushchev. Englewood Cliffs: Prentice-Hall. pp. 163-179.

--- (1980): "Elite Perspectives and the Explanation of Soviet Foreign Policy". In: Erik P. Hoffmann and Frederic J. Fleron, Jr. (Eds.): The Conduct of Soviet Foreign Policy. New York: Aldine Publishing. pp. 18-30. (first published 1970 in the Journal of International Affairs)

--- (1983): "Words and Deeds in Soviet Foreign Policy: The Case of Soviet Military Expenditures". In: American Political Science Review, Vol. 77, No. 2. pp. 358-367.